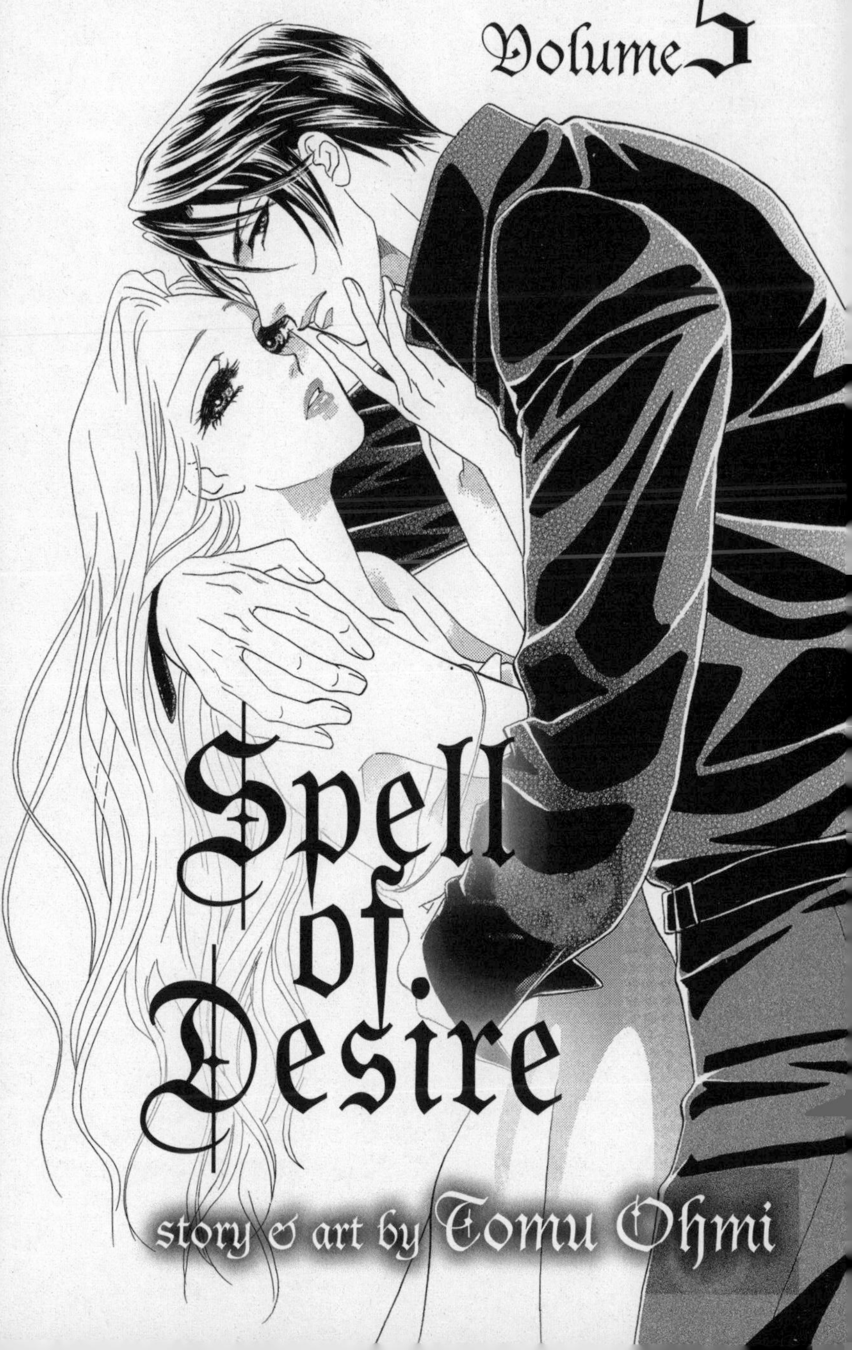
Volume 5
Spell of Desire
story & art by Tomu Ohmi

Spell of Desire
Volume 5

Contents

story

Kaoruko's peaceful life is changed forever by the arrival of Kaname, a knight charged with protecting her after she is unwillingly entrusted with immense magic belonging to her mother, known as the Witch Queen. The Witch Queen's power is beyond Kaoruko's ability to control—except when Kaname kisses her!

Kaoruko and Kaname are drawn to each other and declare their love...a love that means Kaname has betrayed his vows to the Witch Queen, making him a fallen knight. And now the time for the Witch Queen's reawakening—and thus her judgment—is drawing near...

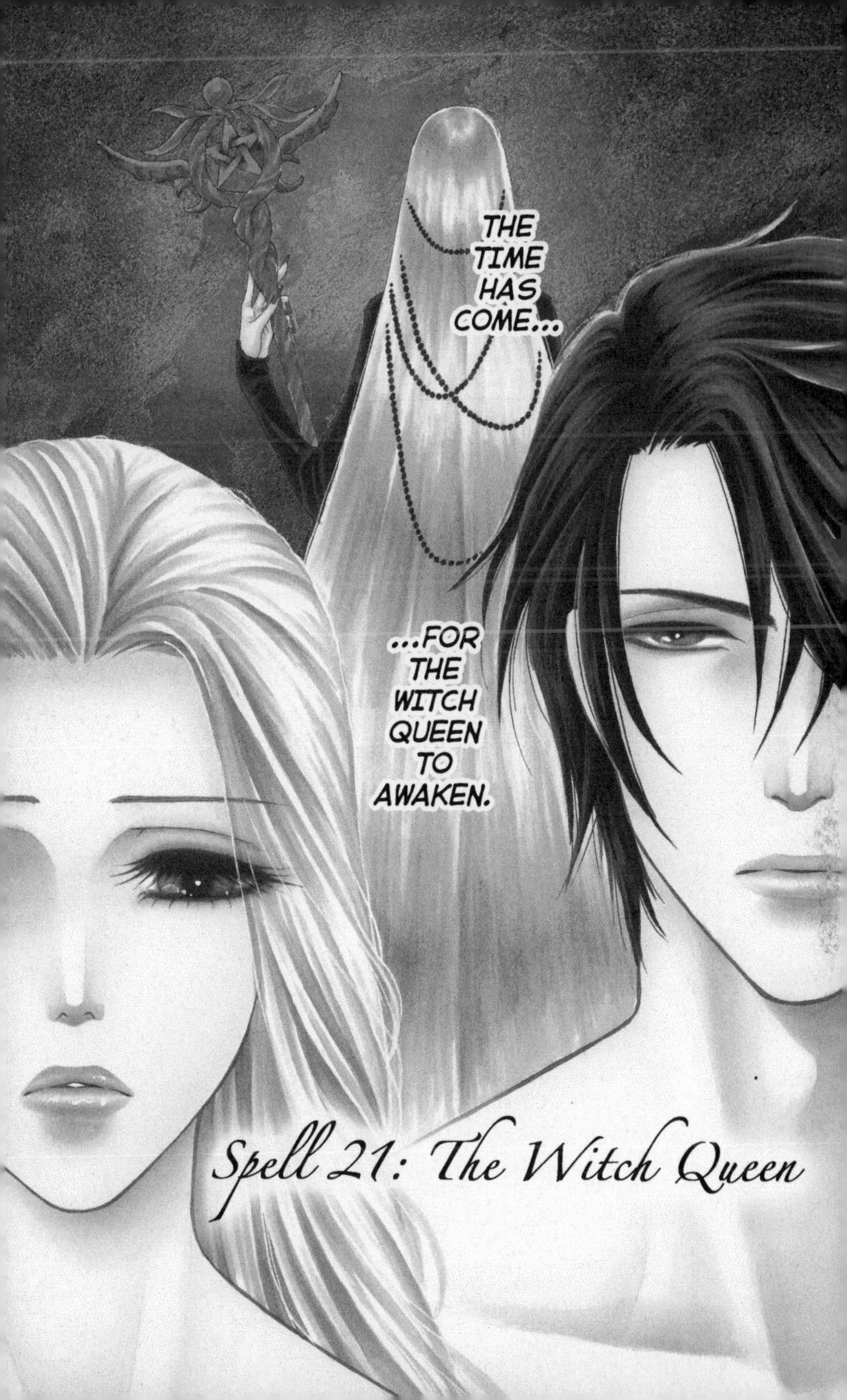
THE TIME HAS COME...
...FOR THE WITCH QUEEN TO AWAKEN.
Spell 21: The Witch Queen

Those of you who read this in the magazine can see that I was given the color page at the front and that the frontispiece was a two-page spread.

That frontispiece became the cover of volume 4. I was also allowed to use the front color page in the magazine issue that ran chapter 1 as the volume 1 graphic novel cover. Thank you!

Including these two cuties. ♪

It's fun drawing cover illustrations! ♪

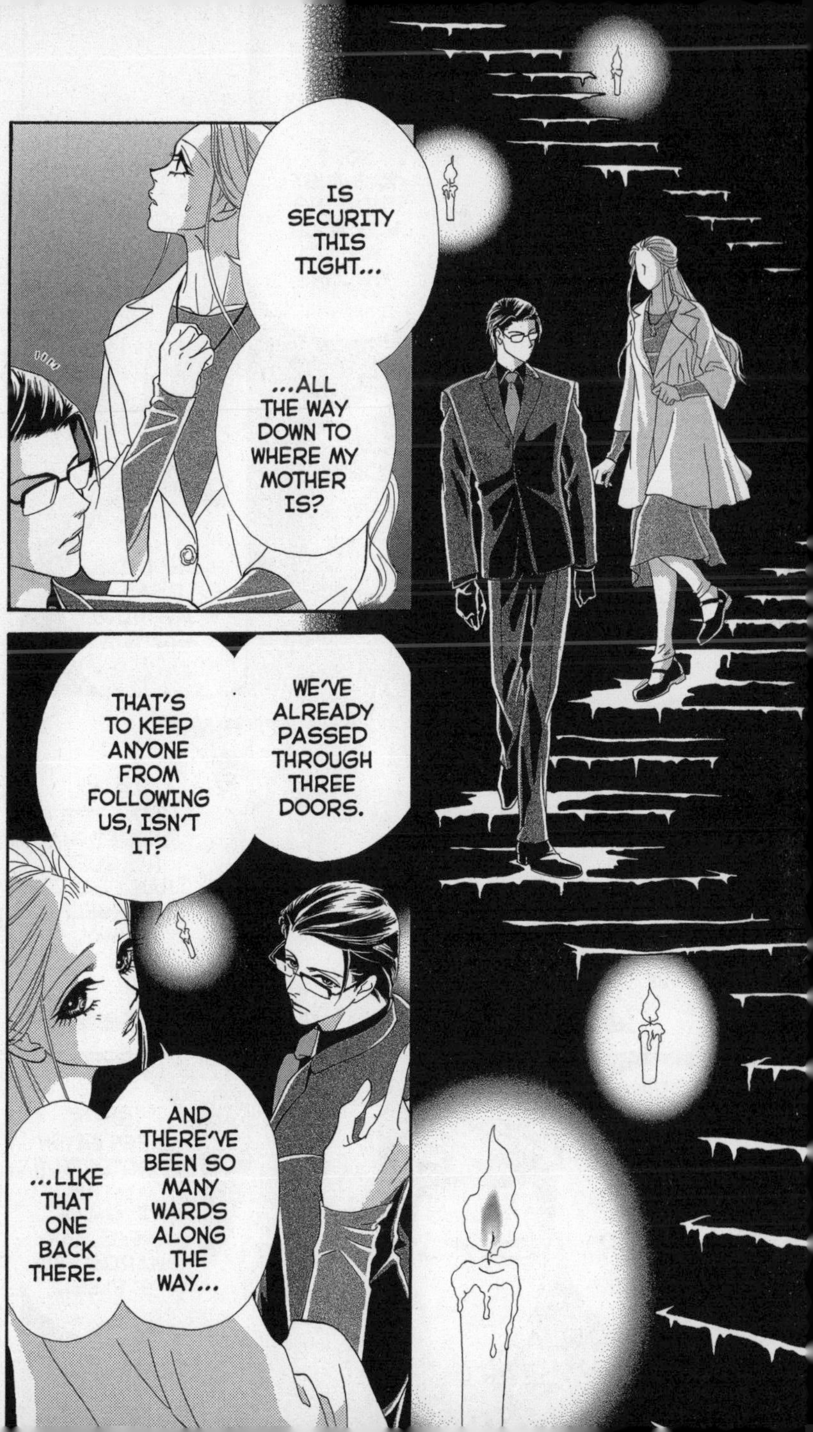
IS SECURITY THIS TIGHT...
...ALL THE WAY DOWN TO WHERE MY MOTHER IS?
WE'VE ALREADY PASSED THROUGH THREE DOORS.
THAT'S TO KEEP ANYONE FROM FOLLOWING US, ISN'T IT?
AND THERE'VE BEEN SO MANY WARDS ALONG THE WAY...
...LIKE THAT ONE BACK THERE.

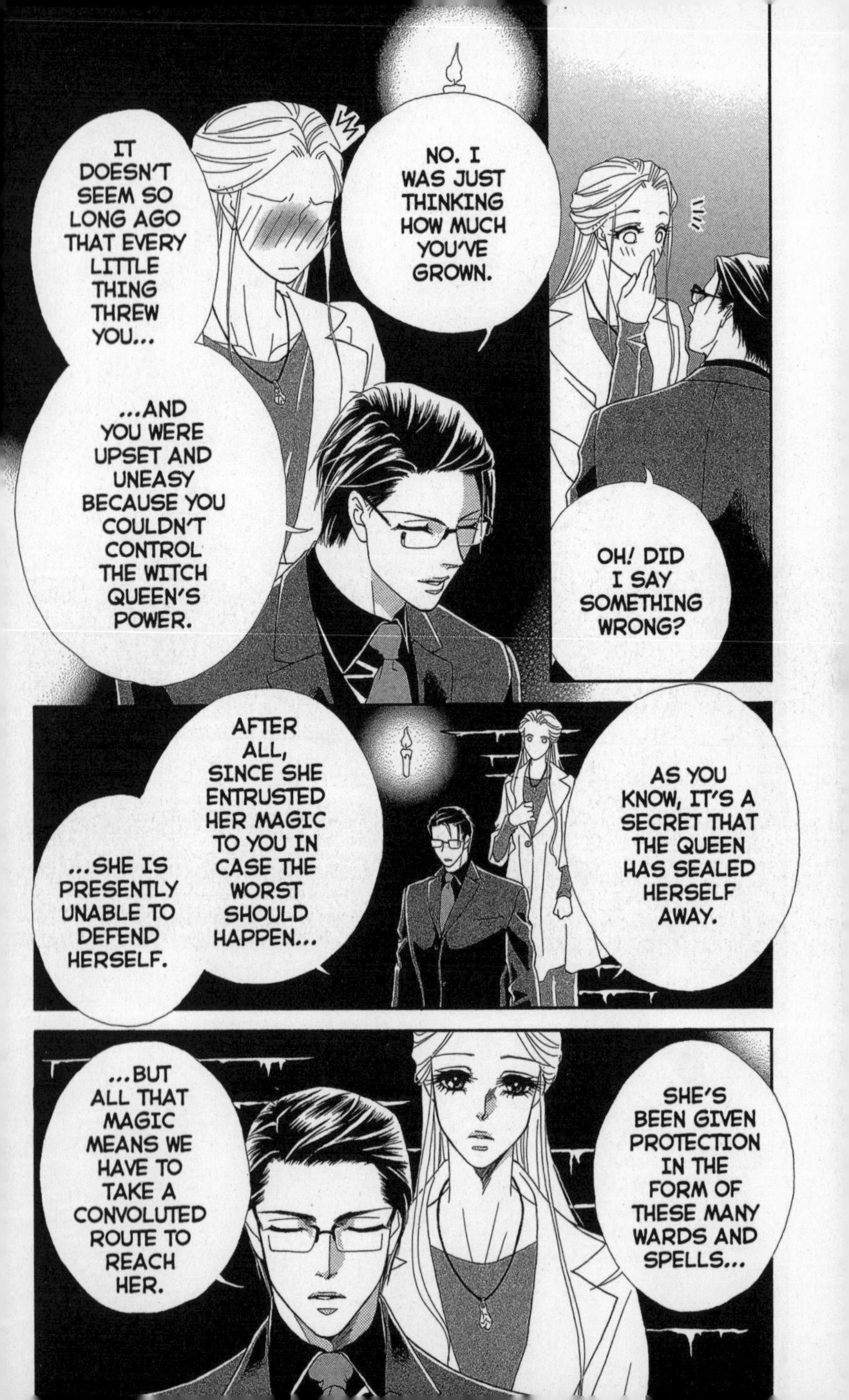
OH! DID I SAY SOMETHING WRONG?
NO. I WAS JUST THINKING HOW MUCH YOU'VE GROWN.
IT DOESN'T SEEM SO LONG AGO THAT EVERY LITTLE THING THREW YOU...
...AND YOU WERE UPSET AND UNEASY BECAUSE YOU COULDN'T CONTROL THE WITCH QUEEN'S POWER.
AS YOU KNOW, IT'S A SECRET THAT THE QUEEN HAS SEALED HERSELF AWAY.
AFTER ALL, SINCE SHE ENTRUSTED HER MAGIC TO YOU IN CASE THE WORST SHOULD HAPPEN...
...SHE IS PRESENTLY UNABLE TO DEFEND HERSELF.
SHE'S BEEN GIVEN PROTECTION IN THE FORM OF THESE MANY WARDS AND SPELLS...
...BUT ALL THAT MAGIC MEANS WE HAVE TO TAKE A CONVOLUTED ROUTE TO REACH HER.

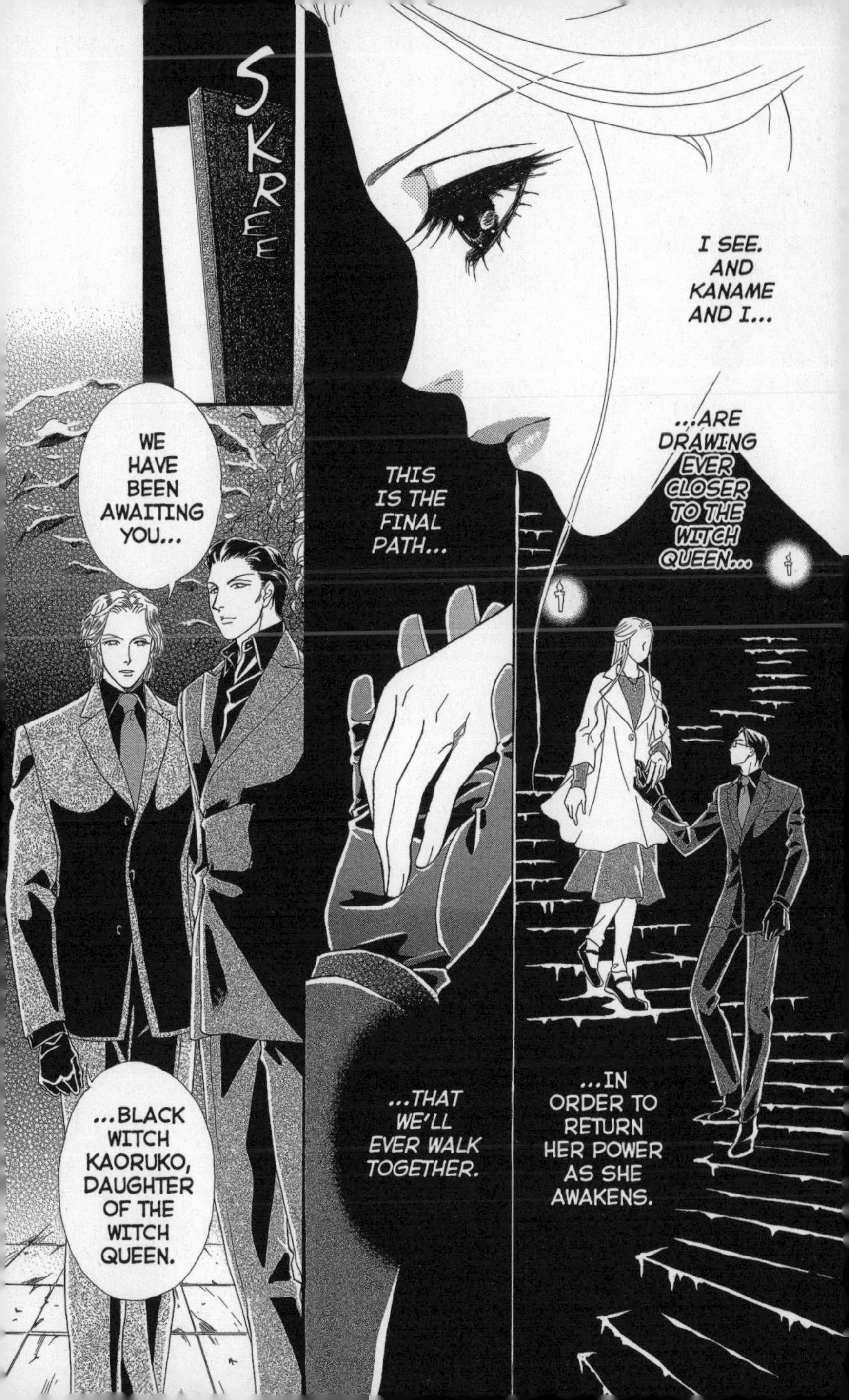
I SEE. AND KANAME AND I...
...ARE DRAWING EVER CLOSER TO THE WITCH QUEEN...
THIS IS THE FINAL PATH...
...IN ORDER TO RETURN HER POWER AS SHE AWAKENS.
...THAT WE'LL EVER WALK TOGETHER.
SKREE
WE HAVE BEEN AWAITING YOU...
...BLACK WITCH KAORUKO, DAUGHTER OF THE WITCH QUEEN.

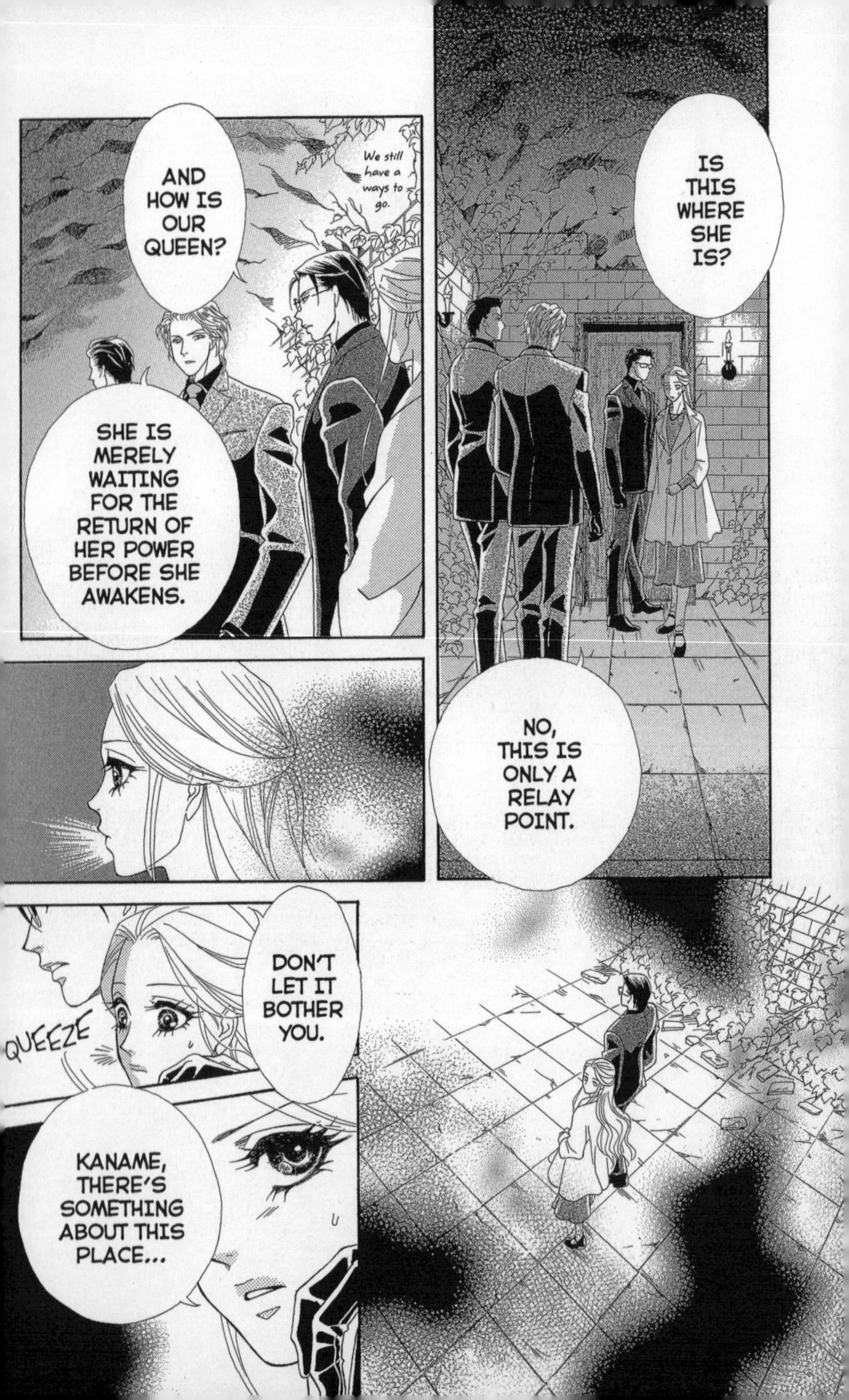
IS THIS WHERE SHE IS?
NO, THIS IS ONLY A RELAY POINT.
We still have a ways to go.
AND HOW IS OUR QUEEN?
SHE IS MERELY WAITING FOR THE RETURN OF HER POWER BEFORE SHE AWAKENS.
DON'T LET IT BOTHER YOU.
QUEEZE
KANAME, THERE'S SOMETHING ABOUT THIS PLACE...

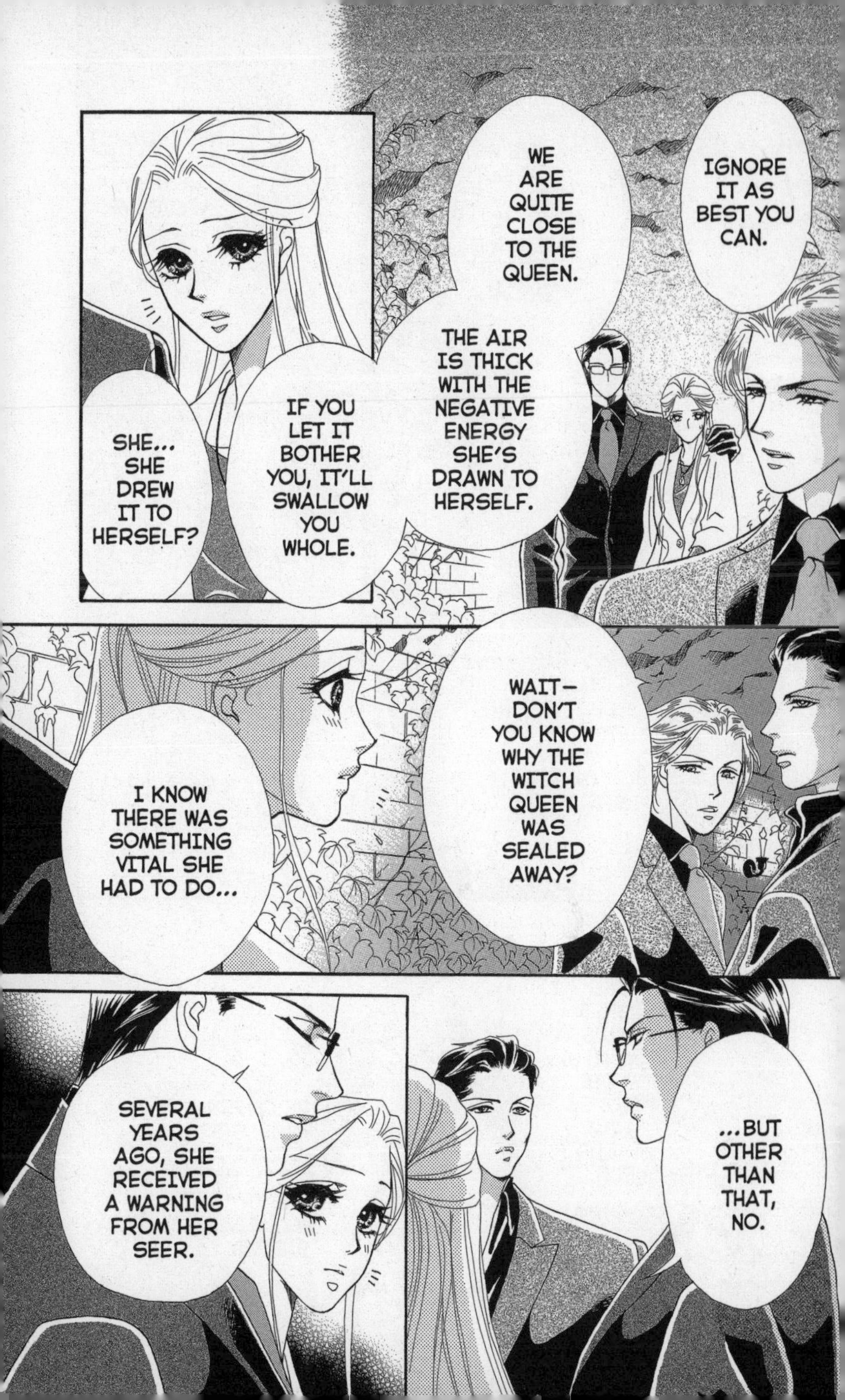
IGNORE IT AS BEST YOU CAN.
WE ARE QUITE CLOSE TO THE QUEEN.
THE AIR IS THICK WITH THE NEGATIVE ENERGY SHE'S DRAWN TO HERSELF.
IF YOU LET IT BOTHER YOU, IT'LL SWALLOW YOU WHOLE.
SHE... SHE DREW IT TO HERSELF?
WAIT—DON'T YOU KNOW WHY THE WITCH QUEEN WAS SEALED AWAY?
I KNOW THERE WAS SOMETHING VITAL SHE HAD TO DO...
...BUT OTHER THAN THAT, NO.
SEVERAL YEARS AGO, SHE RECEIVED A WARNING FROM HER SEER.

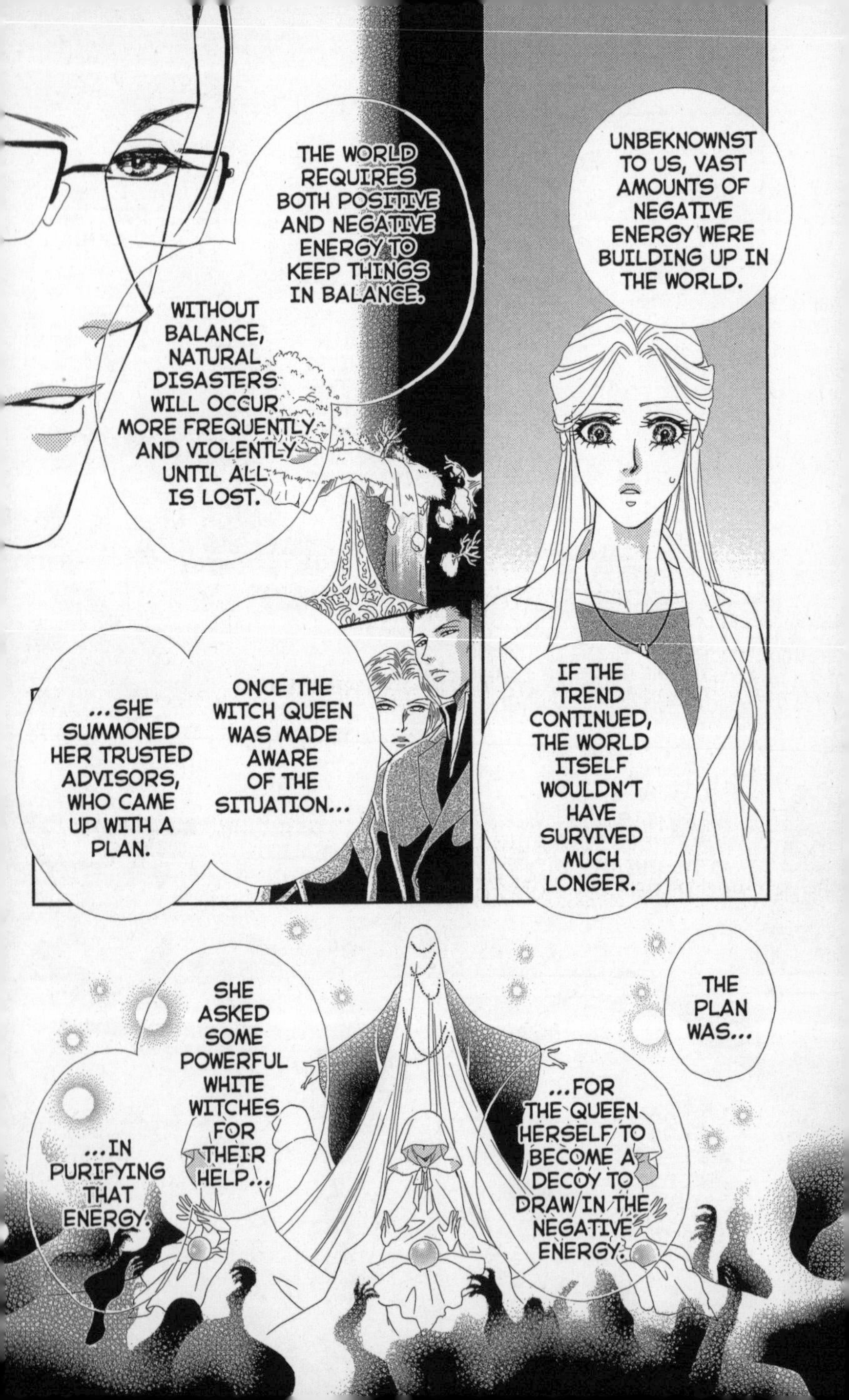
UNBEKNOWNST TO US, VAST AMOUNTS OF NEGATIVE ENERGY WERE BUILDING UP IN THE WORLD.
IF THE TREND CONTINUED, THE WORLD ITSELF WOULDN'T HAVE SURVIVED MUCH LONGER.
THE WORLD REQUIRES BOTH POSITIVE AND NEGATIVE ENERGY TO KEEP THINGS IN BALANCE.
WITHOUT BALANCE, NATURAL DISASTERS WILL OCCUR MORE FREQUENTLY AND VIOLENTLY UNTIL ALL IS LOST.
ONCE THE WITCH QUEEN WAS MADE AWARE OF THE SITUATION...
...SHE SUMMONED HER TRUSTED ADVISORS, WHO CAME UP WITH A PLAN.
THE PLAN WAS...
...FOR THE QUEEN HERSELF TO BECOME A DECOY TO DRAW IN THE NEGATIVE ENERGY.
SHE ASKED SOME POWERFUL WHITE WITCHES FOR THEIR HELP...
...IN PURIFYING THAT ENERGY.

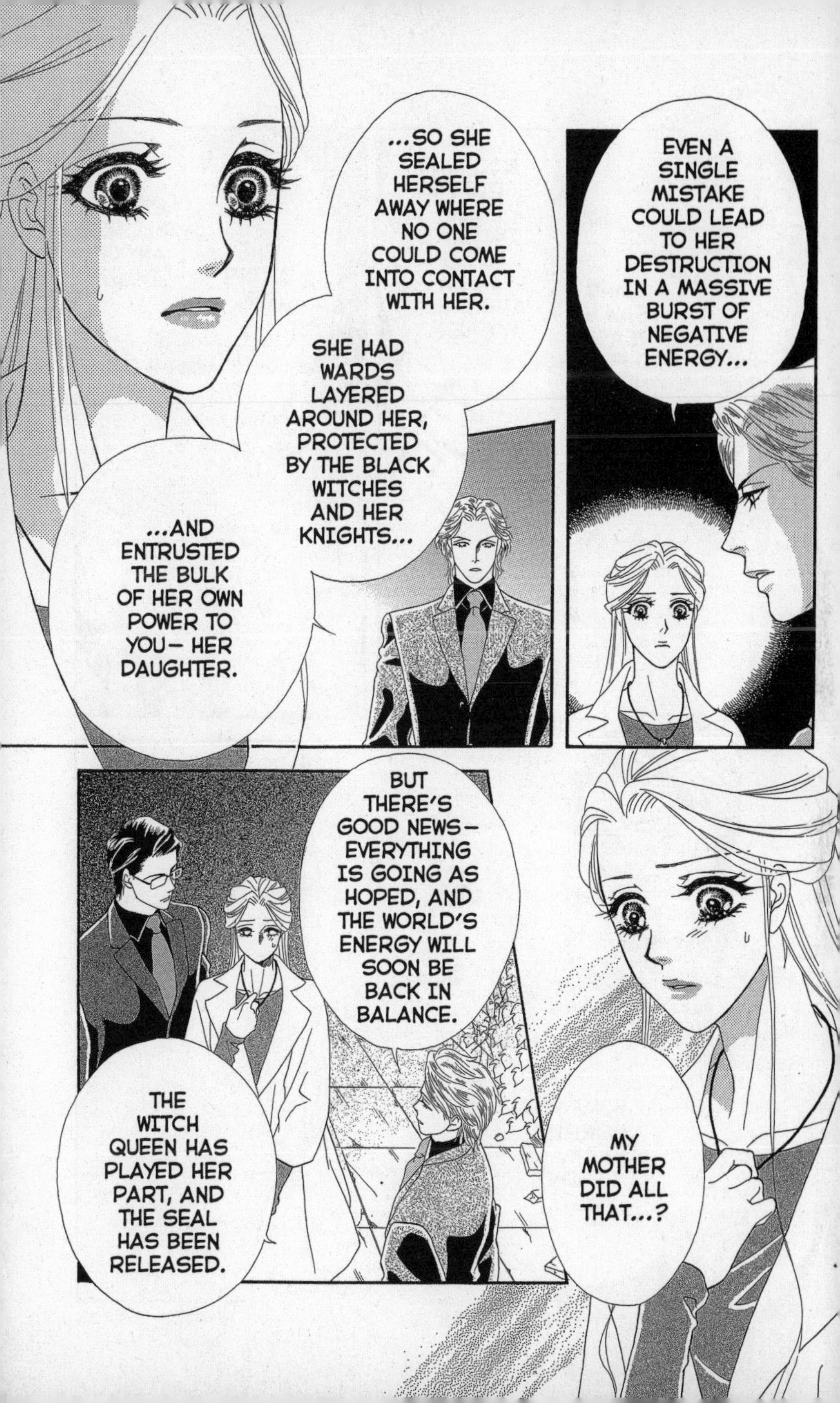
EVEN A SINGLE MISTAKE COULD LEAD TO HER DESTRUCTION IN A MASSIVE BURST OF NEGATIVE ENERGY...
...SO SHE SEALED HERSELF AWAY WHERE NO ONE COULD COME INTO CONTACT WITH HER.
SHE HAD WARDS LAYERED AROUND HER, PROTECTED BY THE BLACK WITCHES AND HER KNIGHTS...
...AND ENTRUSTED THE BULK OF HER OWN POWER TO YOU— HER DAUGHTER.
MY MOTHER DID ALL THAT...?
BUT THERE'S GOOD NEWS— EVERYTHING IS GOING AS HOPED, AND THE WORLD'S ENERGY WILL SOON BE BACK IN BALANCE.
THE WITCH QUEEN HAS PLAYED HER PART, AND THE SEAL HAS BEEN RELEASED.

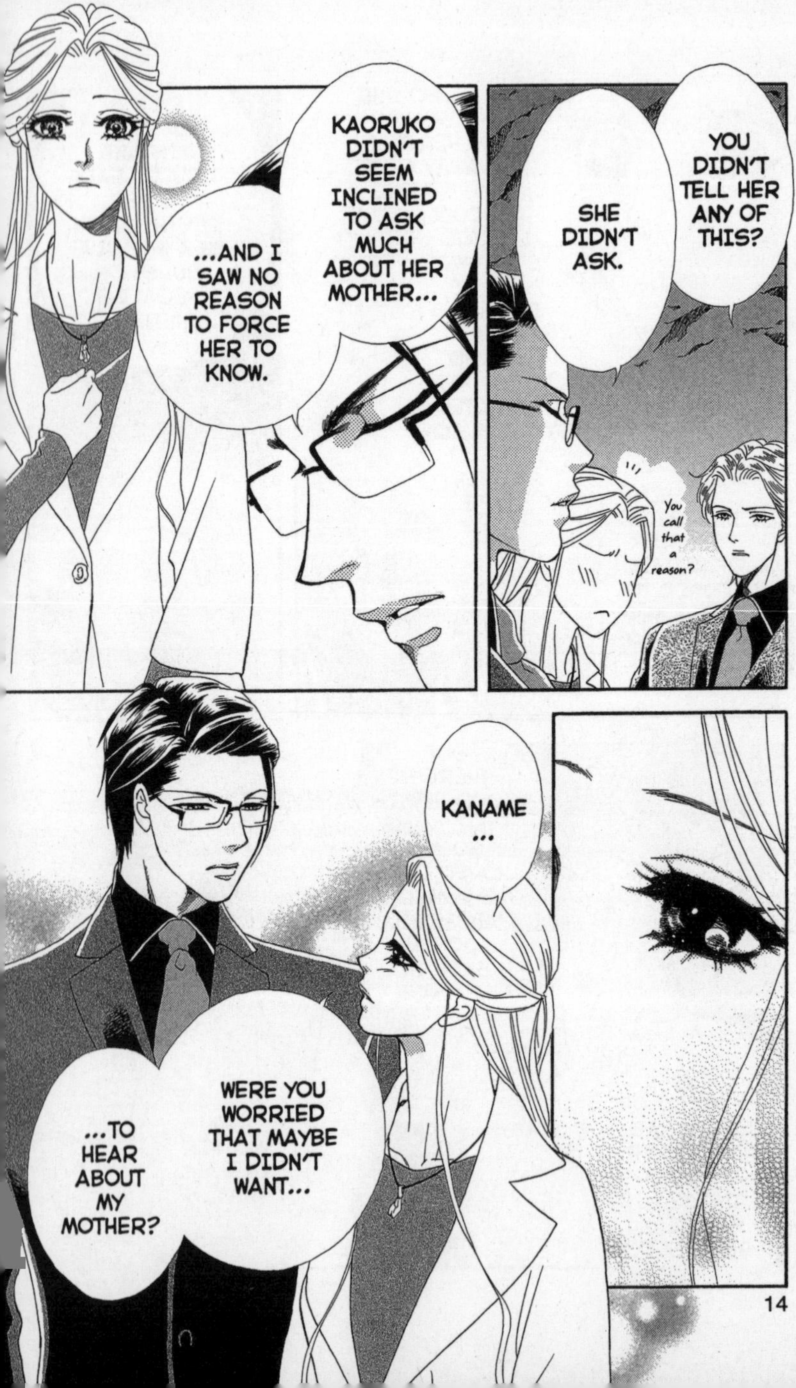
YOU DIDN'T TELL HER ANY OF THIS?
SHE DIDN'T ASK.
You call that a reason?
KAORUKO DIDN'T SEEM INCLINED TO ASK MUCH ABOUT HER MOTHER...
...AND I SAW NO REASON TO FORCE HER TO KNOW.
KANAME...
WERE YOU WORRIED THAT MAYBE I DIDN'T WANT...
...TO HEAR ABOUT MY MOTHER?

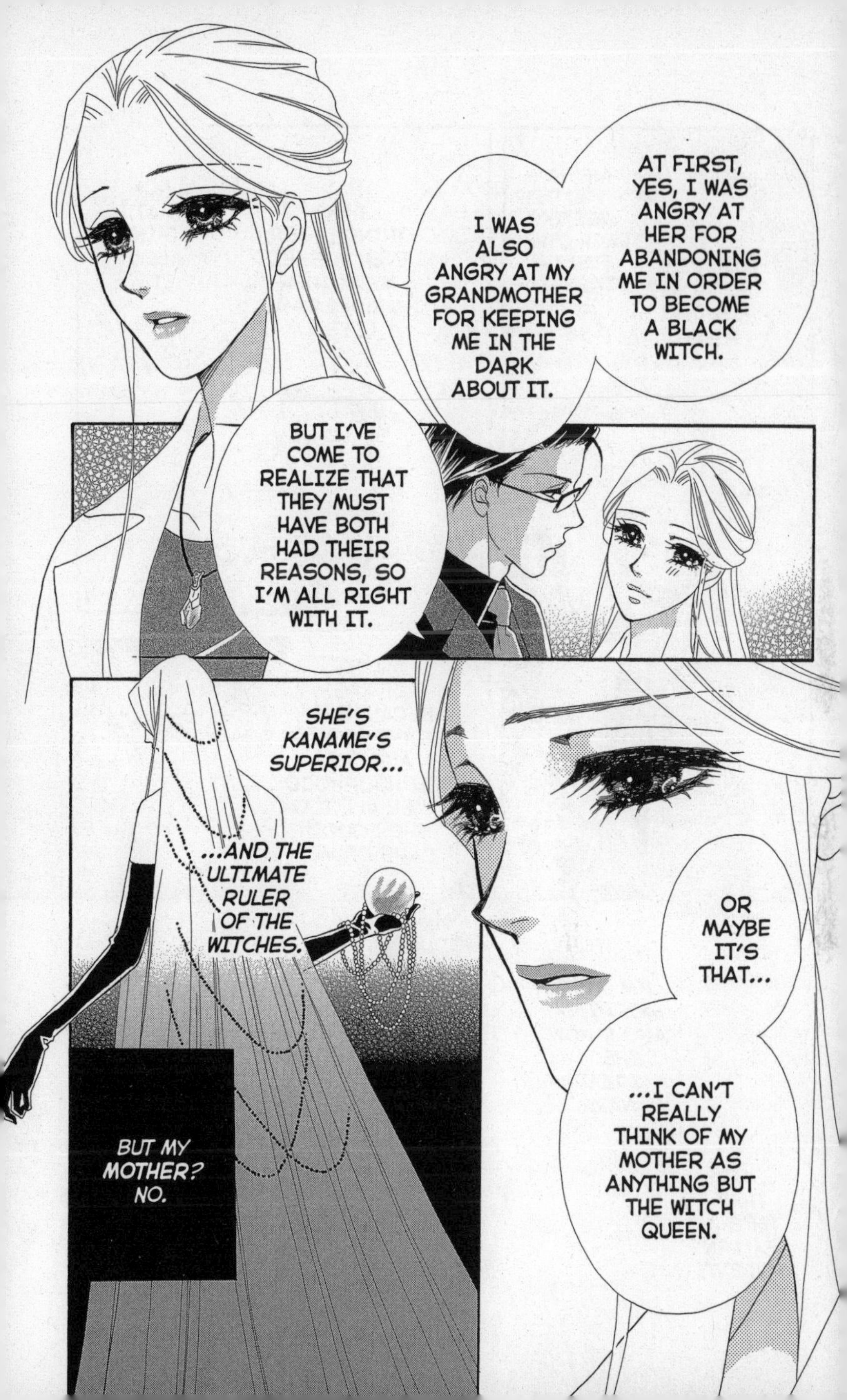
AT FIRST, YES, I WAS ANGRY AT HER FOR ABANDONING ME IN ORDER TO BECOME A BLACK WITCH.
I WAS ALSO ANGRY AT MY GRANDMOTHER FOR KEEPING ME IN THE DARK ABOUT IT.
BUT I'VE COME TO REALIZE THAT THEY MUST HAVE BOTH HAD THEIR REASONS, SO I'M ALL RIGHT WITH IT.
OR MAYBE IT'S THAT...
...I CAN'T REALLY THINK OF MY MOTHER AS ANYTHING BUT THE WITCH QUEEN.
SHE'S KANAME'S SUPERIOR...
...AND THE ULTIMATE RULER OF THE WITCHES.
BUT MY MOTHER? NO.

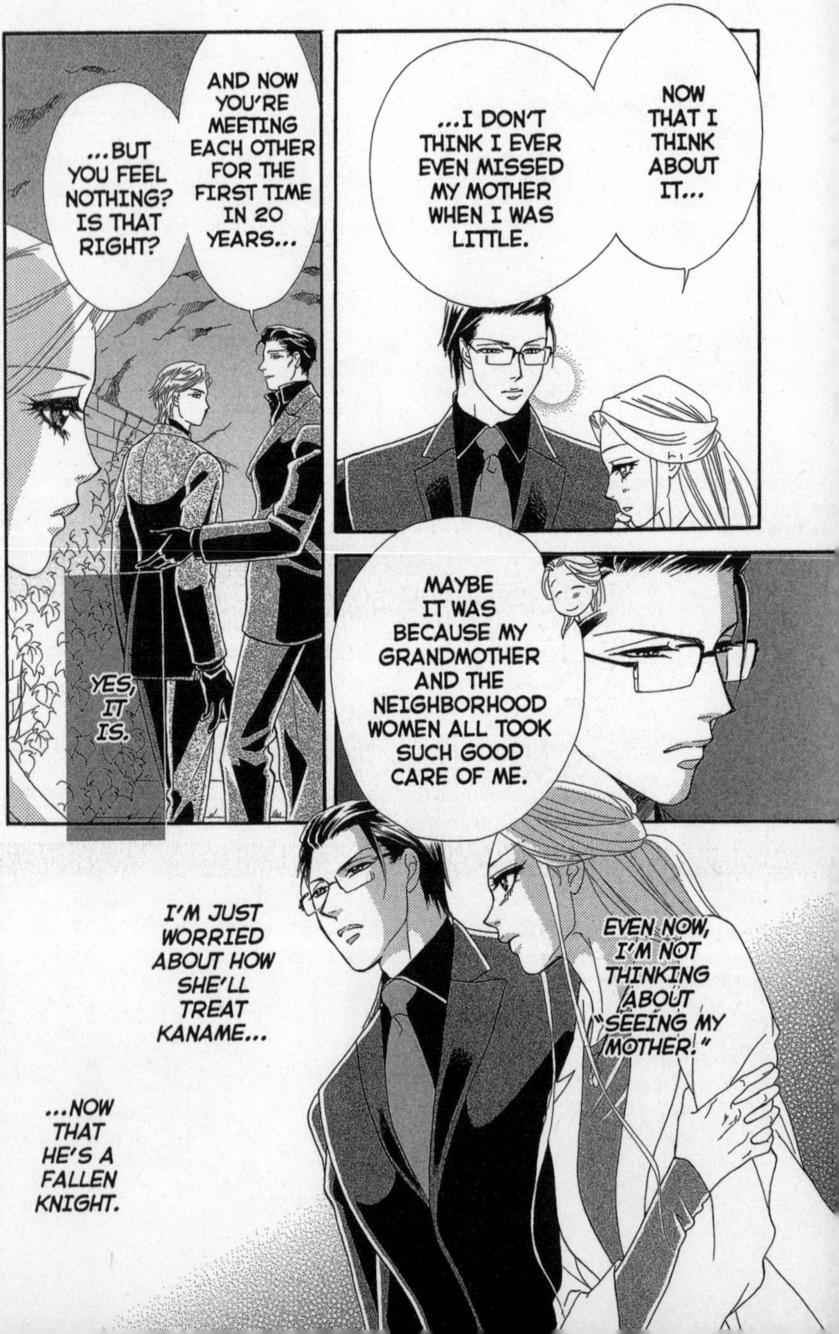
NOW THAT I THINK ABOUT IT...
...I DON'T THINK I EVER EVEN MISSED MY MOTHER WHEN I WAS LITTLE.
MAYBE IT WAS BECAUSE MY GRANDMOTHER AND THE NEIGHBORHOOD WOMEN ALL TOOK SUCH GOOD CARE OF ME.
AND NOW YOU'RE MEETING EACH OTHER FOR THE FIRST TIME IN 20 YEARS...
...BUT YOU FEEL NOTHING? IS THAT RIGHT?
YES, IT IS.
EVEN NOW, I'M NOT THINKING ABOUT "SEEING MY MOTHER."
I'M JUST WORRIED ABOUT HOW SHE'LL TREAT KANAME...
...NOW THAT HE'S A FALLEN KNIGHT.

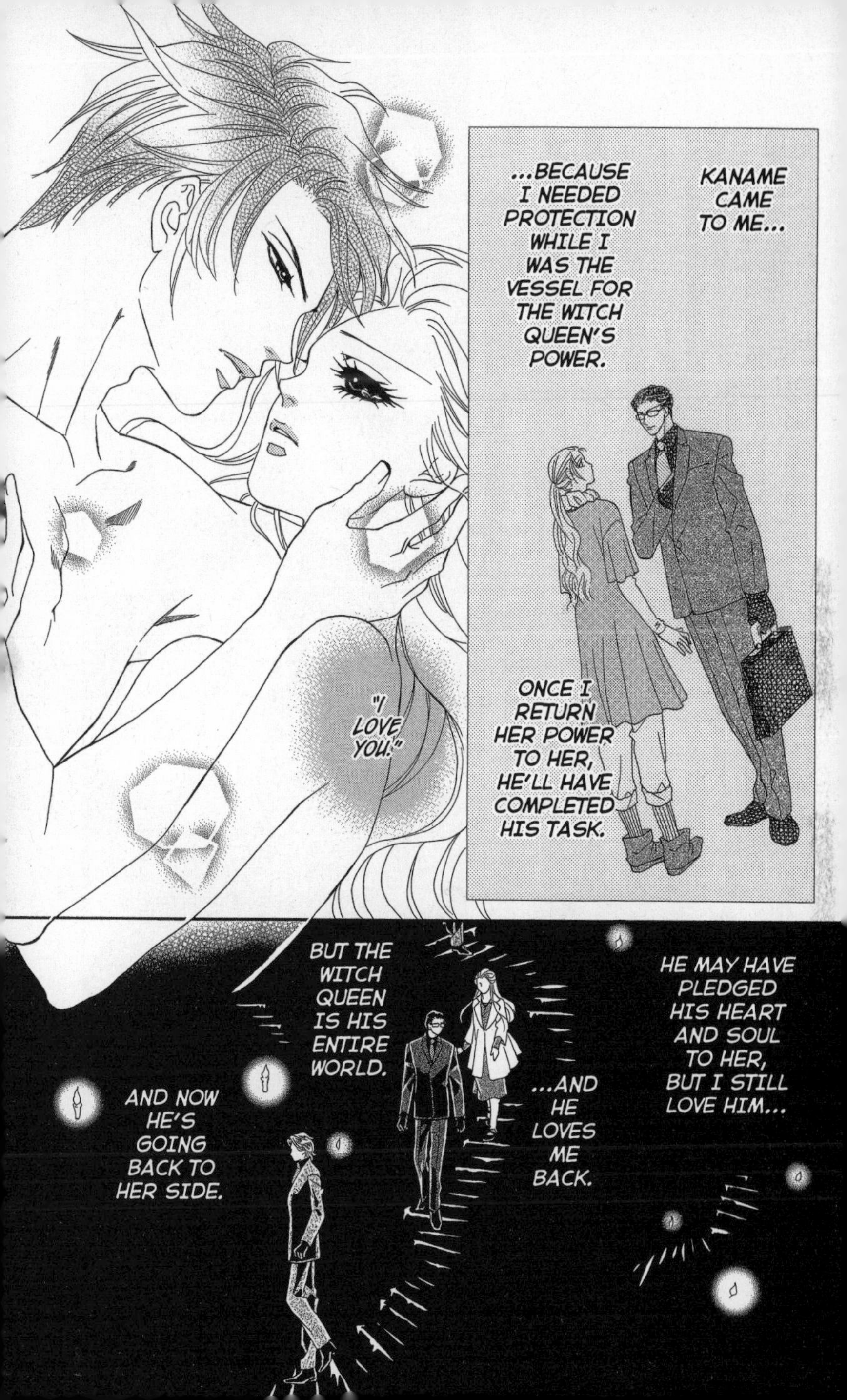
KANAME CAME TO ME...
...BECAUSE I NEEDED PROTECTION WHILE I WAS THE VESSEL FOR THE WITCH QUEEN'S POWER.
ONCE I RETURN HER POWER TO HER, HE'LL HAVE COMPLETED HIS TASK.
"I LOVE YOU."
HE MAY HAVE PLEDGED HIS HEART AND SOUL TO HER, BUT I STILL LOVE HIM...
...AND HE LOVES ME BACK.
BUT THE WITCH QUEEN IS HIS ENTIRE WORLD.
AND NOW HE'S GOING BACK TO HER SIDE.

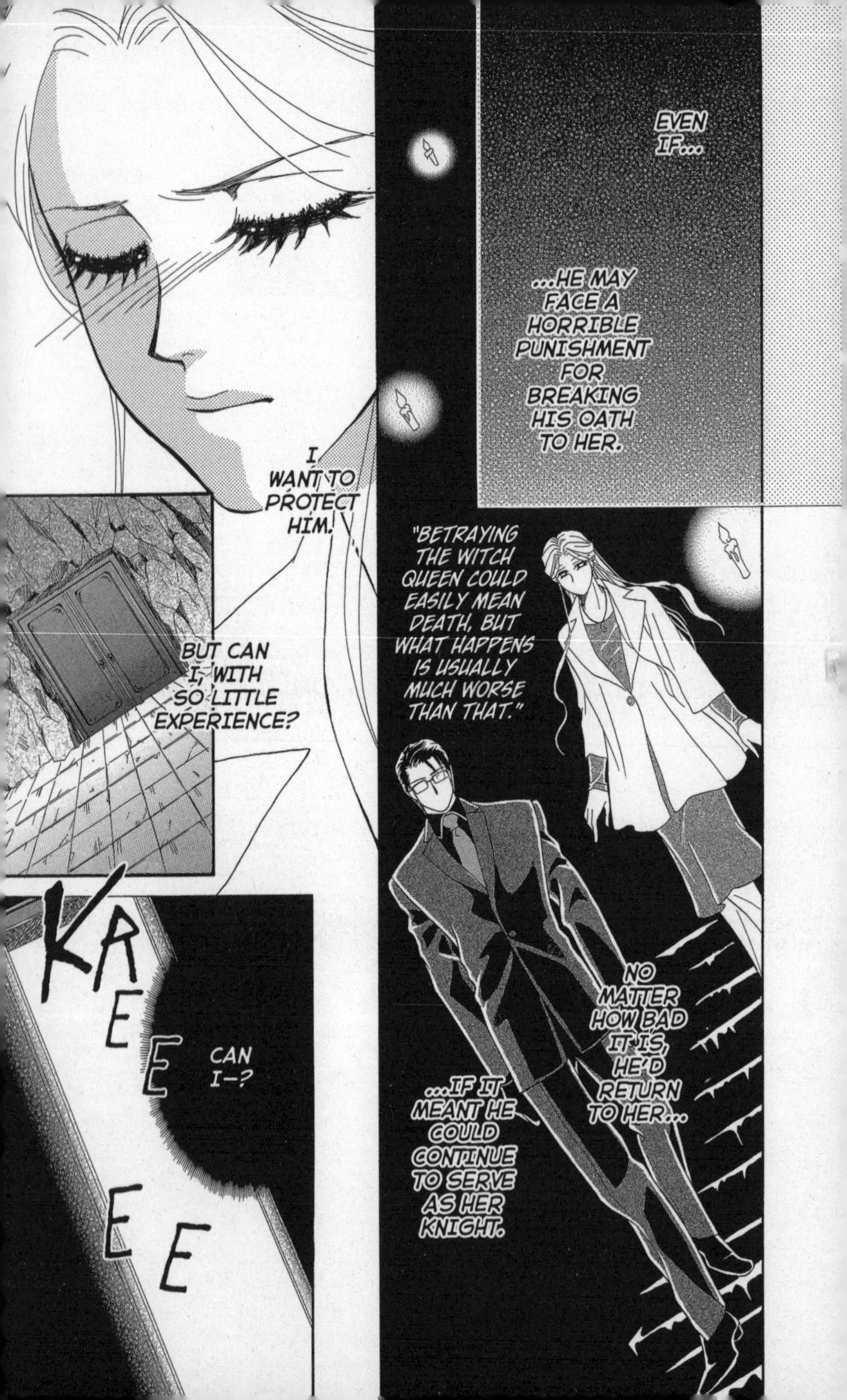
EVEN IF...
...HE MAY FACE A HORRIBLE PUNISHMENT FOR BREAKING HIS OATH TO HER.
"BETRAYING THE WITCH QUEEN COULD EASILY MEAN DEATH, BUT WHAT HAPPENS IS USUALLY MUCH WORSE THAN THAT."
NO MATTER HOW BAD IT IS, HE'D RETURN TO HER...
...IF IT MEANT HE COULD CONTINUE TO SERVE AS HER KNIGHT.
I WANT TO PROTECT HIM.
BUT CAN I, WITH SO LITTLE EXPERIENCE?
KREEEEE
CAN I-?

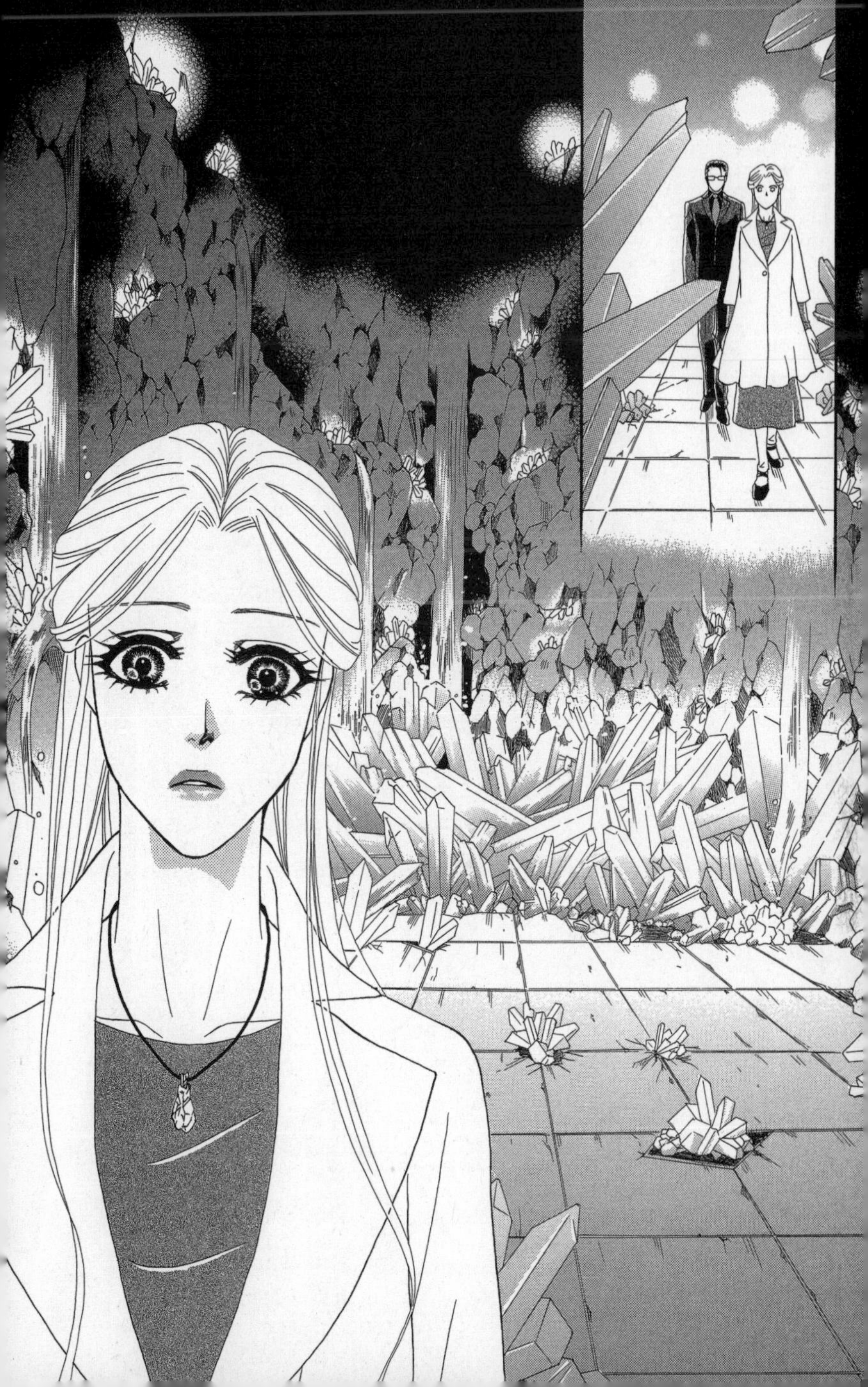

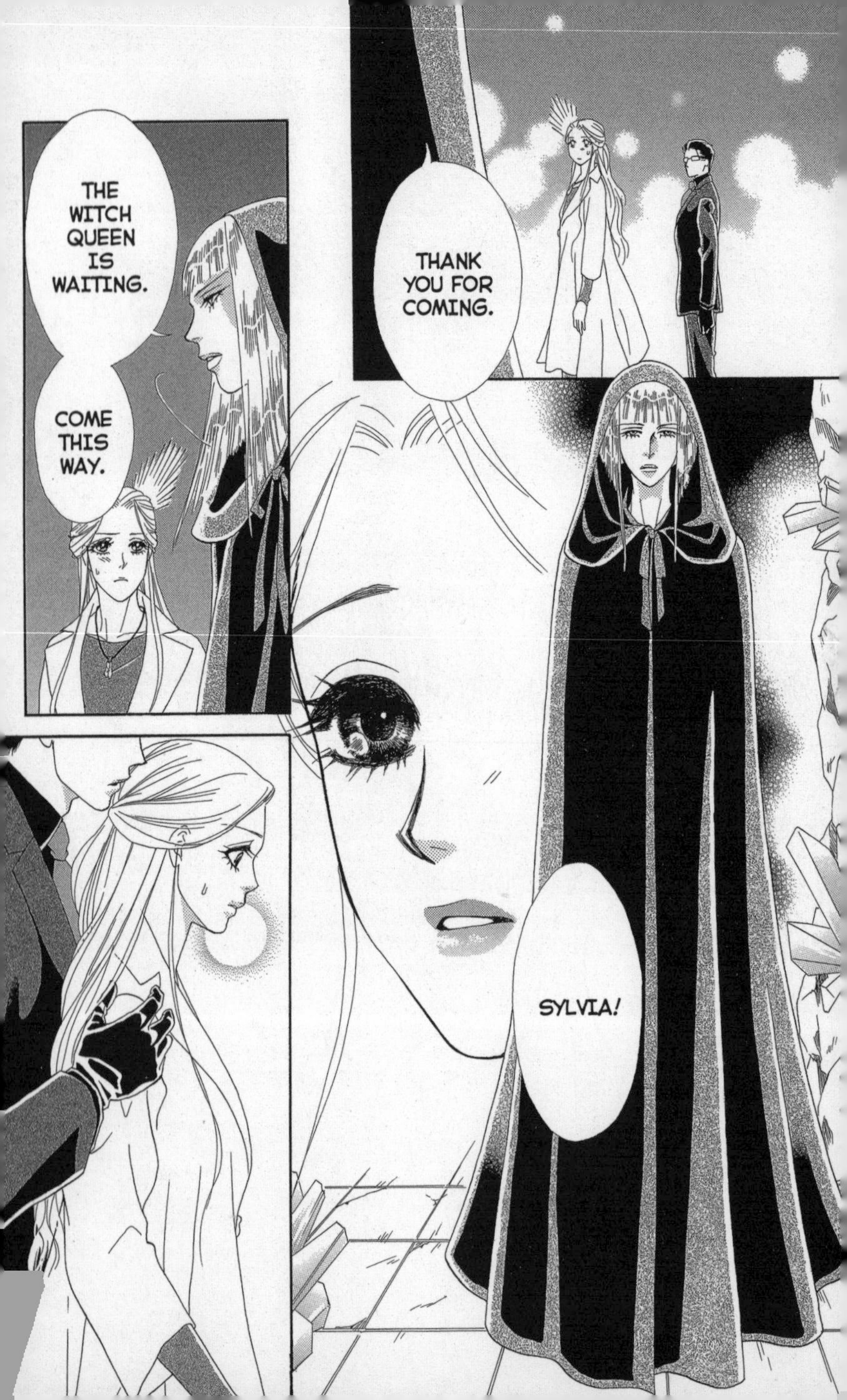
THANK YOU FOR COMING.
SYLVIA!
THE WITCH QUEEN IS WAITING.
COME THIS WAY.

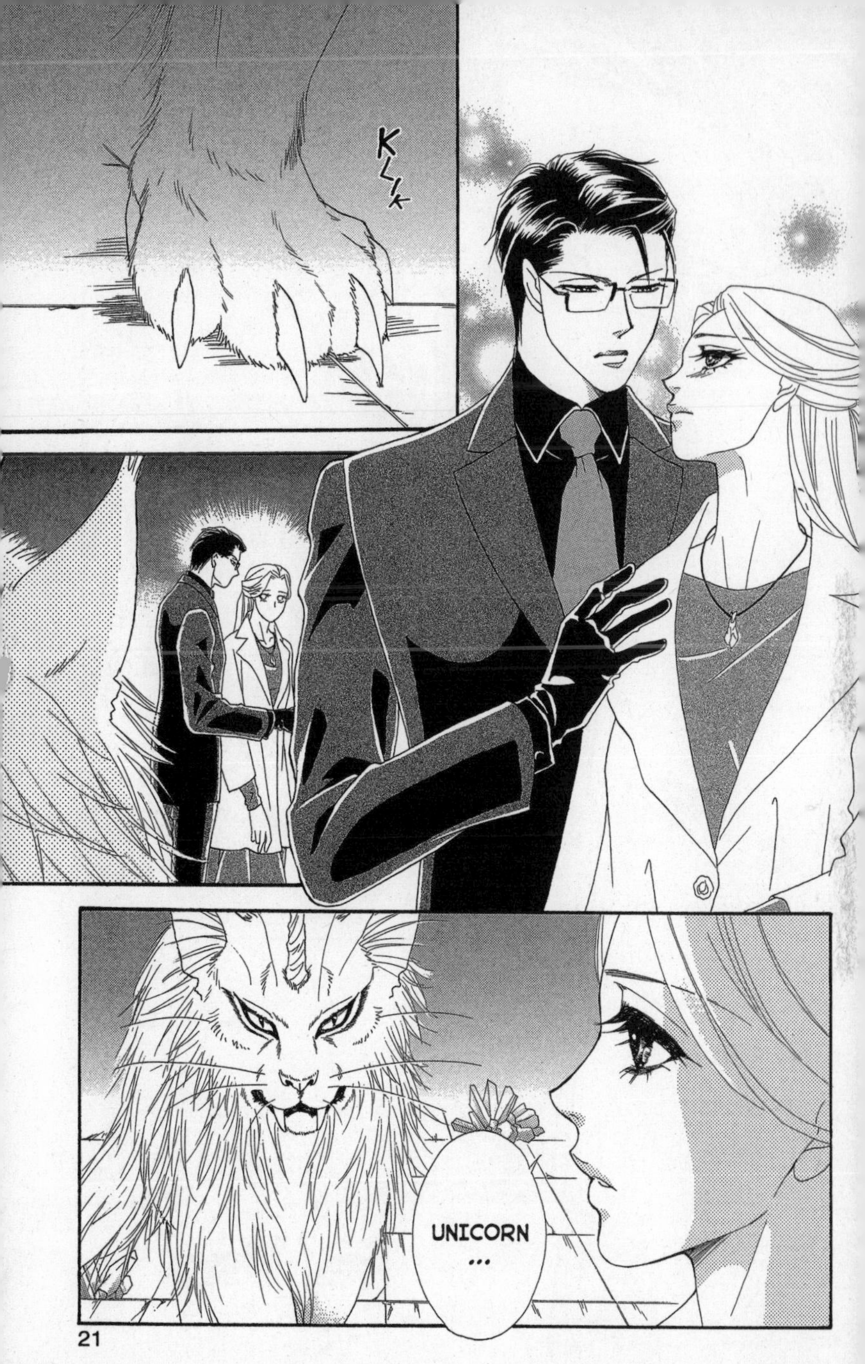
KLIK
UNICORN
...

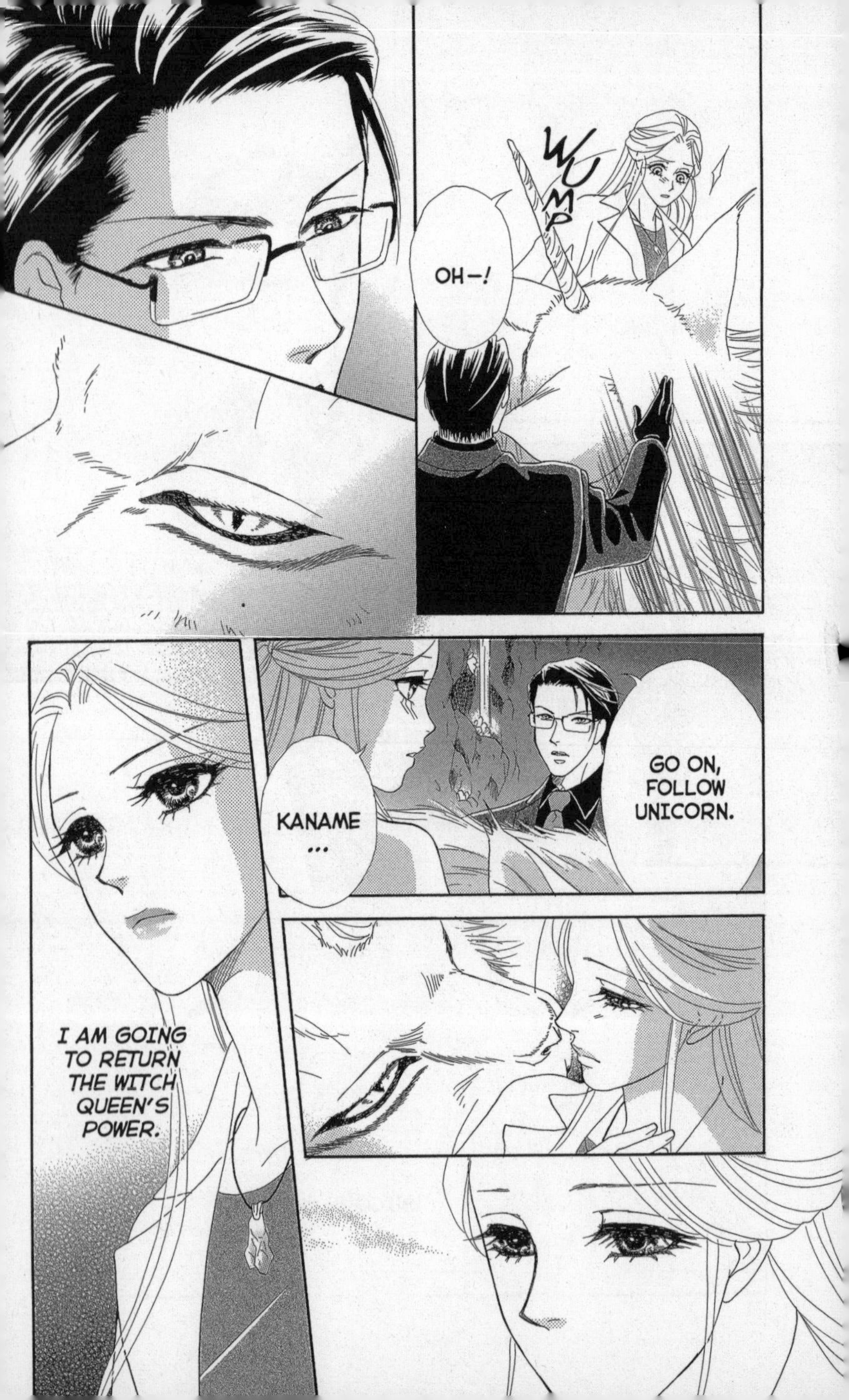
WUMP
OH–!
GO ON, FOLLOW UNICORN.
KANAME ...
I AM GOING TO RETURN THE WITCH QUEEN'S POWER.

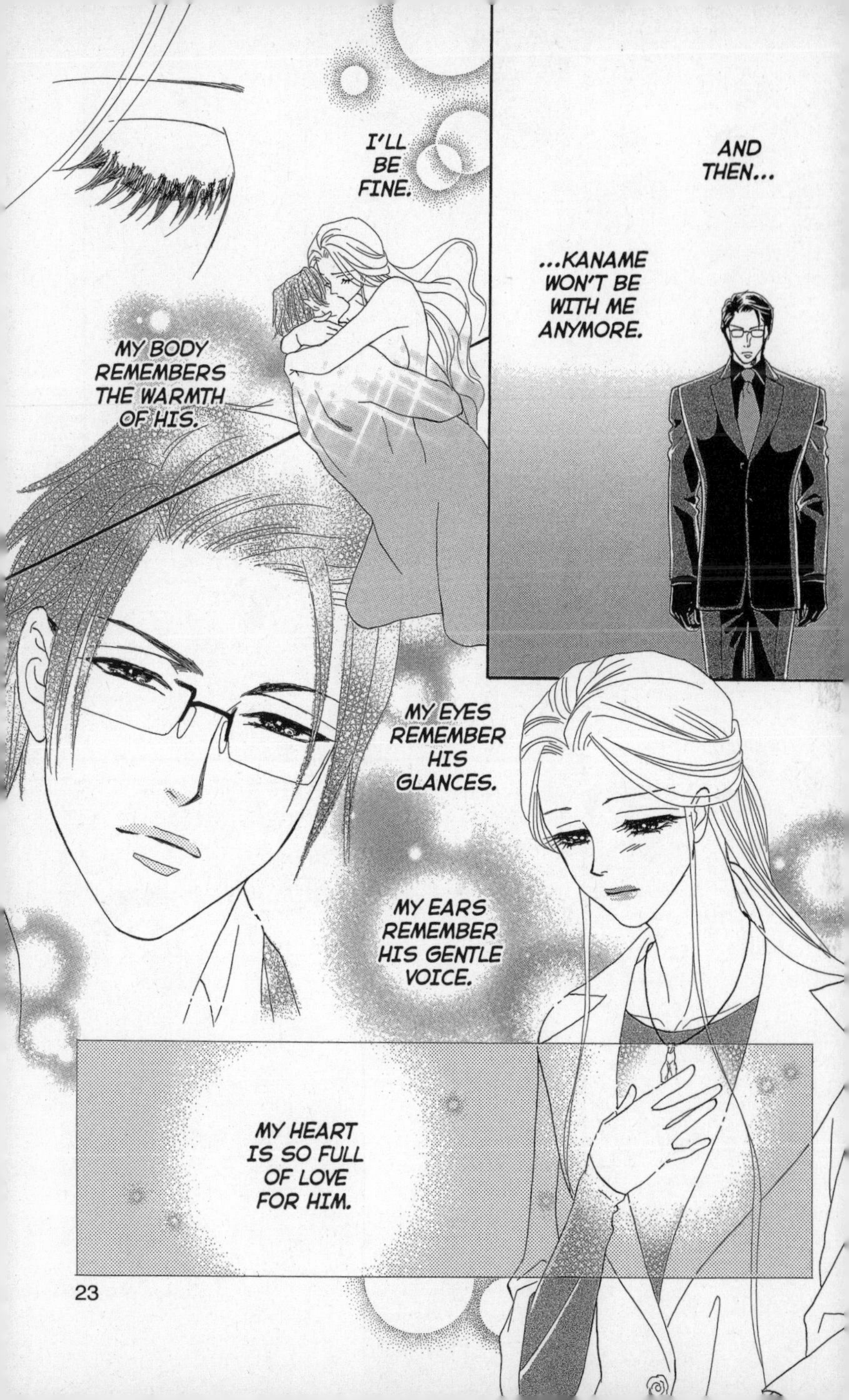
AND THEN...
...KANAME WON'T BE WITH ME ANYMORE.
I'LL BE FINE.
MY BODY REMEMBERS THE WARMTH OF HIS.
MY EYES REMEMBER HIS GLANCES.
MY EARS REMEMBER HIS GENTLE VOICE.
MY HEART IS SO FULL OF LOVE FOR HIM.

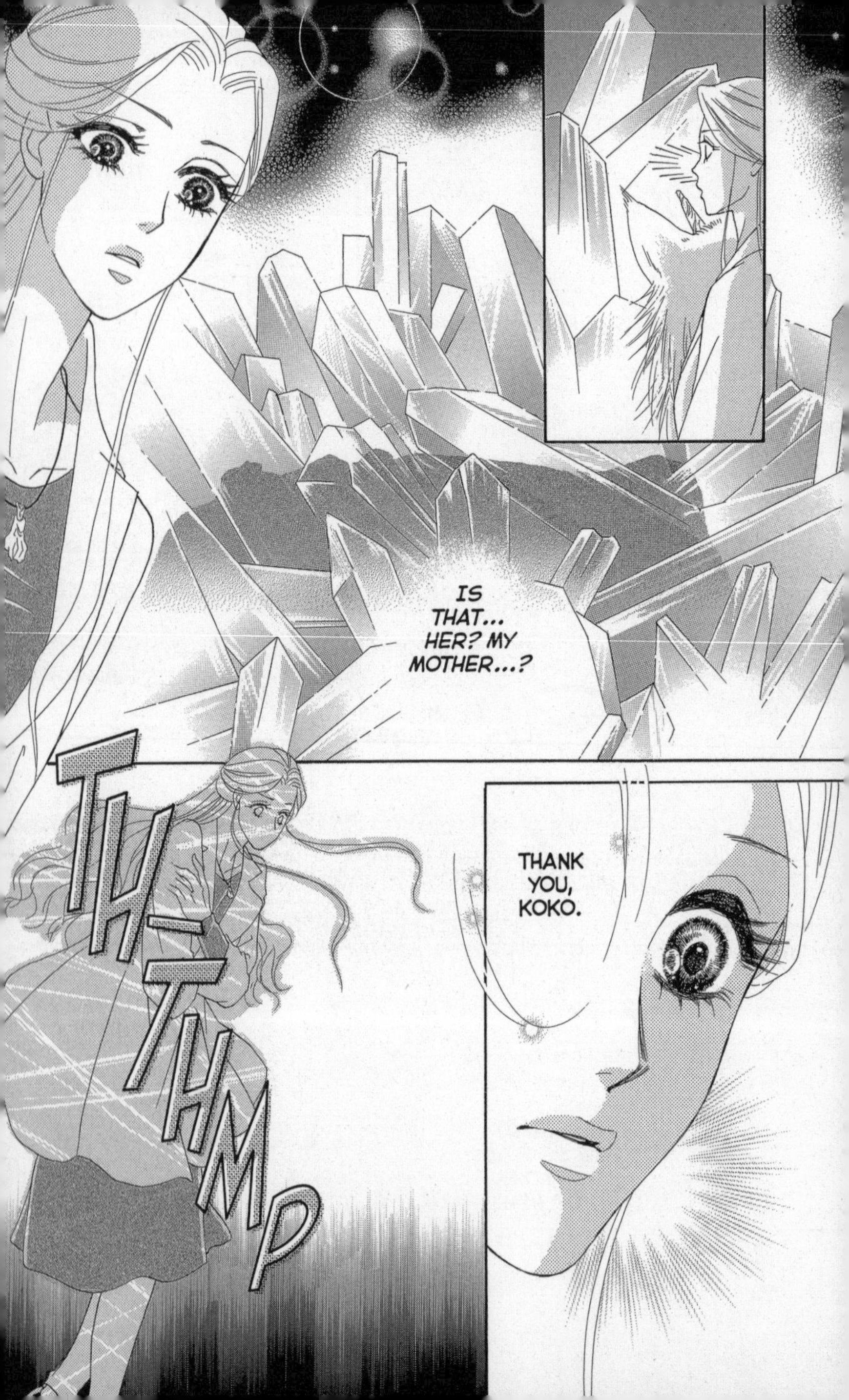
IS THAT... HER? MY MOTHER...?
THANK YOU, KOKO.
TH-THMP

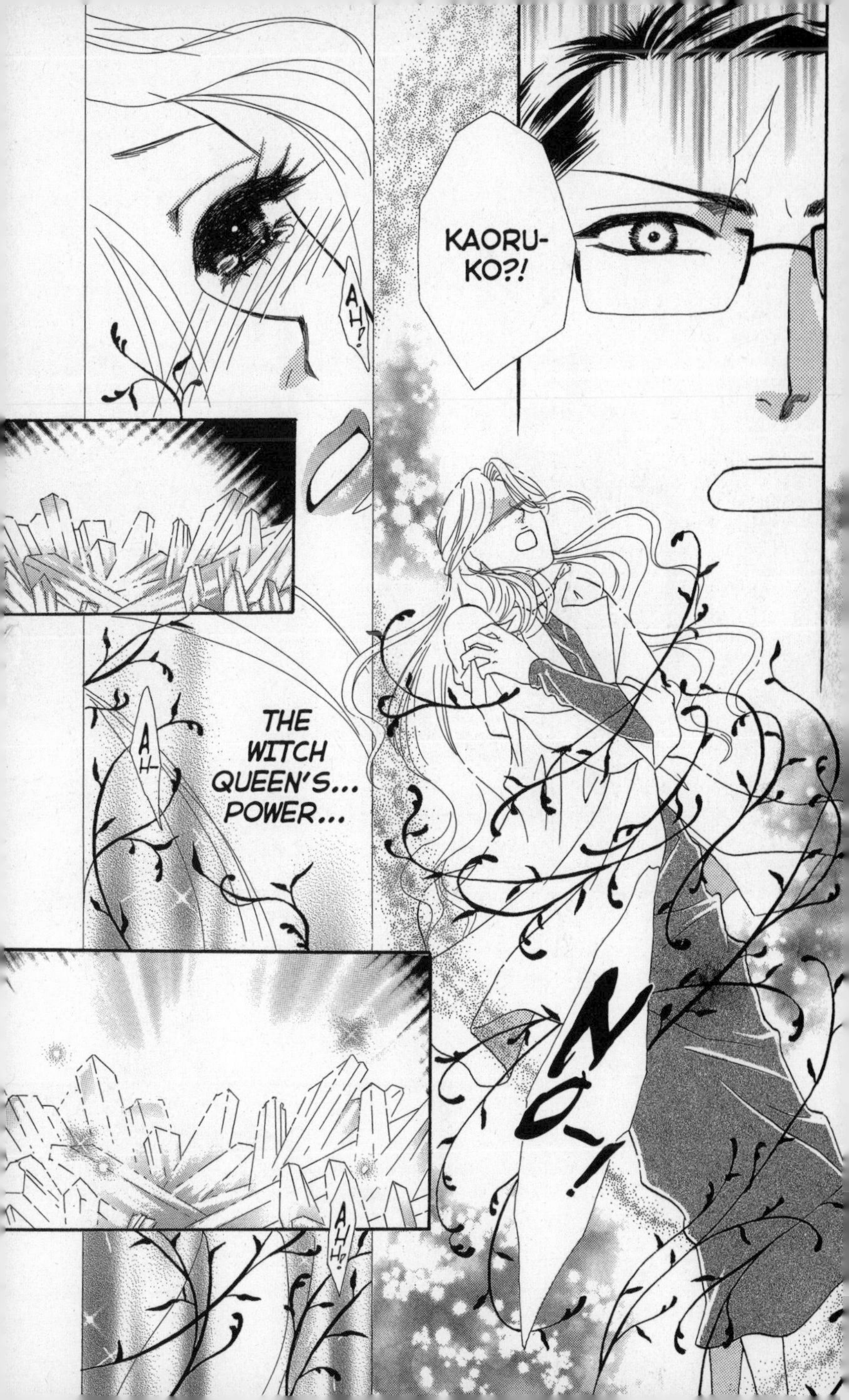
KAORU-KO?!
AH!?
THE WITCH QUEEN'S... POWER...
AH
AHH!?
NO-!

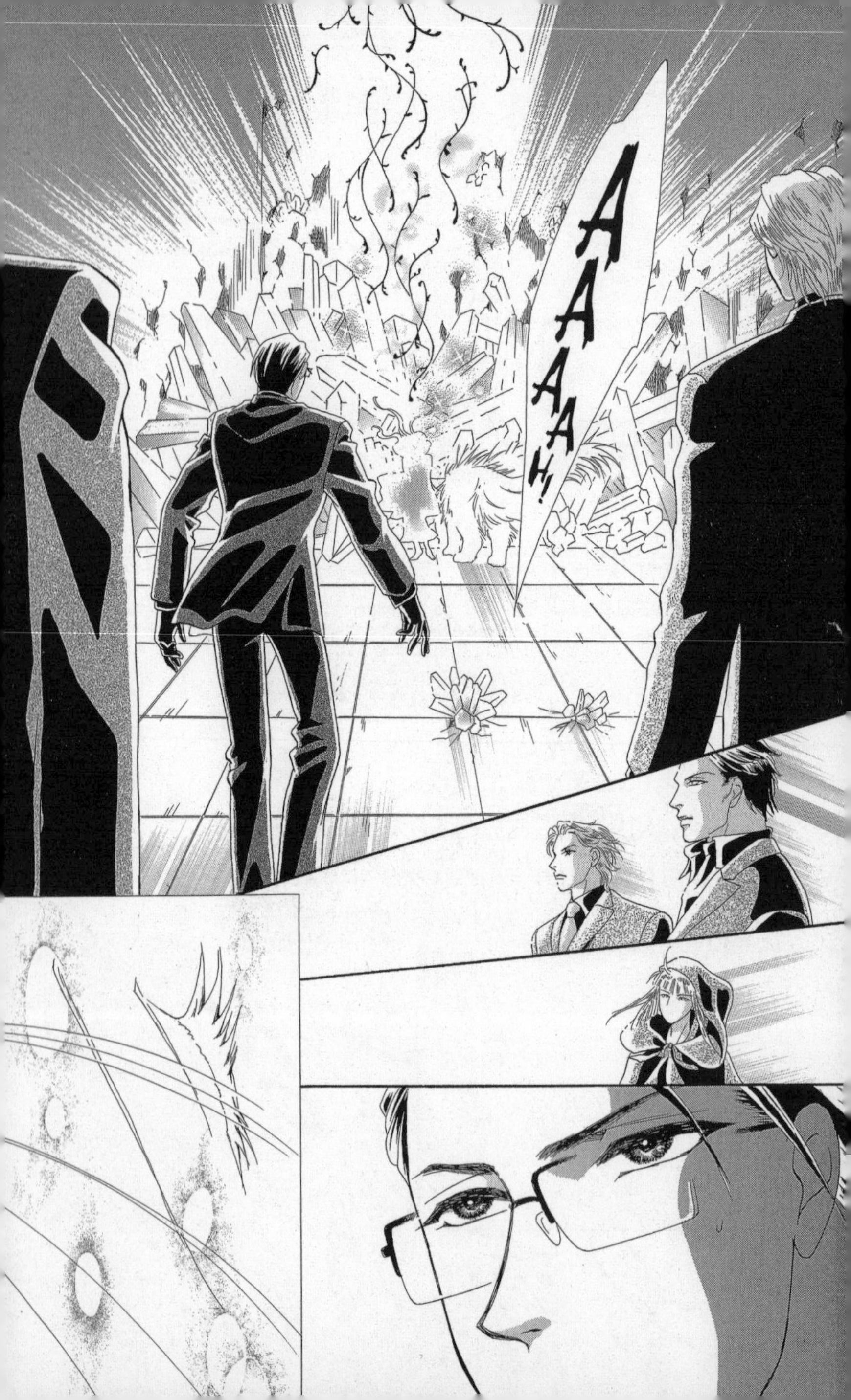
AAAAAH!

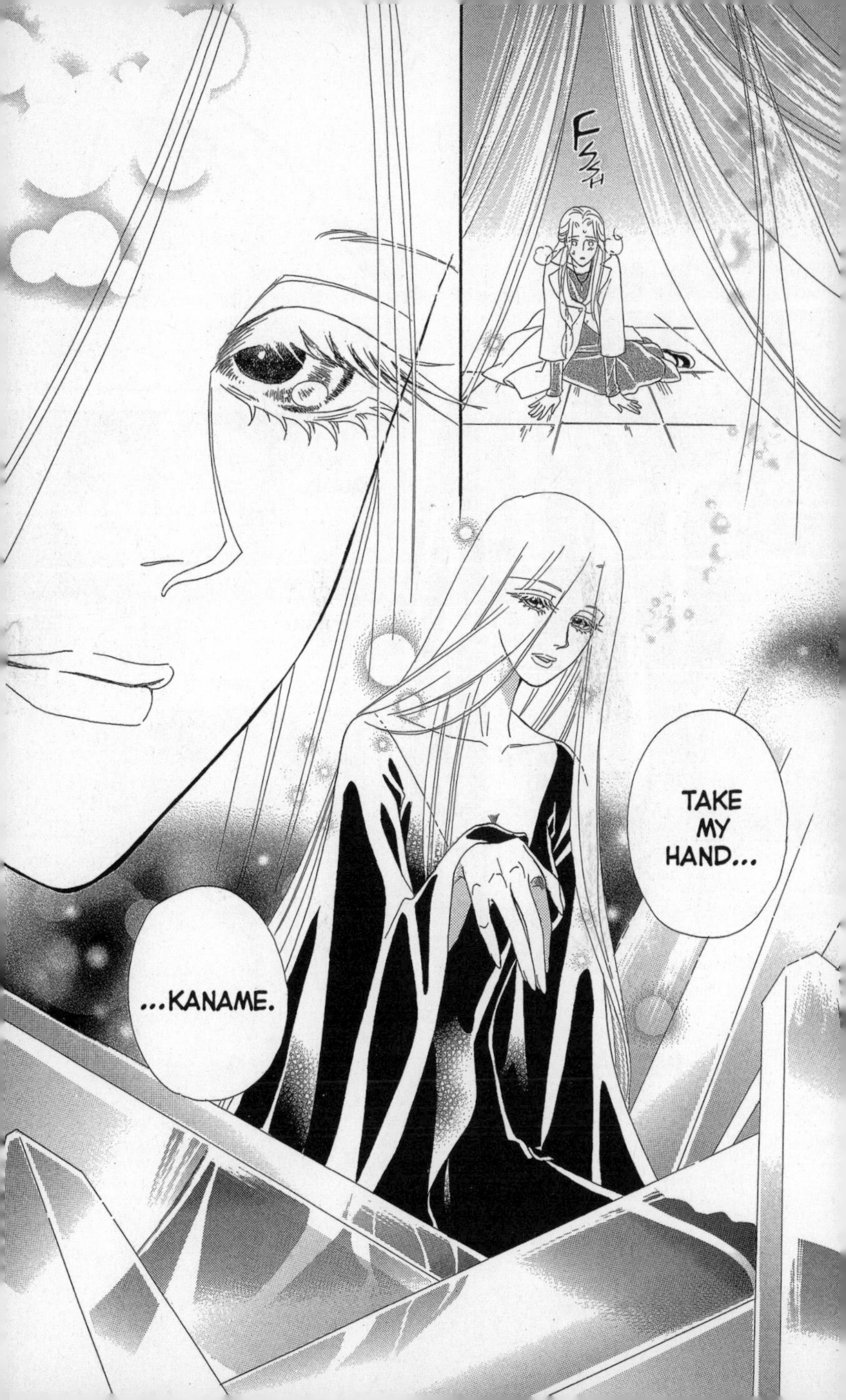
FSSH
TAKE MY HAND...
...KANAME.

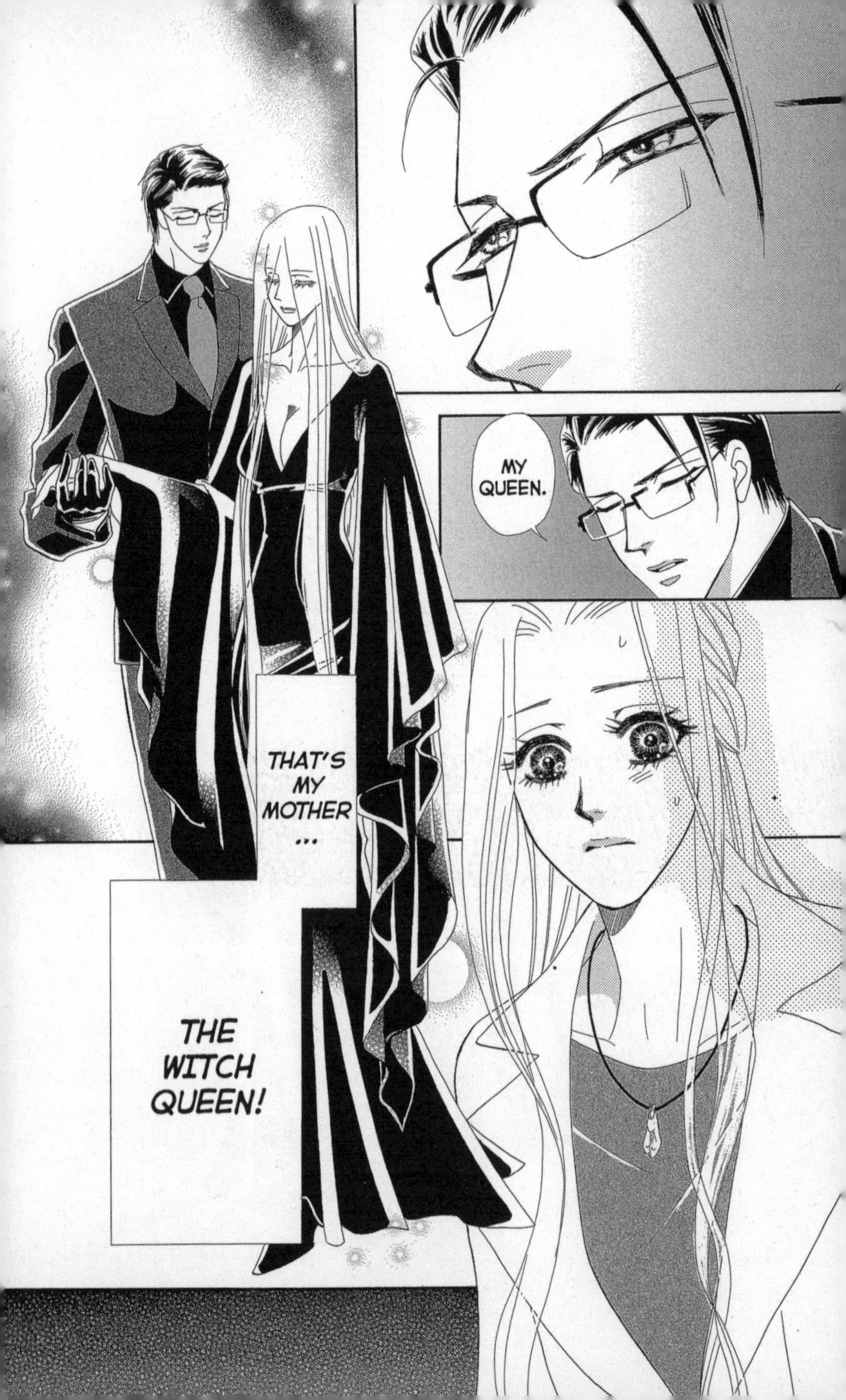
MY QUEEN.
THAT'S MY MOTHER...
THE WITCH QUEEN!

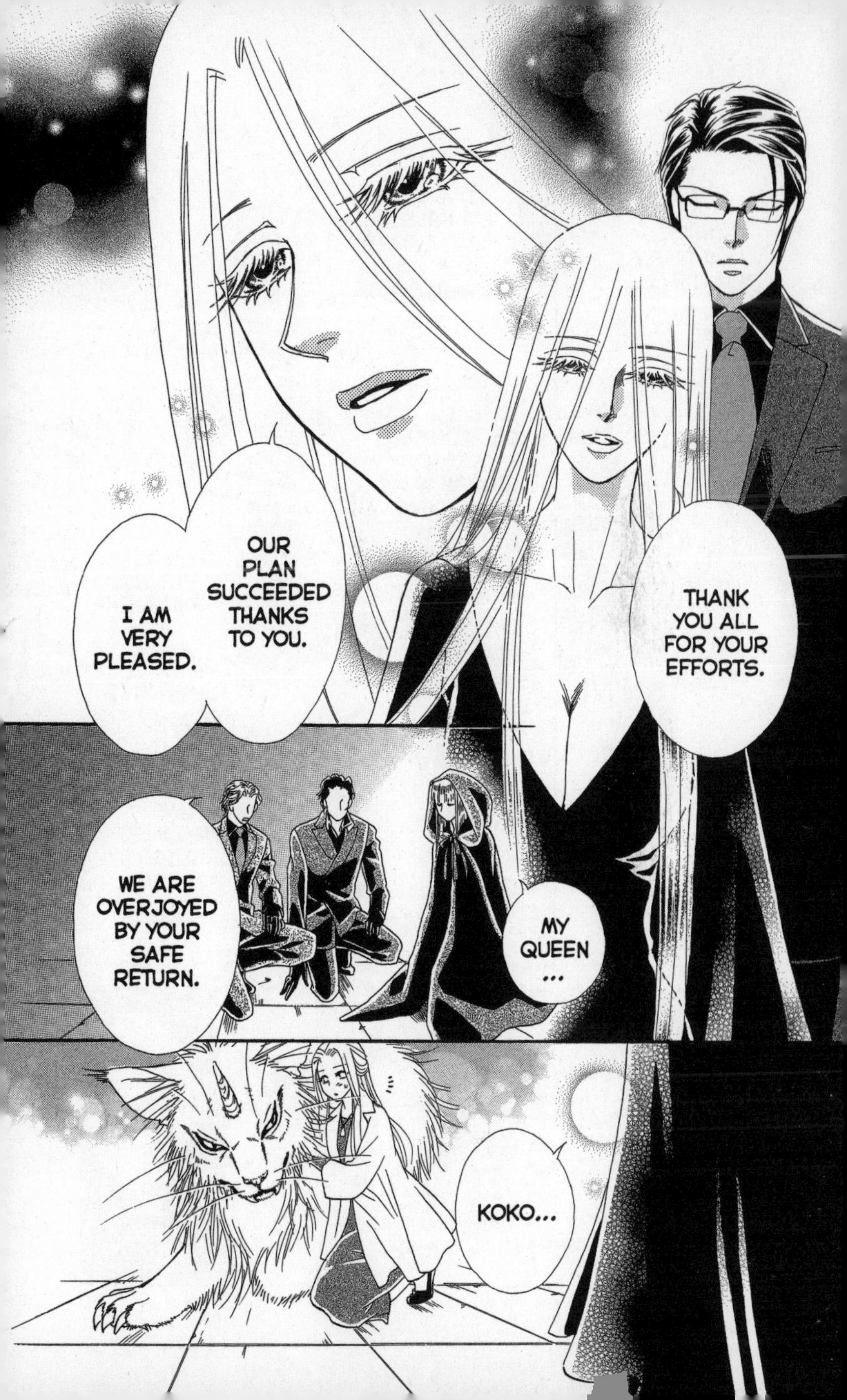
THANK YOU ALL FOR YOUR EFFORTS.
OUR PLAN SUCCEEDED THANKS TO YOU.
I AM VERY PLEASED.
MY QUEEN...
WE ARE OVERJOYED BY YOUR SAFE RETURN.
KOKO...

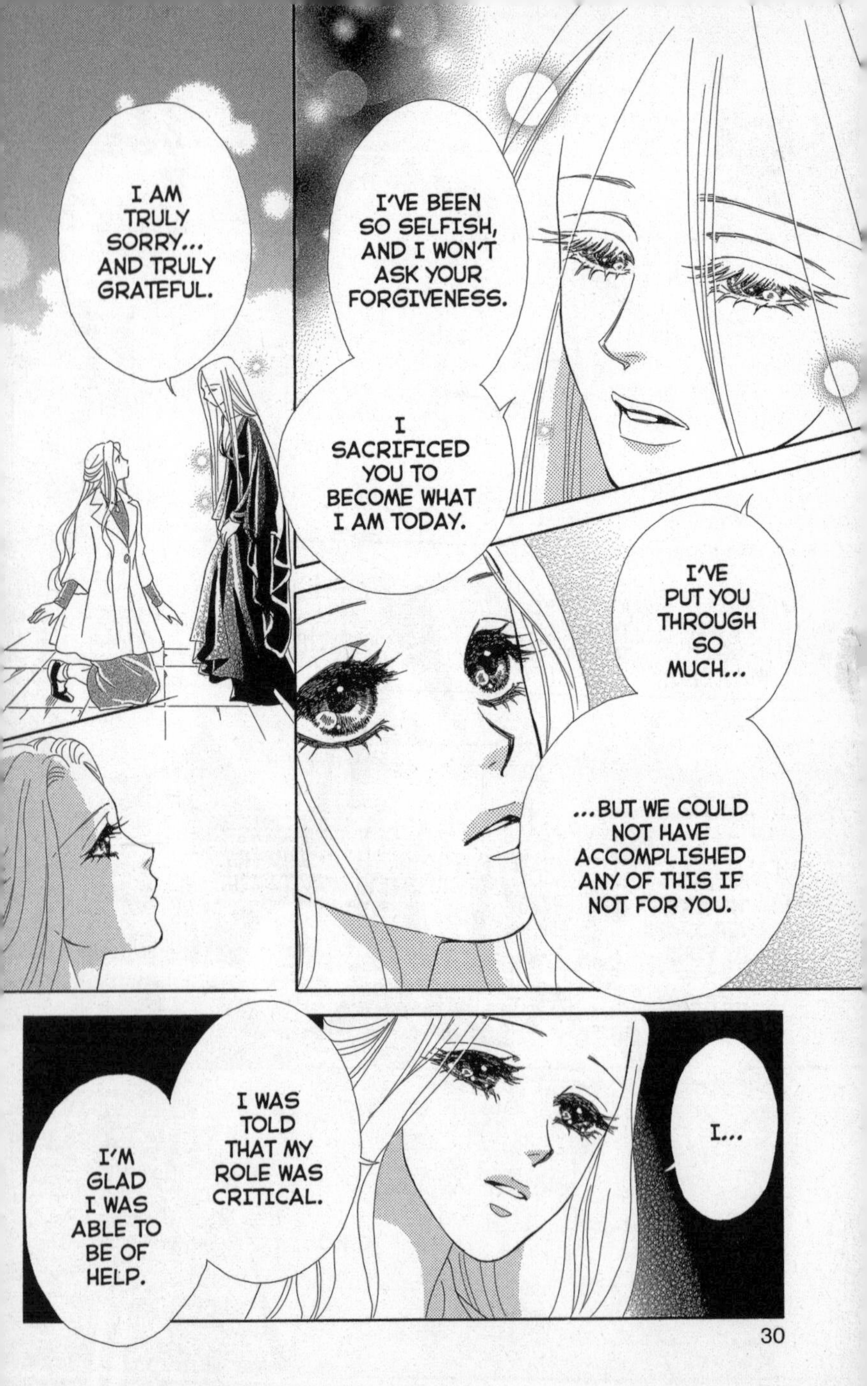
I'VE BEEN SO SELFISH, AND I WON'T ASK YOUR FORGIVENESS.
I SACRIFICED YOU TO BECOME WHAT I AM TODAY.
I AM TRULY SORRY... AND TRULY GRATEFUL.
I'VE PUT YOU THROUGH SO MUCH...
...BUT WE COULD NOT HAVE ACCOMPLISHED ANY OF THIS IF NOT FOR YOU.
I...
I WAS TOLD THAT MY ROLE WAS CRITICAL.
I'M GLAD I WAS ABLE TO BE OF HELP.

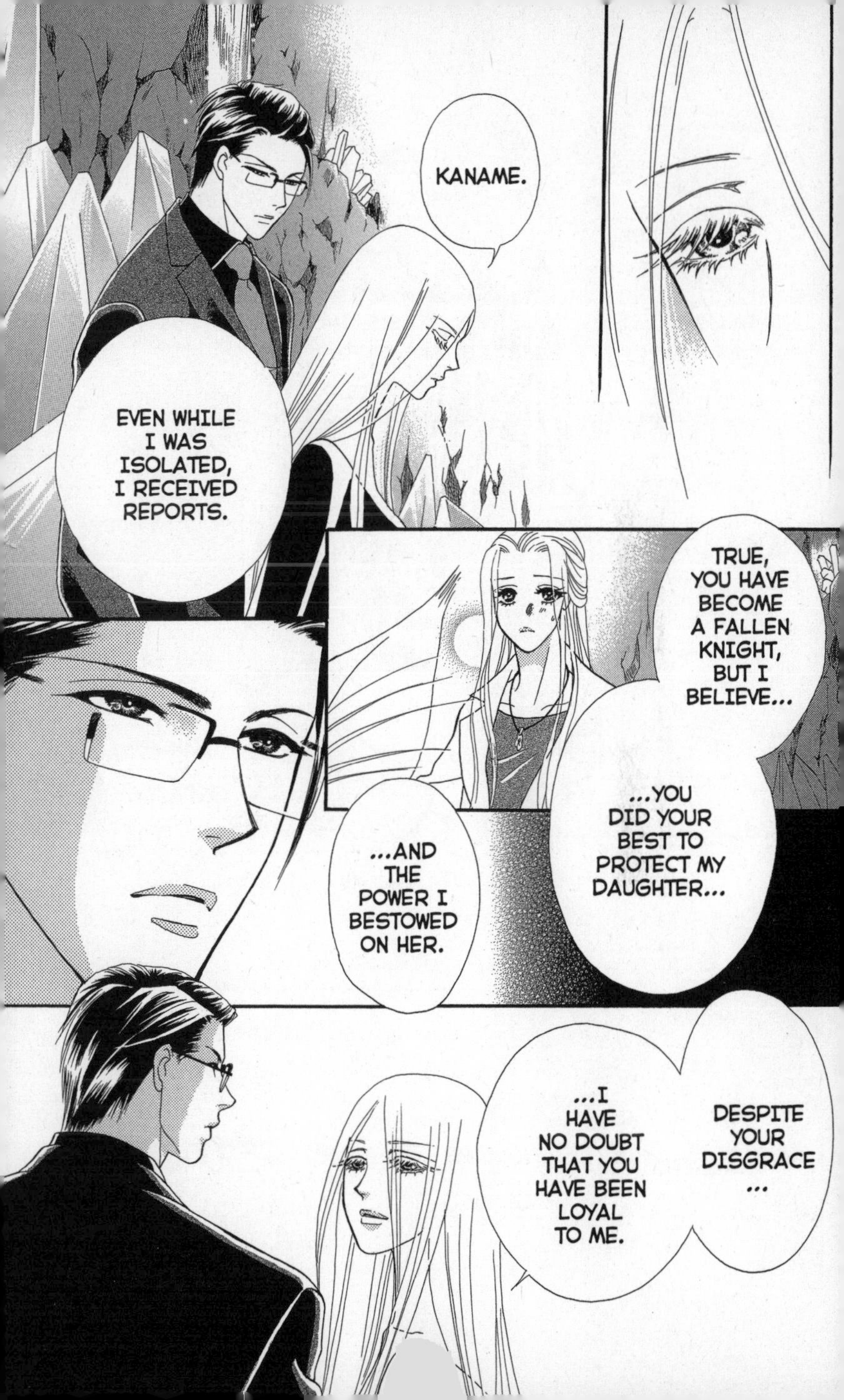
KANAME.
EVEN WHILE I WAS ISOLATED, I RECEIVED REPORTS.
TRUE, YOU HAVE BECOME A FALLEN KNIGHT, BUT I BELIEVE...
...YOU DID YOUR BEST TO PROTECT MY DAUGHTER...
...AND THE POWER I BESTOWED ON HER.
DESPITE YOUR DISGRACE ...
...I HAVE NO DOUBT THAT YOU HAVE BEEN LOYAL TO ME.

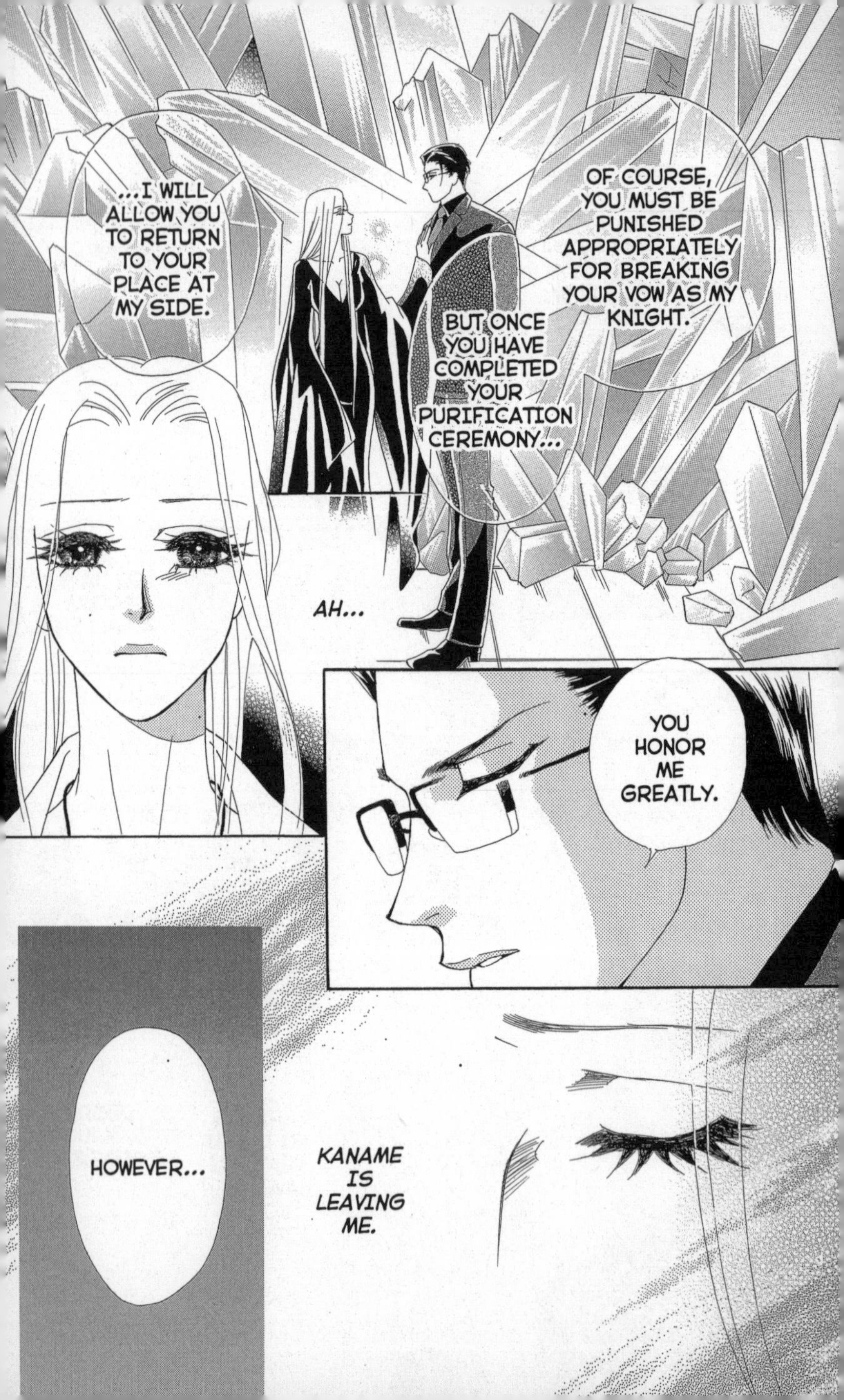
OF COURSE, YOU MUST BE PUNISHED APPROPRIATELY FOR BREAKING YOUR VOW AS MY KNIGHT.
BUT ONCE YOU HAVE COMPLETED YOUR PURIFICATION CEREMONY...
...I WILL ALLOW YOU TO RETURN TO YOUR PLACE AT MY SIDE.
YOU HONOR ME GREATLY.
AH...
KANAME IS LEAVING ME.
HOWEVER...

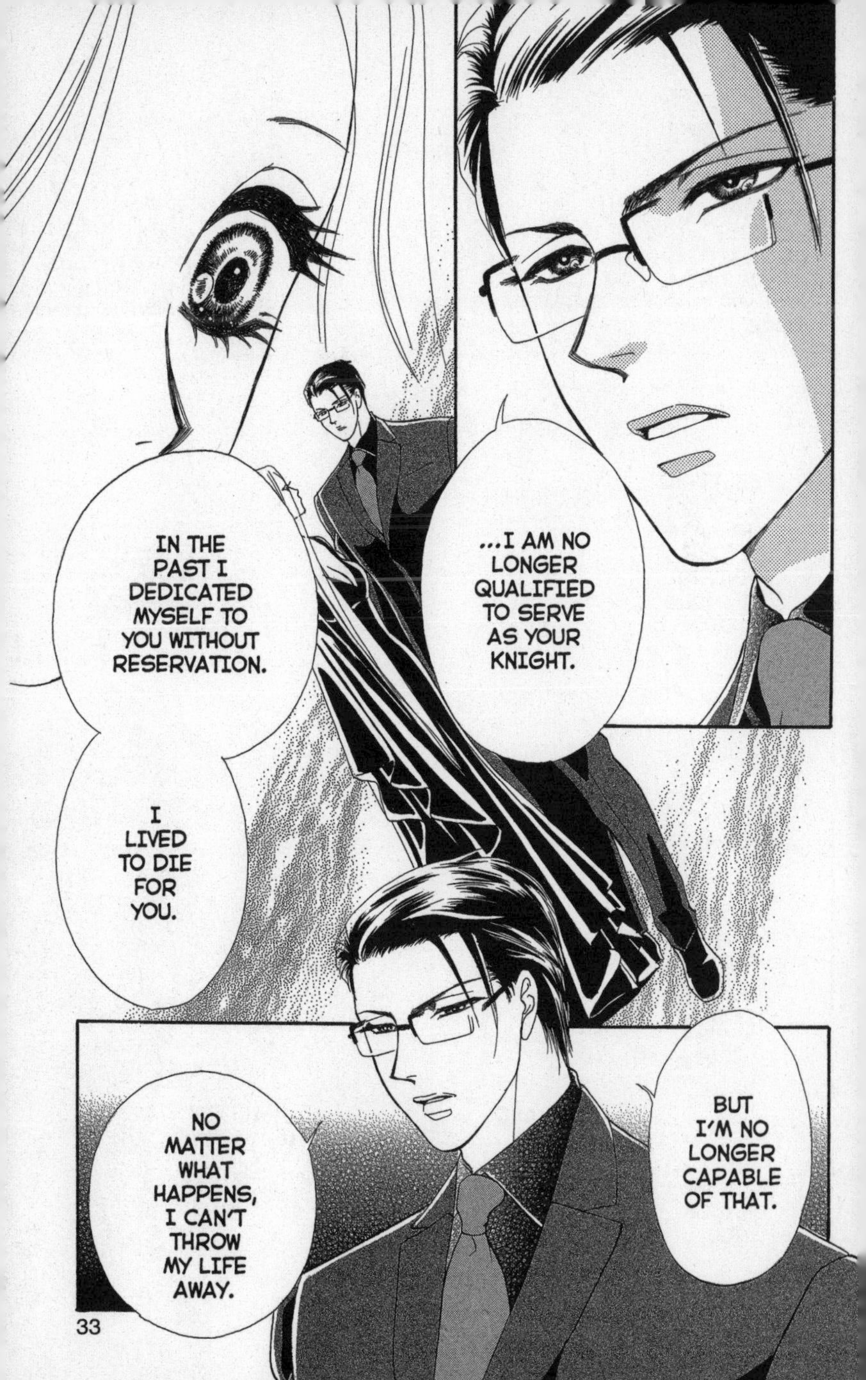
...I AM NO LONGER QUALIFIED TO SERVE AS YOUR KNIGHT.
IN THE PAST I DEDICATED MYSELF TO YOU WITHOUT RESERVATION.
I LIVED TO DIE FOR YOU.
BUT I'M NO LONGER CAPABLE OF THAT.
NO MATTER WHAT HAPPENS, I CAN'T THROW MY LIFE AWAY.

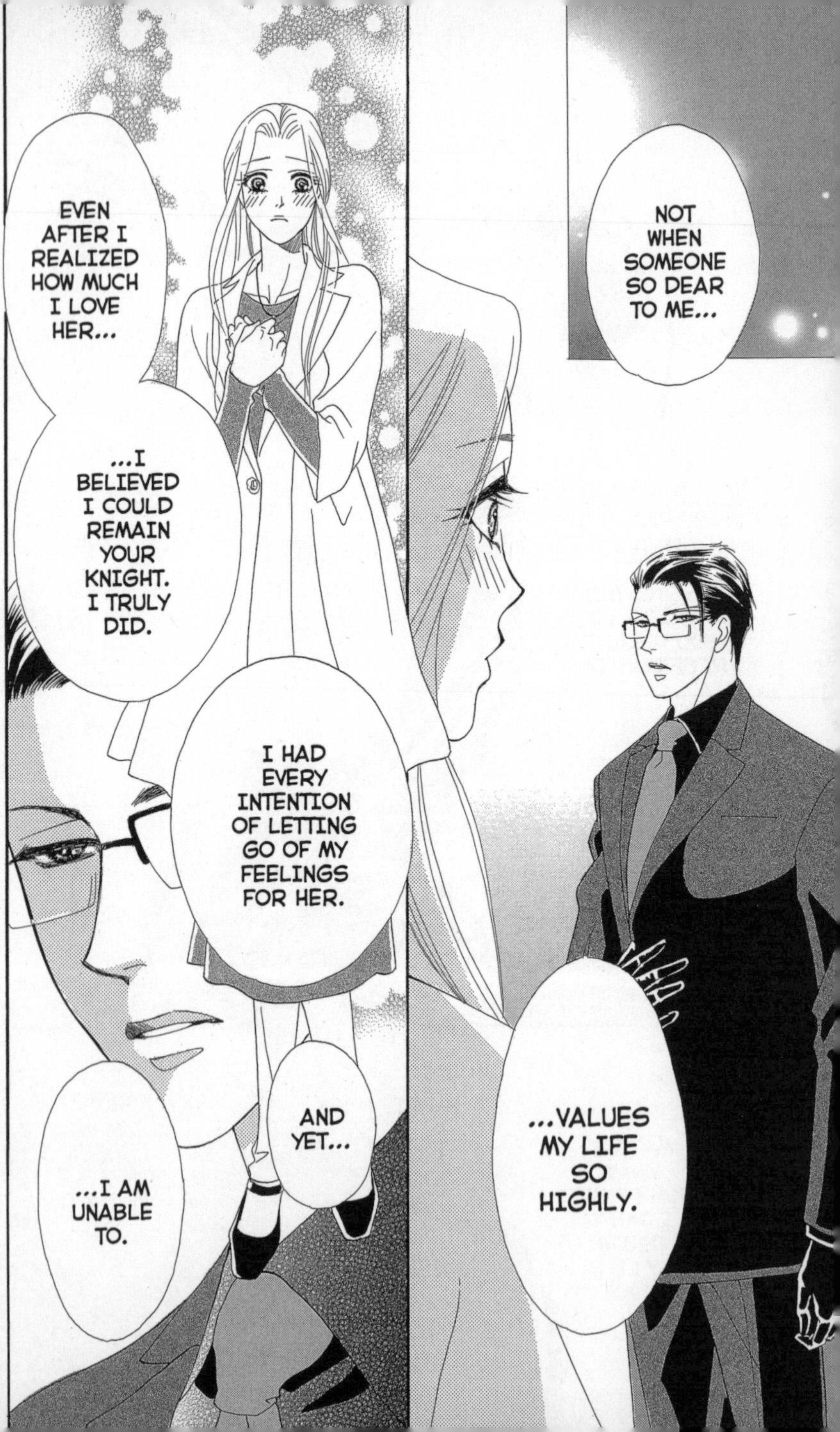
NOT WHEN SOMEONE SO DEAR TO ME...
...VALUES MY LIFE SO HIGHLY.
EVEN AFTER I REALIZED HOW MUCH I LOVE HER...
...I BELIEVED I COULD REMAIN YOUR KNIGHT. I TRULY DID.
I HAD EVERY INTENTION OF LETTING GO OF MY FEELINGS FOR HER.
AND YET...
...I AM UNABLE TO.

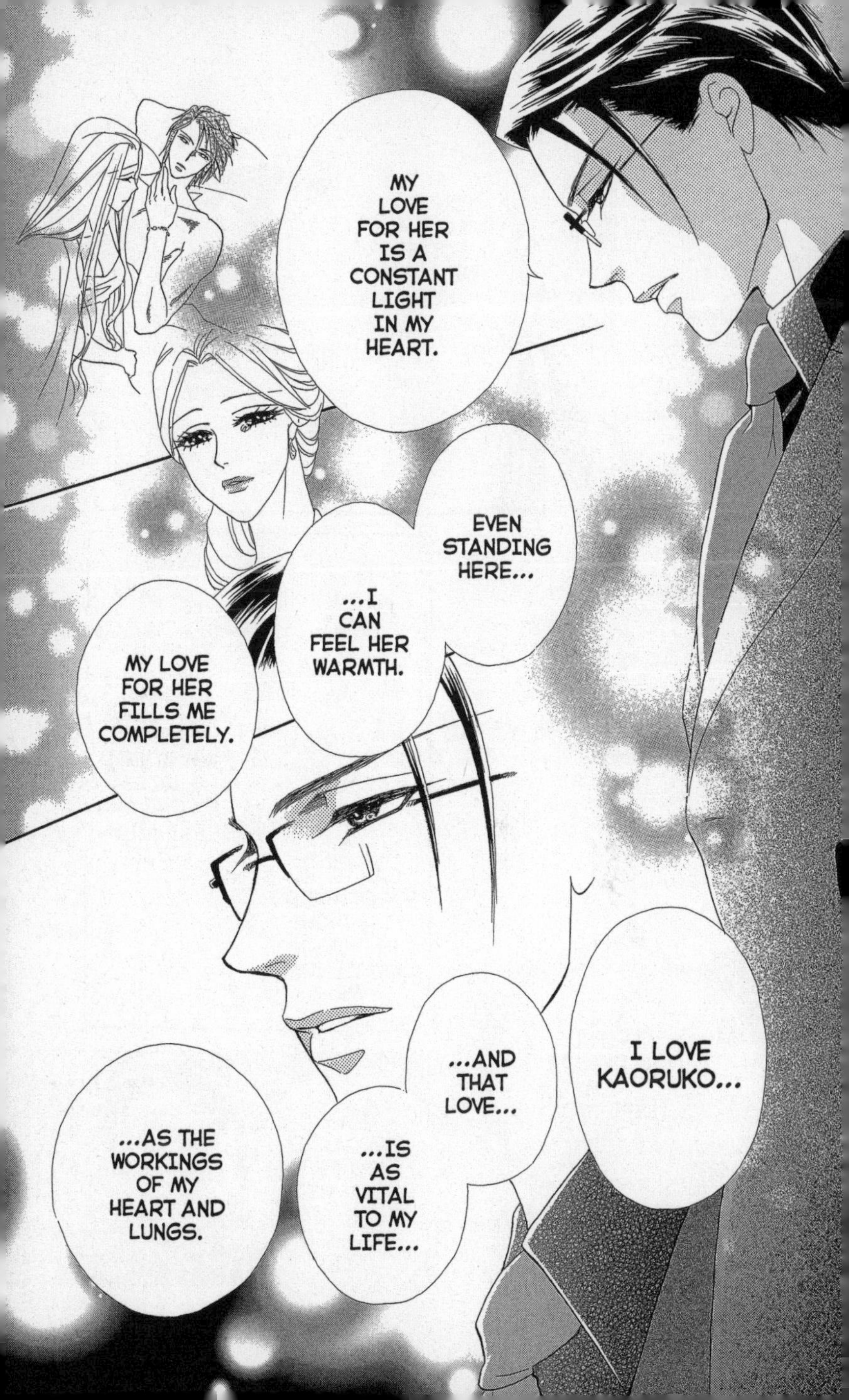
MY LOVE FOR HER IS A CONSTANT LIGHT IN MY HEART.
EVEN STANDING HERE...
...I CAN FEEL HER WARMTH.
MY LOVE FOR HER FILLS ME COMPLETELY.
I LOVE KAORUKO...
...AND THAT LOVE...
...IS AS VITAL TO MY LIFE...
...AS THE WORKINGS OF MY HEART AND LUNGS.

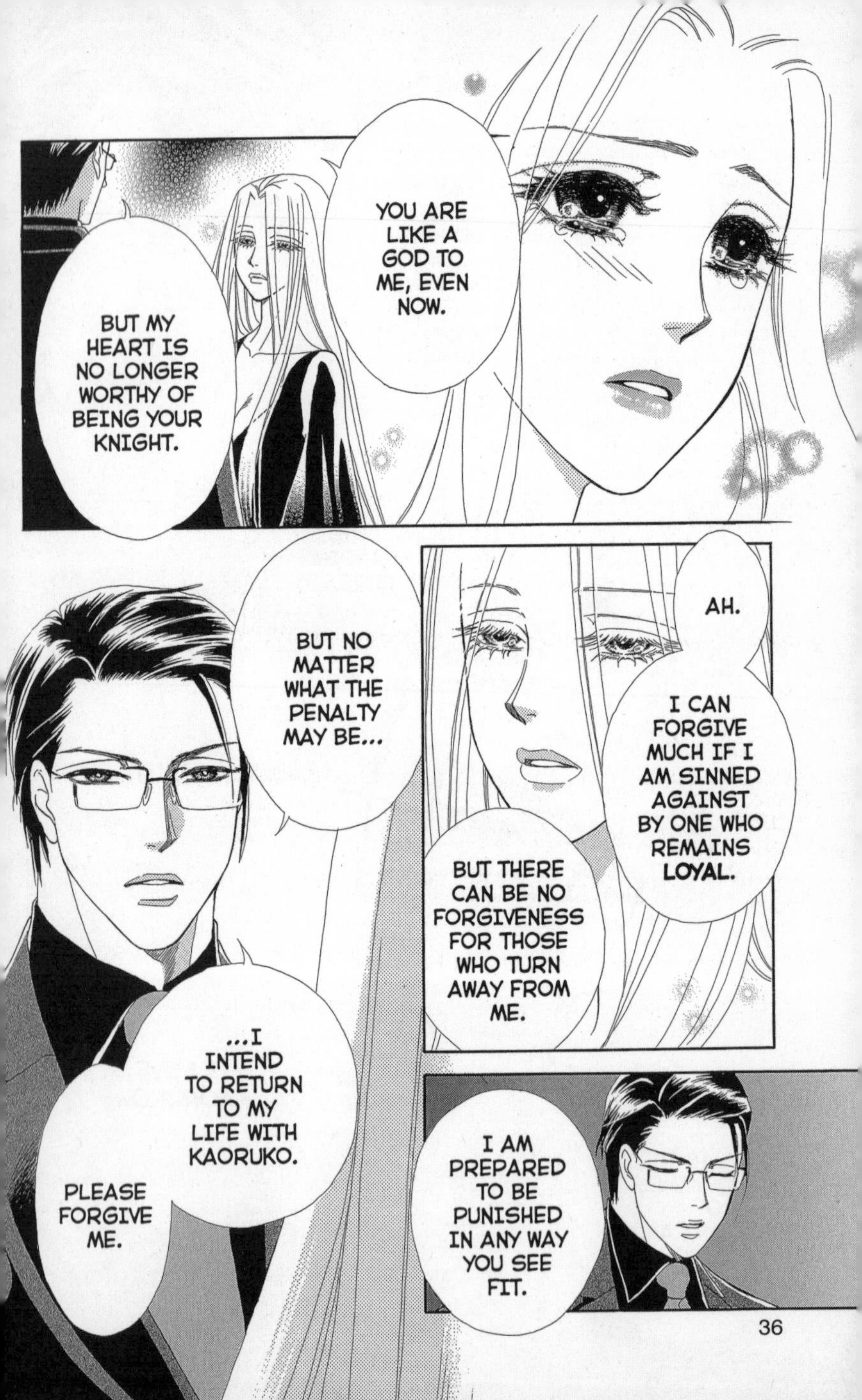
YOU ARE LIKE A GOD TO ME, EVEN NOW.
BUT MY HEART IS NO LONGER WORTHY OF BEING YOUR KNIGHT.
AH.
I CAN FORGIVE MUCH IF I AM SINNED AGAINST BY ONE WHO REMAINS LOYAL.
BUT THERE CAN BE NO FORGIVENESS FOR THOSE WHO TURN AWAY FROM ME.
I AM PREPARED TO BE PUNISHED IN ANY WAY YOU SEE FIT.
BUT NO MATTER WHAT THE PENALTY MAY BE...
...I INTEND TO RETURN TO MY LIFE WITH KAORUKO.
PLEASE FORGIVE ME.

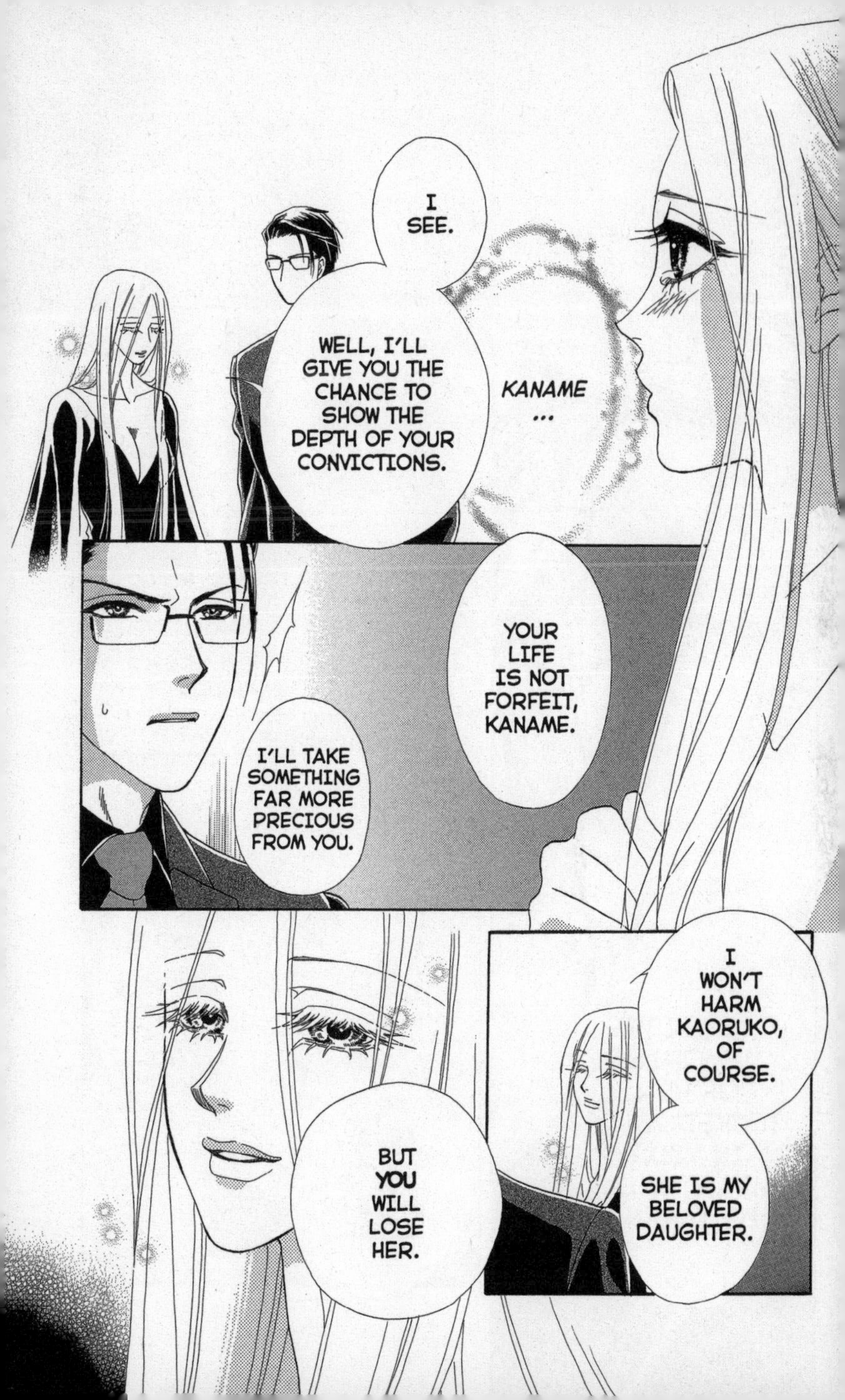
KANAME …
I SEE.
WELL, I'LL GIVE YOU THE CHANCE TO SHOW THE DEPTH OF YOUR CONVICTIONS.
YOUR LIFE IS NOT FORFEIT, KANAME.
I'LL TAKE SOMETHING FAR MORE PRECIOUS FROM YOU.
I WON'T HARM KAORUKO, OF COURSE.
SHE IS MY BELOVED DAUGHTER.
BUT YOU WILL LOSE HER.

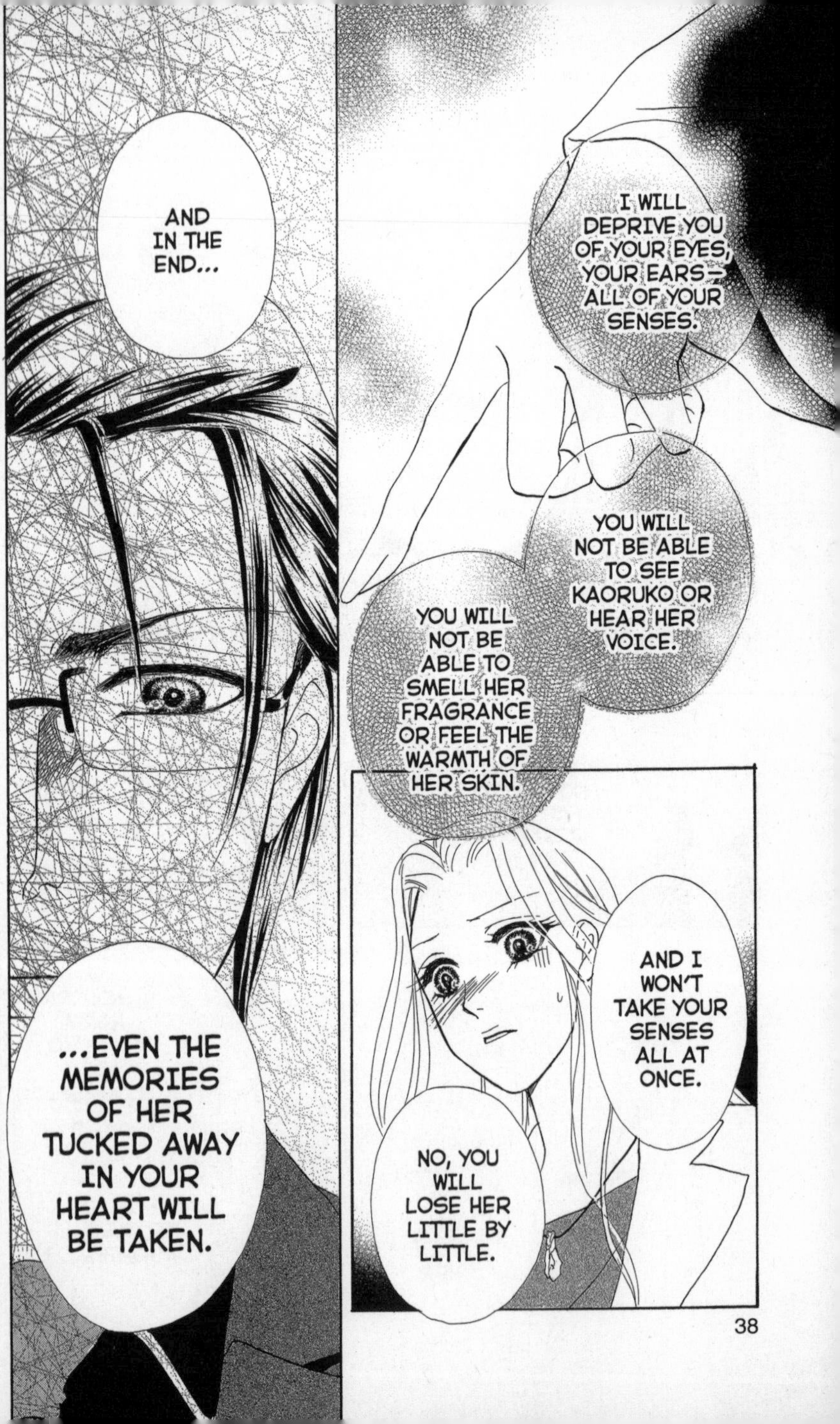
I WILL DEPRIVE YOU OF YOUR EYES, YOUR EARS— ALL OF YOUR SENSES.
YOU WILL NOT BE ABLE TO SEE KAORUKO OR HEAR HER VOICE.
YOU WILL NOT BE ABLE TO SMELL HER FRAGRANCE OR FEEL THE WARMTH OF HER SKIN.
AND I WON'T TAKE YOUR SENSES ALL AT ONCE.
NO, YOU WILL LOSE HER LITTLE BY LITTLE.
AND IN THE END...
...EVEN THE MEMORIES OF HER TUCKED AWAY IN YOUR HEART WILL BE TAKEN.

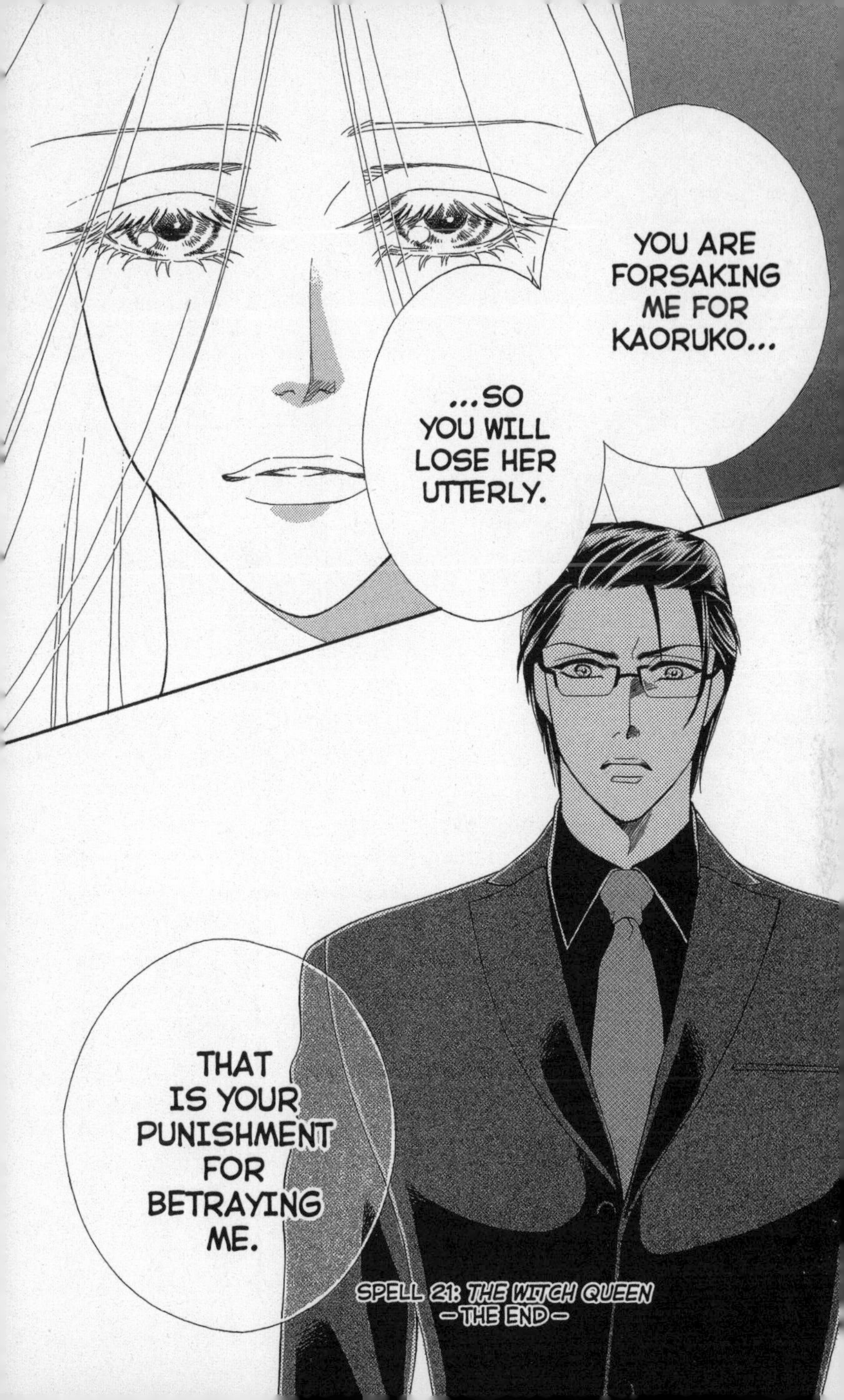
YOU ARE FORSAKING ME FOR KAORUKO...
...SO YOU WILL LOSE HER UTTERLY.
THAT IS YOUR PUNISHMENT FOR BETRAYING ME.
SPELL 21: THE WITCH QUEEN
–THE END–

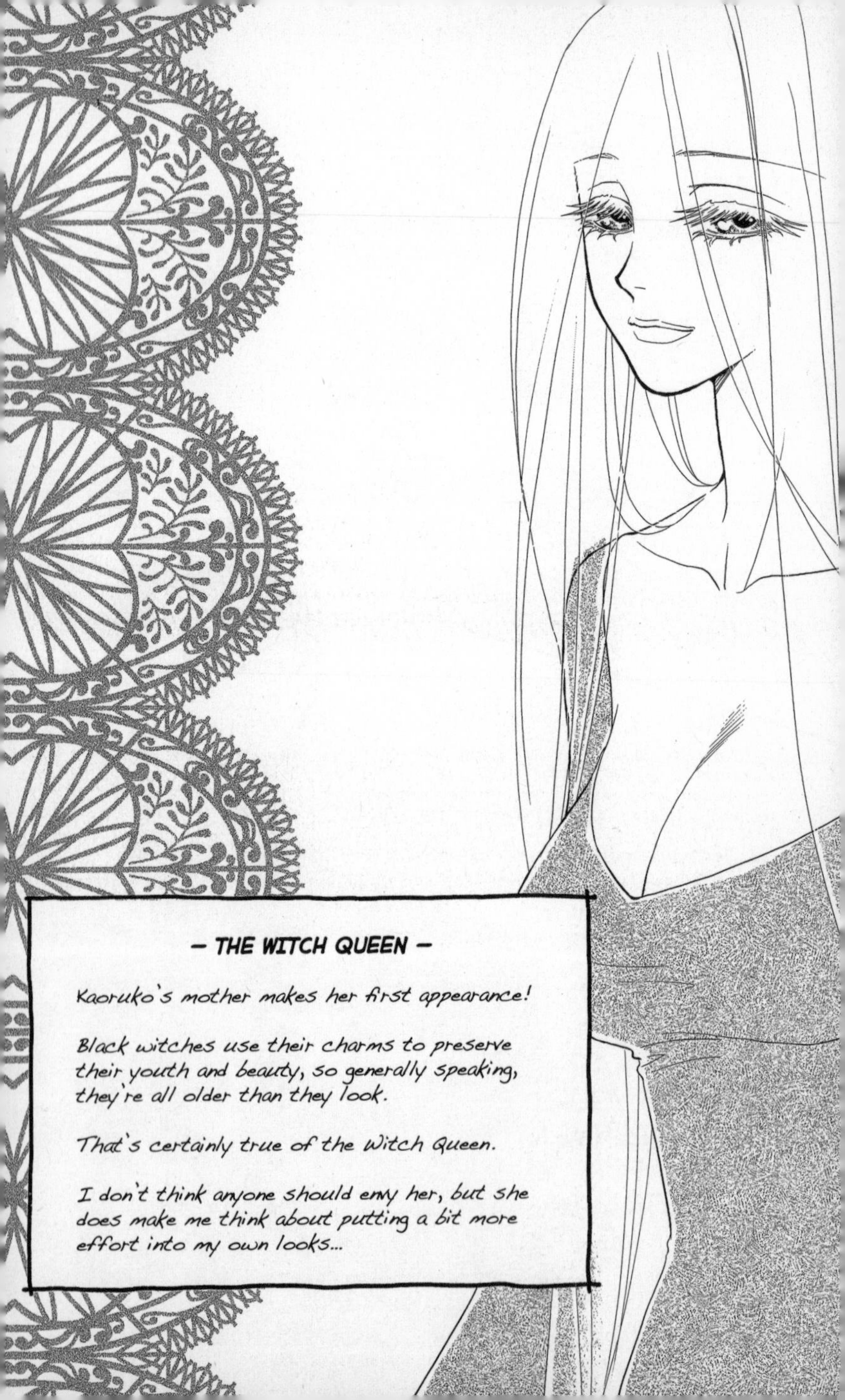

– THE WITCH QUEEN –

Kaoruko's mother makes her first appearance!

Black witches use their charms to preserve their youth and beauty, so generally speaking, they're all older than they look.

That's certainly true of the Witch Queen.

I don't think anyone should envy her, but she does make me think about putting a bit more effort into my own looks...

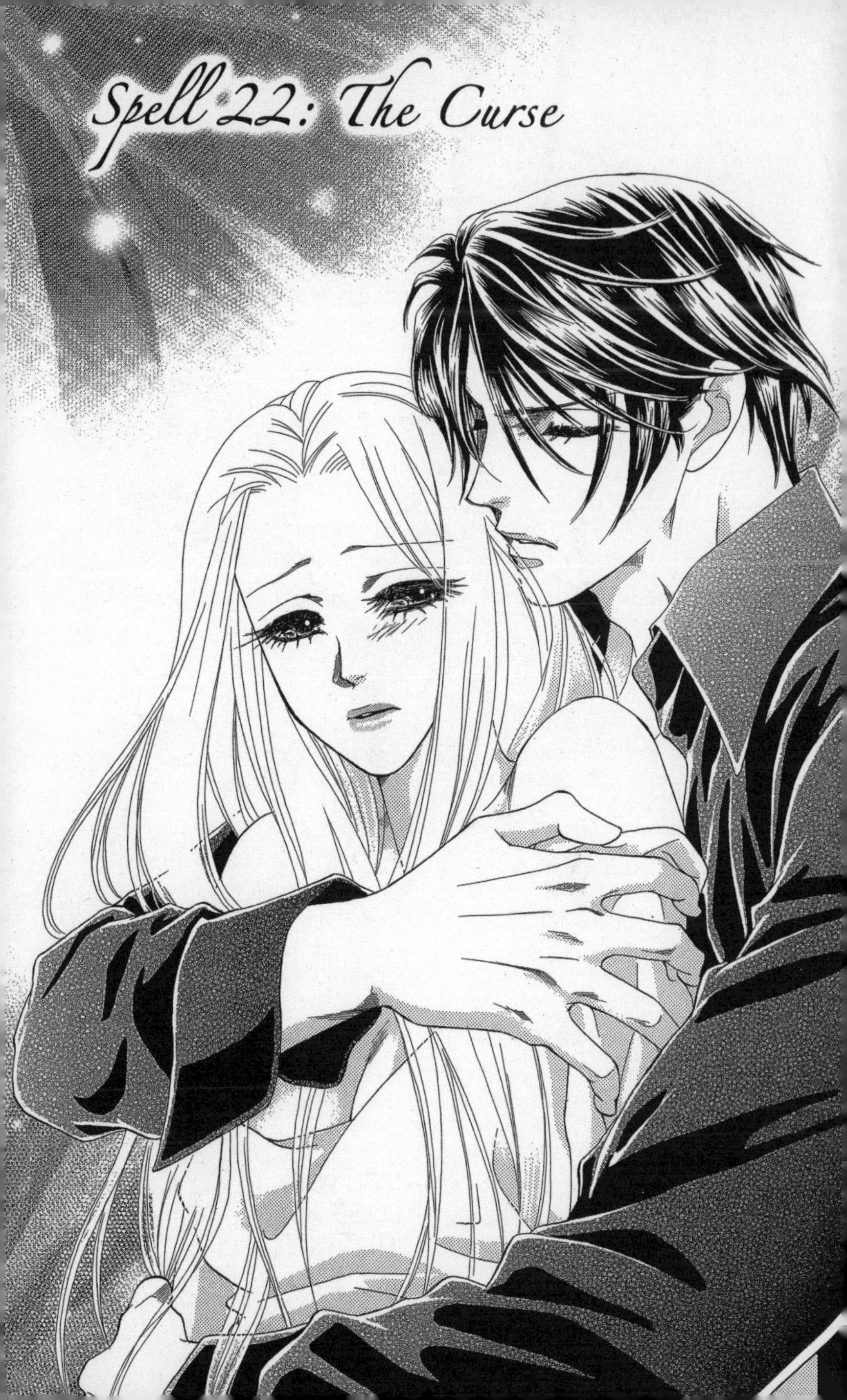
Spell 22: The Curse

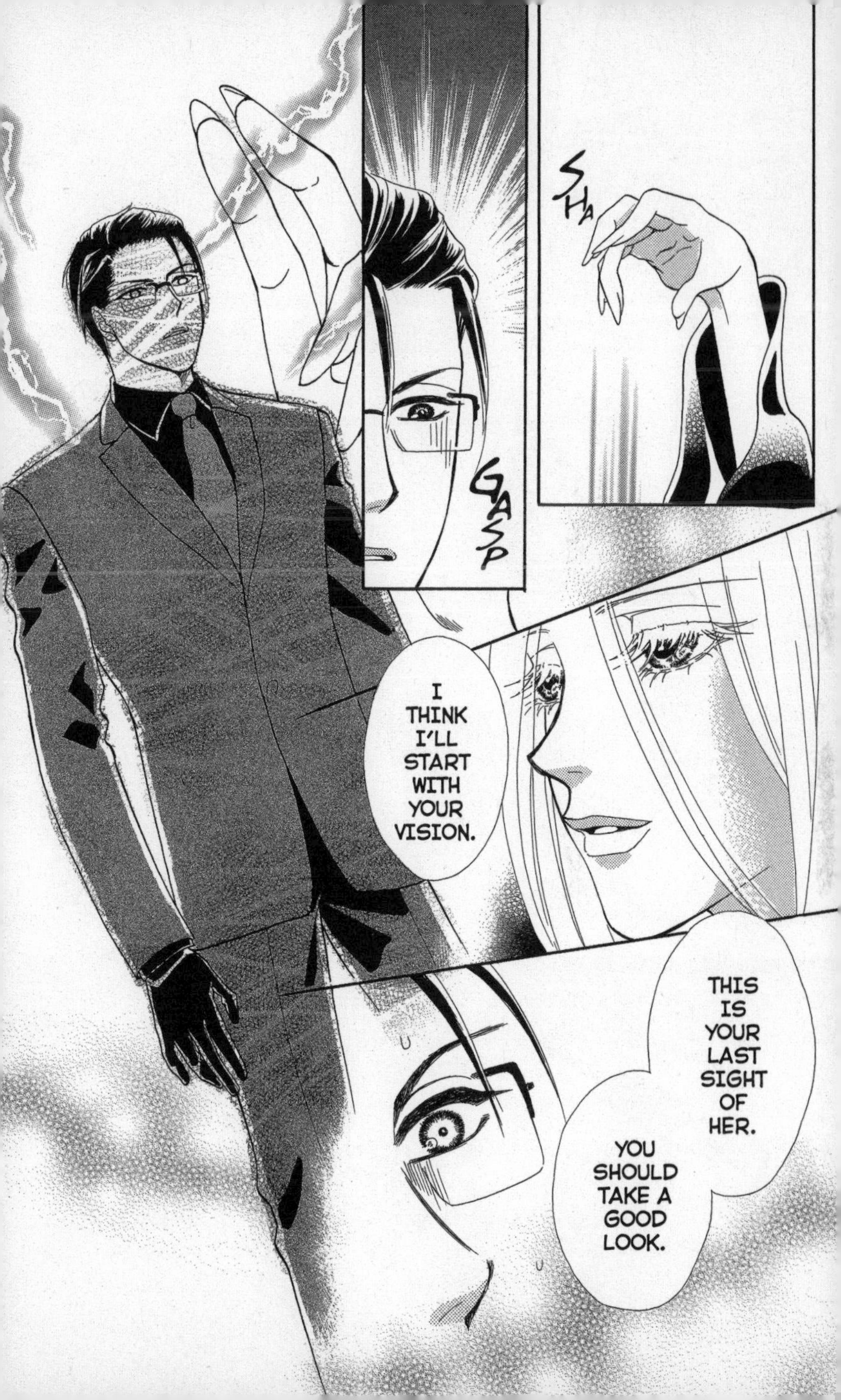
SHA
GASP
I THINK I'LL START WITH YOUR VISION.
THIS IS YOUR LAST SIGHT OF HER.
YOU SHOULD TAKE A GOOD LOOK.

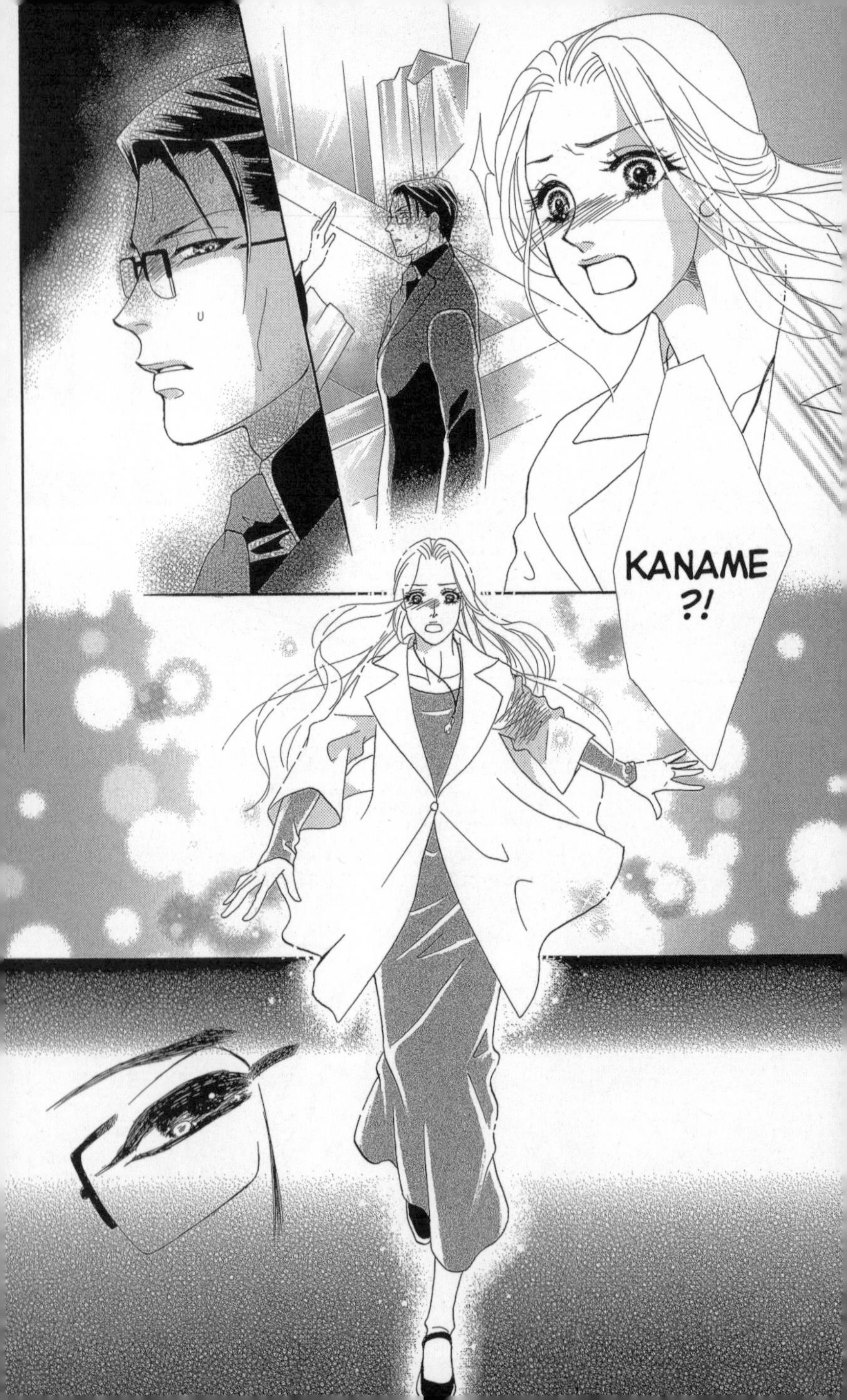
KANAME ?!

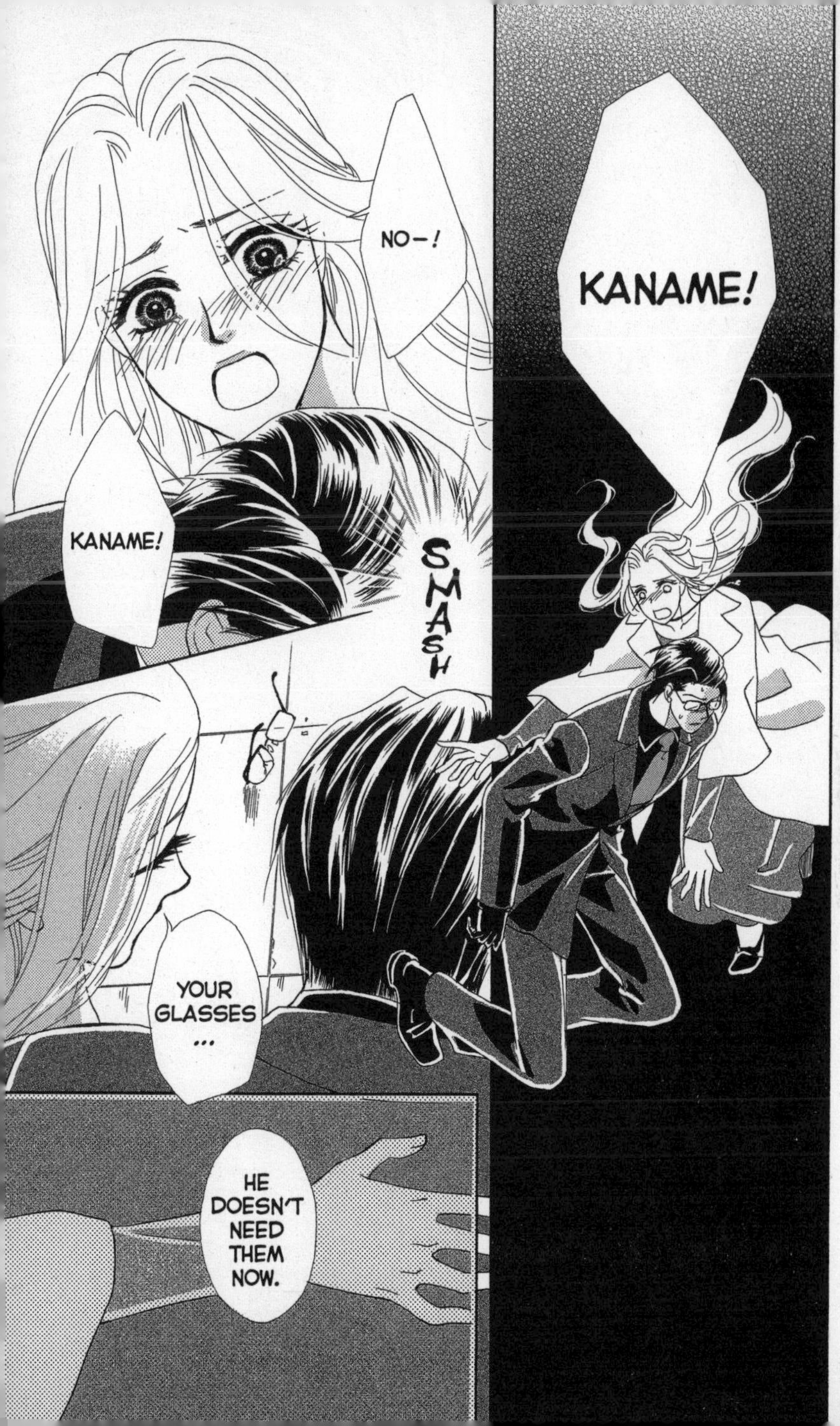
KANAME!
NO-!
KANAME!
SMASH
YOUR GLASSES ...
HE DOESN'T NEED THEM NOW.

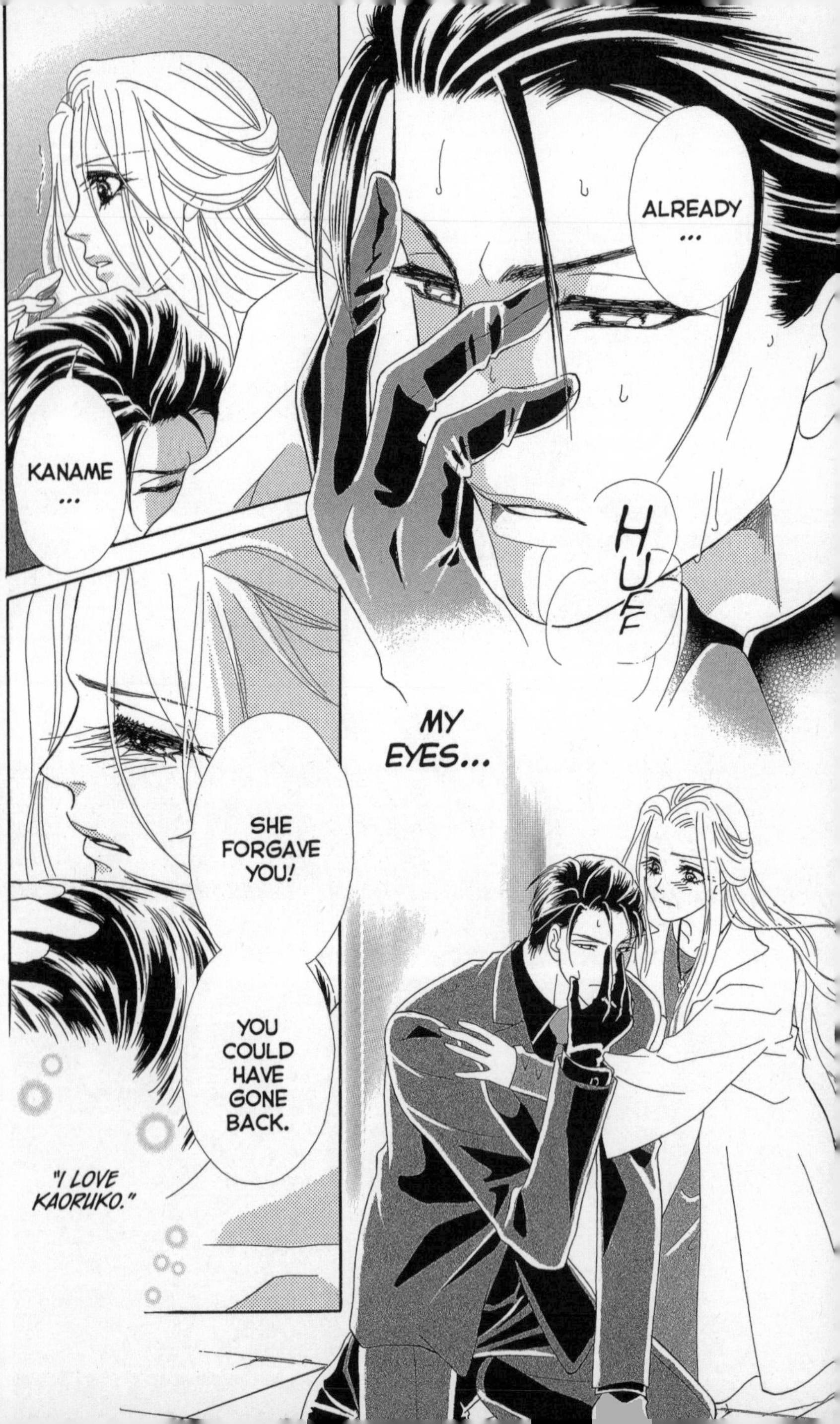
ALREADY ...
HUFF
KANAME ...
MY EYES...
SHE FORGAVE YOU!
YOU COULD HAVE GONE BACK.
"I LOVE KAORUKO."

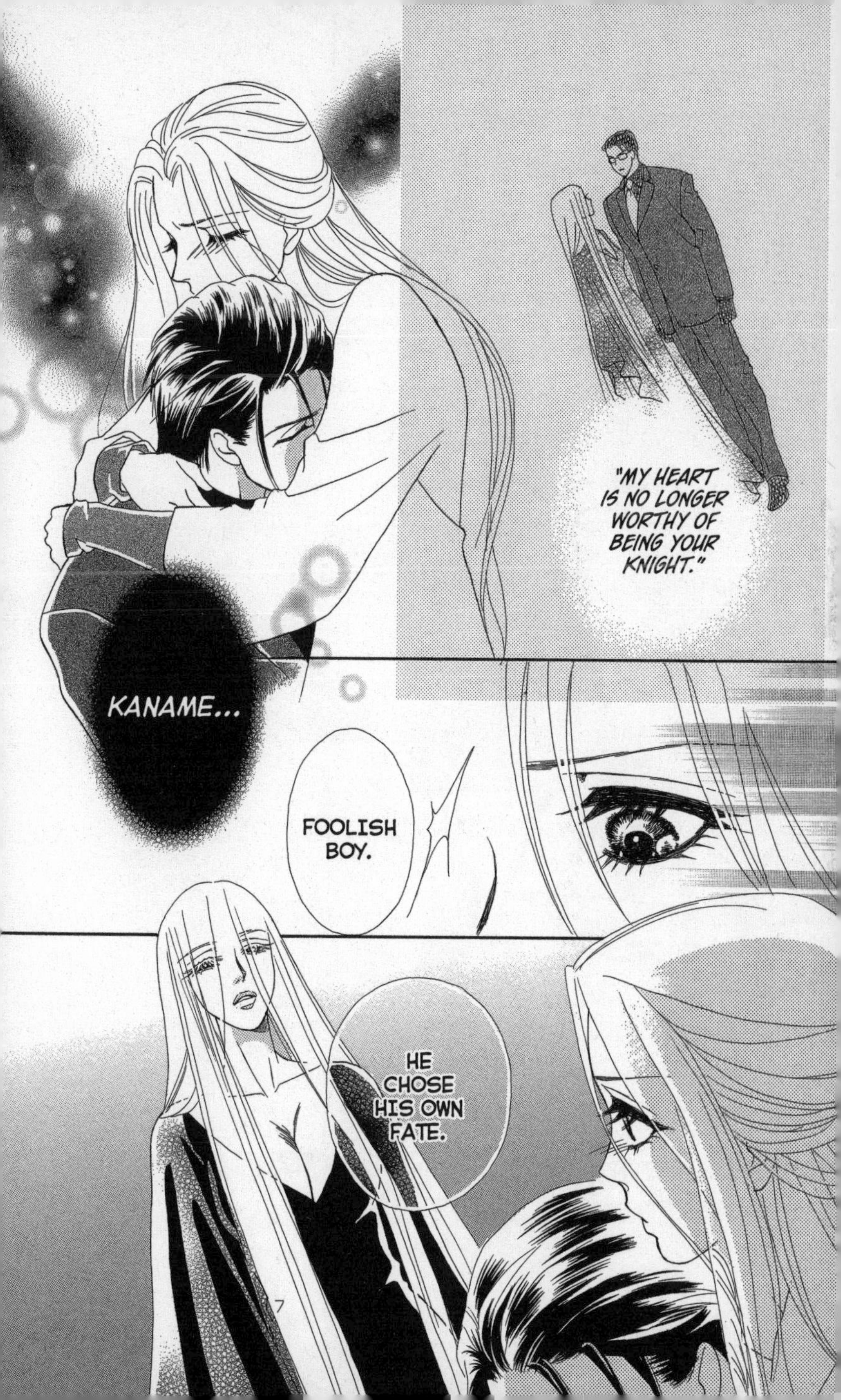
"MY HEART IS NO LONGER WORTHY OF BEING YOUR KNIGHT."
KANAME...
FOOLISH BOY.
HE CHOSE HIS OWN FATE.

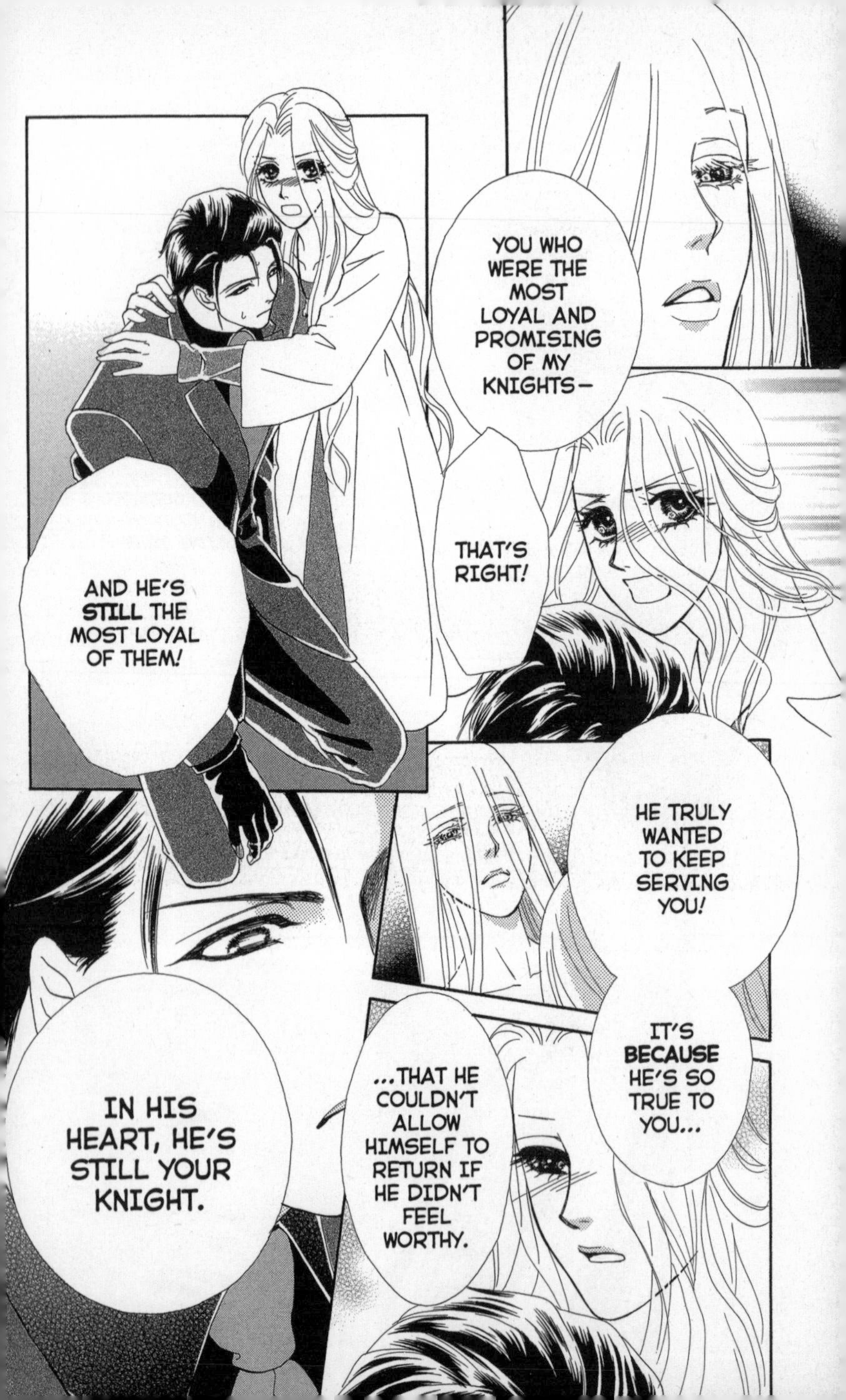
YOU WHO WERE THE MOST LOYAL AND PROMISING OF MY KNIGHTS—
THAT'S RIGHT!
AND HE'S **STILL** THE MOST LOYAL OF THEM!
HE TRULY WANTED TO KEEP SERVING YOU!
IT'S **BECAUSE** HE'S SO TRUE TO YOU...
...THAT HE COULDN'T ALLOW HIMSELF TO RETURN IF HE DIDN'T FEEL WORTHY.
IN HIS HEART, HE'S STILL YOUR KNIGHT.

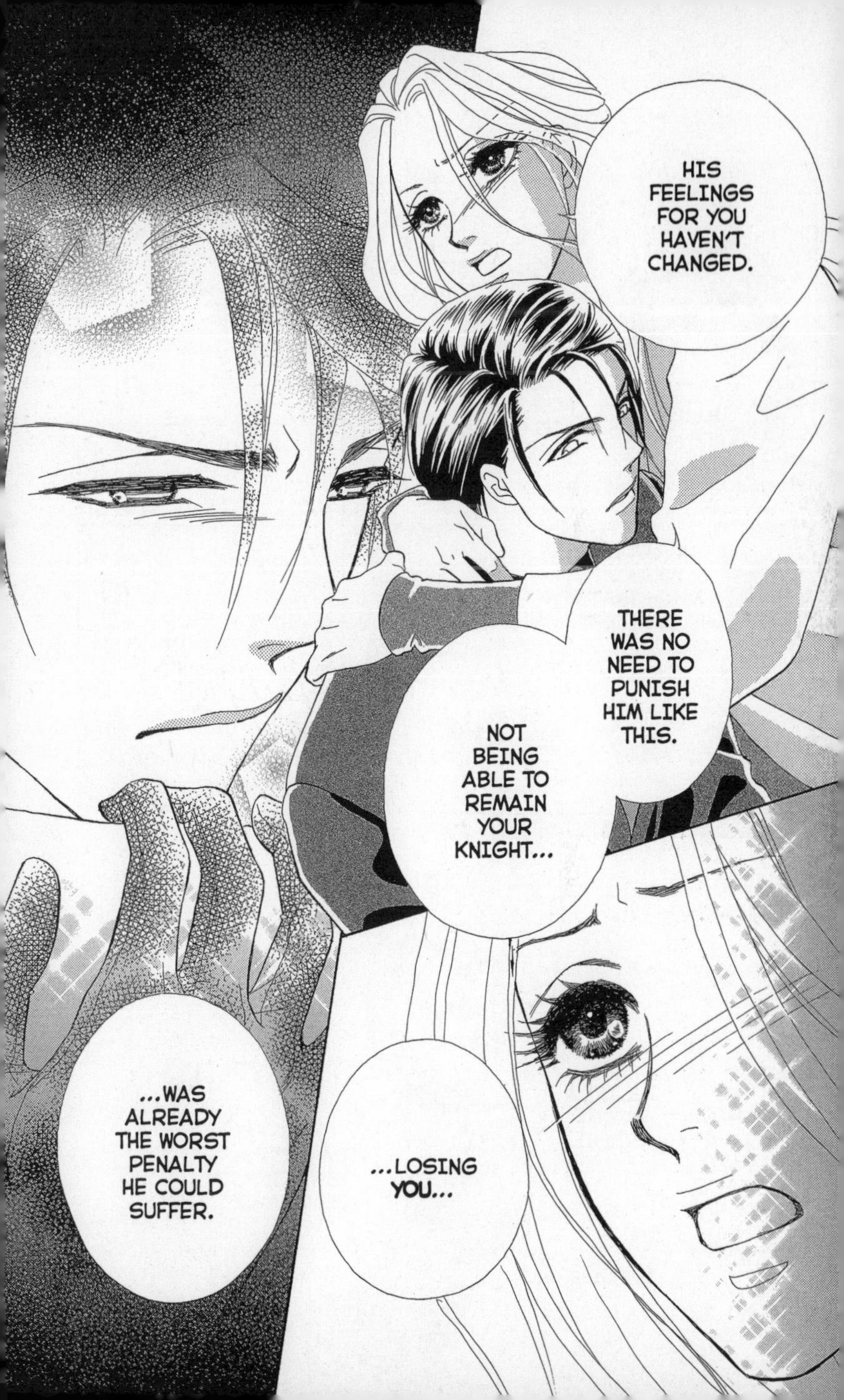
HIS FEELINGS FOR YOU HAVEN'T CHANGED.
THERE WAS NO NEED TO PUNISH HIM LIKE THIS.
NOT BEING ABLE TO REMAIN YOUR KNIGHT...
...LOSING YOU...
...WAS ALREADY THE WORST PENALTY HE COULD SUFFER.

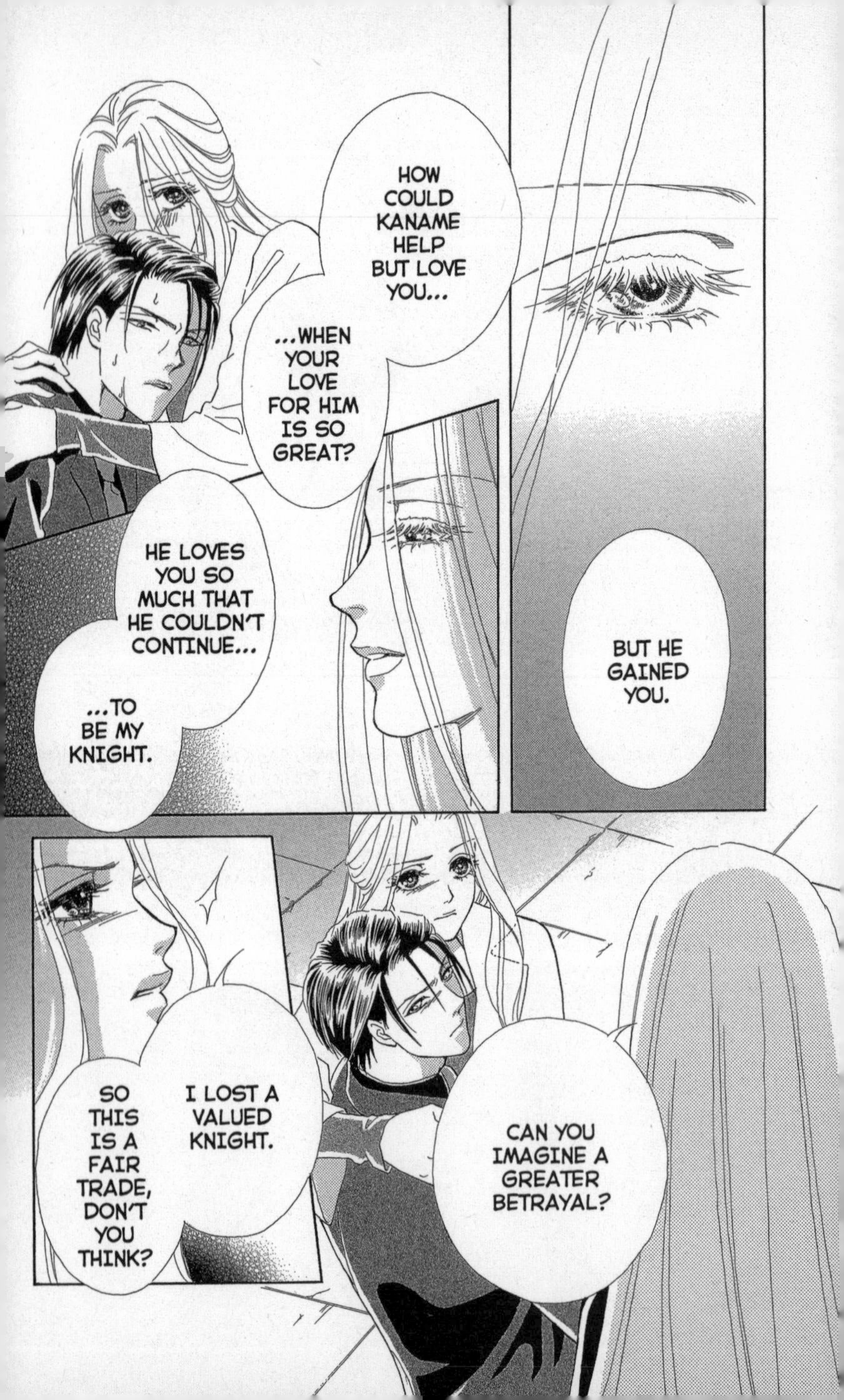
BUT HE GAINED YOU.
HOW COULD KANAME HELP BUT LOVE YOU...
...WHEN YOUR LOVE FOR HIM IS SO GREAT?
HE LOVES YOU SO MUCH THAT HE COULDN'T CONTINUE...
...TO BE MY KNIGHT.
CAN YOU IMAGINE A GREATER BETRAYAL?
I LOST A VALUED KNIGHT.
SO THIS IS A FAIR TRADE, DON'T YOU THINK?

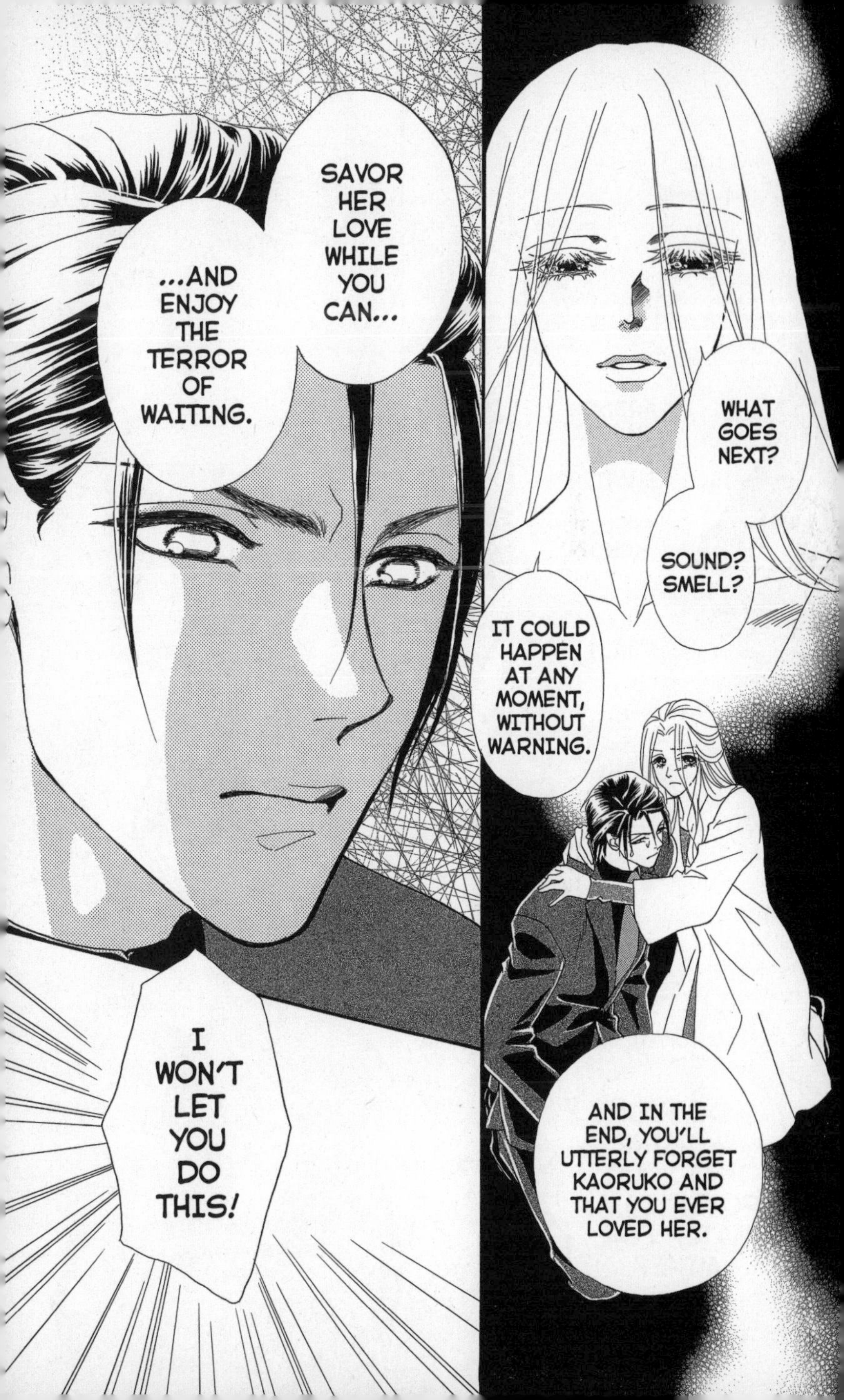
WHAT GOES NEXT?
SOUND? SMELL?
IT COULD HAPPEN AT ANY MOMENT, WITHOUT WARNING.
AND IN THE END, YOU'LL UTTERLY FORGET KAORUKO AND THAT YOU EVER LOVED HER.
SAVOR HER LOVE WHILE YOU CAN...
...AND ENJOY THE TERROR OF WAITING.
I WON'T LET YOU DO THIS!

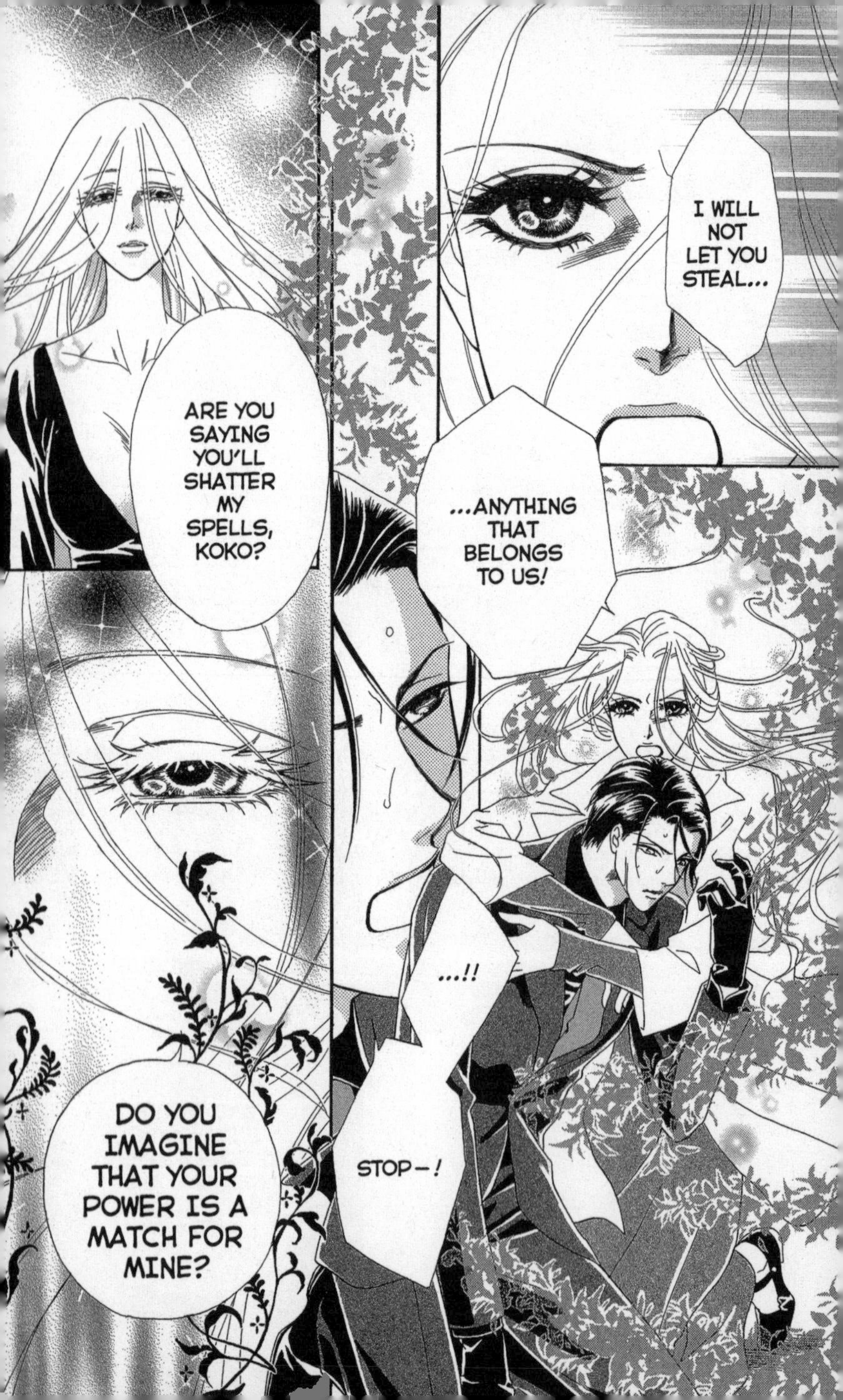
I WILL NOT LET YOU STEAL...
...ANYTHING THAT BELONGS TO US!
ARE YOU SAYING YOU'LL SHATTER MY SPELLS, KOKO?
...!!
STOP—!
DO YOU IMAGINE THAT YOUR POWER IS A MATCH FOR MINE?

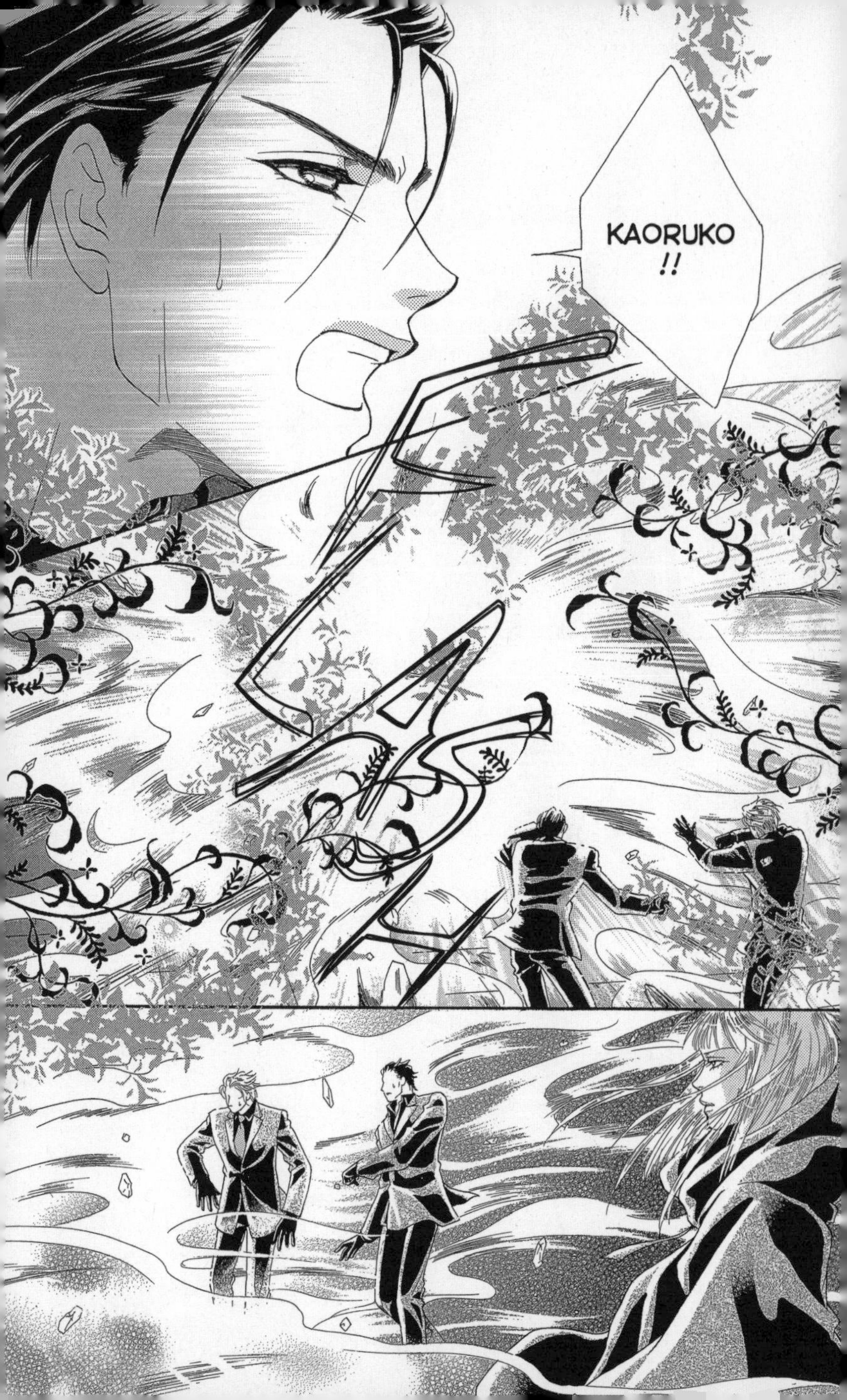
KAORUKO
!!

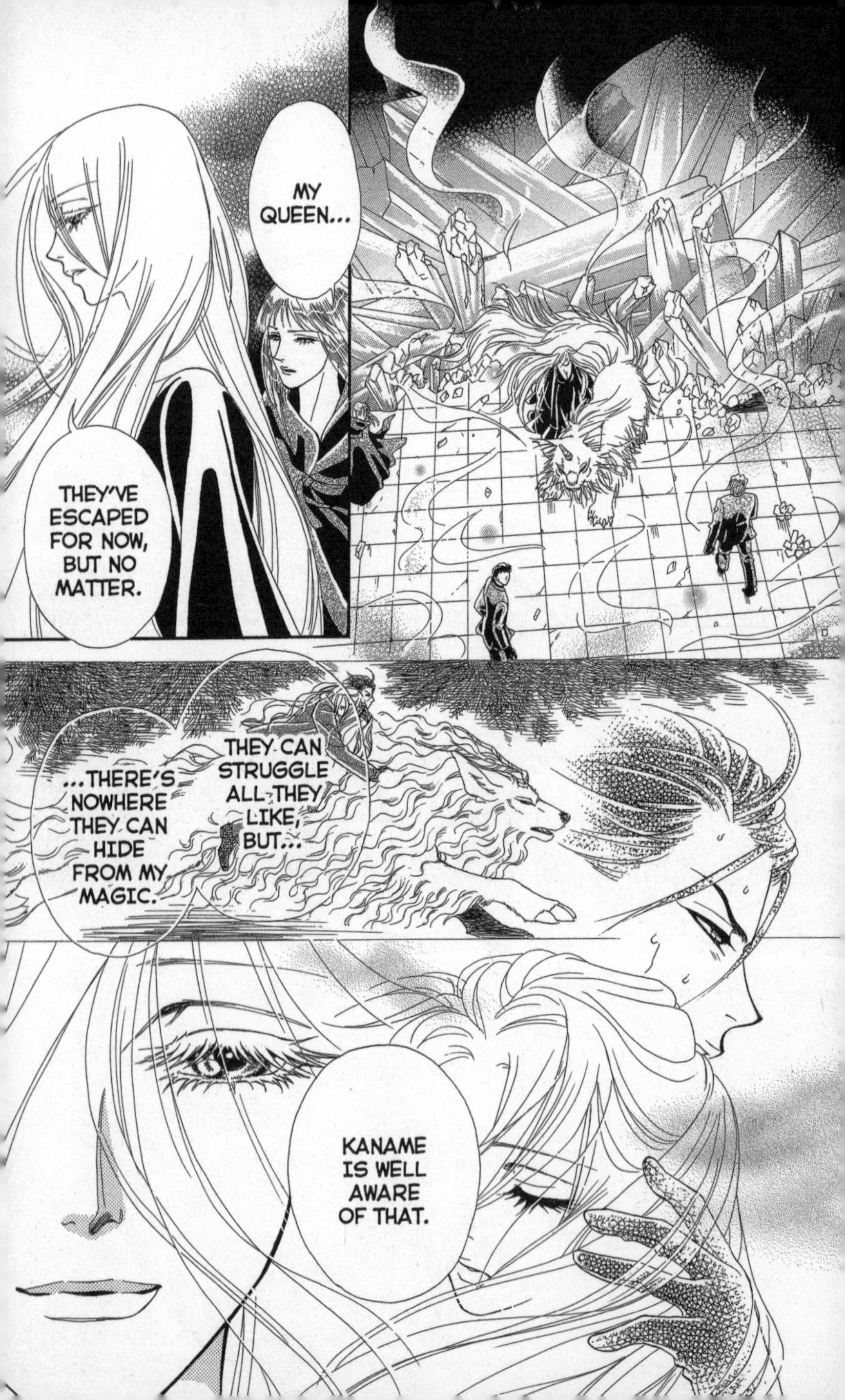
MY QUEEN...
THEY'VE ESCAPED FOR NOW, BUT NO MATTER.
THEY CAN STRUGGLE ALL THEY LIKE, BUT...
...THERE'S NOWHERE THEY CAN HIDE FROM MY MAGIC.
KANAME IS WELL AWARE OF THAT.

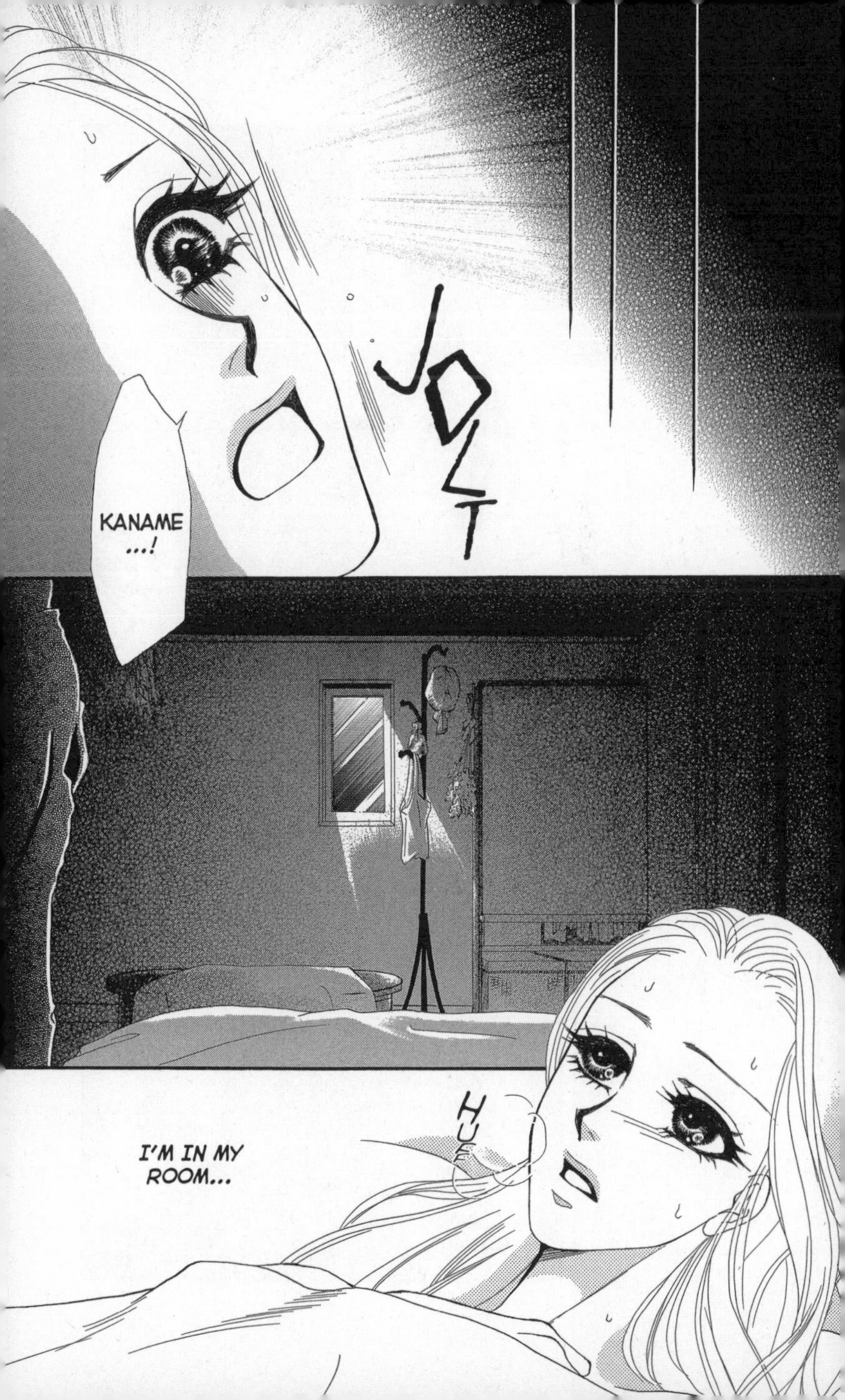
JOLT
KANAME ...!
HUFF
I'M IN MY ROOM...

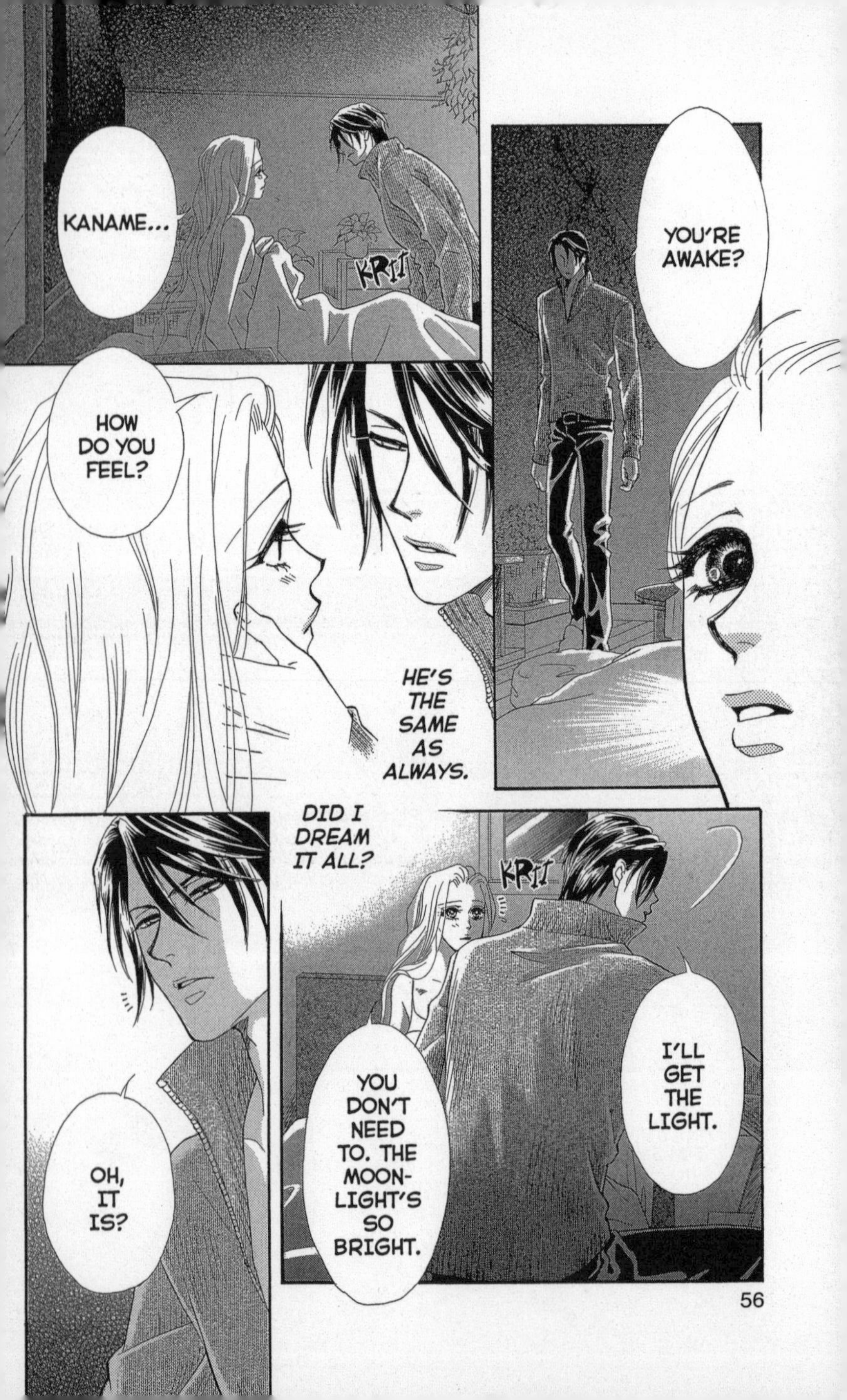
YOU'RE AWAKE?
KANAME...
KRIT
HOW DO YOU FEEL?
HE'S THE SAME AS ALWAYS.
DID I DREAM IT ALL?
KRIT
I'LL GET THE LIGHT.
YOU DON'T NEED TO. THE MOON-LIGHT'S SO BRIGHT.
OH, IT IS?

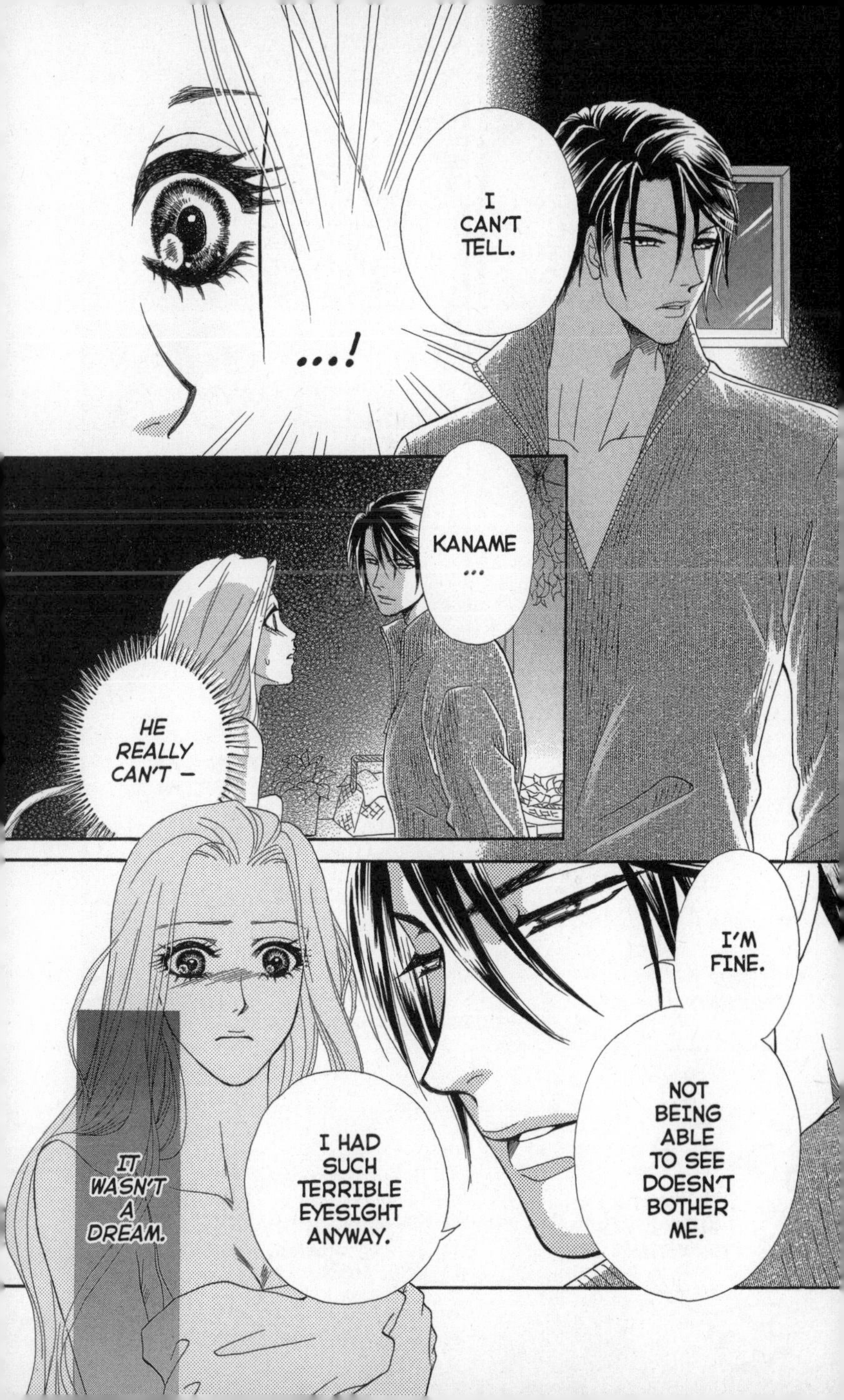
I CAN'T TELL.
...!
KANAME ...
HE REALLY CAN'T –
I'M FINE.
NOT BEING ABLE TO SEE DOESN'T BOTHER ME.
I HAD SUCH TERRIBLE EYESIGHT ANYWAY.
IT WASN'T A DREAM.

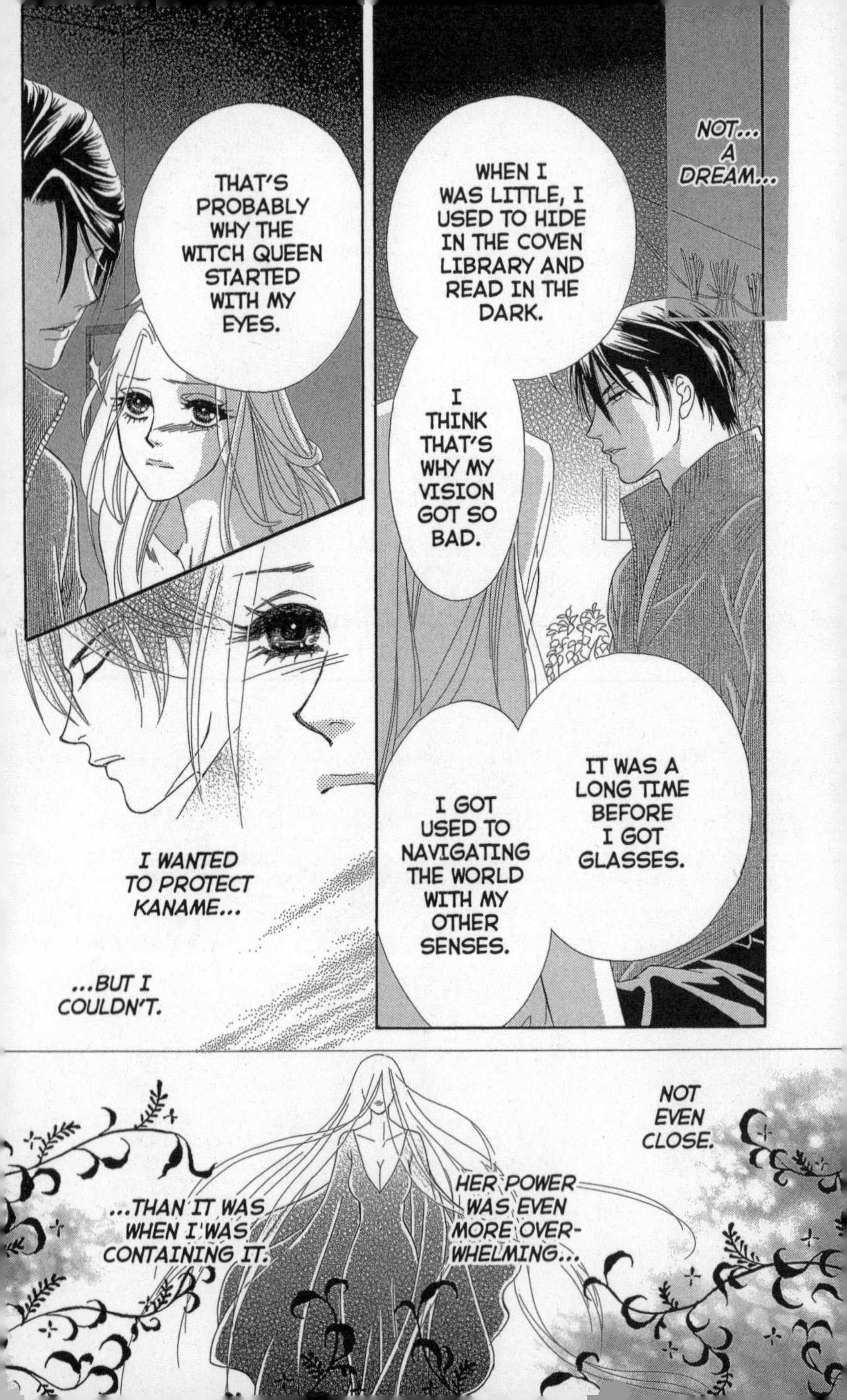

NOT... A DREAM...
WHEN I WAS LITTLE, I USED TO HIDE IN THE COVEN LIBRARY AND READ IN THE DARK.
I THINK THAT'S WHY MY VISION GOT SO BAD.
IT WAS A LONG TIME BEFORE I GOT GLASSES.
I GOT USED TO NAVIGATING THE WORLD WITH MY OTHER SENSES.
THAT'S PROBABLY WHY THE WITCH QUEEN STARTED WITH MY EYES.
I WANTED TO PROTECT KANAME...
...BUT I COULDN'T.
NOT EVEN CLOSE.
HER POWER WAS EVEN MORE OVER-WHELMING...
...THAN IT WAS WHEN I WAS CONTAINING IT.

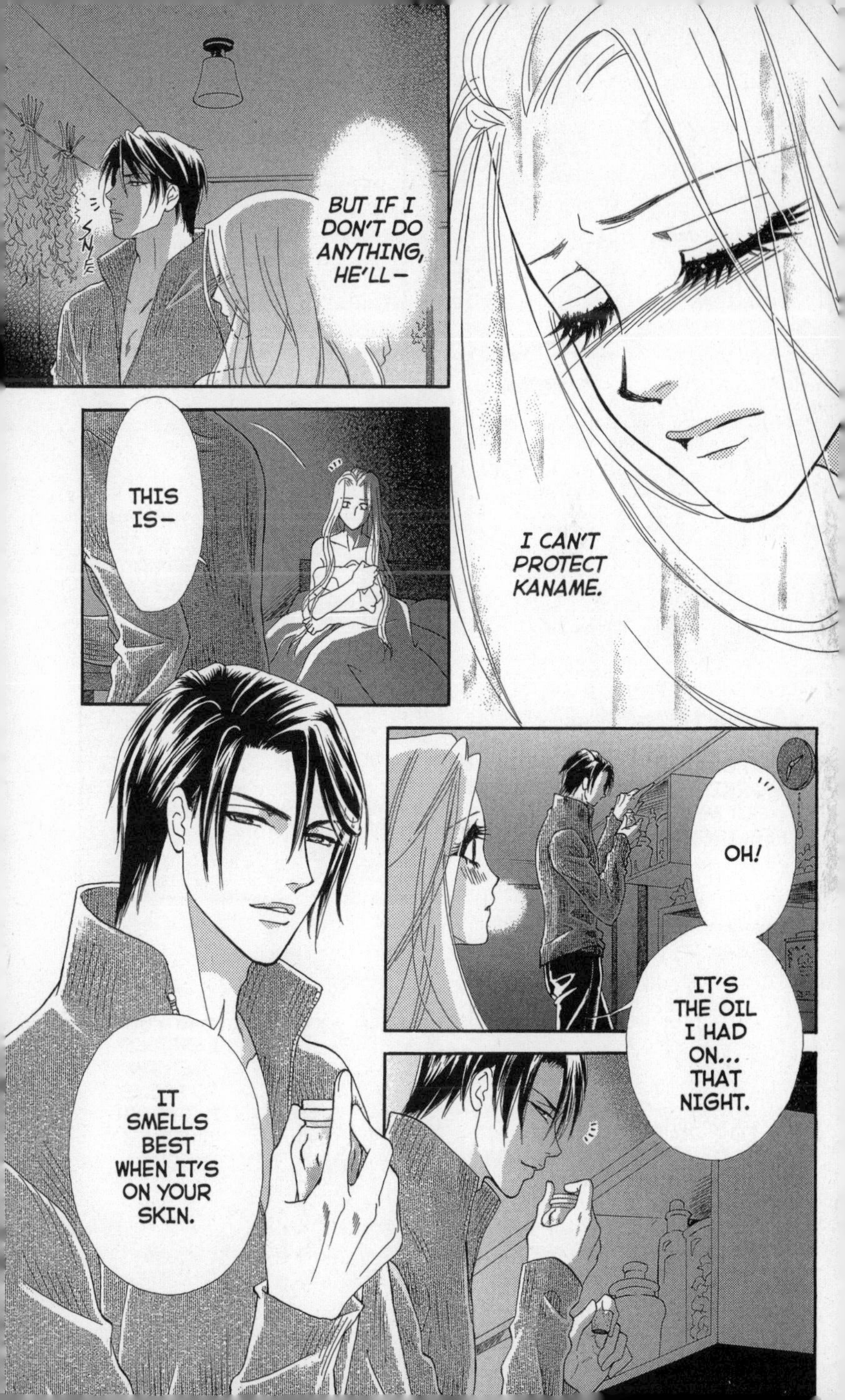
I CAN'T PROTECT KANAME.
SNIF
BUT IF I DON'T DO ANYTHING, HE'LL—
THIS IS—
OH!
IT'S THE OIL I HAD ON... THAT NIGHT.
IT SMELLS BEST WHEN IT'S ON YOUR SKIN.

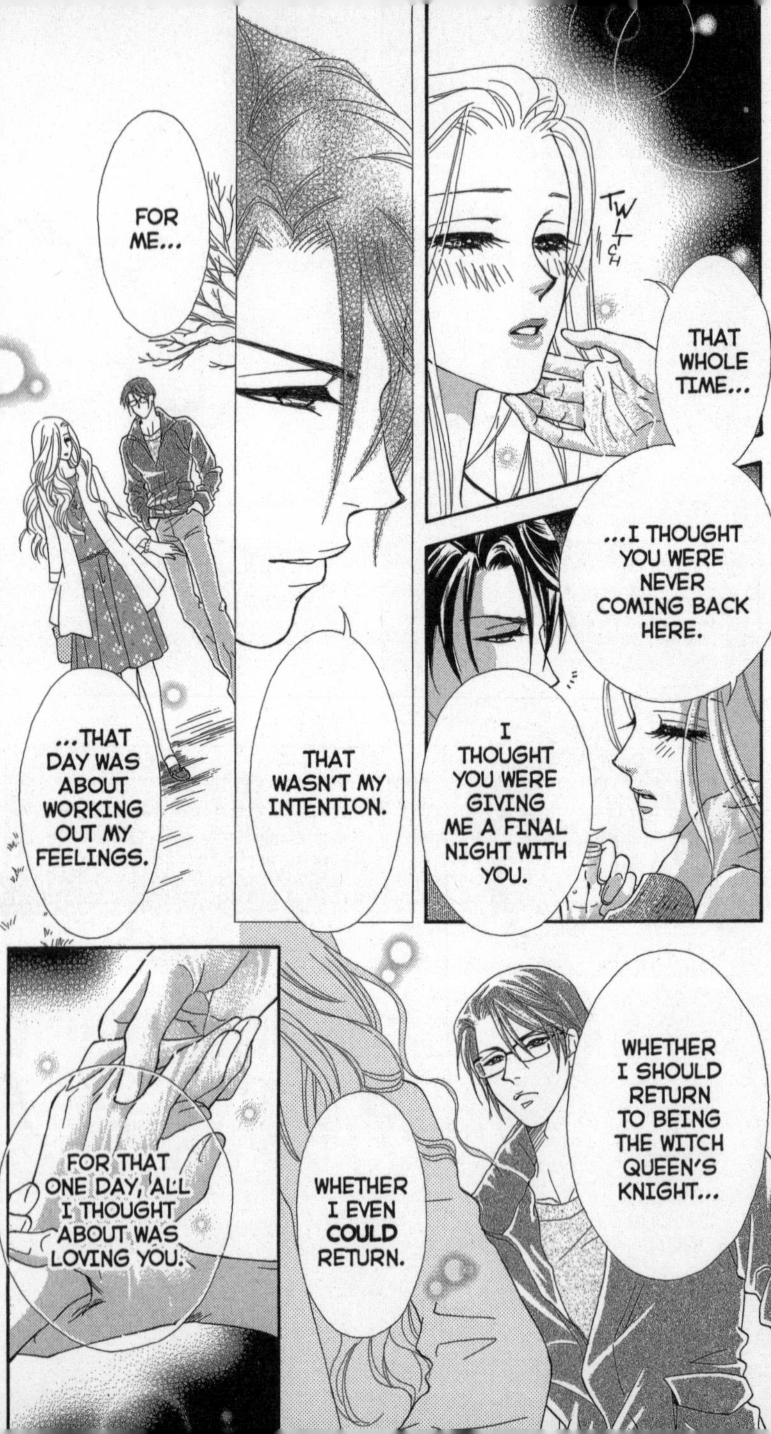
TWITCH
THAT WHOLE TIME...
...I THOUGHT YOU WERE NEVER COMING BACK HERE.
I THOUGHT YOU WERE GIVING ME A FINAL NIGHT WITH YOU.
THAT WASN'T MY INTENTION.
FOR ME...
...THAT DAY WAS ABOUT WORKING OUT MY FEELINGS.
WHETHER I SHOULD RETURN TO BEING THE WITCH QUEEN'S KNIGHT...
WHETHER I EVEN **COULD** RETURN.
FOR THAT ONE DAY, ALL I THOUGHT ABOUT WAS LOVING YOU.

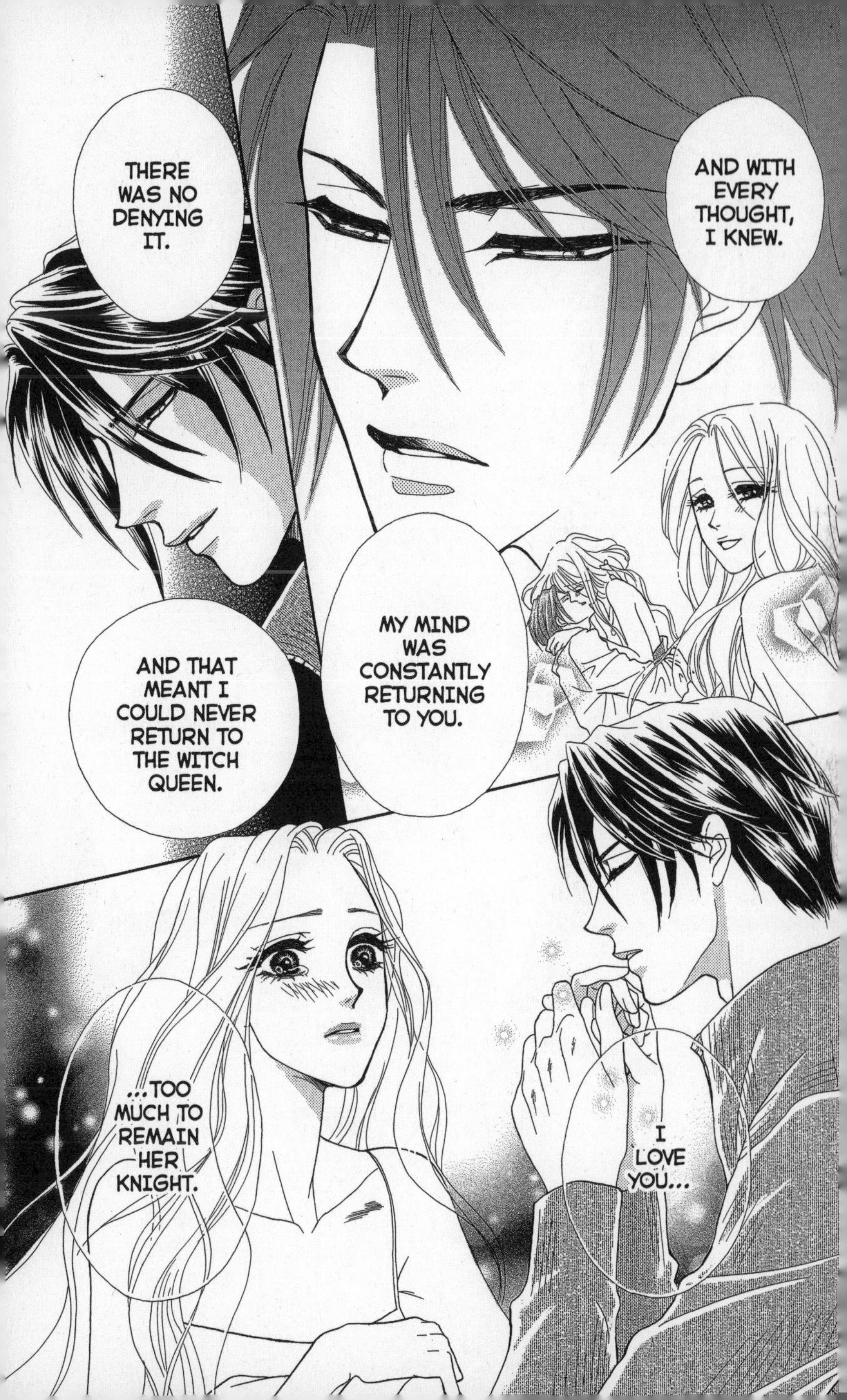
AND WITH EVERY THOUGHT, I KNEW.
THERE WAS NO DENYING IT.
MY MIND WAS CONSTANTLY RETURNING TO YOU.
AND THAT MEANT I COULD NEVER RETURN TO THE WITCH QUEEN.
I LOVE YOU...
...TOO MUCH TO REMAIN HER KNIGHT.

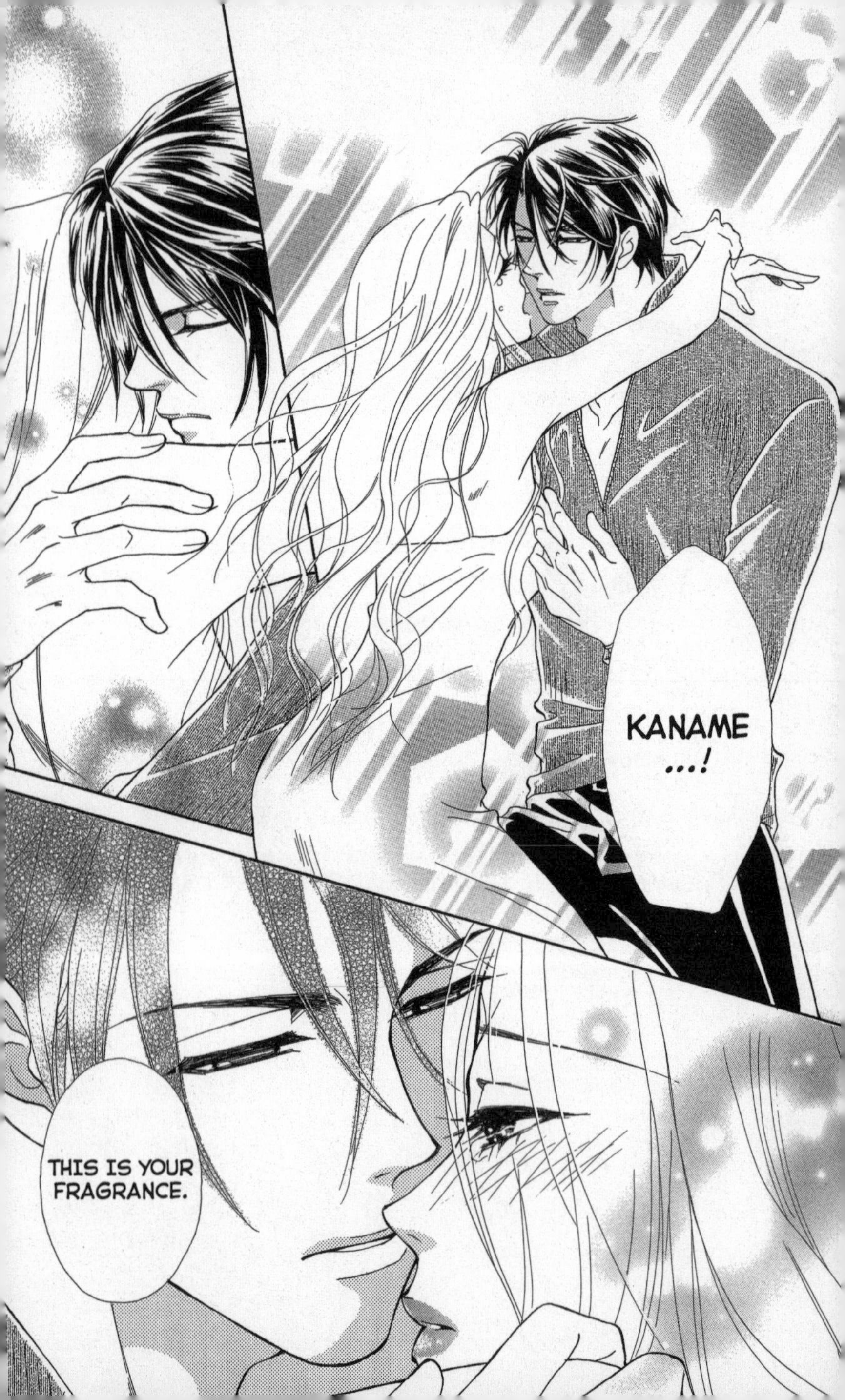
KANAME ...!
THIS IS YOUR FRAGRANCE.

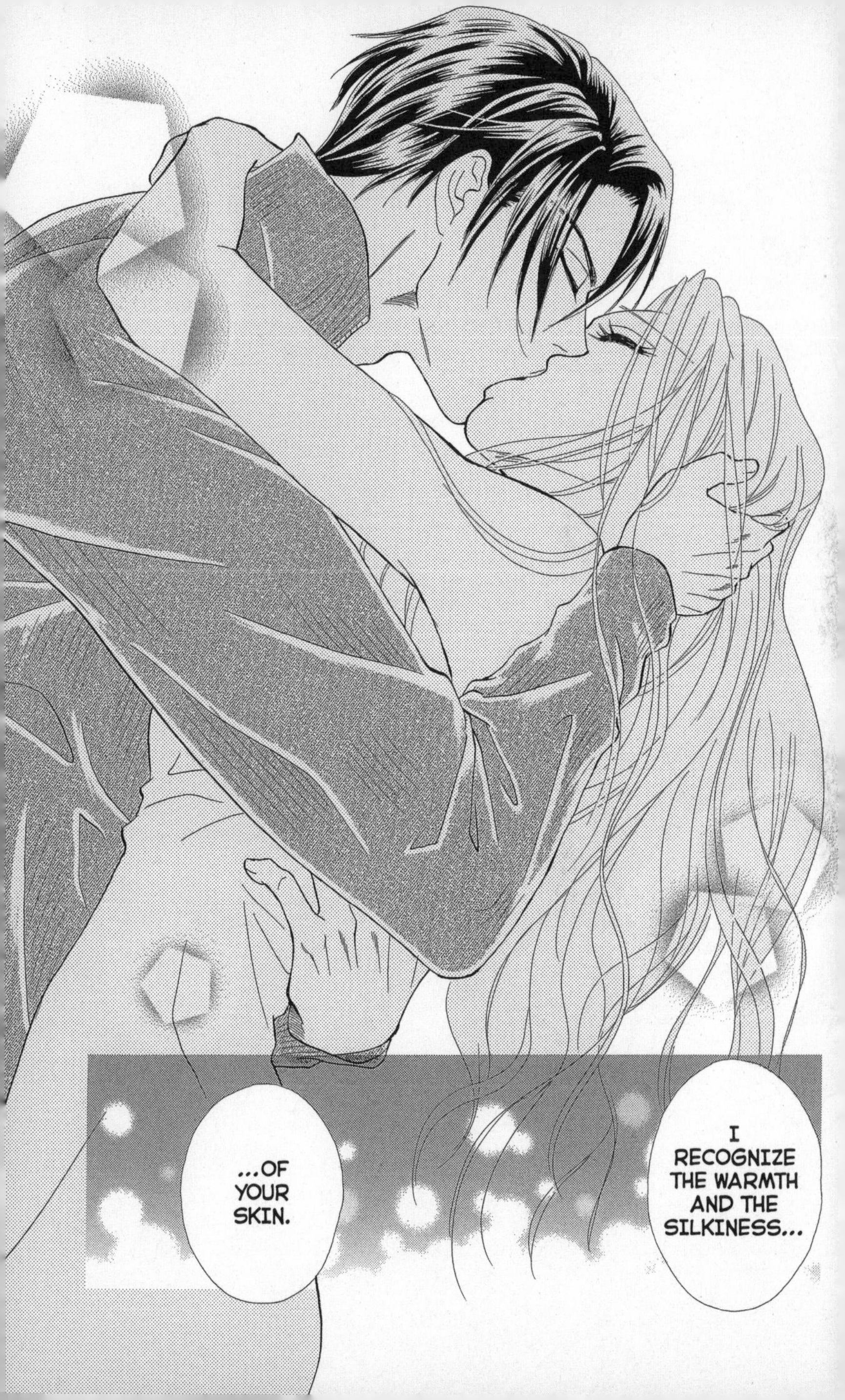
I RECOGNIZE THE WARMTH AND THE SILKINESS...
...OF YOUR SKIN.

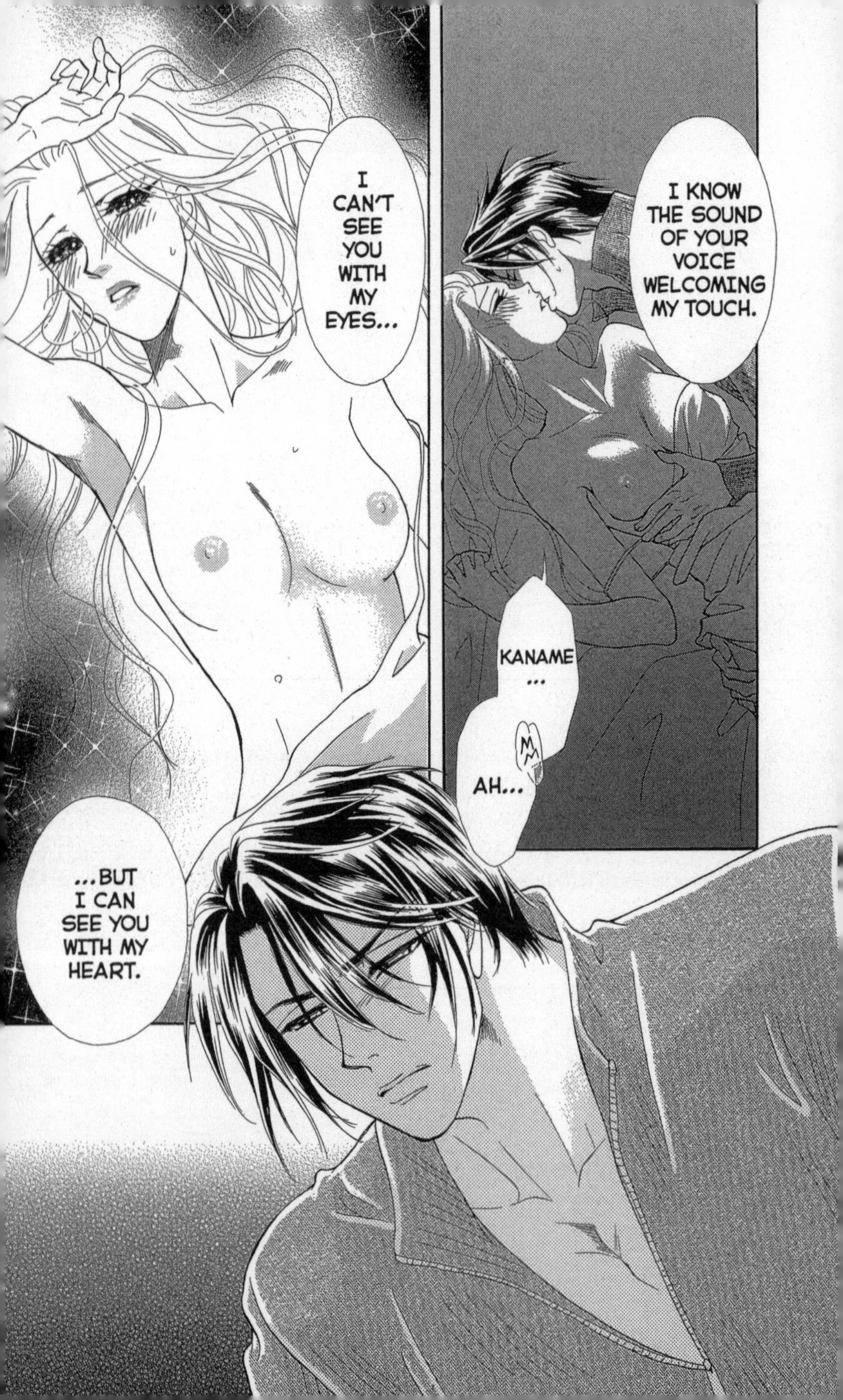
I KNOW THE SOUND OF YOUR VOICE WELCOMING MY TOUCH.
I CAN'T SEE YOU WITH MY EYES...
KANAME...
AH...
...BUT I CAN SEE YOU WITH MY HEART.

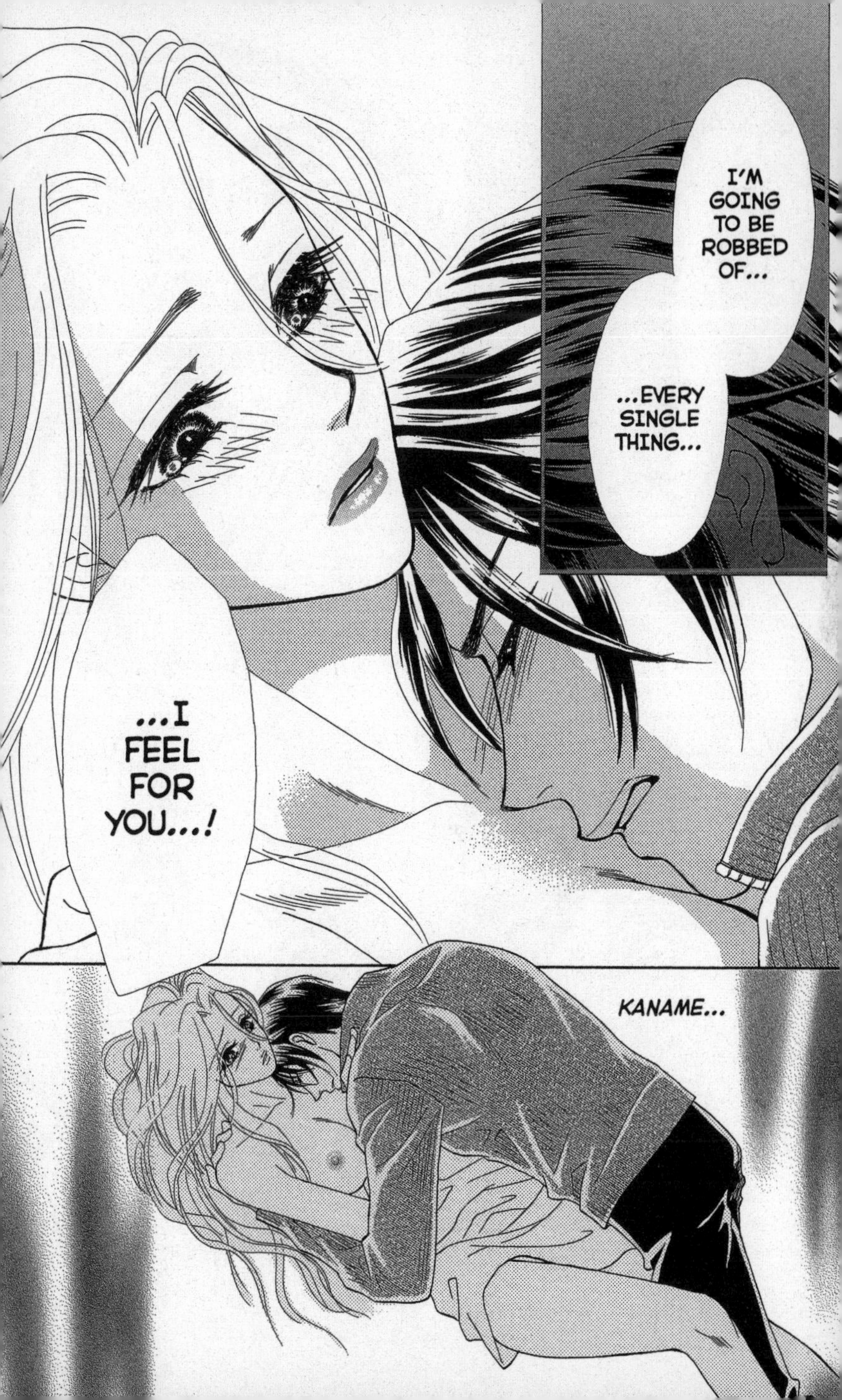

I'M GOING TO BE ROBBED OF...
...EVERY SINGLE THING...
...I FEEL FOR YOU...!
KANAME...

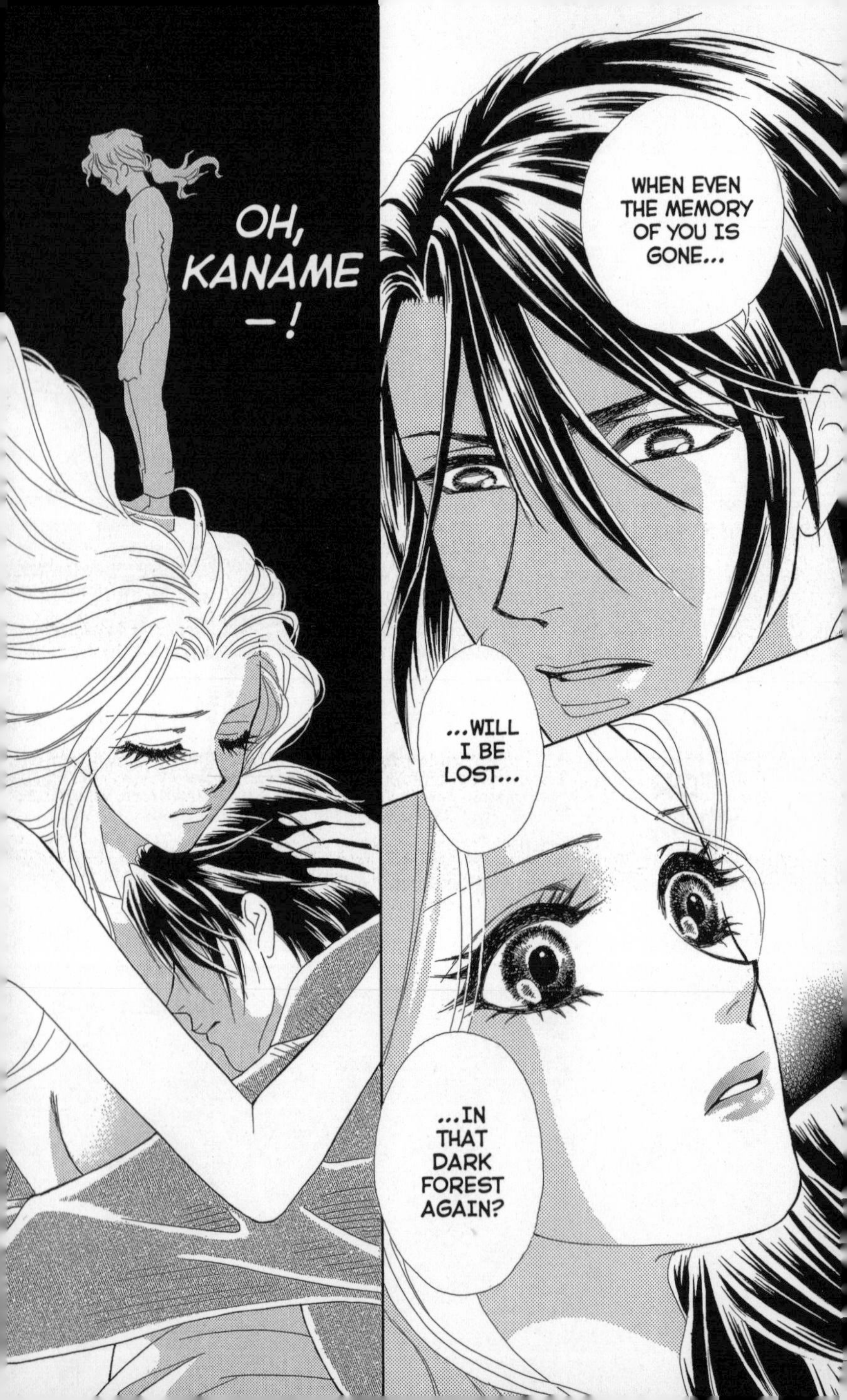
WHEN EVEN THE MEMORY OF YOU IS GONE...
...WILL I BE LOST...
...IN THAT DARK FOREST AGAIN?
OH, KANAME—!

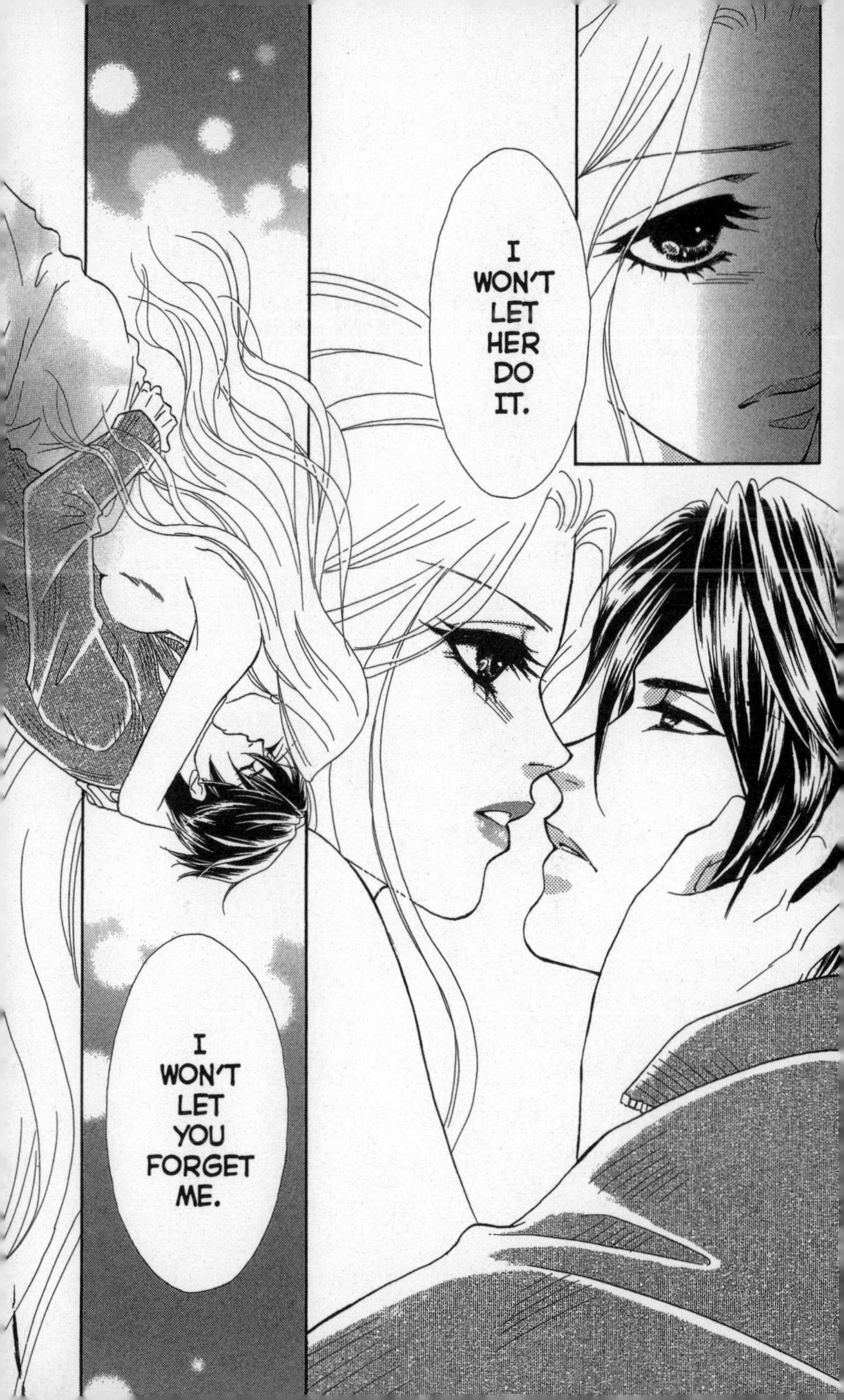
I WON'T LET HER DO IT.
I WON'T LET YOU FORGET ME.

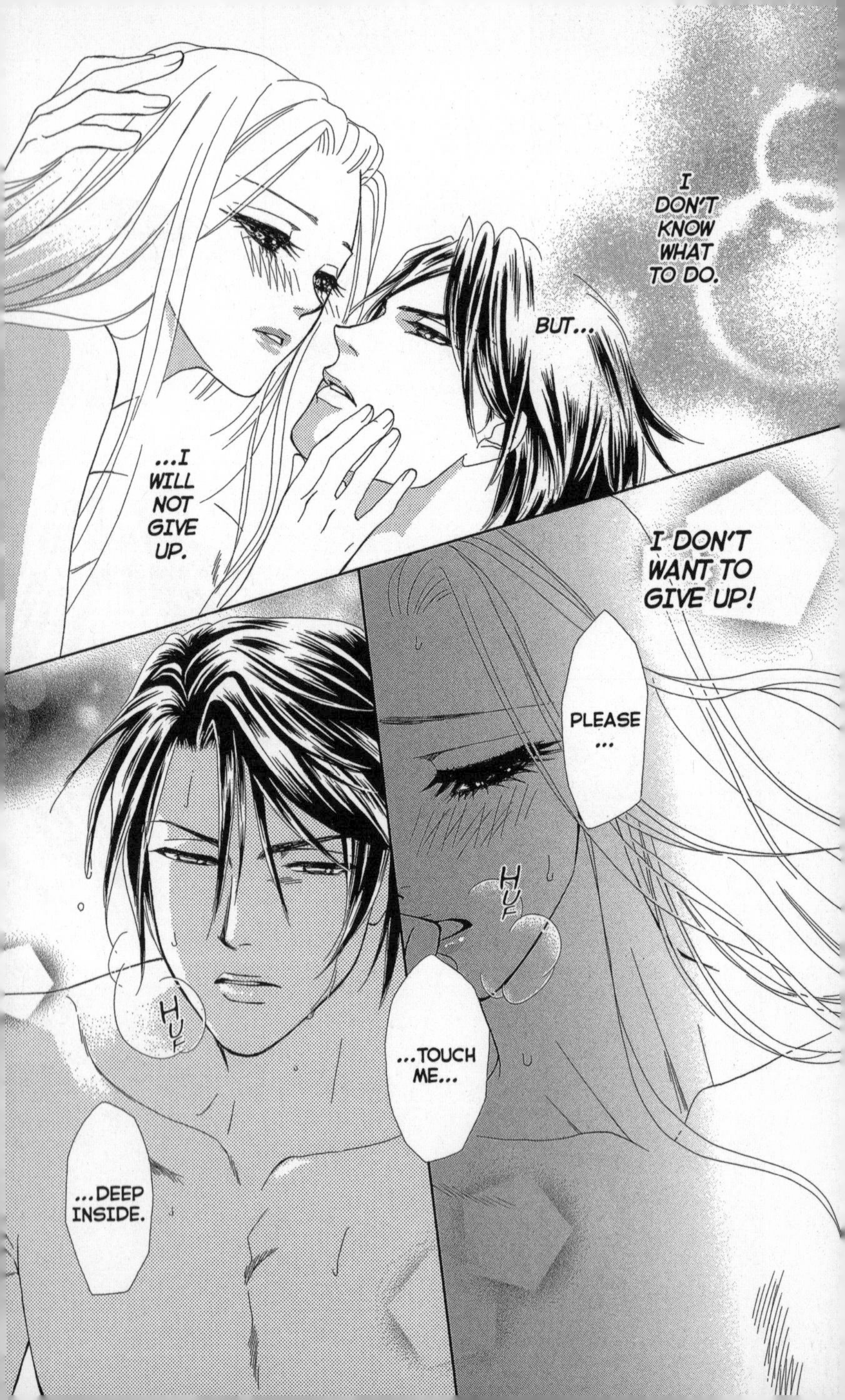
I DON'T KNOW WHAT TO DO.
BUT...
...I WILL NOT GIVE UP.
I DON'T WANT TO GIVE UP!
PLEASE...
HUF
...TOUCH ME...
HUF
...DEEP INSIDE.

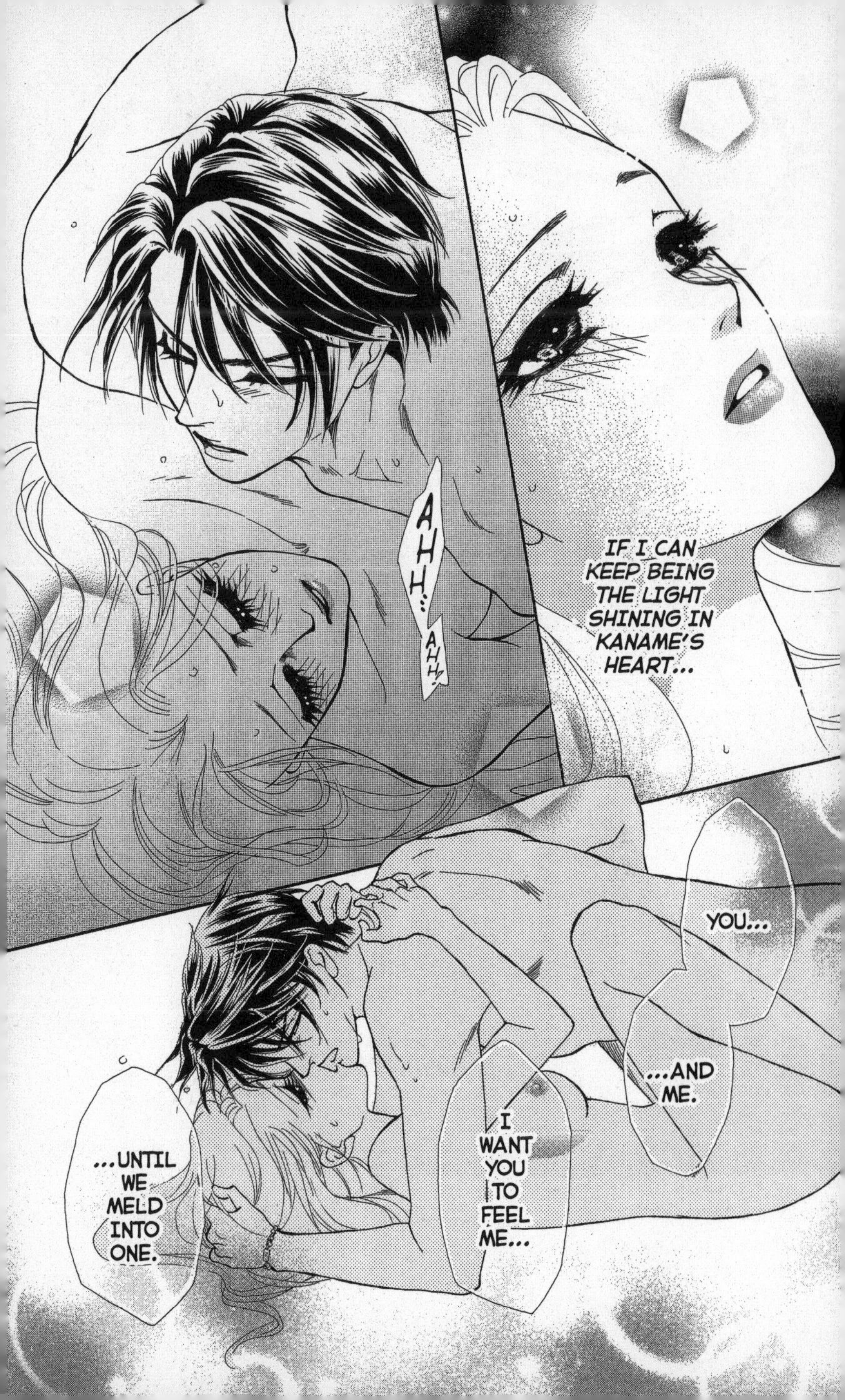
IF I CAN KEEP BEING THE LIGHT SHINING IN KANAME'S HEART...
AHH..
AHH!
YOU...
...AND ME.
I WANT YOU TO FEEL ME...
...UNTIL WE MELD INTO ONE.

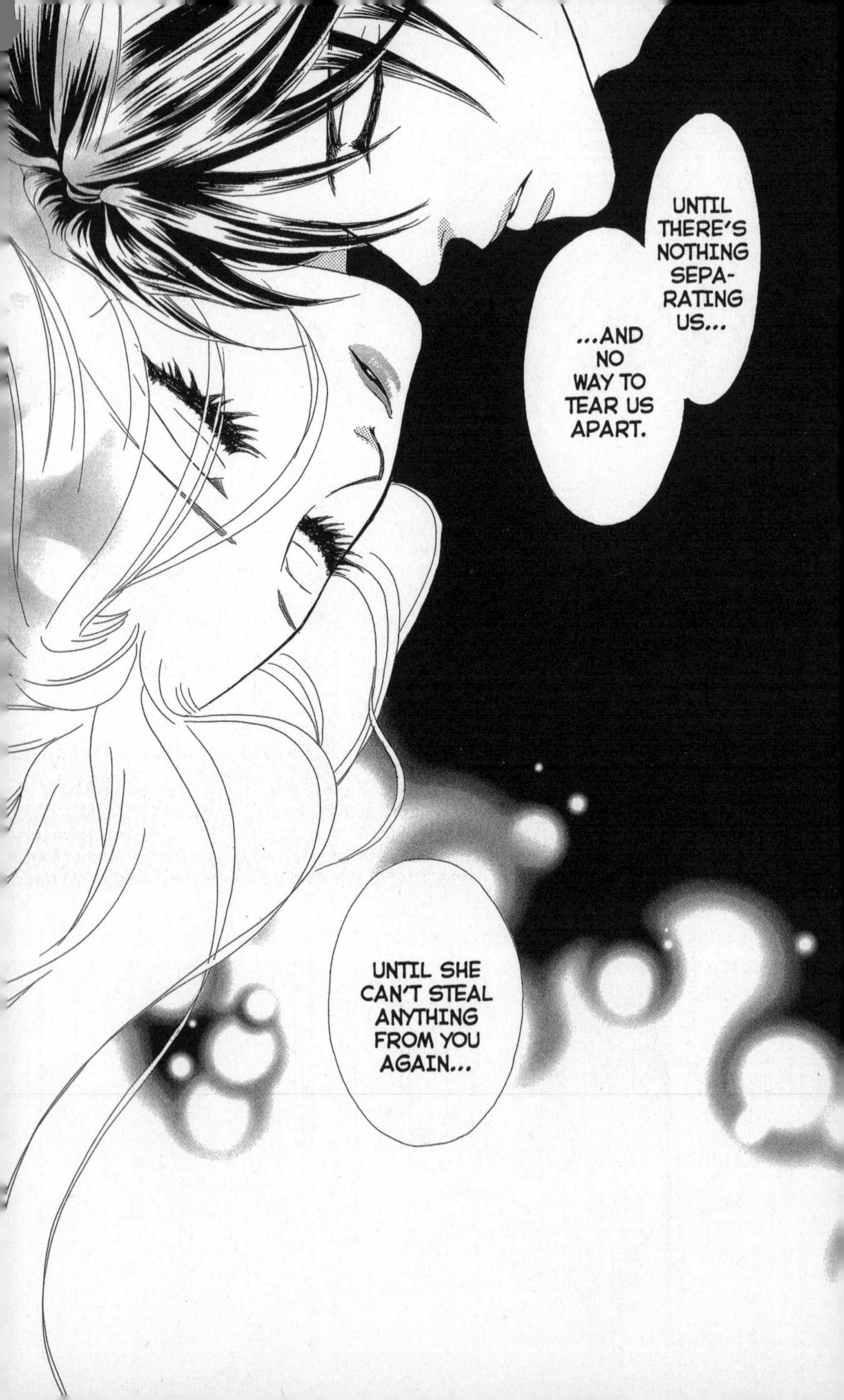
UNTIL THERE'S NOTHING SEPA- RATING US...
...AND NO WAY TO TEAR US APART.
UNTIL SHE CAN'T STEAL ANYTHING FROM YOU AGAIN...

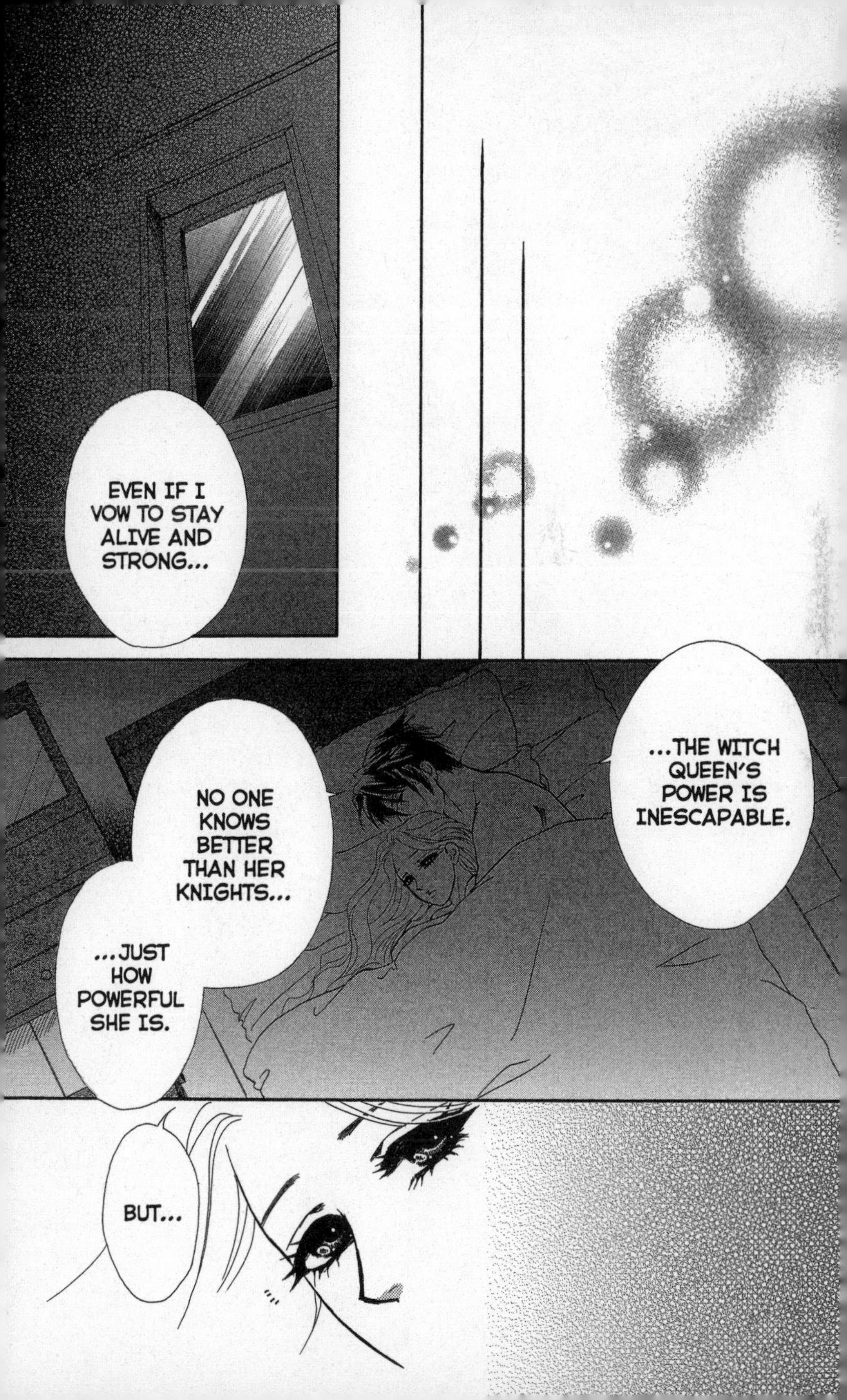
EVEN IF I VOW TO STAY ALIVE AND STRONG...
...THE WITCH QUEEN'S POWER IS INESCAPABLE.
NO ONE KNOWS BETTER THAN HER KNIGHTS...
...JUST HOW POWERFUL SHE IS.
BUT...

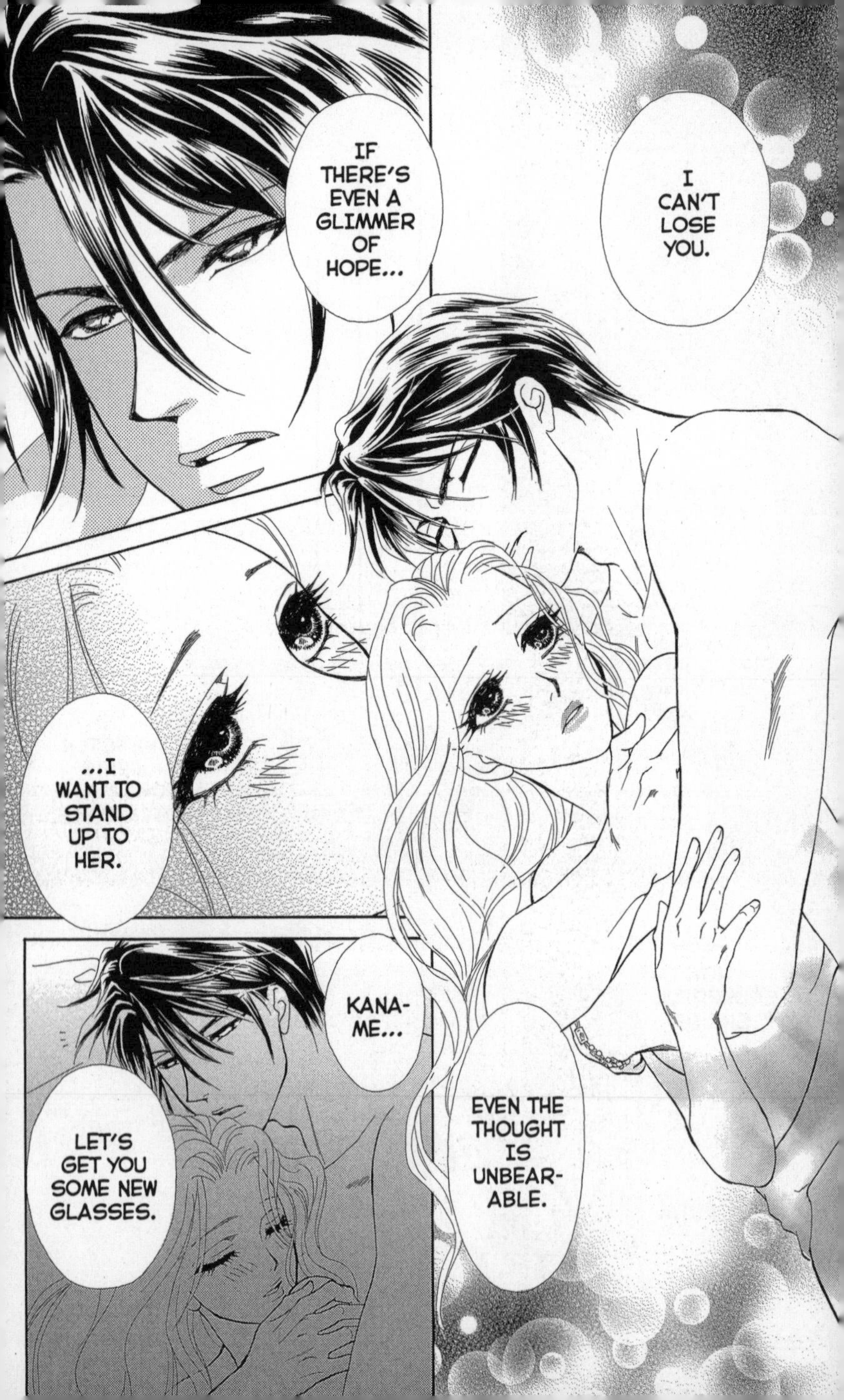
I CAN'T LOSE YOU.
EVEN THE THOUGHT IS UNBEARABLE.
IF THERE'S EVEN A GLIMMER OF HOPE...
...I WANT TO STAND UP TO HER.
KANAME...
LET'S GET YOU SOME NEW GLASSES.

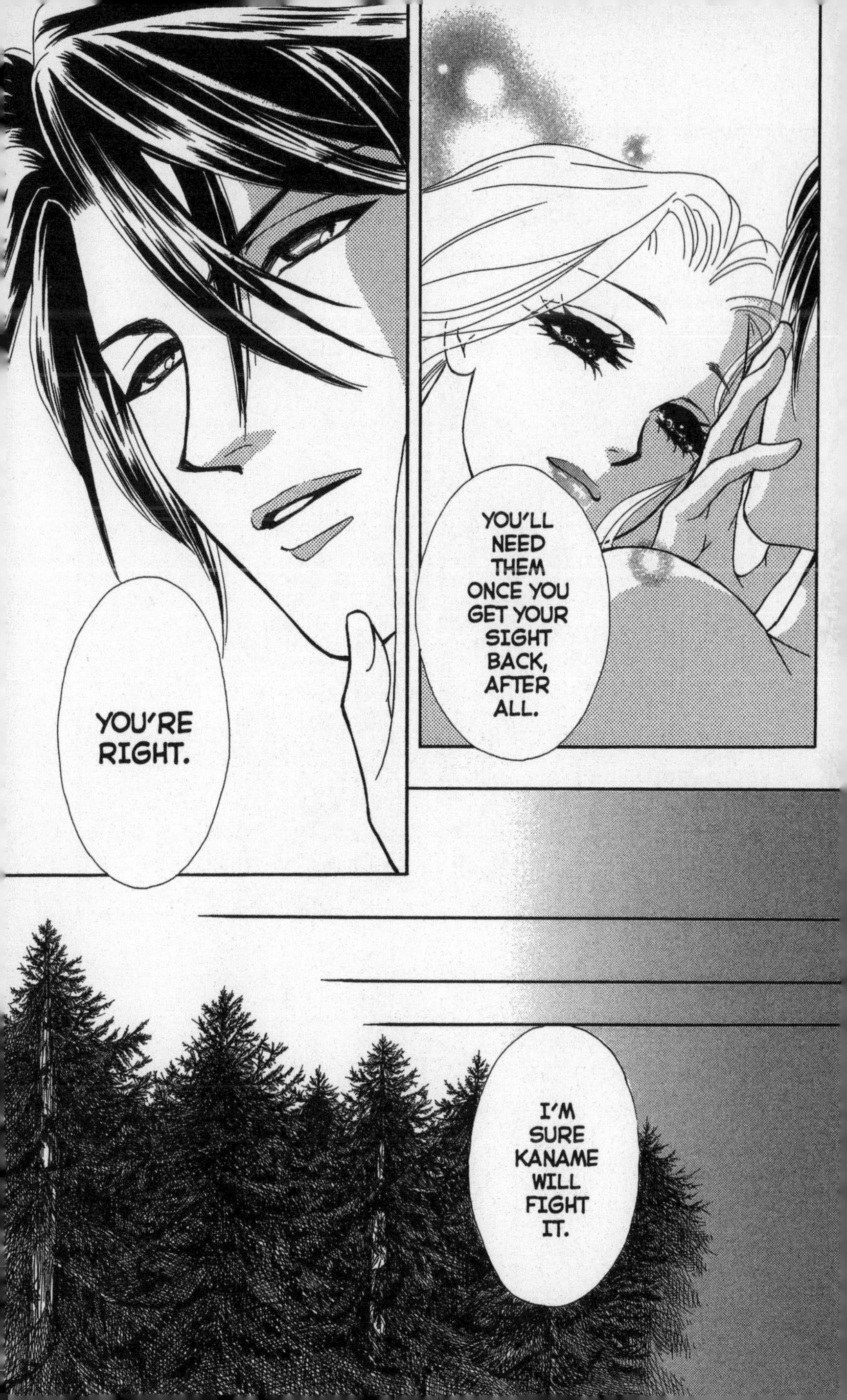
YOU'LL NEED THEM ONCE YOU GET YOUR SIGHT BACK, AFTER ALL.
YOU'RE RIGHT.
I'M SURE KANAME WILL FIGHT IT.

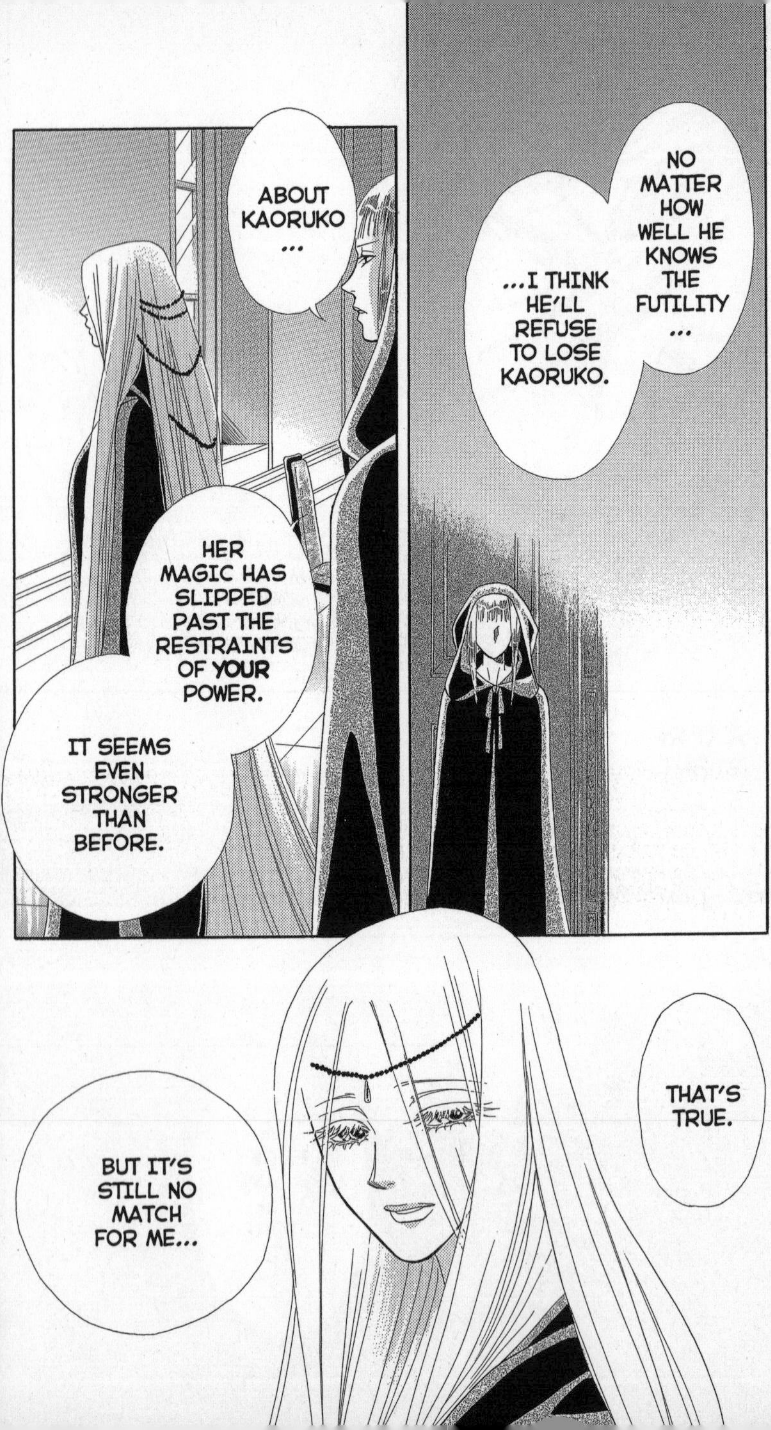
NO MATTER HOW WELL HE KNOWS THE FUTILITY...
...I THINK HE'LL REFUSE TO LOSE KAORUKO.
ABOUT KAORUKO...
HER MAGIC HAS SLIPPED PAST THE RESTRAINTS OF **YOUR** POWER.
IT SEEMS EVEN STRONGER THAN BEFORE.
THAT'S TRUE.
BUT IT'S STILL NO MATCH FOR ME...

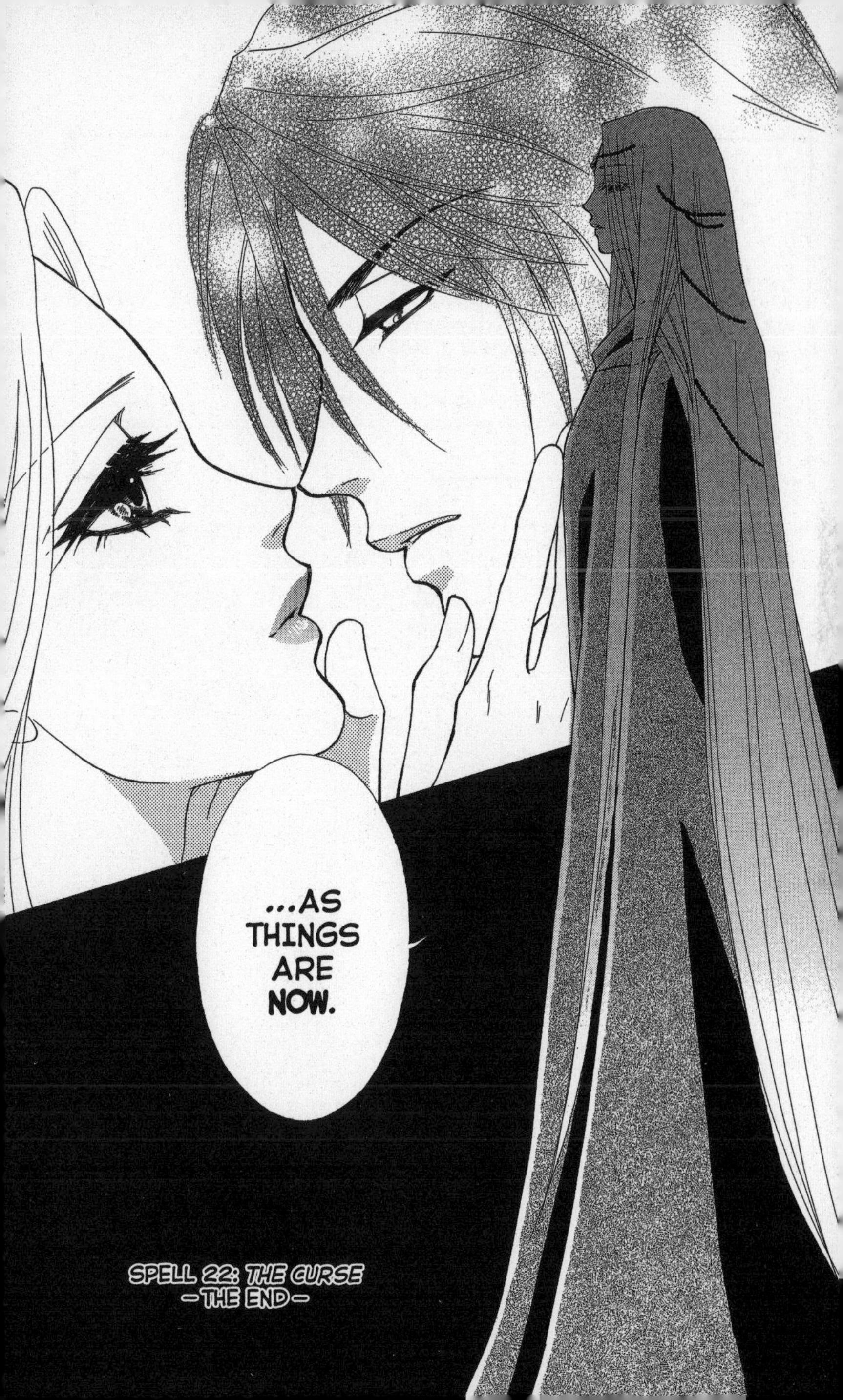
...AS THINGS ARE NOW.
SPELL 22: THE CURSE
-THE END-

– THE CURSE –

Without his glasses, Kaname can only see about a foot in front of him. He moves as though he can see, but he's extremely nearsighted. Plus, he has astigmatism.

He wears glasses, but it seems like he's honed all of his other senses so that he doesn't need to rely on his vision. Even if he were a ninja, that'd be impressive!
(Laugh)

I'd like to do it with my glasses on.

Not happening.

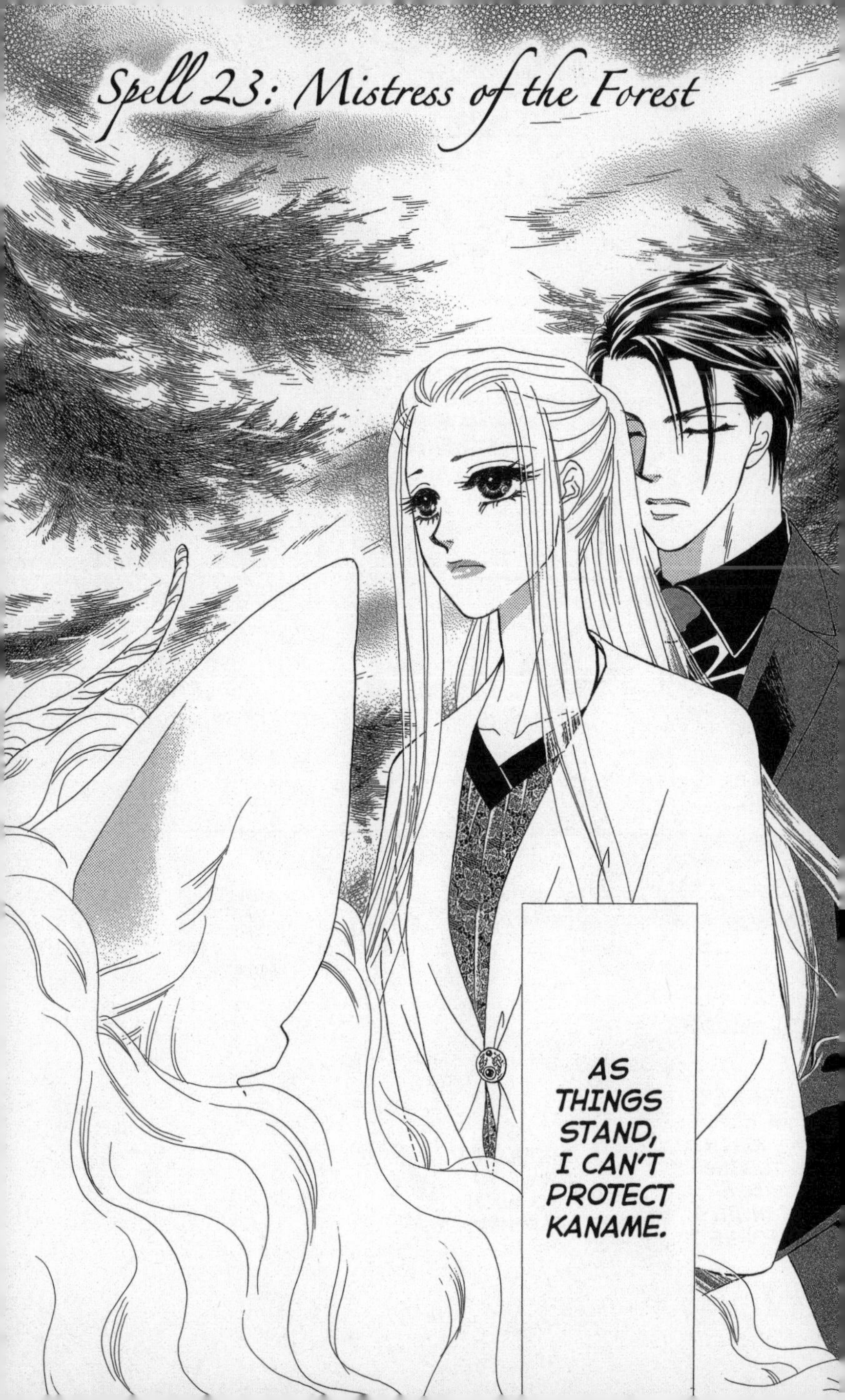
Spell 23: Mistress of the Forest
AS THINGS STAND, I CAN'T PROTECT KANAME.

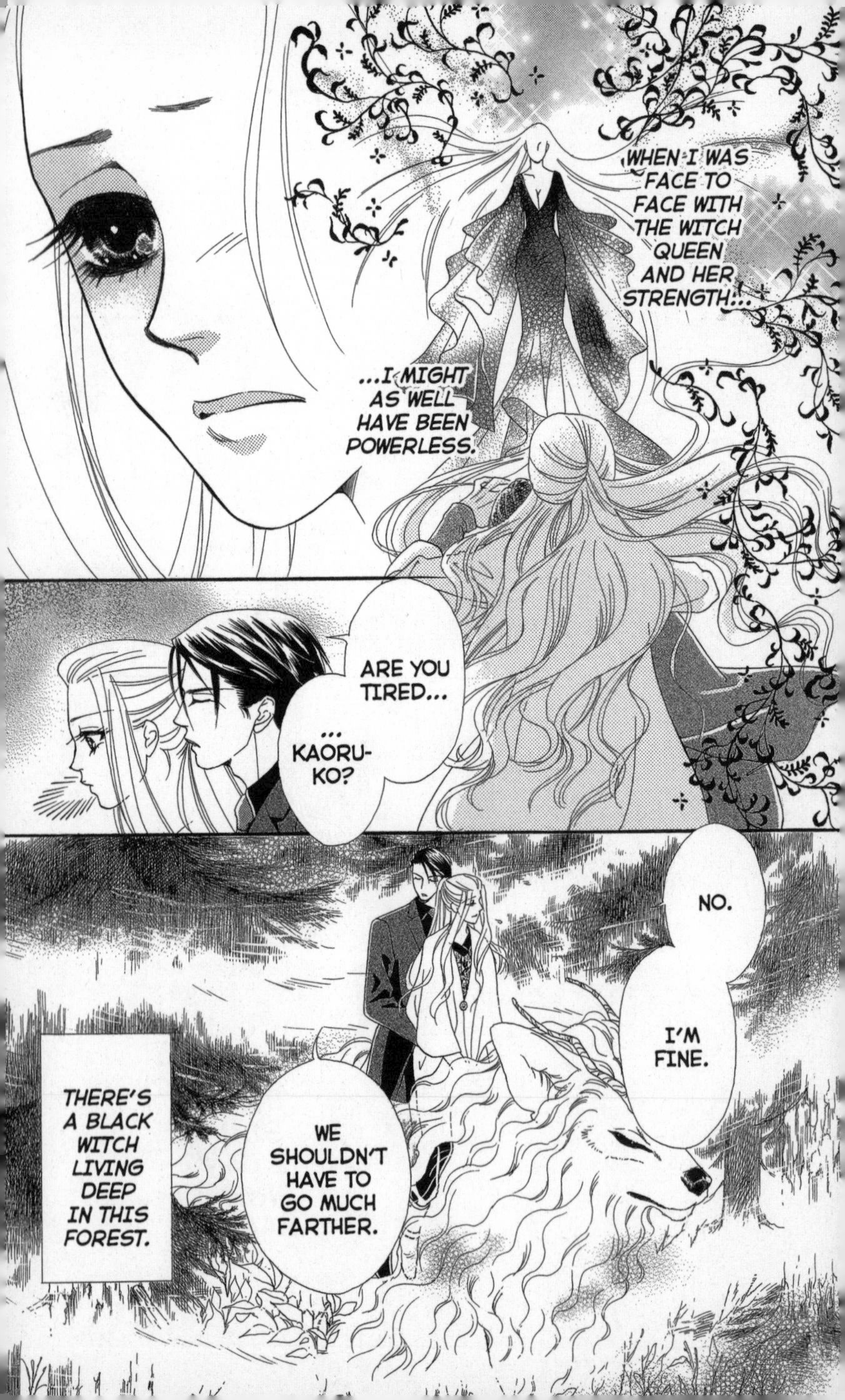
WHEN I WAS FACE TO FACE WITH THE WITCH QUEEN AND HER STRENGTH...
...I MIGHT AS WELL HAVE BEEN POWERLESS.
ARE YOU TIRED...
...KAORU-KO?
NO.
I'M FINE.
WE SHOULDN'T HAVE TO GO MUCH FARTHER.
THERE'S A BLACK WITCH LIVING DEEP IN THIS FOREST.

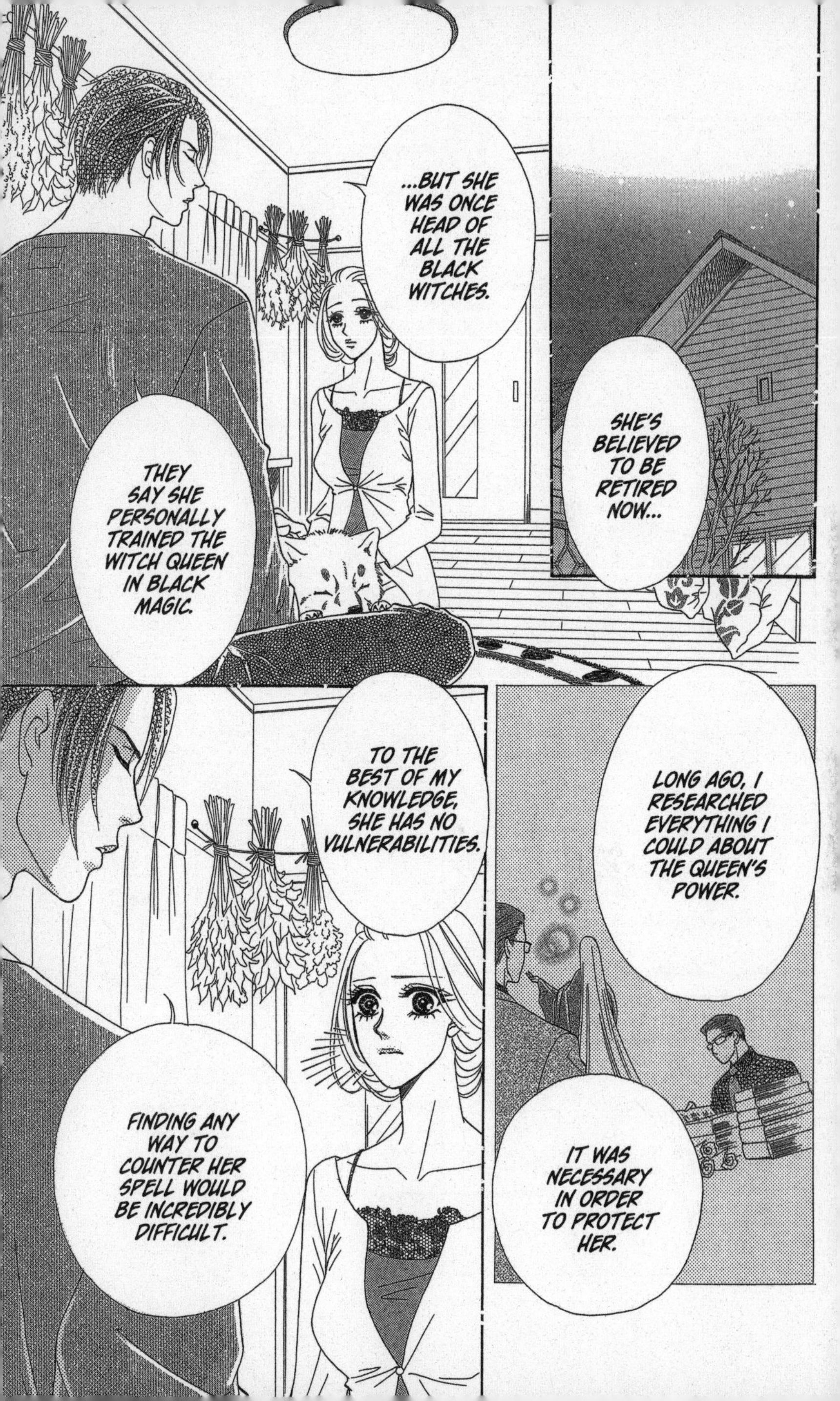
SHE'S BELIEVED TO BE RETIRED NOW...
...BUT SHE WAS ONCE HEAD OF ALL THE BLACK WITCHES.
THEY SAY SHE PERSONALLY TRAINED THE WITCH QUEEN IN BLACK MAGIC.
LONG AGO, I RESEARCHED EVERYTHING I COULD ABOUT THE QUEEN'S POWER.
IT WAS NECESSARY IN ORDER TO PROTECT HER.
TO THE BEST OF MY KNOWLEDGE, SHE HAS NO VULNERABILITIES.
FINDING ANY WAY TO COUNTER HER SPELL WOULD BE INCREDIBLY DIFFICULT.

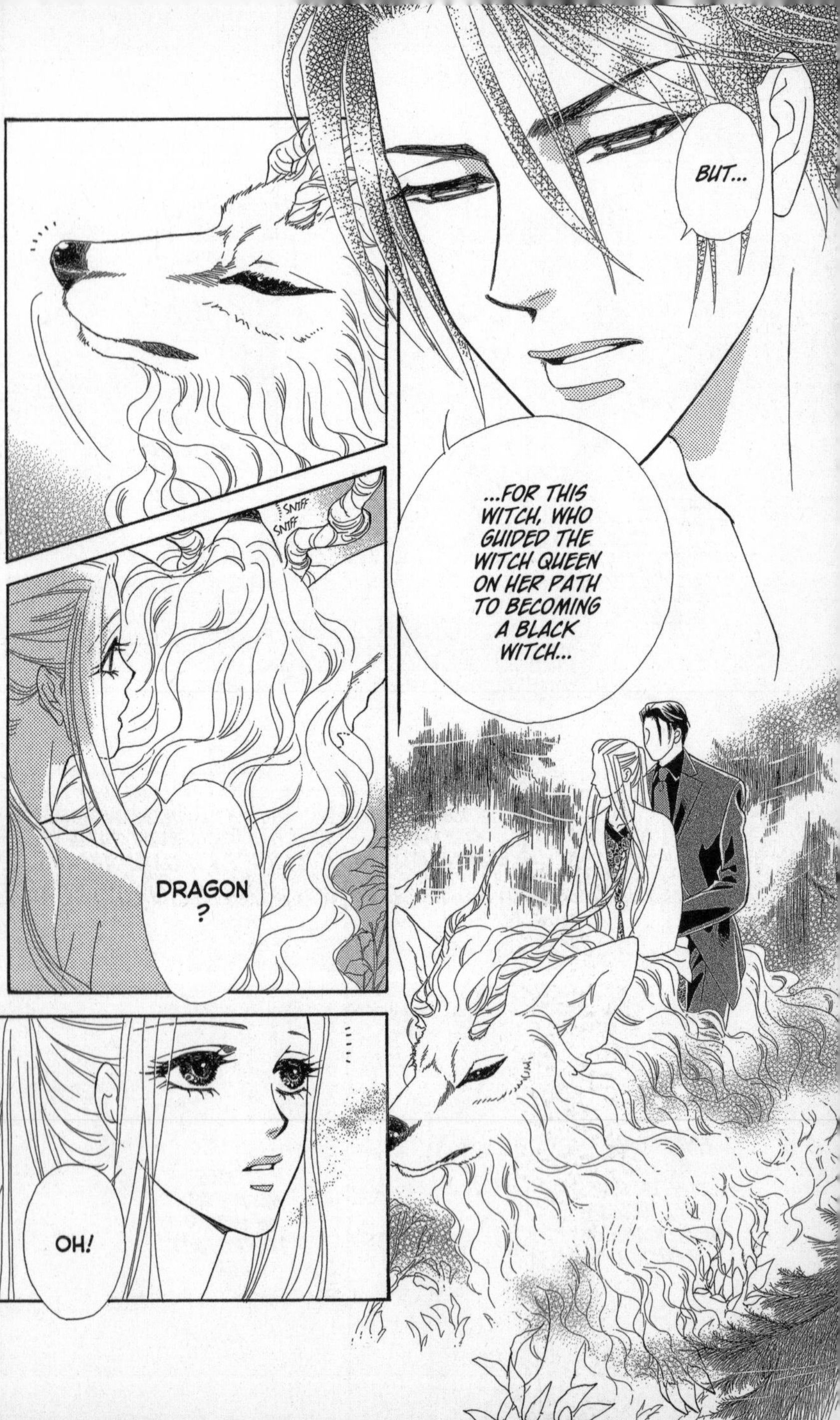
BUT...
...FOR THIS WITCH, WHO GUIDED THE WITCH QUEEN ON HER PATH TO BECOMING A BLACK WITCH...
SNIFF SNIFF
DRAGON?
OH!

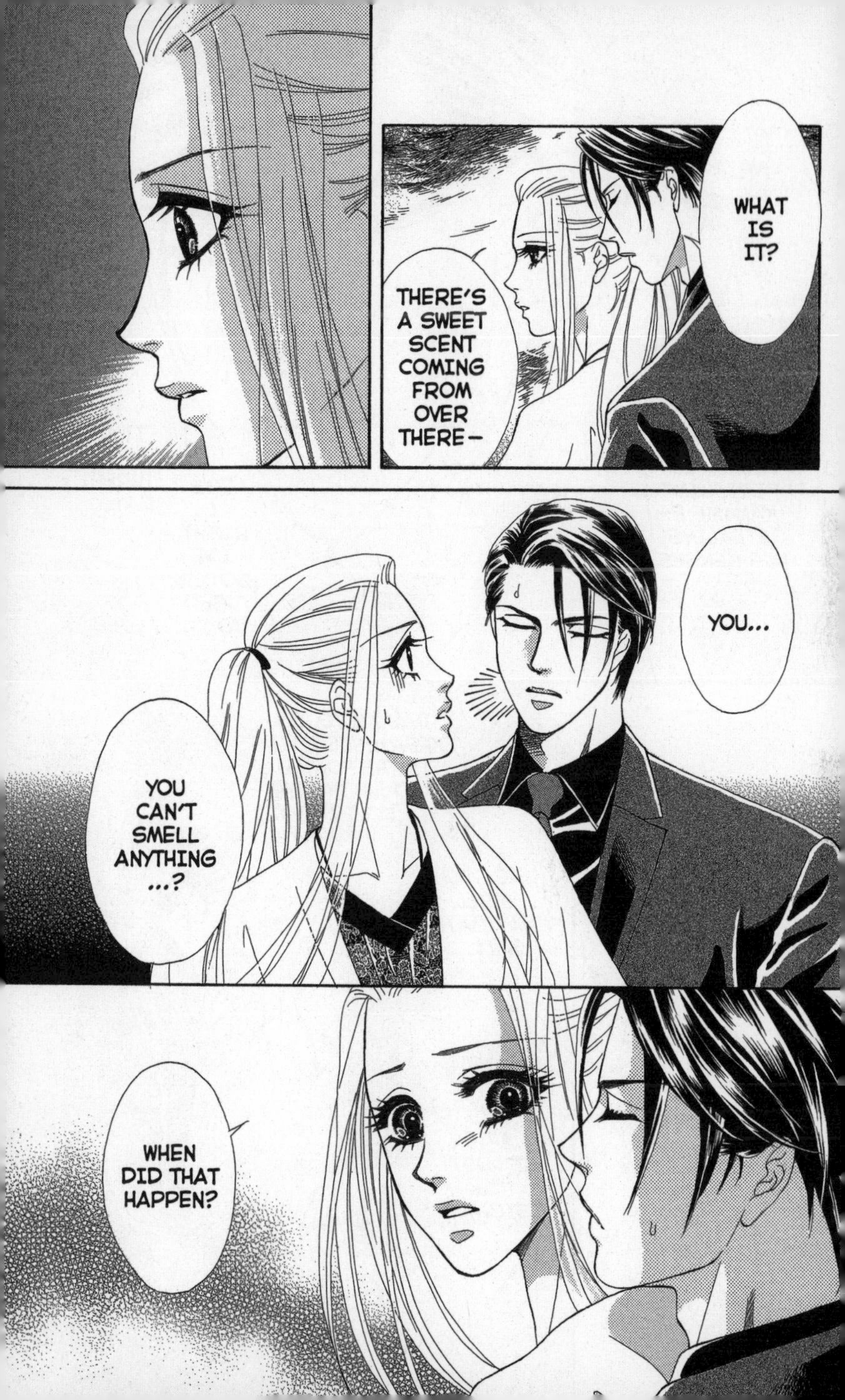
WHAT IS IT?
THERE'S A SWEET SCENT COMING FROM OVER THERE—
YOU...
YOU CAN'T SMELL ANYTHING ...?
WHEN DID THAT HAPPEN?

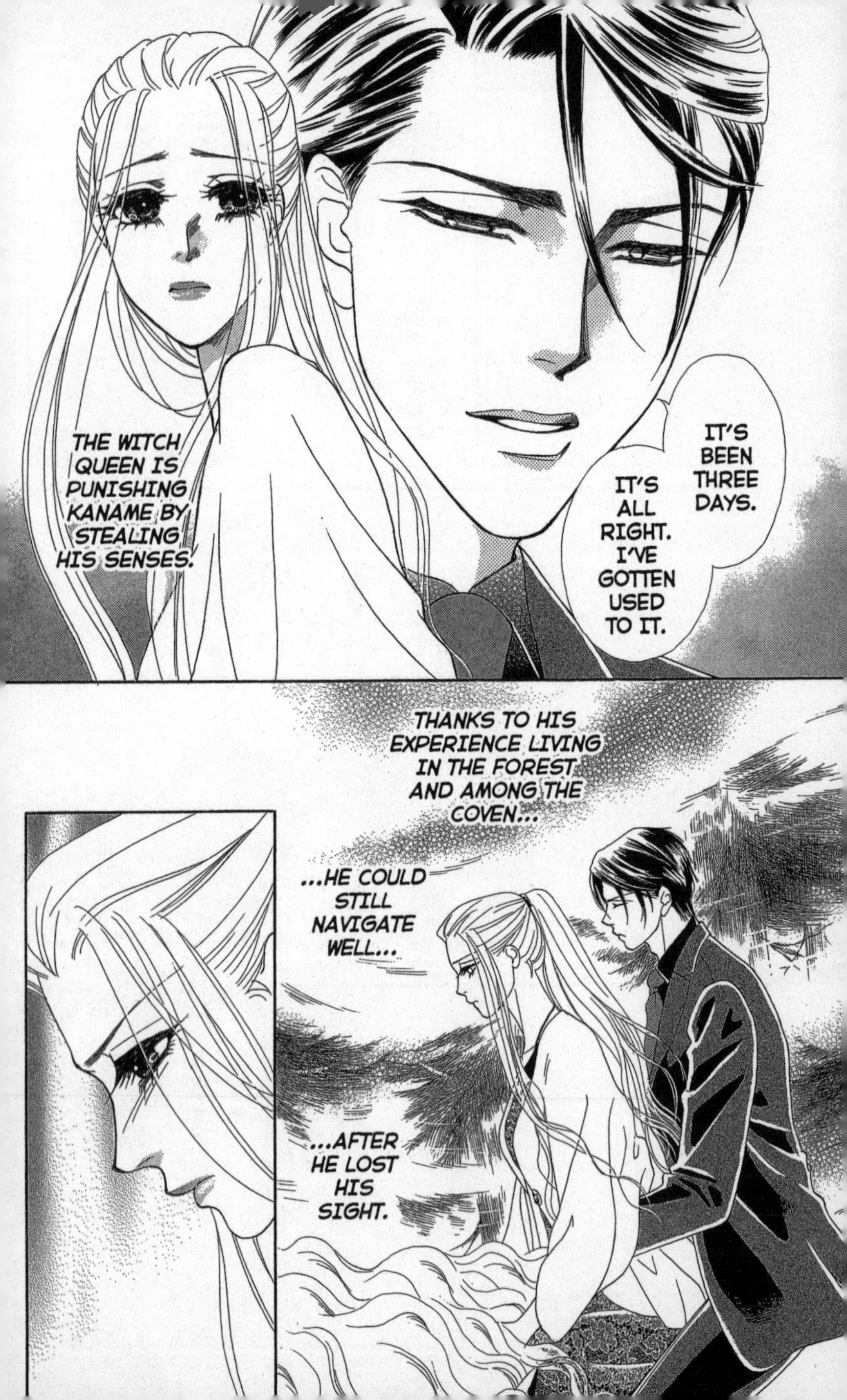
IT'S BEEN THREE DAYS.
IT'S ALL RIGHT. I'VE GOTTEN USED TO IT.
THE WITCH QUEEN IS PUNISHING KANAME BY STEALING HIS SENSES.
THANKS TO HIS EXPERIENCE LIVING IN THE FOREST AND AMONG THE COVEN...
...HE COULD STILL NAVIGATE WELL...
...AFTER HE LOST HIS SIGHT.

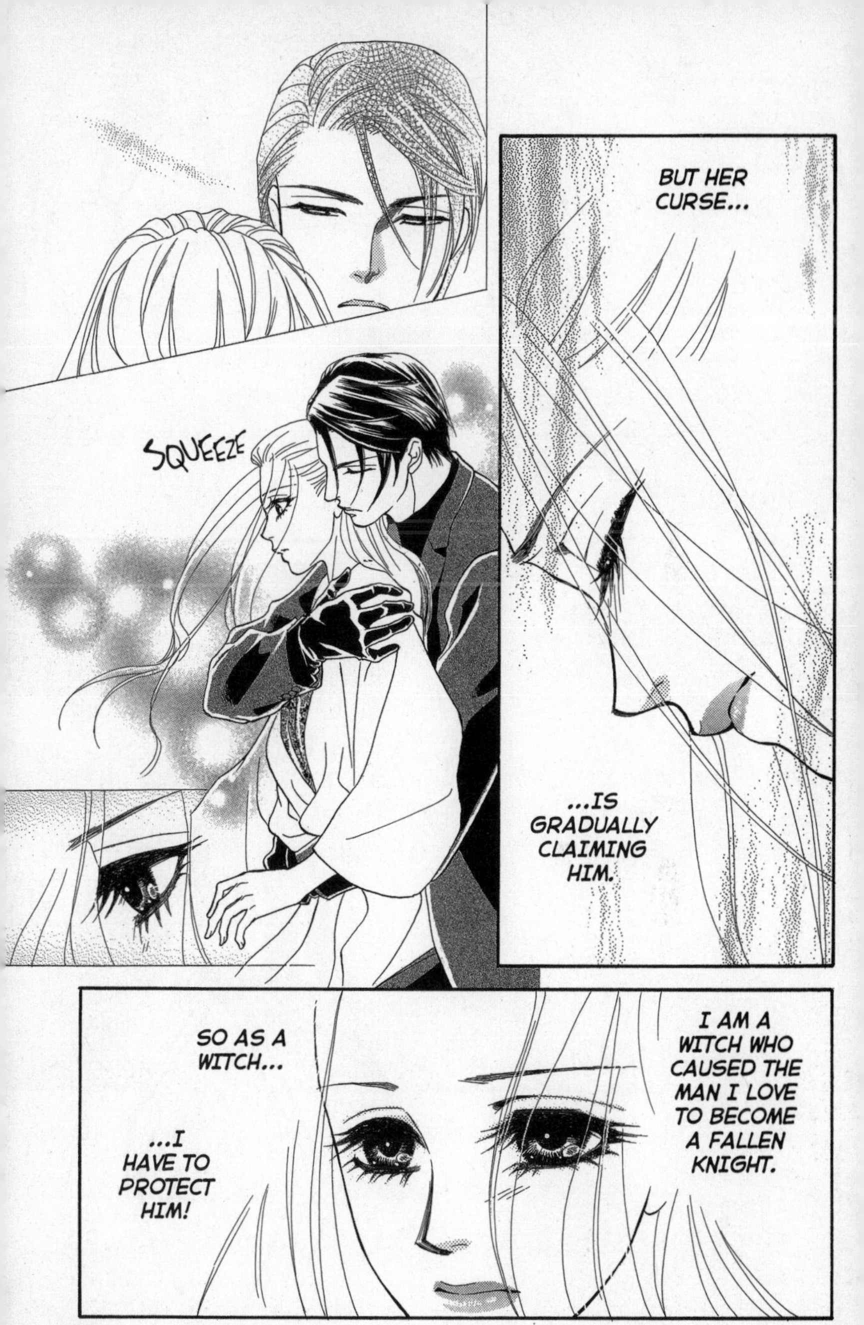
BUT HER CURSE...
...IS GRADUALLY CLAIMING HIM.
SQUEEZE
I AM A WITCH WHO CAUSED THE MAN I LOVE TO BECOME A FALLEN KNIGHT.
SO AS A WITCH...
...I HAVE TO PROTECT HIM!

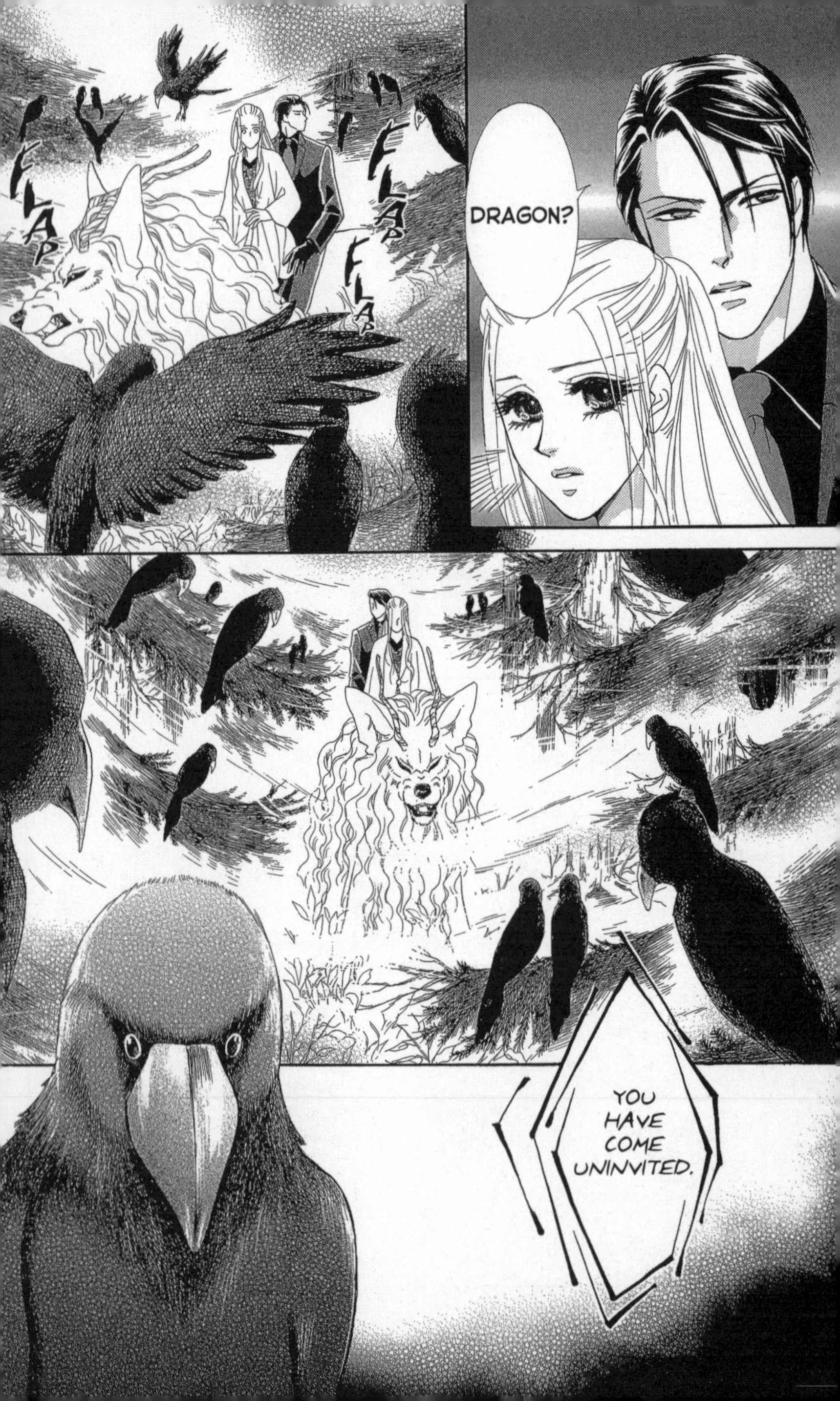
DRAGON?
FLAP
FLAP
FLAP
YOU HAVE COME UNINVITED.

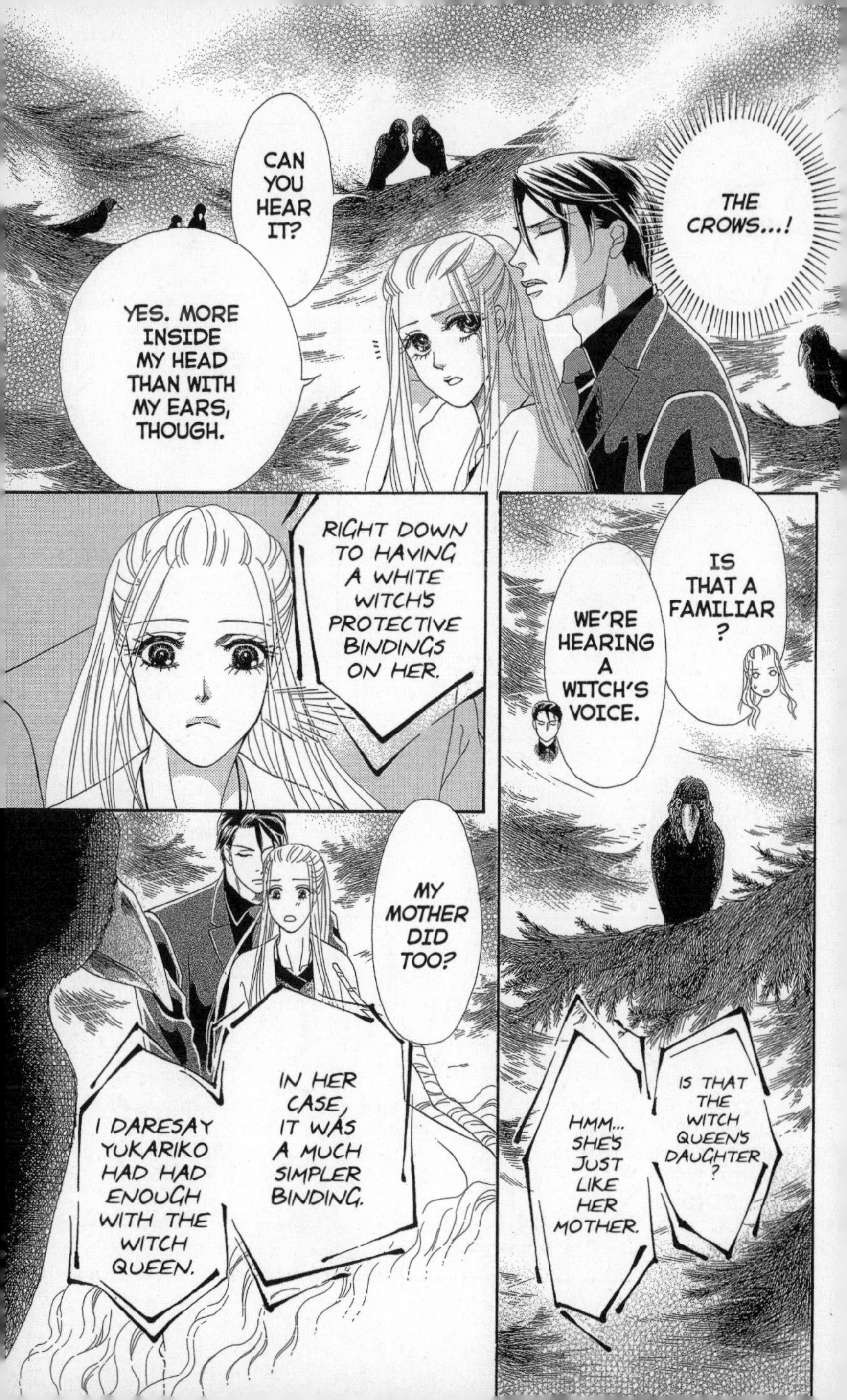
THE CROWS...!
CAN YOU HEAR IT?
YES. MORE INSIDE MY HEAD THAN WITH MY EARS, THOUGH.
IS THAT A FAMILIAR?
WE'RE HEARING A WITCH'S VOICE.
IS THAT THE WITCH QUEEN'S DAUGHTER?
HMM... SHE'S JUST LIKE HER MOTHER.
RIGHT DOWN TO HAVING A WHITE WITCH'S PROTECTIVE BINDINGS ON HER.
MY MOTHER DID TOO?
IN HER CASE, IT WAS A MUCH SIMPLER BINDING.
I DARESAY YUKARIKO HAD HAD ENOUGH WITH THE WITCH QUEEN.

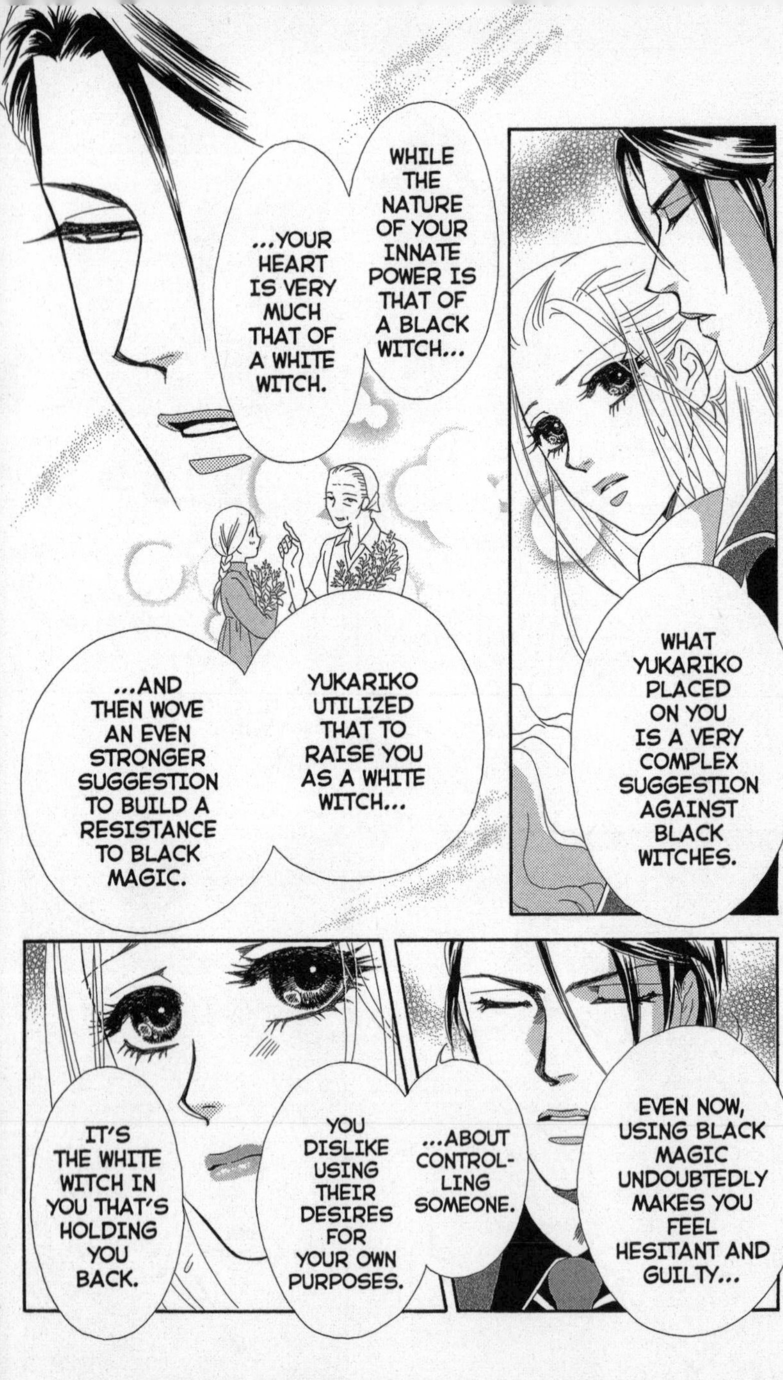
WHILE THE NATURE OF YOUR INNATE POWER IS THAT OF A BLACK WITCH...
...YOUR HEART IS VERY MUCH THAT OF A WHITE WITCH.
WHAT YUKARIKO PLACED ON YOU IS A VERY COMPLEX SUGGESTION AGAINST BLACK WITCHES.
YUKARIKO UTILIZED THAT TO RAISE YOU AS A WHITE WITCH...
...AND THEN WOVE AN EVEN STRONGER SUGGESTION TO BUILD A RESISTANCE TO BLACK MAGIC.
EVEN NOW, USING BLACK MAGIC UNDOUBTEDLY MAKES YOU FEEL HESITANT AND GUILTY...
...ABOUT CONTROL-LING SOMEONE.
YOU DISLIKE USING THEIR DESIRES FOR YOUR OWN PURPOSES.
IT'S THE WHITE WITCH IN YOU THAT'S HOLDING YOU BACK.

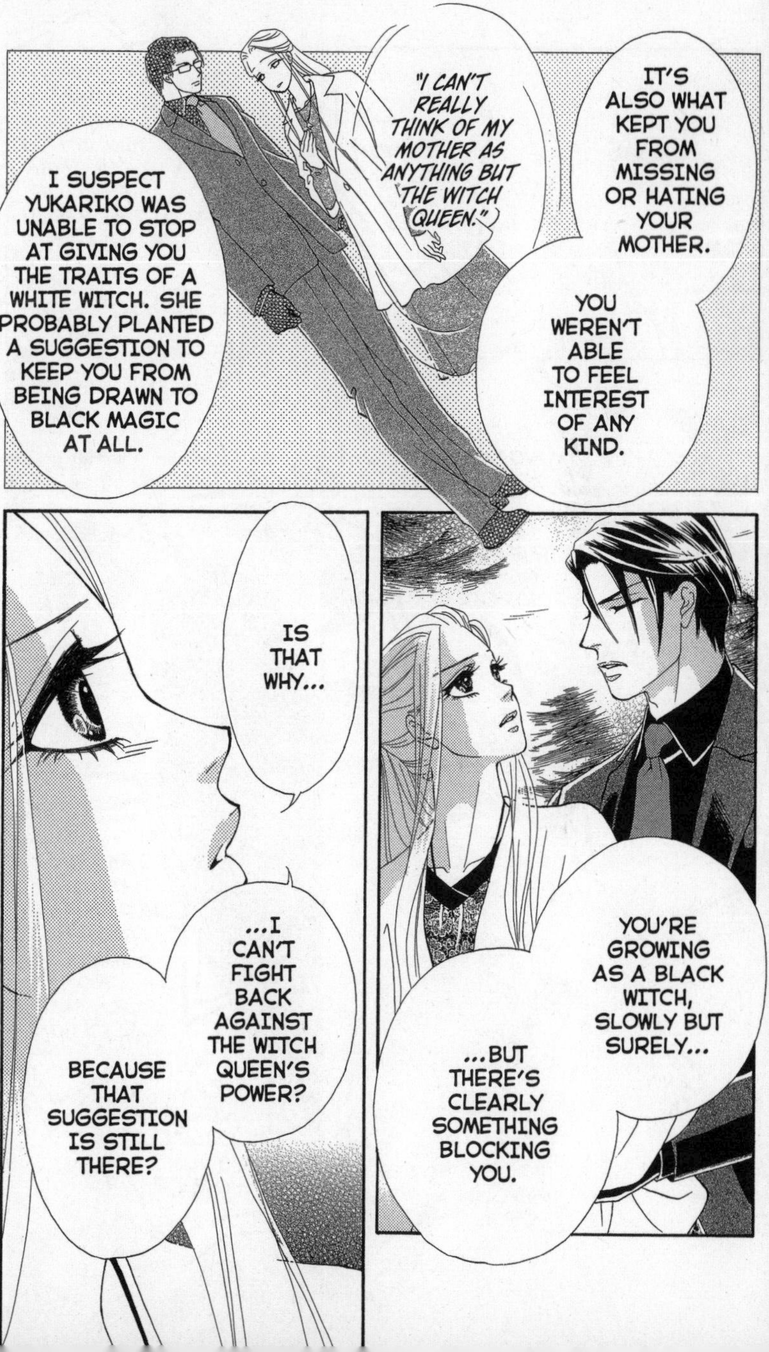
"I CAN'T REALLY THINK OF MY MOTHER AS ANYTHING BUT THE WITCH QUEEN."
IT'S ALSO WHAT KEPT YOU FROM MISSING OR HATING YOUR MOTHER.
YOU WEREN'T ABLE TO FEEL INTEREST OF ANY KIND.
I SUSPECT YUKARIKO WAS UNABLE TO STOP AT GIVING YOU THE TRAITS OF A WHITE WITCH. SHE PROBABLY PLANTED A SUGGESTION TO KEEP YOU FROM BEING DRAWN TO BLACK MAGIC AT ALL.
YOU'RE GROWING AS A BLACK WITCH, SLOWLY BUT SURELY...
...BUT THERE'S CLEARLY SOMETHING BLOCKING YOU.
IS THAT WHY...
...I CAN'T FIGHT BACK AGAINST THE WITCH QUEEN'S POWER?
BECAUSE THAT SUGGESTION IS STILL THERE?

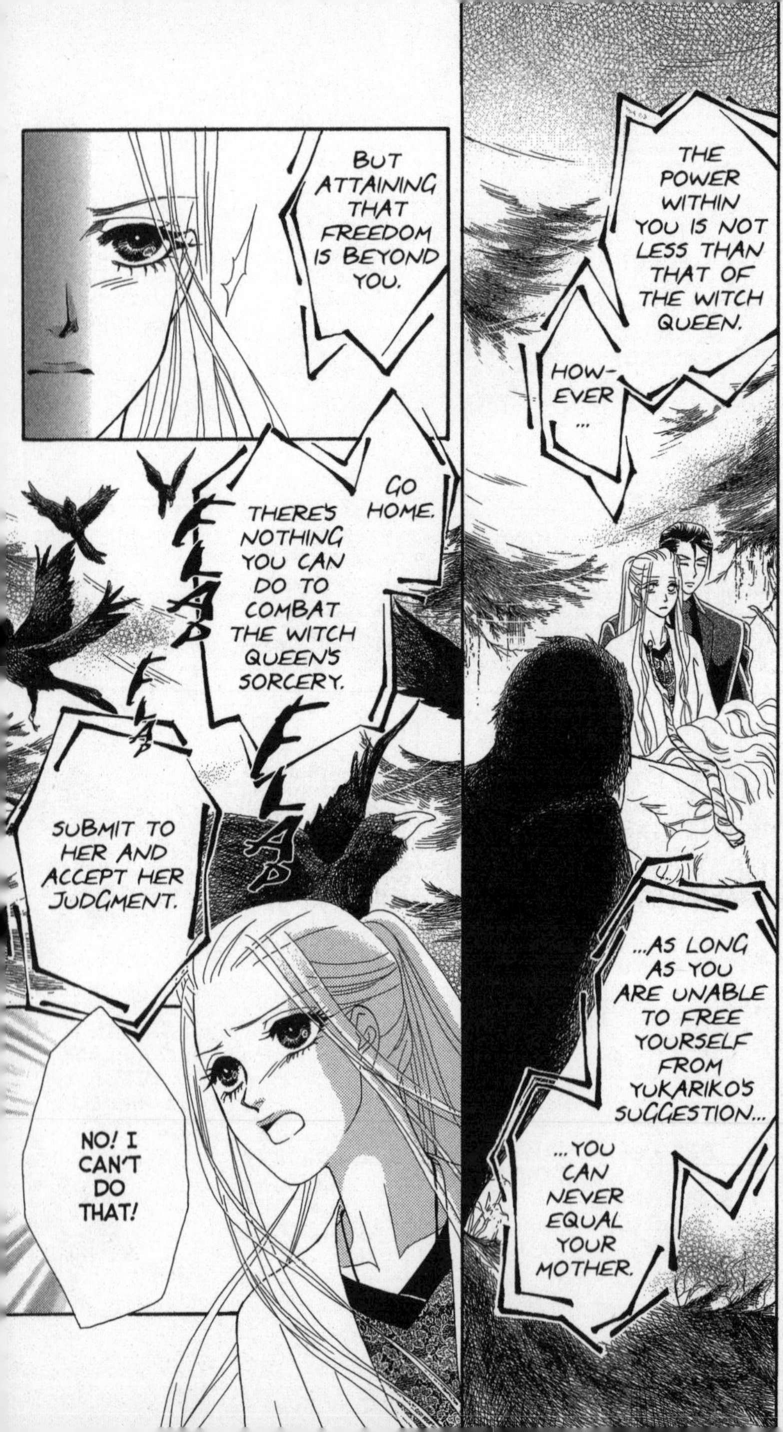
THE POWER WITHIN YOU IS NOT LESS THAN THAT OF THE WITCH QUEEN.
HOW-EVER ...
...AS LONG AS YOU ARE UNABLE TO FREE YOURSELF FROM YUKARIKO'S SUGGESTION...
...YOU CAN NEVER EQUAL YOUR MOTHER.
BUT ATTAINING THAT FREEDOM IS BEYOND YOU.
GO HOME.
THERE'S NOTHING YOU CAN DO TO COMBAT THE WITCH QUEEN'S SORCERY.
FLAP
FLAP
FLAP
SUBMIT TO HER AND ACCEPT HER JUDGMENT.
NO! I CAN'T DO THAT!

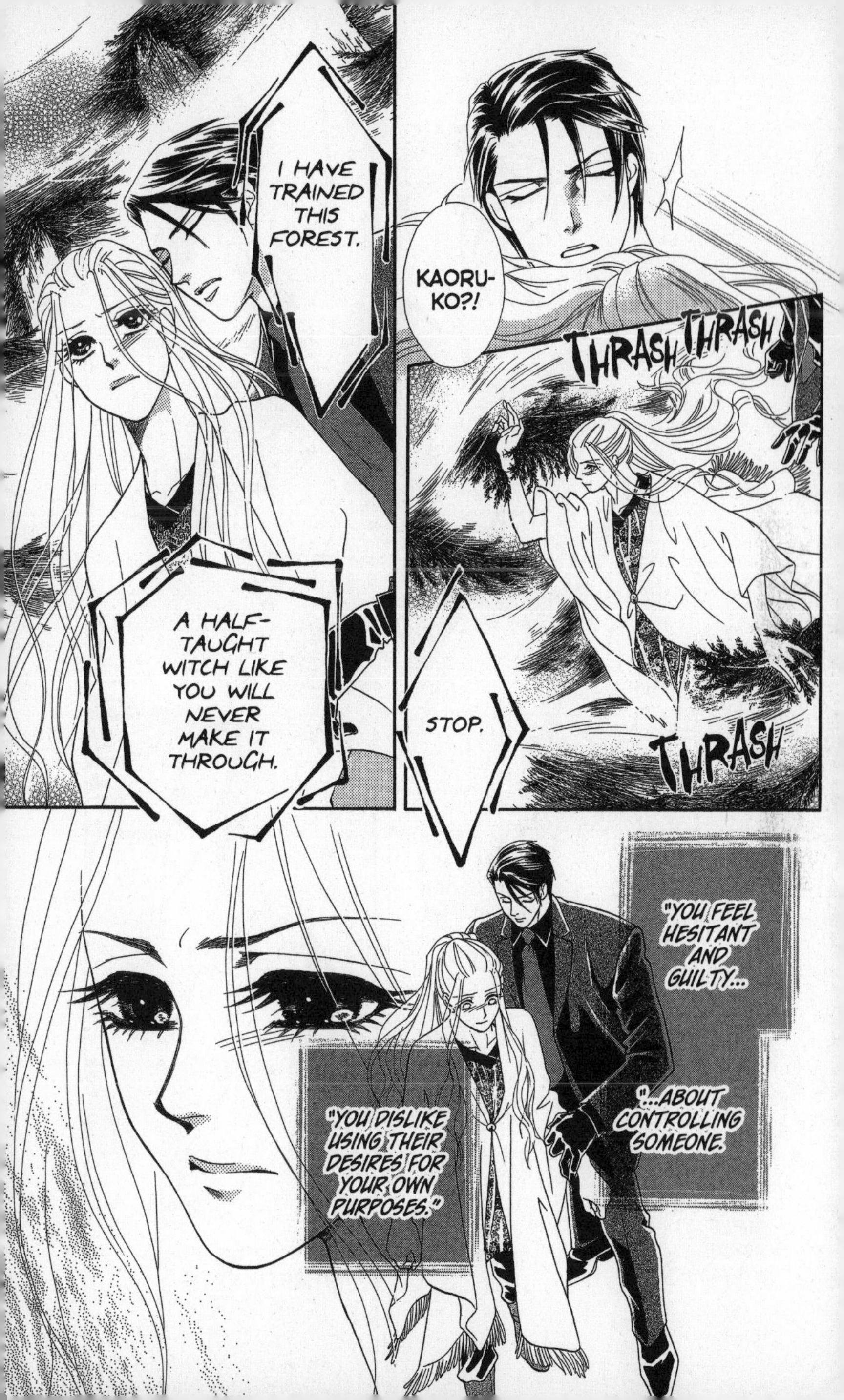
KAORU-KO?!
THRASH THRASH
STOP.
THRASH
I HAVE TRAINED THIS FOREST.
A HALF-TAUGHT WITCH LIKE YOU WILL NEVER MAKE IT THROUGH.
"YOU FEEL HESITANT AND GUILTY...
"...ABOUT CONTROLLING SOMEONE.
"YOU DISLIKE USING THEIR DESIRES FOR YOUR OWN PURPOSES."

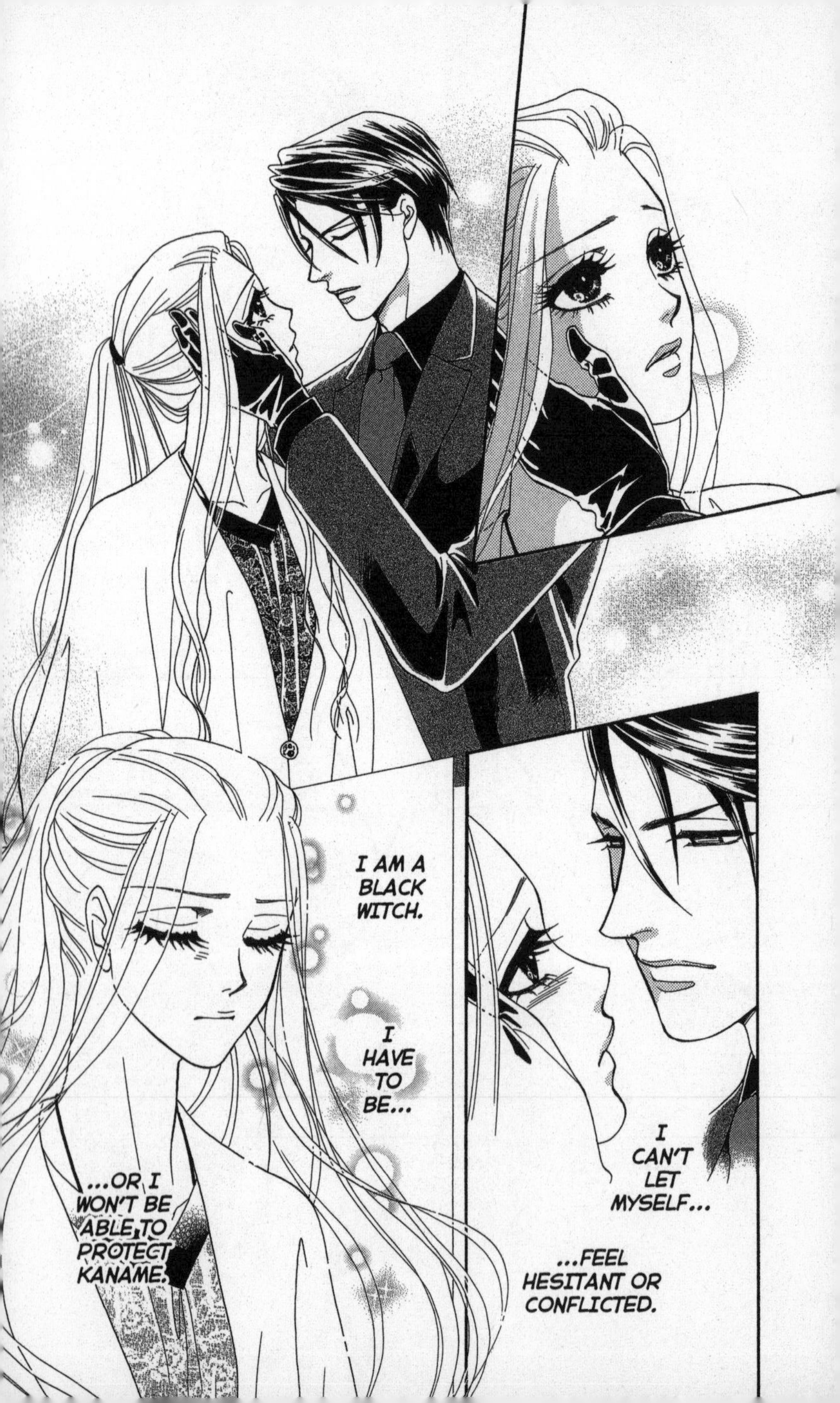
I CAN'T LET MYSELF...
...FEEL HESITANT OR CONFLICTED.
I AM A BLACK WITCH.
I HAVE TO BE...
...OR I WON'T BE ABLE TO PROTECT KANAME.

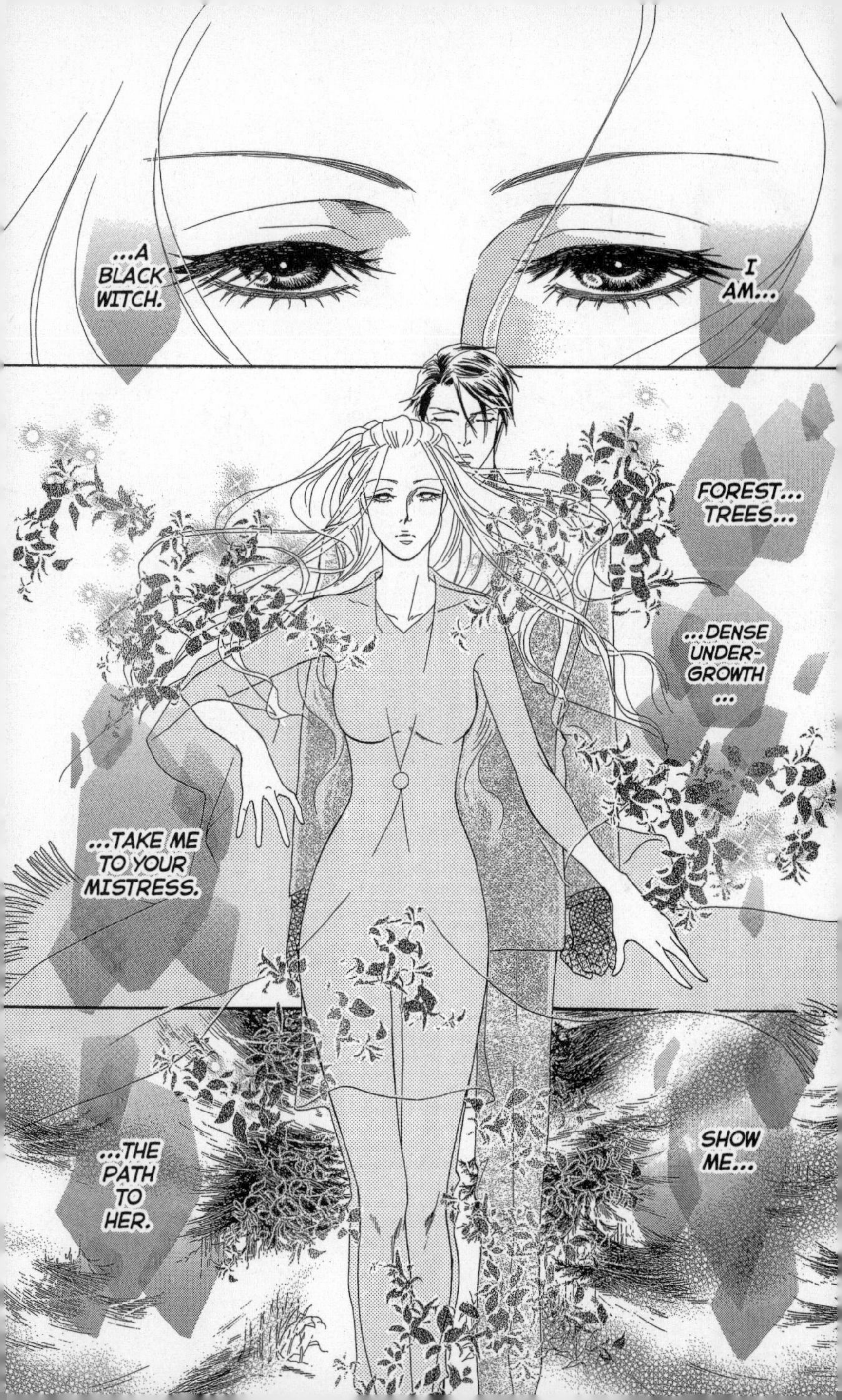
I AM...
...A BLACK WITCH.
FOREST... TREES...
...DENSE UNDER-GROWTH ...
...TAKE ME TO YOUR MISTRESS.
SHOW ME...
...THE PATH TO HER.

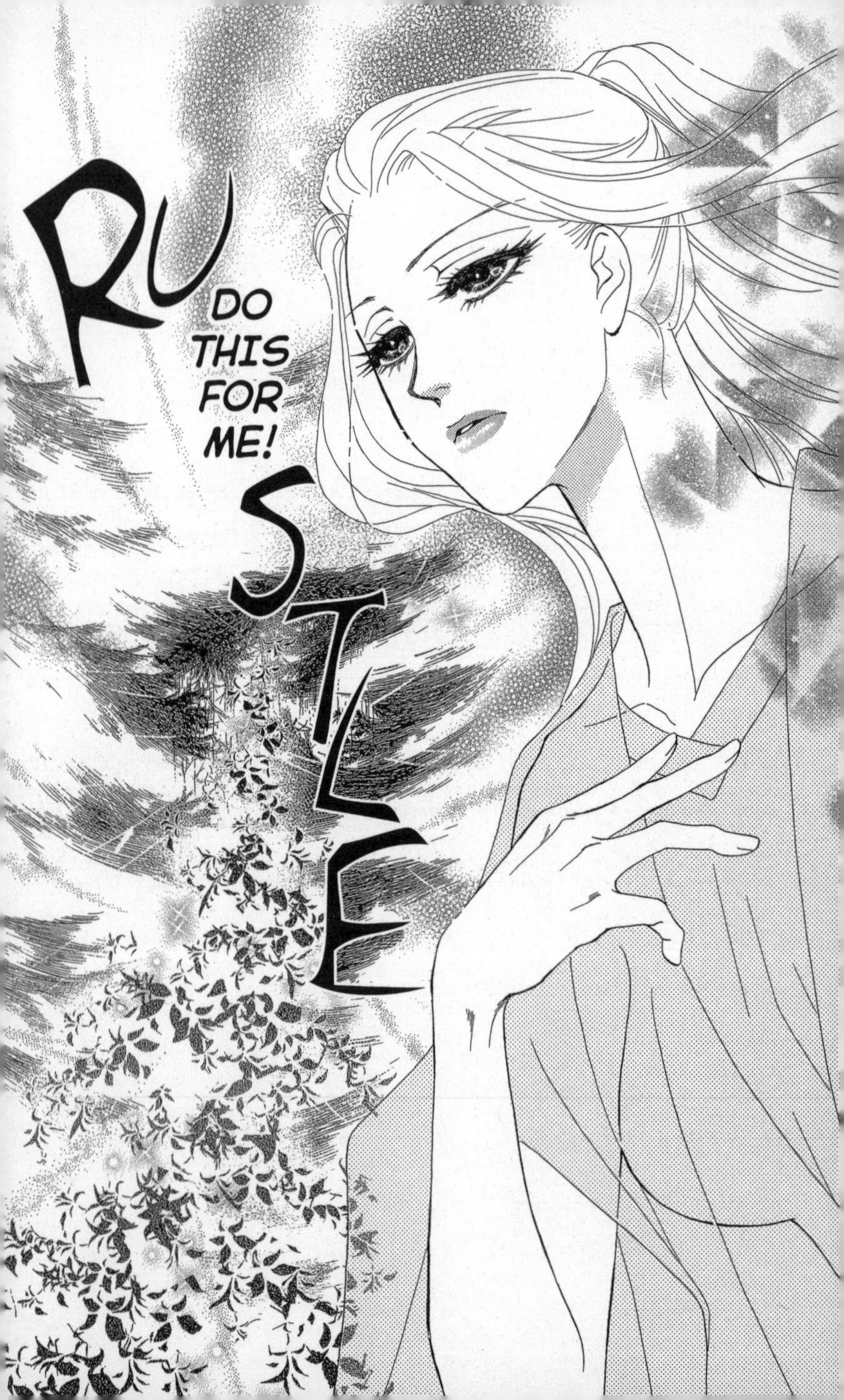
RU
DO THIS FOR ME!
STLE

FLAP

HUF

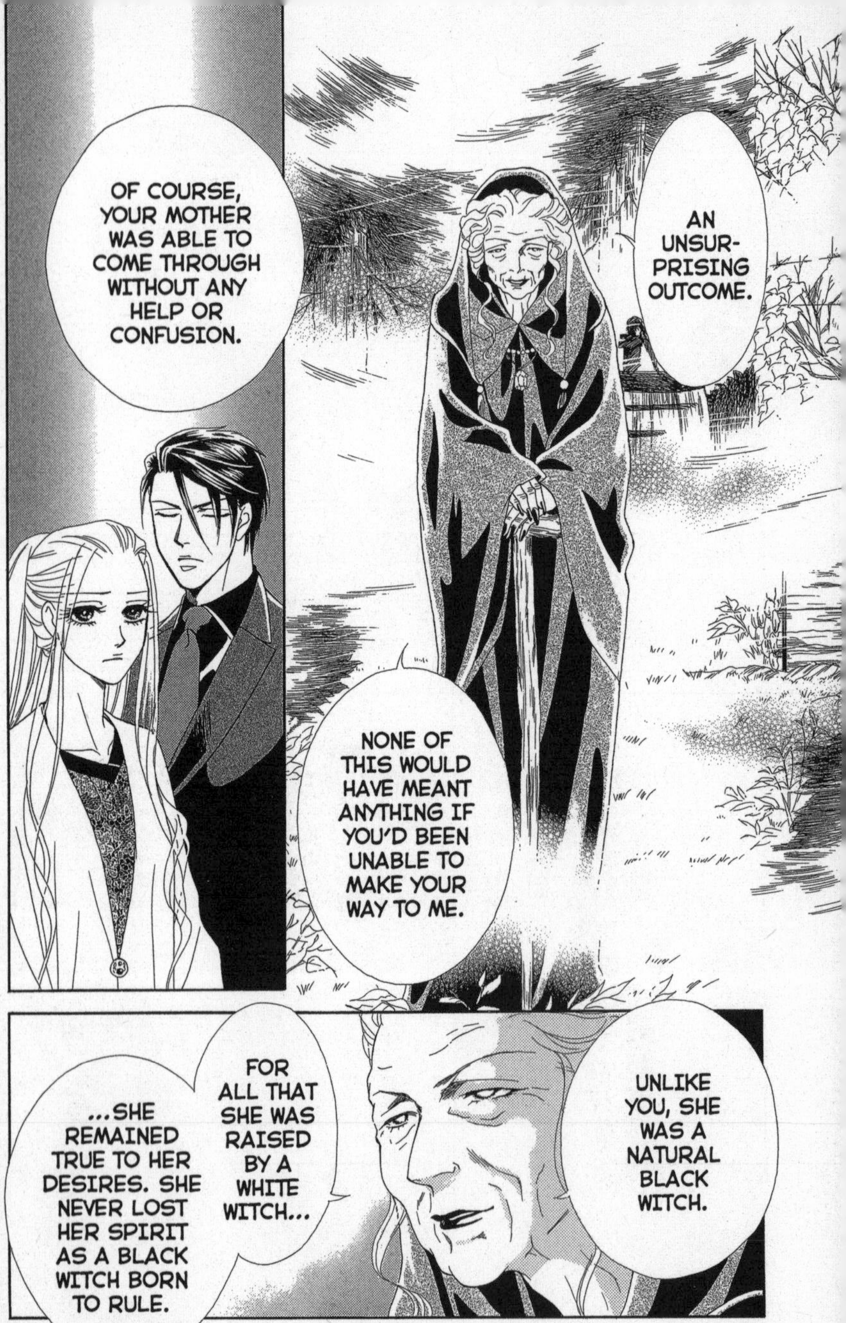
AN UNSURPRISING OUTCOME.
NONE OF THIS WOULD HAVE MEANT ANYTHING IF YOU'D BEEN UNABLE TO MAKE YOUR WAY TO ME.
OF COURSE, YOUR MOTHER WAS ABLE TO COME THROUGH WITHOUT ANY HELP OR CONFUSION.
UNLIKE YOU, SHE WAS A NATURAL BLACK WITCH.
FOR ALL THAT SHE WAS RAISED BY A WHITE WITCH...
...SHE REMAINED TRUE TO HER DESIRES. SHE NEVER LOST HER SPIRIT AS A BLACK WITCH BORN TO RULE.

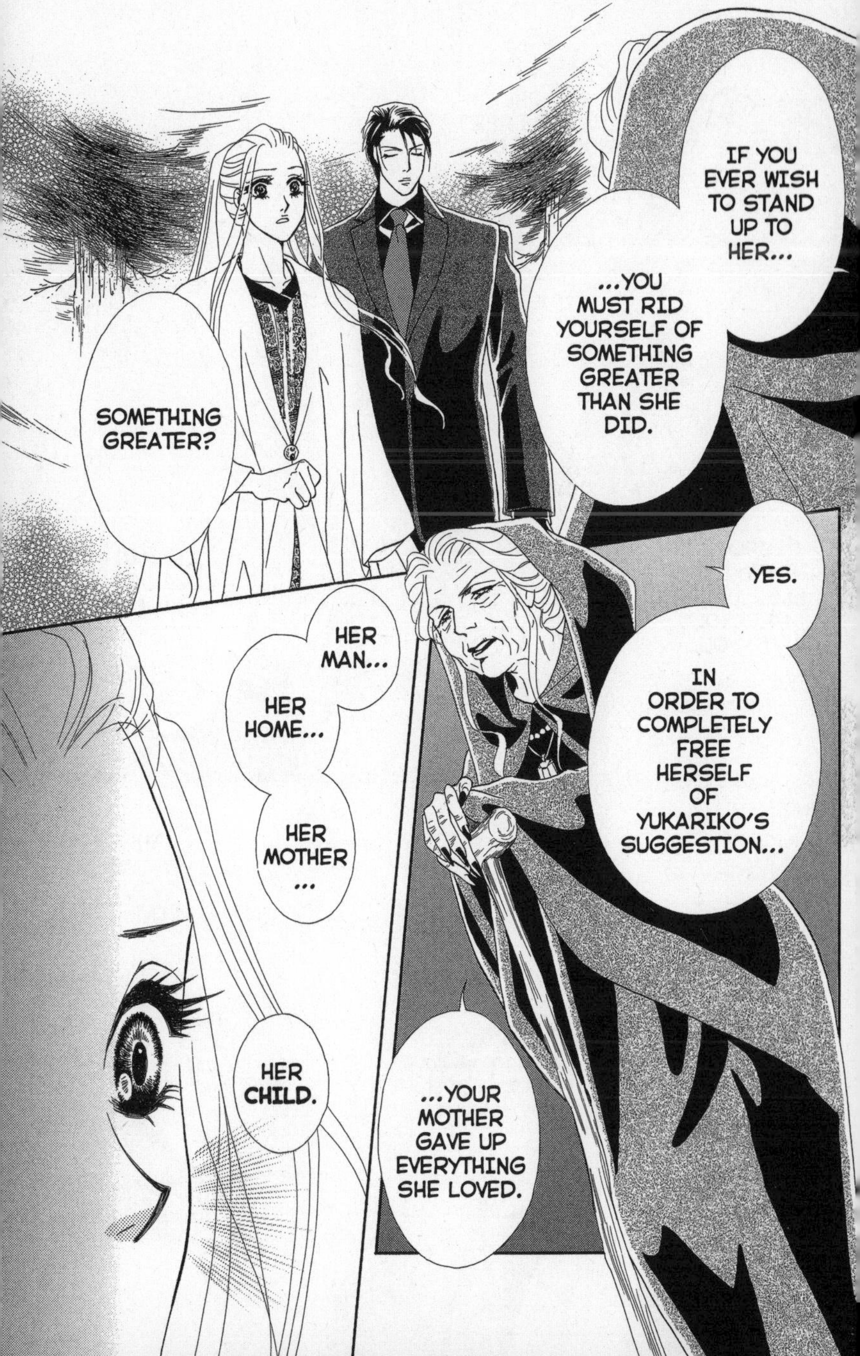
IF YOU EVER WISH TO STAND UP TO HER...
...YOU MUST RID YOURSELF OF SOMETHING GREATER THAN SHE DID.
SOMETHING GREATER?
YES.
IN ORDER TO COMPLETELY FREE HERSELF OF YUKARIKO'S SUGGESTION...
...YOUR MOTHER GAVE UP EVERYTHING SHE LOVED.
HER MAN...
HER HOME...
HER MOTHER...
HER CHILD.

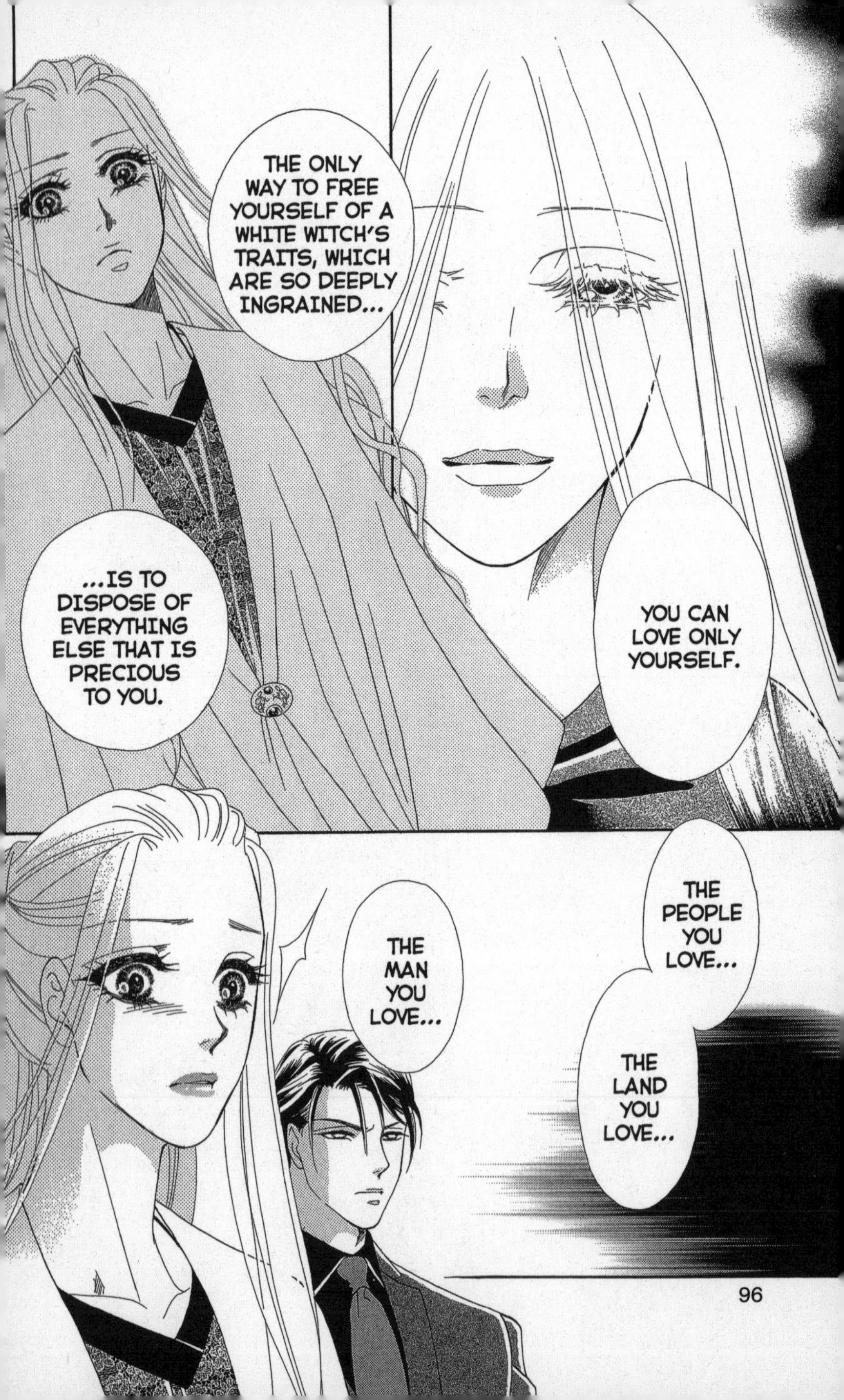
THE ONLY WAY TO FREE YOURSELF OF A WHITE WITCH'S TRAITS, WHICH ARE SO DEEPLY INGRAINED...
...IS TO DISPOSE OF EVERYTHING ELSE THAT IS PRECIOUS TO YOU.
YOU CAN LOVE ONLY YOURSELF.
THE PEOPLE YOU LOVE...
THE LAND YOU LOVE...
THE MAN YOU LOVE...

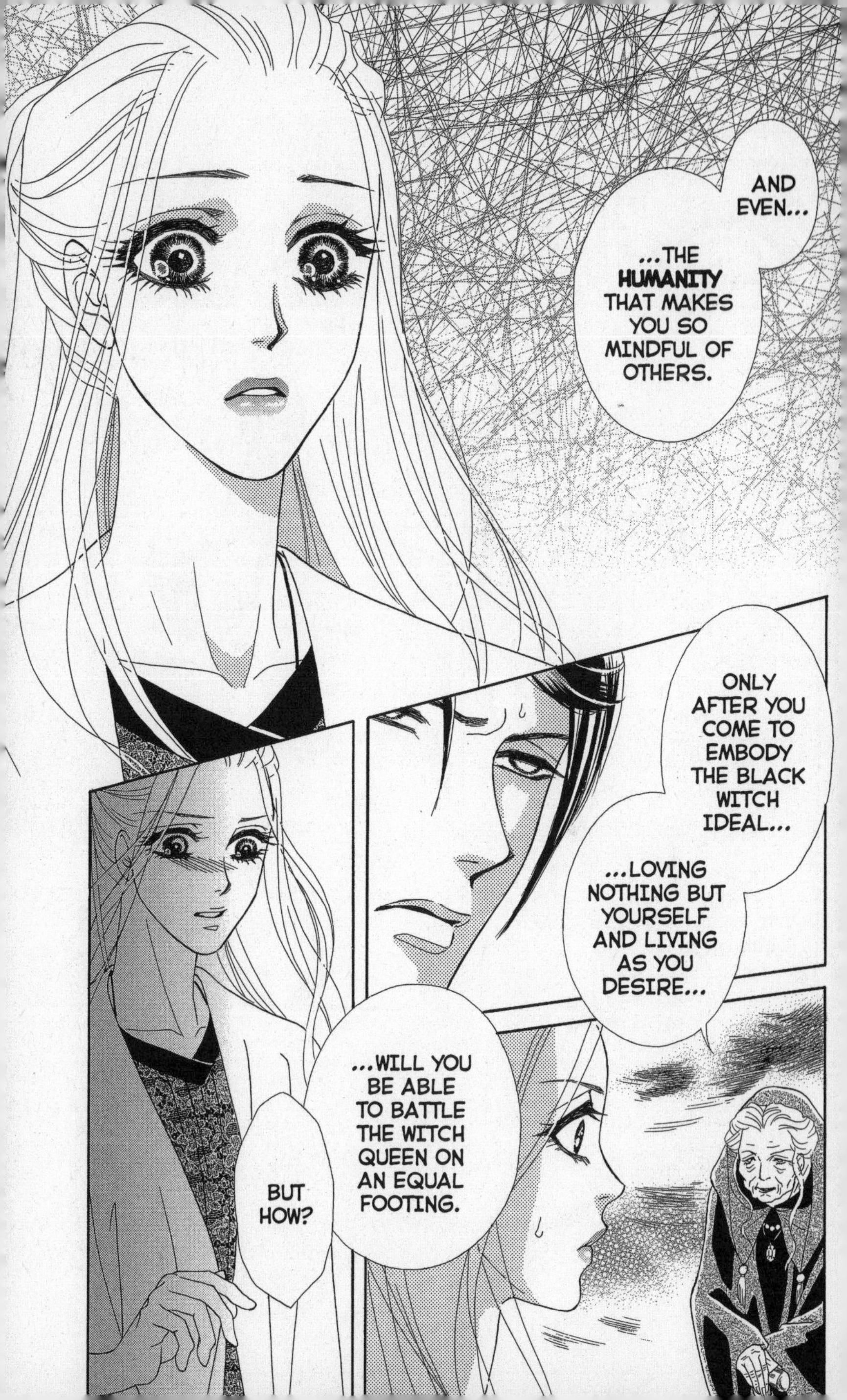
AND EVEN...
...THE **HUMANITY** THAT MAKES YOU SO MINDFUL OF OTHERS.
ONLY AFTER YOU COME TO EMBODY THE BLACK WITCH IDEAL...
...LOVING NOTHING BUT YOURSELF AND LIVING AS YOU DESIRE...
...WILL YOU BE ABLE TO BATTLE THE WITCH QUEEN ON AN EQUAL FOOTING.
BUT HOW?

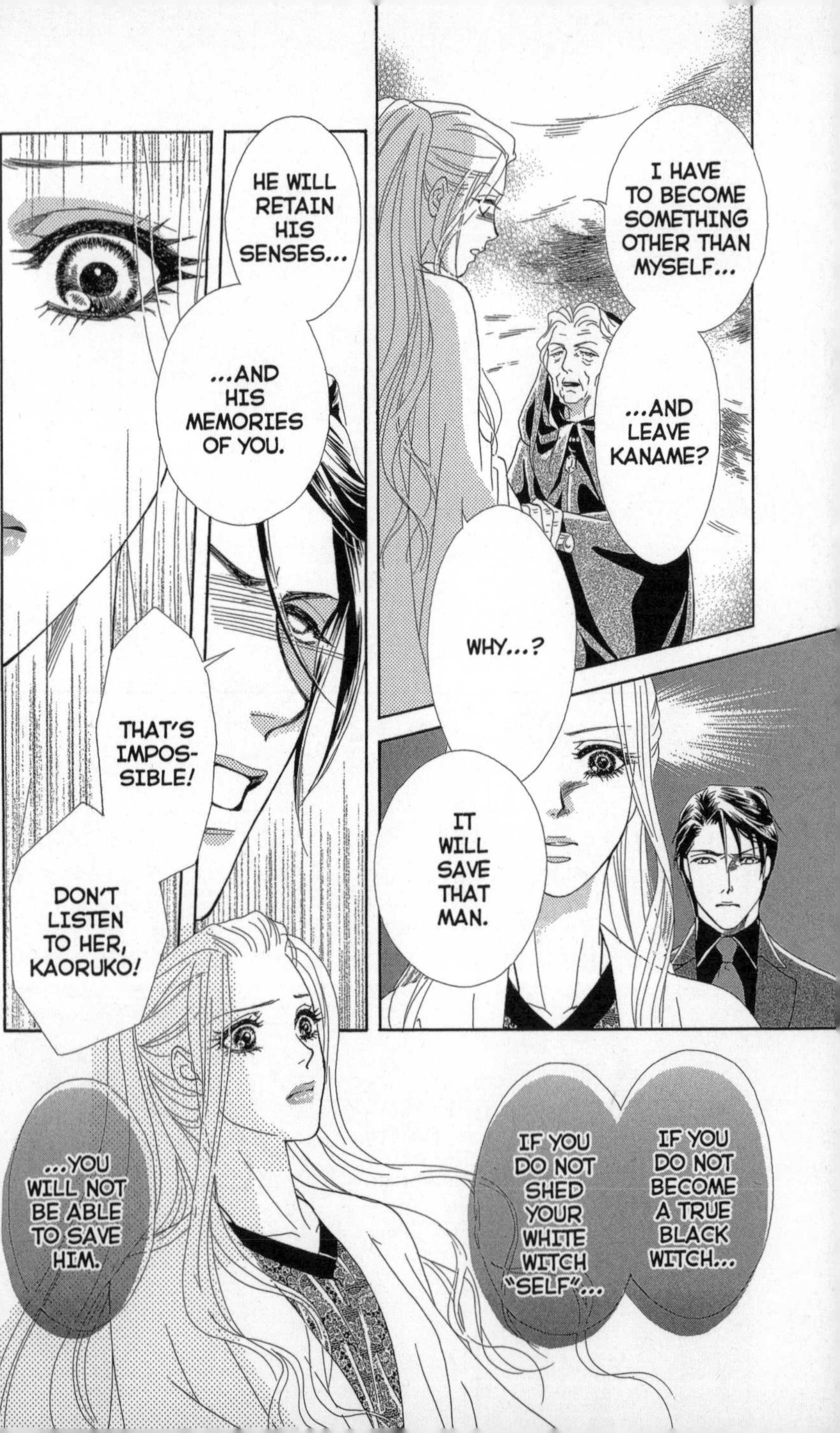
I HAVE TO BECOME SOMETHING OTHER THAN MYSELF...
...AND LEAVE KANAME?
WHY...?
IT WILL SAVE THAT MAN.
HE WILL RETAIN HIS SENSES...
...AND HIS MEMORIES OF YOU.
THAT'S IMPOS-SIBLE!
DON'T LISTEN TO HER, KAORUKO!
IF YOU DO NOT BECOME A TRUE BLACK WITCH...
IF YOU DO NOT SHED YOUR WHITE WITCH "SELF"...
...YOU WILL NOT BE ABLE TO SAVE HIM.

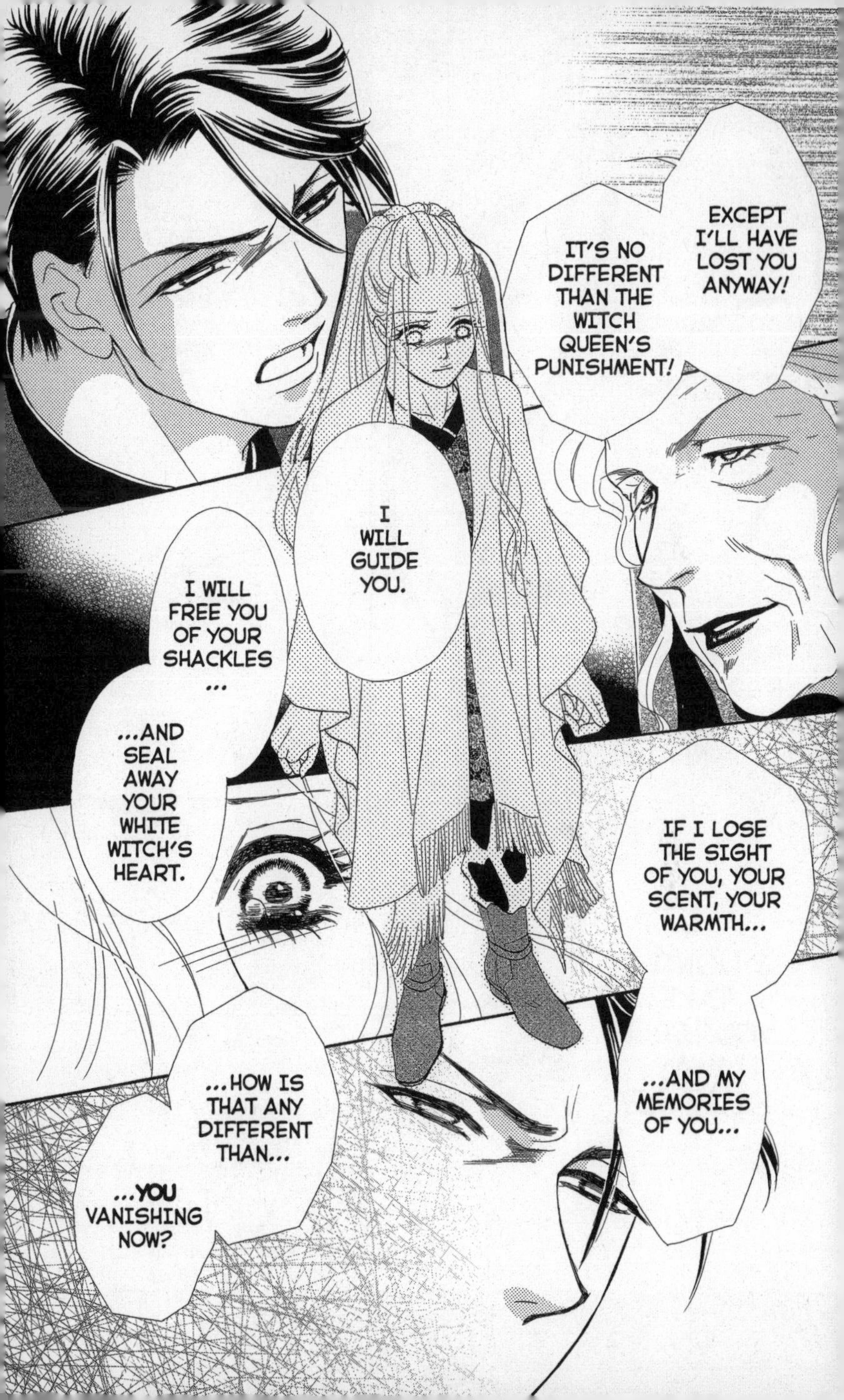
EXCEPT I'LL HAVE LOST YOU ANYWAY!
IT'S NO DIFFERENT THAN THE WITCH QUEEN'S PUNISHMENT!
I WILL GUIDE YOU.
I WILL FREE YOU OF YOUR SHACKLES...
...AND SEAL AWAY YOUR WHITE WITCH'S HEART.
IF I LOSE THE SIGHT OF YOU, YOUR SCENT, YOUR WARMTH...
...AND MY MEMORIES OF YOU...
...HOW IS THAT ANY DIFFERENT THAN...
...YOU VANISHING NOW?

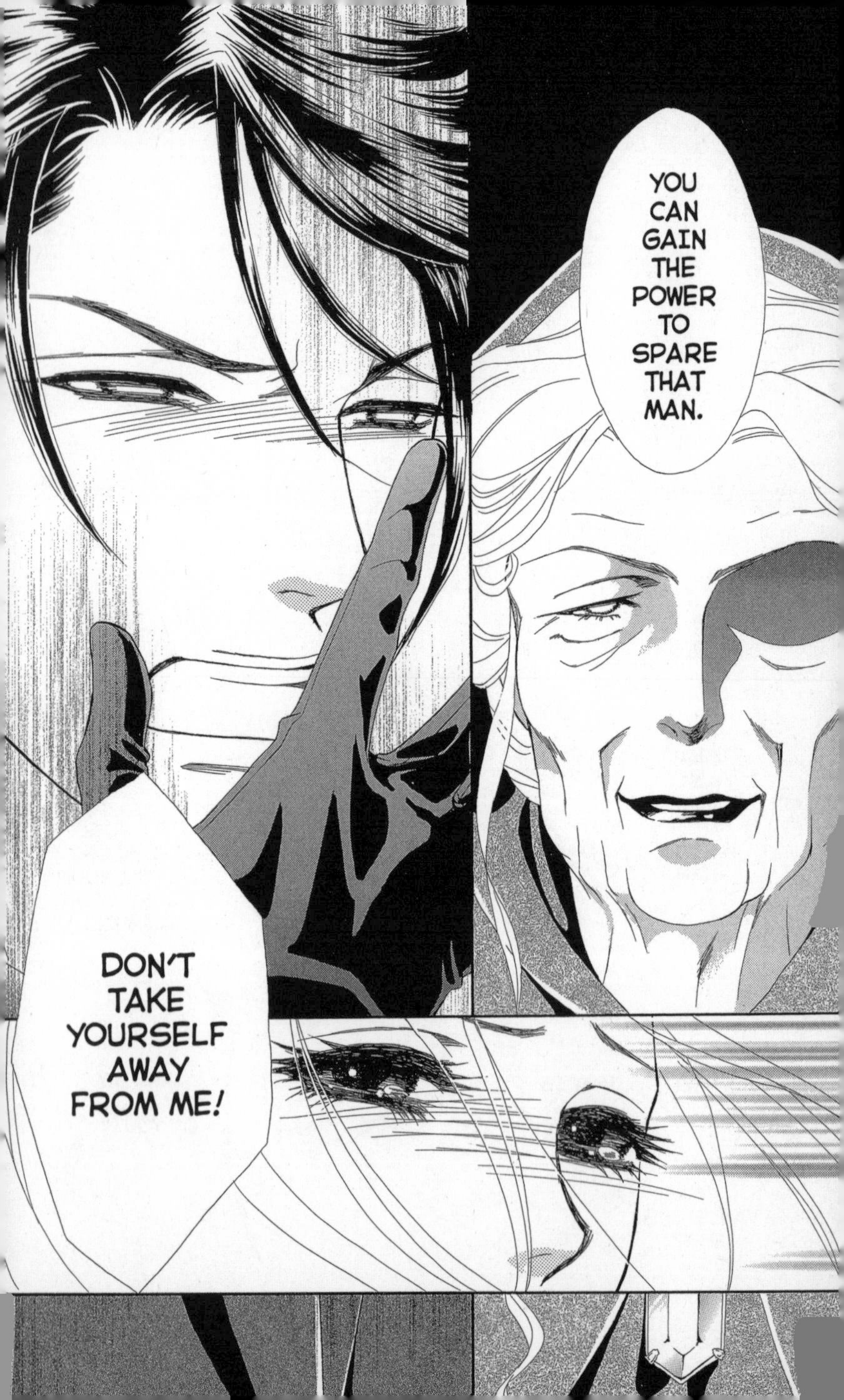
YOU CAN GAIN THE POWER TO SPARE THAT MAN.
DON'T TAKE YOURSELF AWAY FROM ME!

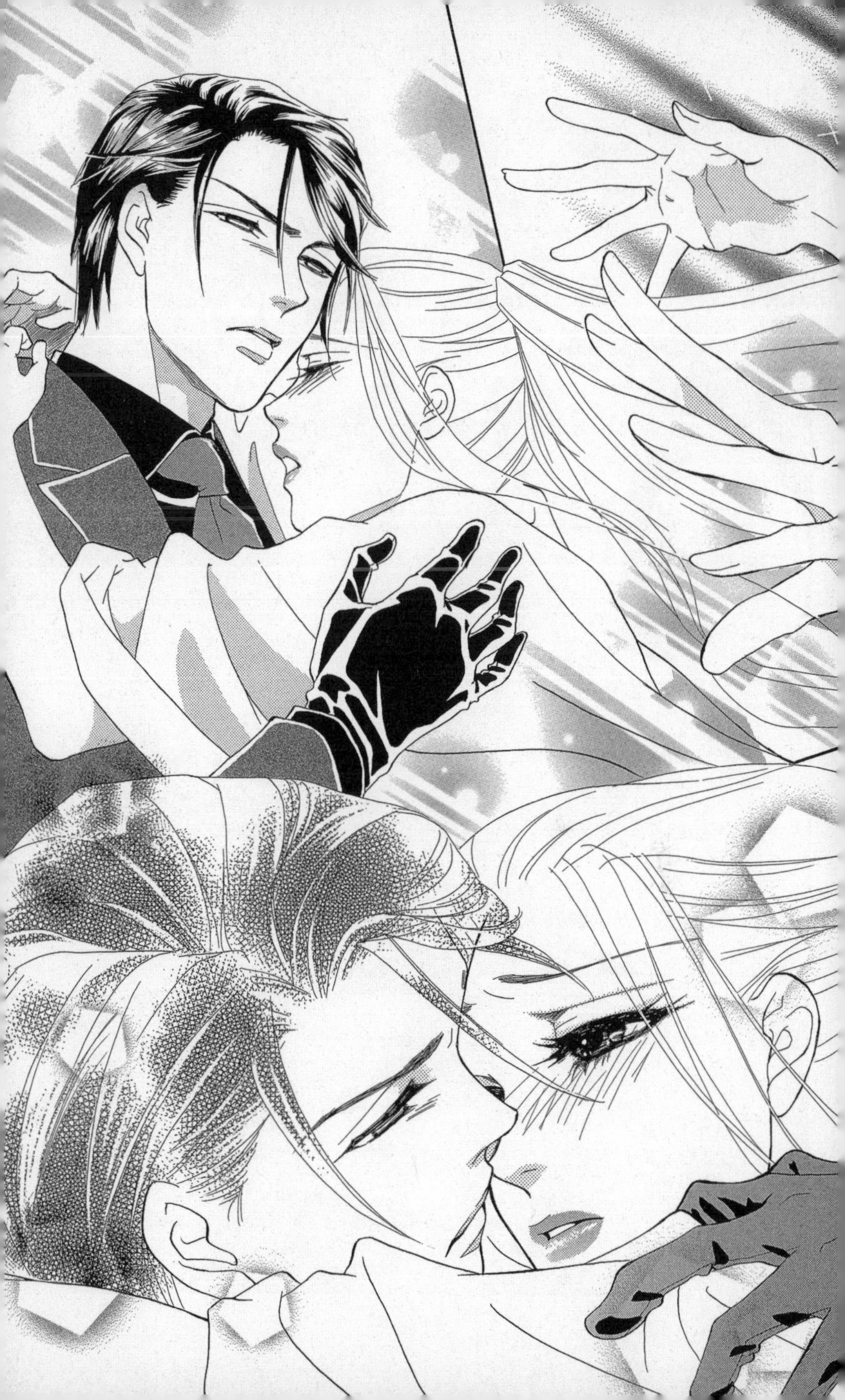

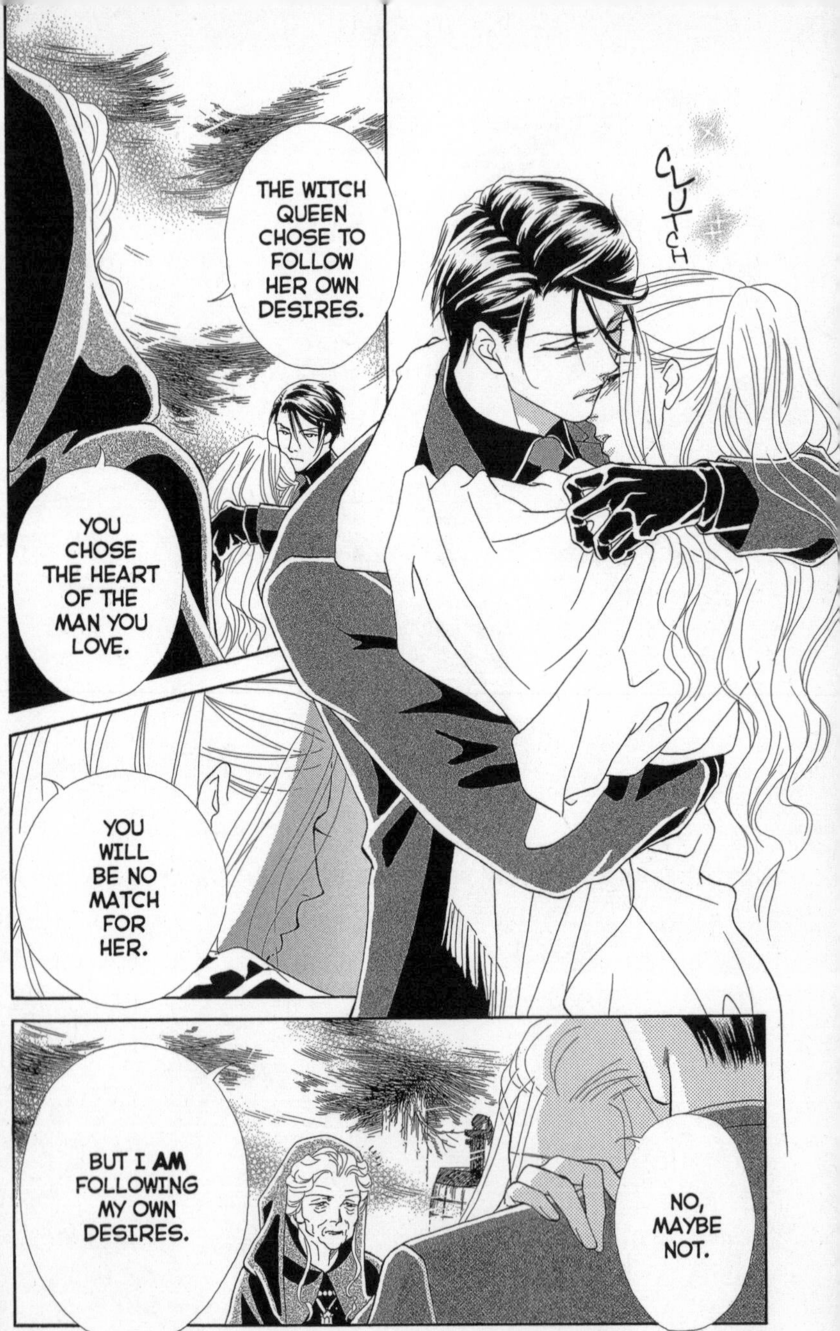
CLUTCH
THE WITCH QUEEN CHOSE TO FOLLOW HER OWN DESIRES.
YOU CHOSE THE HEART OF THE MAN YOU LOVE.
YOU WILL BE NO MATCH FOR HER.
NO, MAYBE NOT.
BUT I **AM** FOLLOWING MY OWN DESIRES.

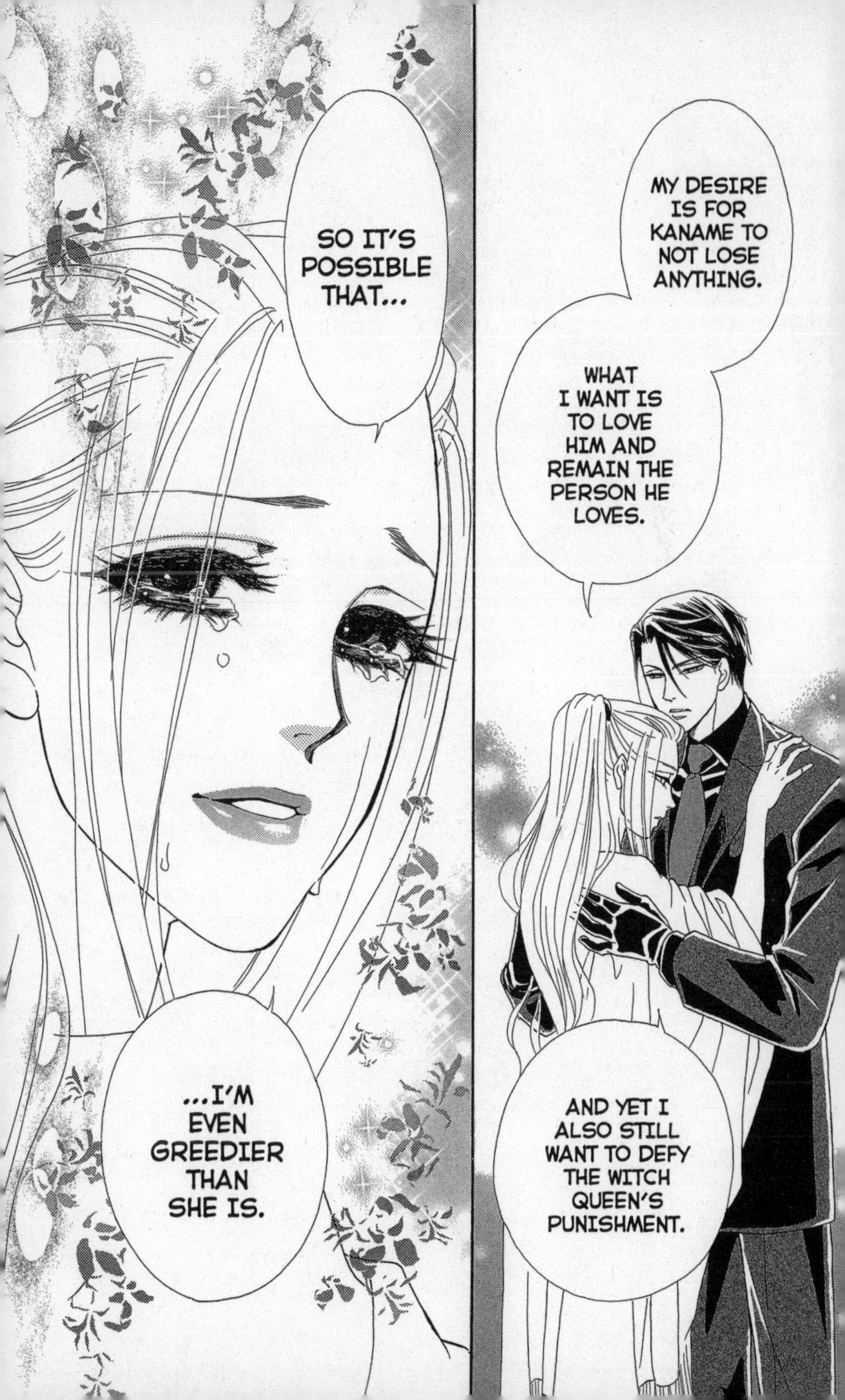
MY DESIRE IS FOR KANAME TO NOT LOSE ANYTHING.
WHAT I WANT IS TO LOVE HIM AND REMAIN THE PERSON HE LOVES.
AND YET I ALSO STILL WANT TO DEFY THE WITCH QUEEN'S PUNISHMENT.
SO IT'S POSSIBLE THAT...
...I'M EVEN GREEDIER THAN SHE IS.

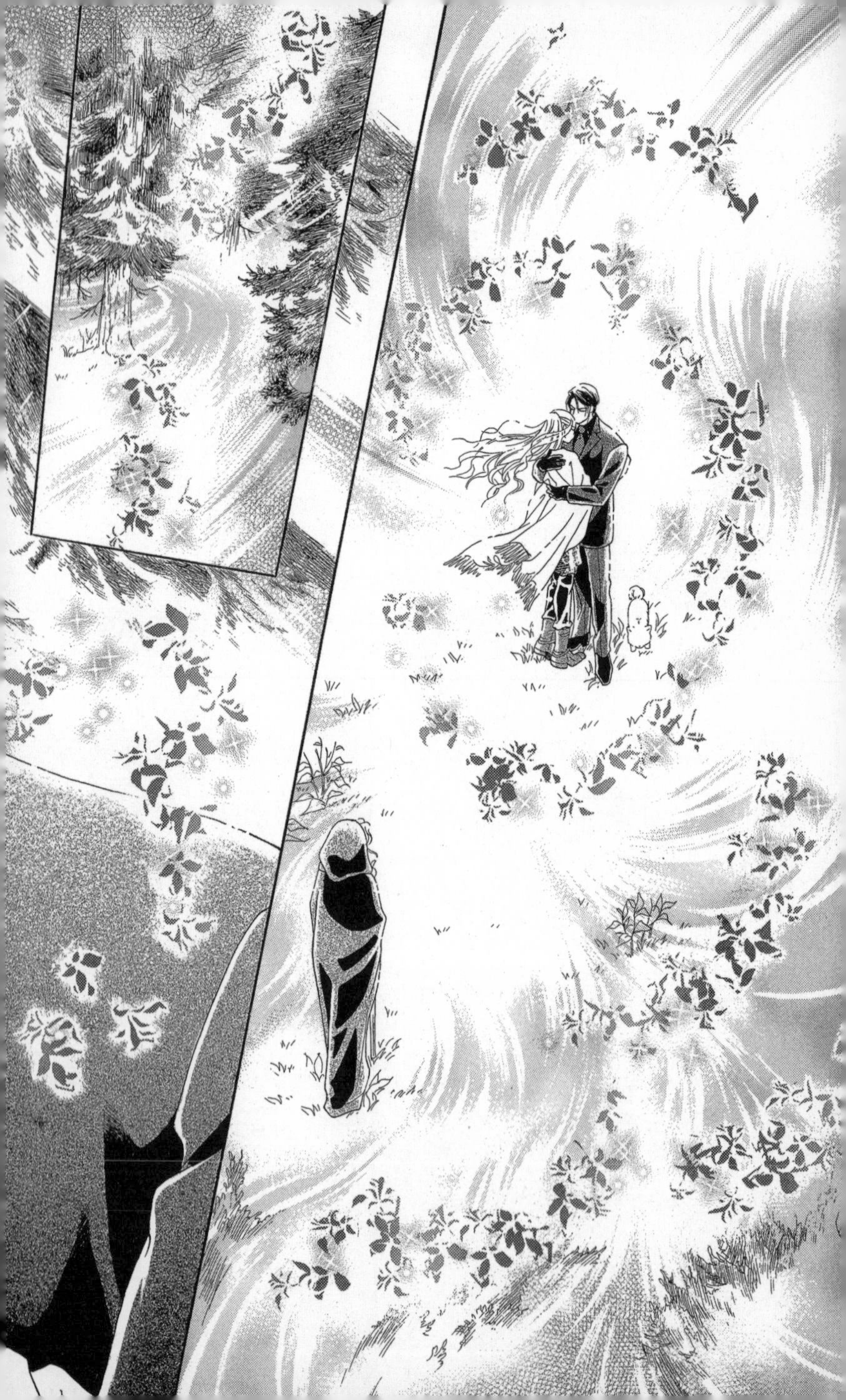

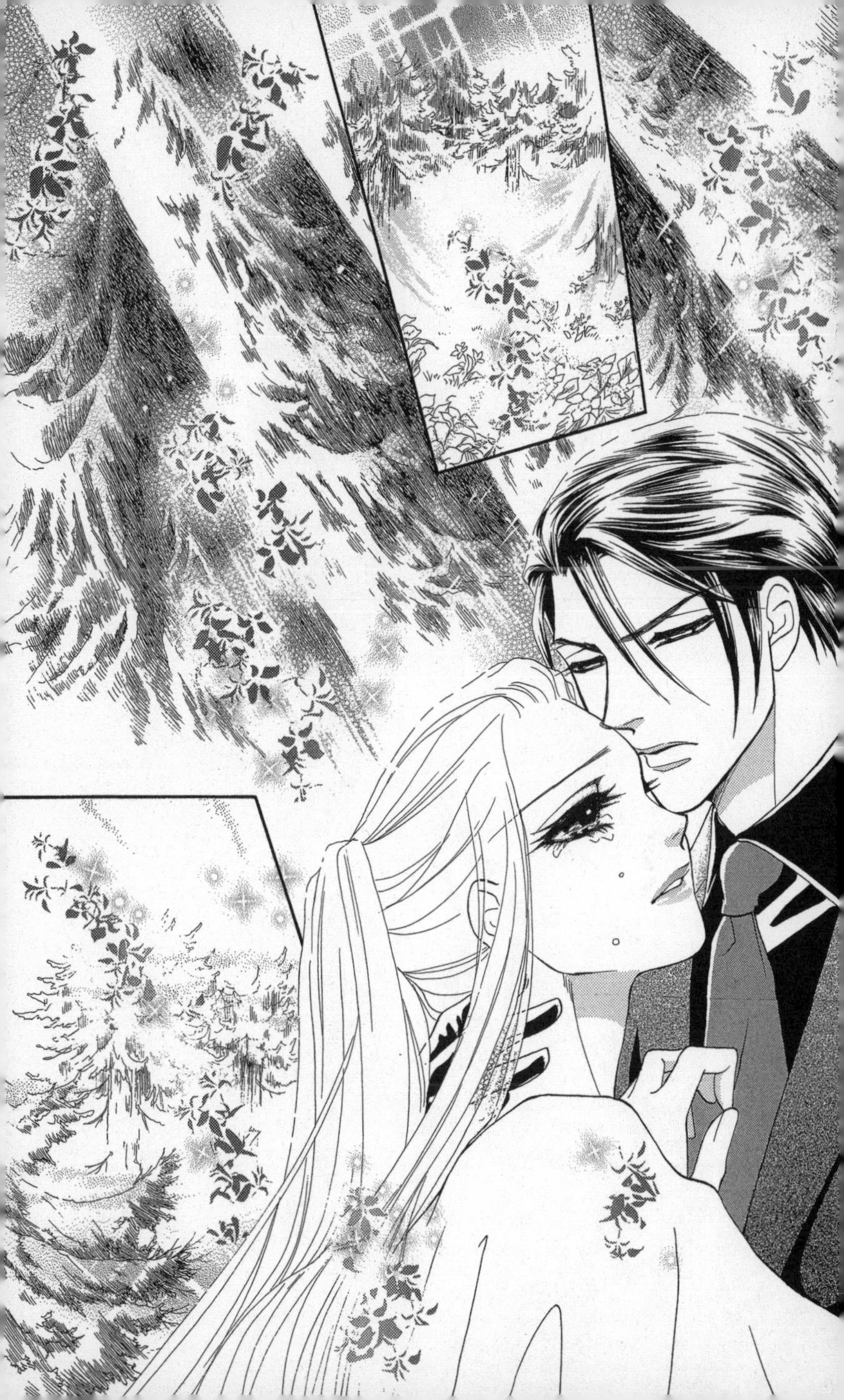

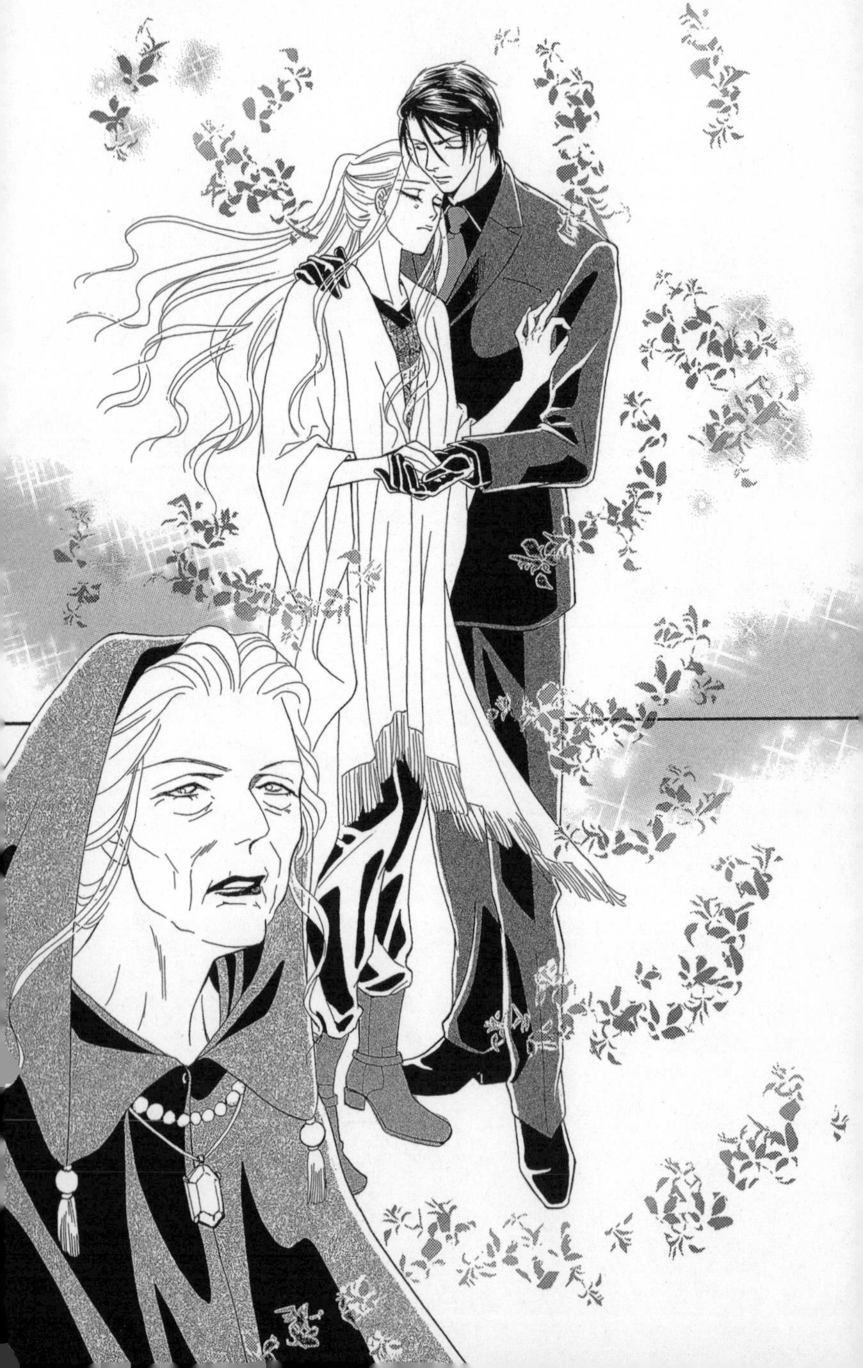

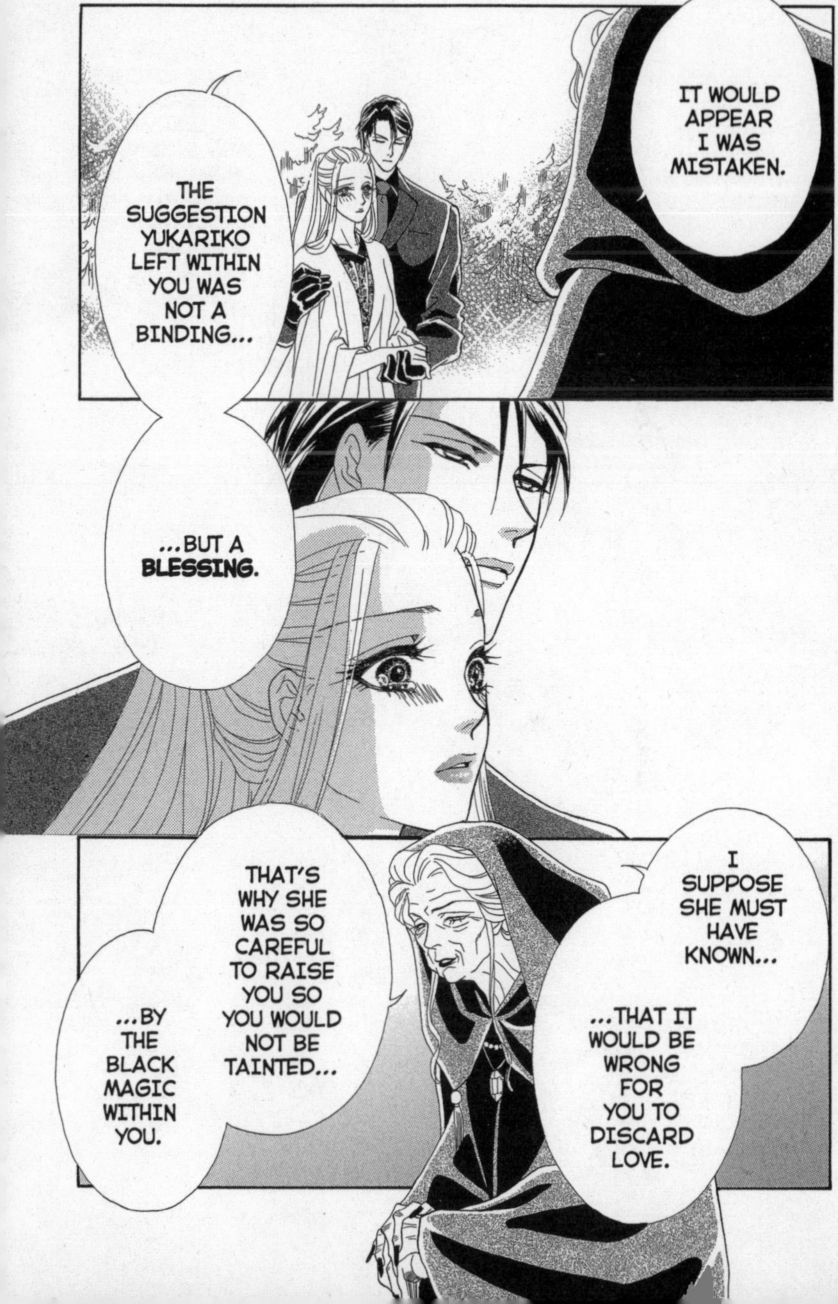
IT WOULD APPEAR I WAS MISTAKEN.
THE SUGGESTION YUKARIKO LEFT WITHIN YOU WAS NOT A BINDING...
...BUT A **BLESSING.**
I SUPPOSE SHE MUST HAVE KNOWN...
...THAT IT WOULD BE WRONG FOR YOU TO DISCARD LOVE.
THAT'S WHY SHE WAS SO CAREFUL TO RAISE YOU SO YOU WOULD NOT BE TAINTED...
...BY THE BLACK MAGIC WITHIN YOU.

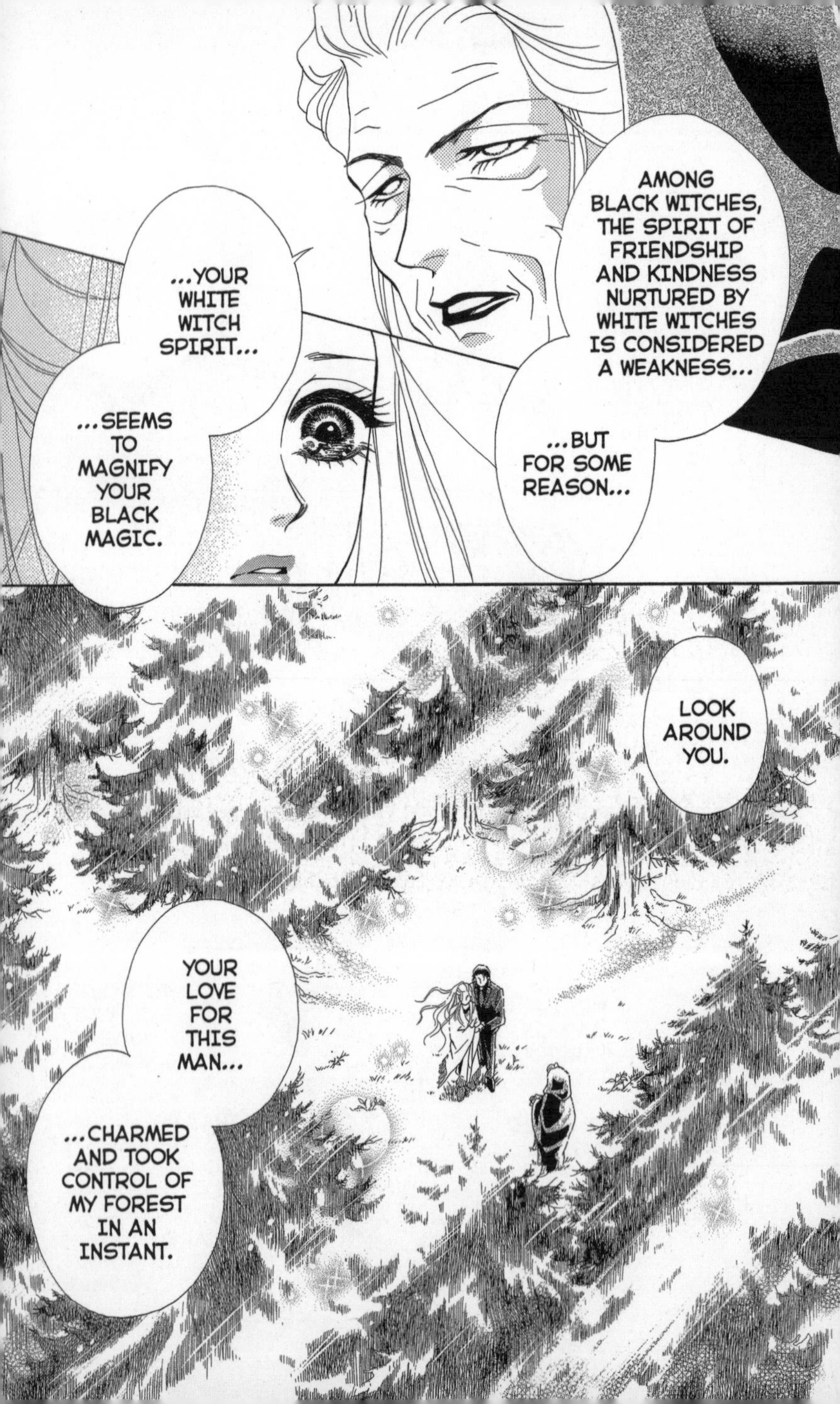
AMONG BLACK WITCHES, THE SPIRIT OF FRIENDSHIP AND KINDNESS NURTURED BY WHITE WITCHES IS CONSIDERED A WEAKNESS...
...BUT FOR SOME REASON...
...YOUR WHITE WITCH SPIRIT...
...SEEMS TO MAGNIFY YOUR BLACK MAGIC.
LOOK AROUND YOU.
YOUR LOVE FOR THIS MAN...
...CHARMED AND TOOK CONTROL OF MY FOREST IN AN INSTANT.

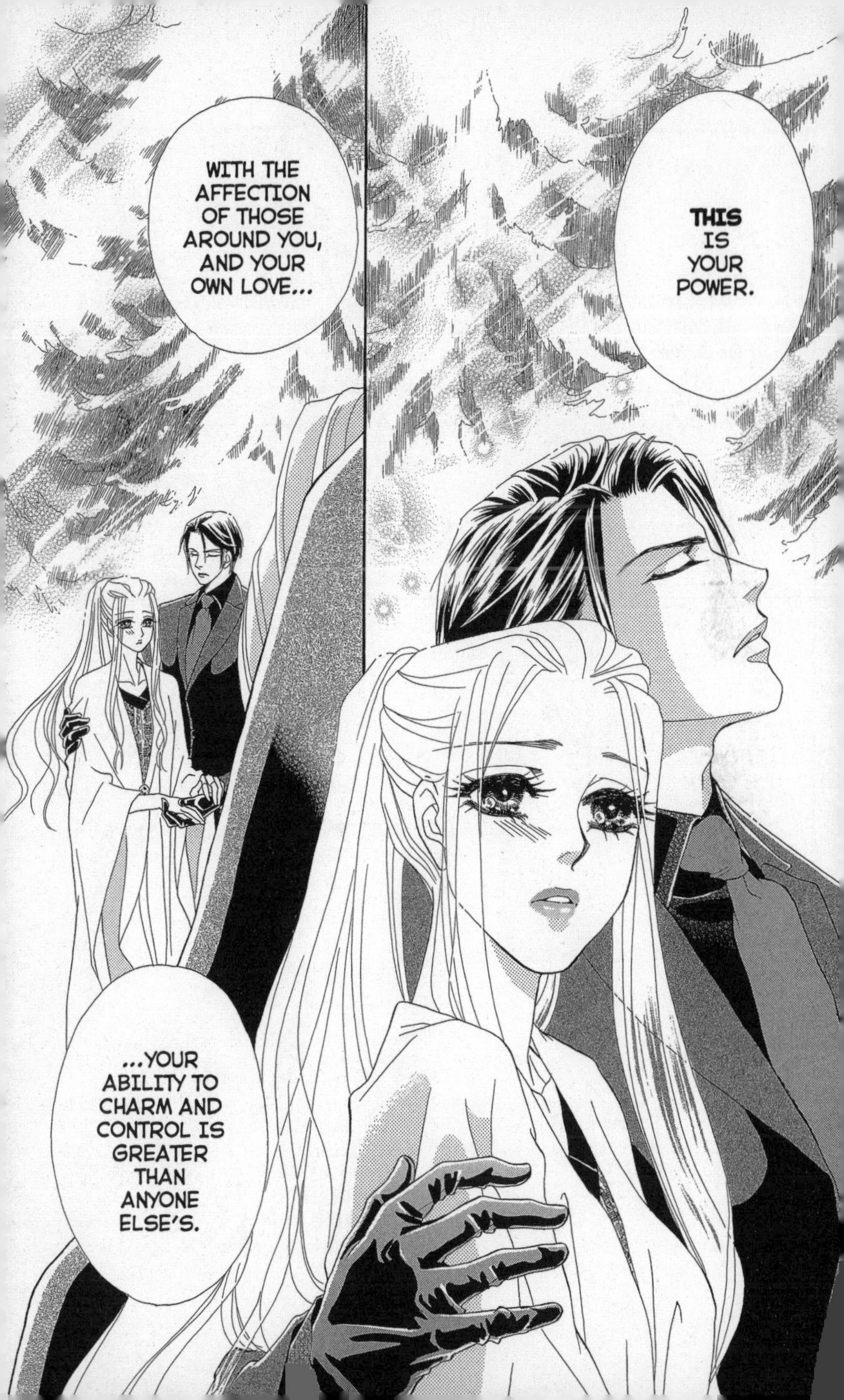
THIS IS YOUR POWER.
WITH THE AFFECTION OF THOSE AROUND YOU, AND YOUR OWN LOVE...
...YOUR ABILITY TO CHARM AND CONTROL IS GREATER THAN ANYONE ELSE'S.

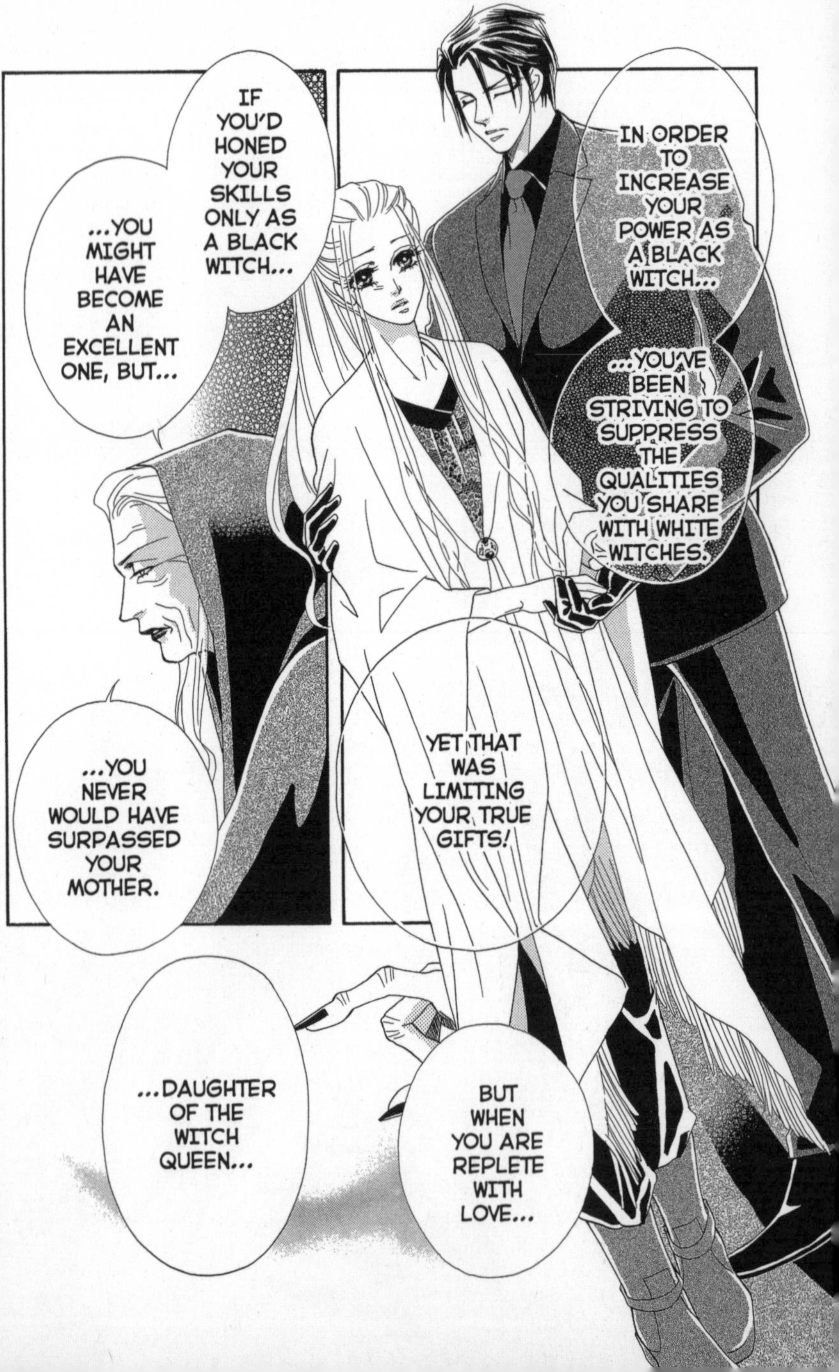
IN ORDER TO INCREASE YOUR POWER AS A BLACK WITCH...
...YOU'VE BEEN STRIVING TO SUPPRESS THE QUALITIES YOU SHARE WITH WHITE WITCHES.
YET THAT WAS LIMITING YOUR TRUE GIFTS!
IF YOU'D HONED YOUR SKILLS ONLY AS A BLACK WITCH...
...YOU MIGHT HAVE BECOME AN EXCELLENT ONE, BUT...
...YOU NEVER WOULD HAVE SURPASSED YOUR MOTHER.
BUT WHEN YOU ARE REPLETE WITH LOVE...
...DAUGHTER OF THE WITCH QUEEN...

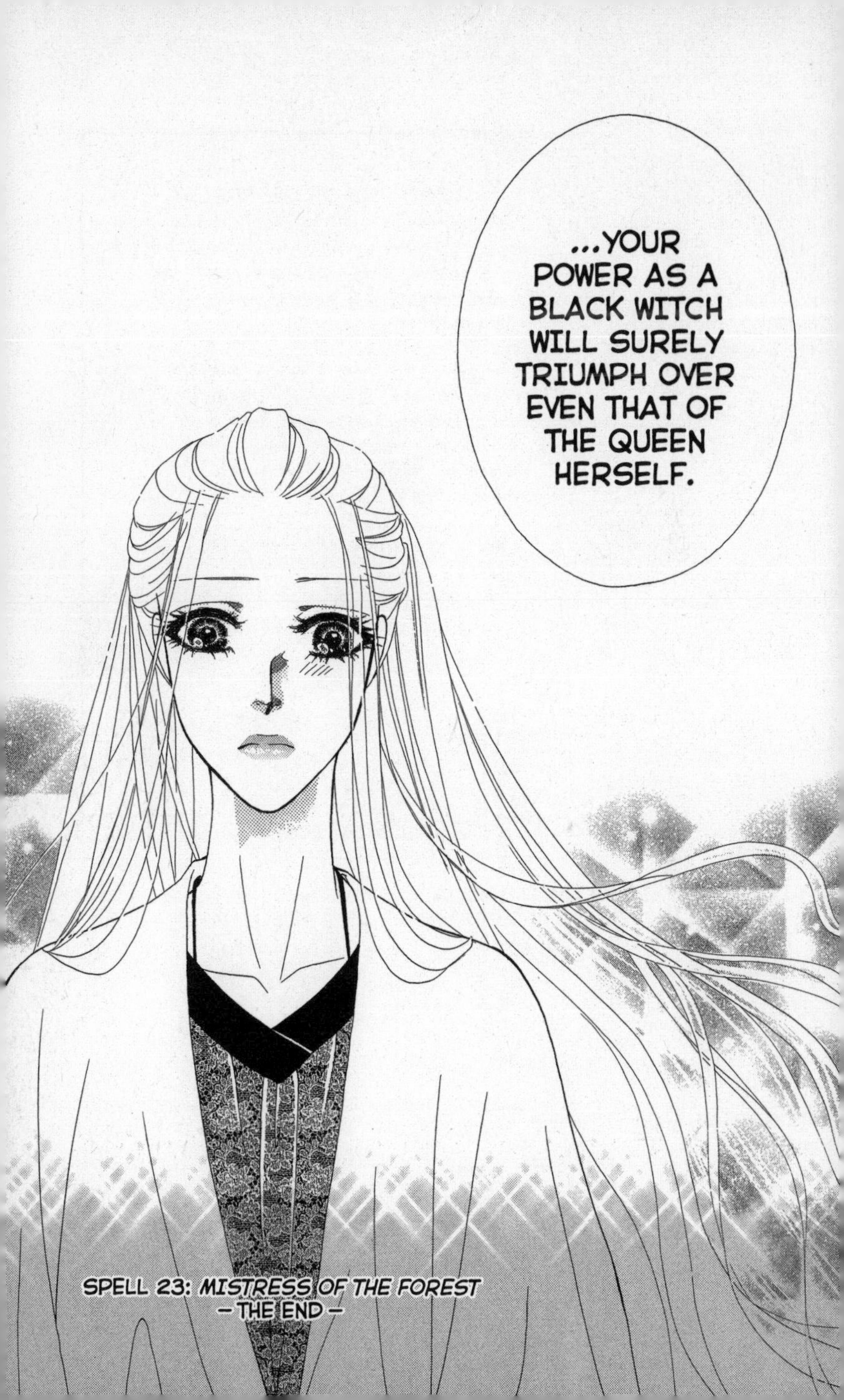
...YOUR POWER AS A BLACK WITCH WILL SURELY TRIUMPH OVER EVEN THAT OF THE QUEEN HERSELF.
SPELL 23: MISTRESS OF THE FOREST
– THE END –

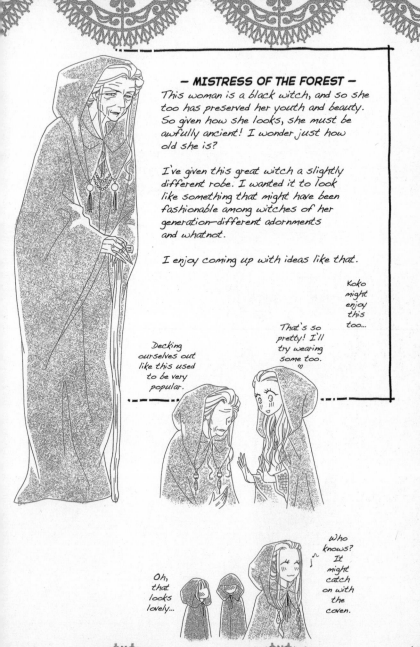

– MISTRESS OF THE FOREST –

This woman is a black witch, and so she too has preserved her youth and beauty. So given how she looks, she must be awfully ancient! I wonder just how old she is?

I've given this great witch a slightly different robe. I wanted it to look like something that might have been fashionable among witches of her generation—different adornments and whatnot.

I enjoy coming up with ideas like that.

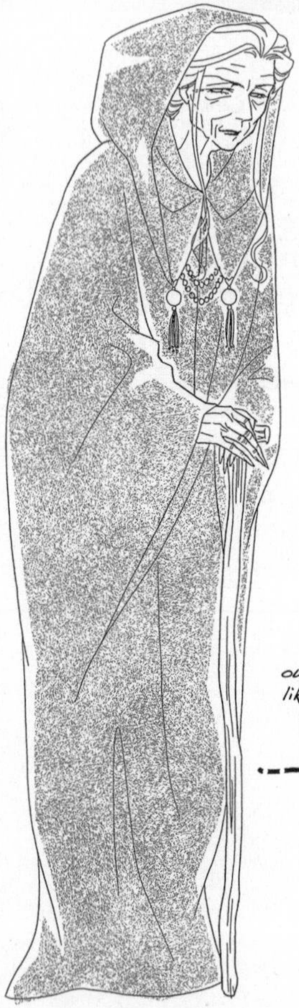

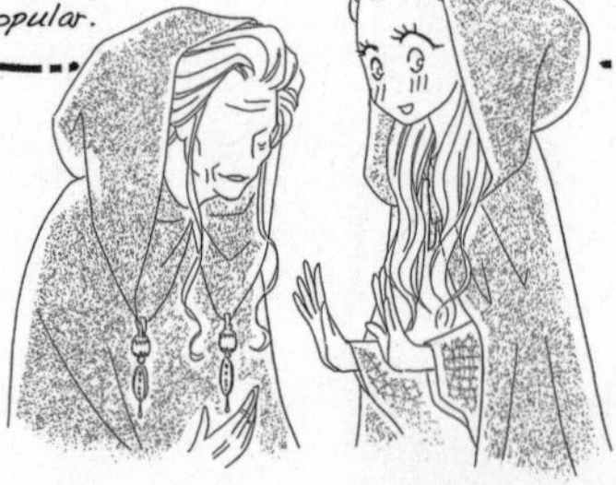
Koko might enjoy this too...
That's so pretty! I'll try wearing some too. ♡
Decking ourselves out like this used to be very popular.

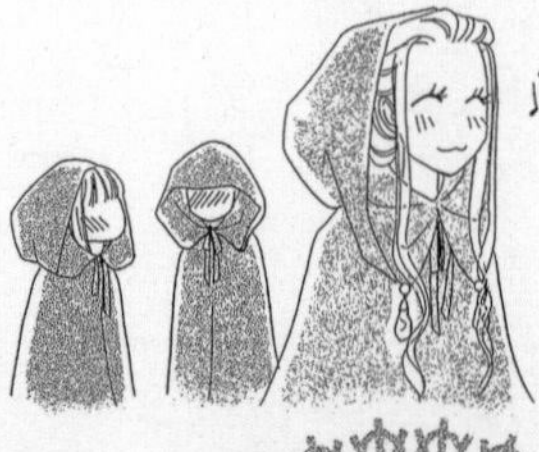
Who knows? It might catch on with the coven.
Oh, that looks lovely...

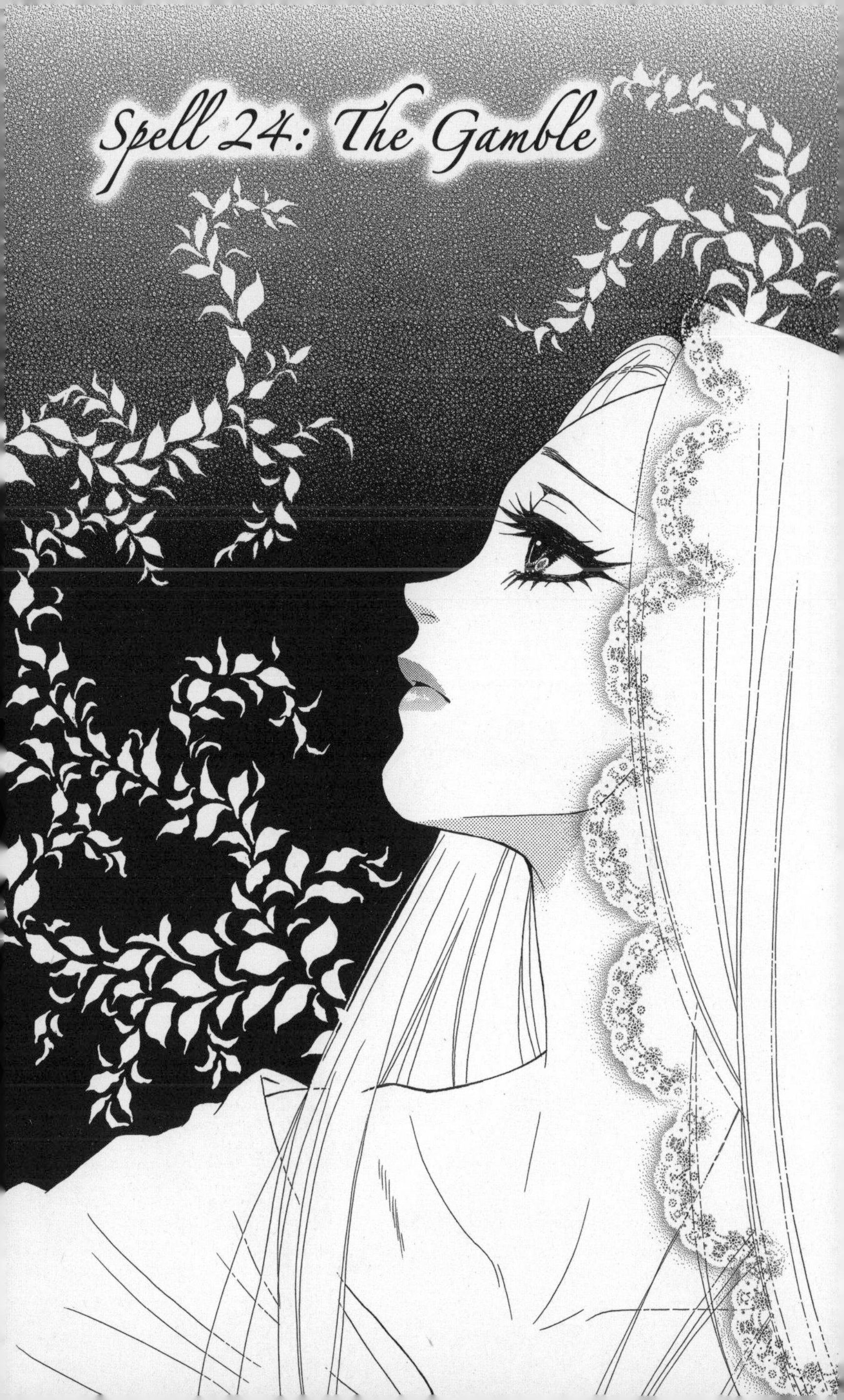
Spell 24: The Gamble

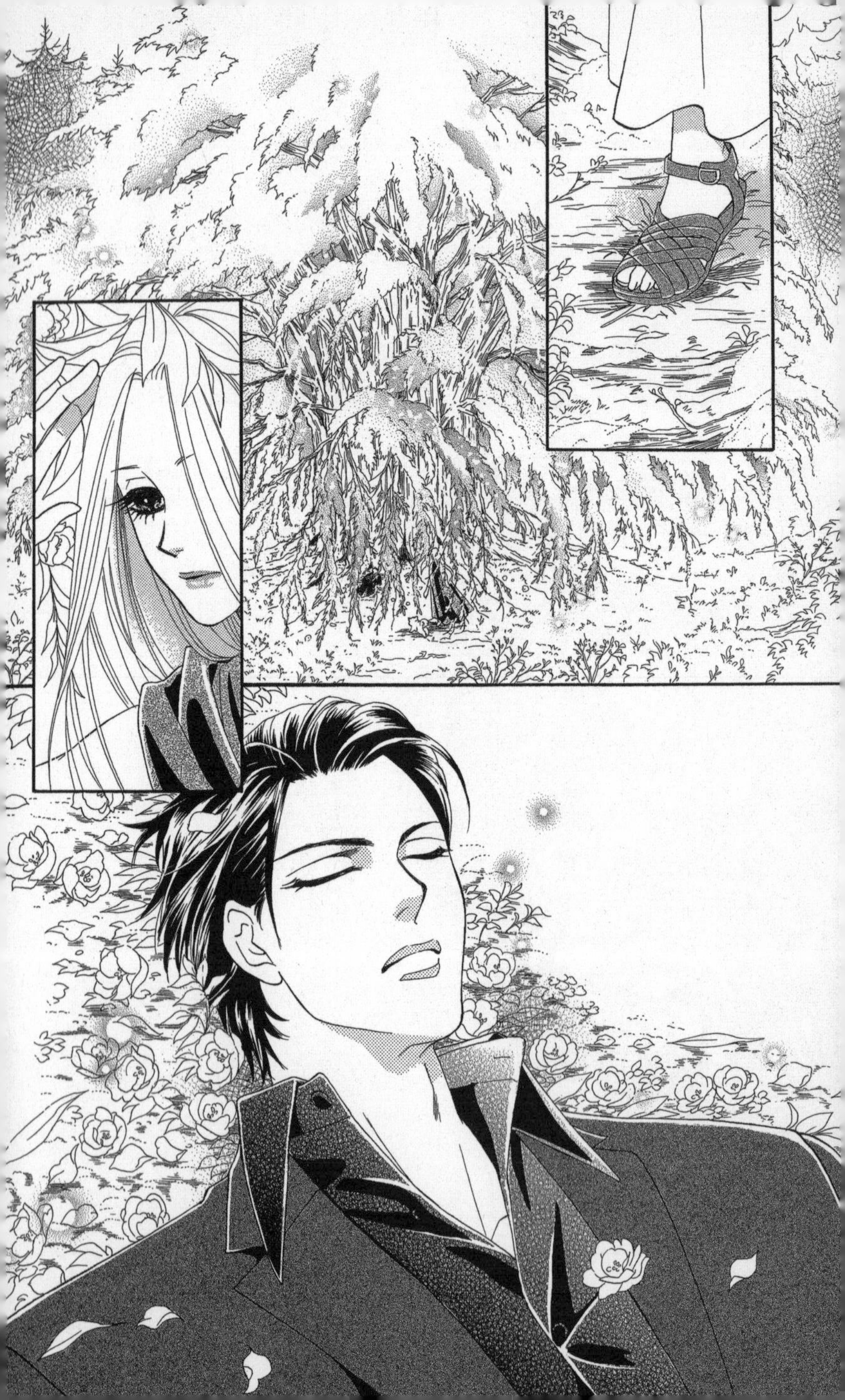

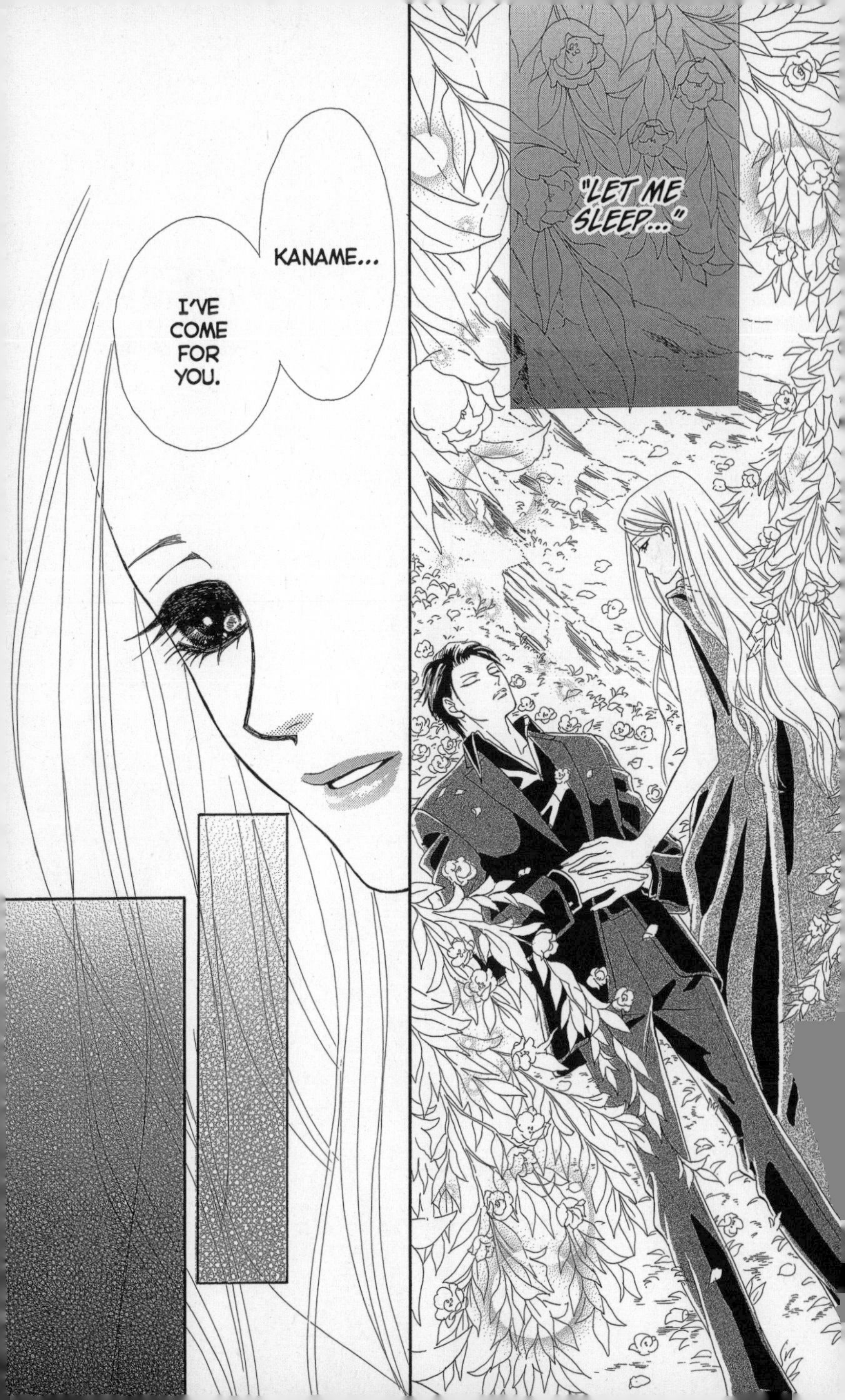
"LET ME SLEEP..."
KANAME... I'VE COME FOR YOU.

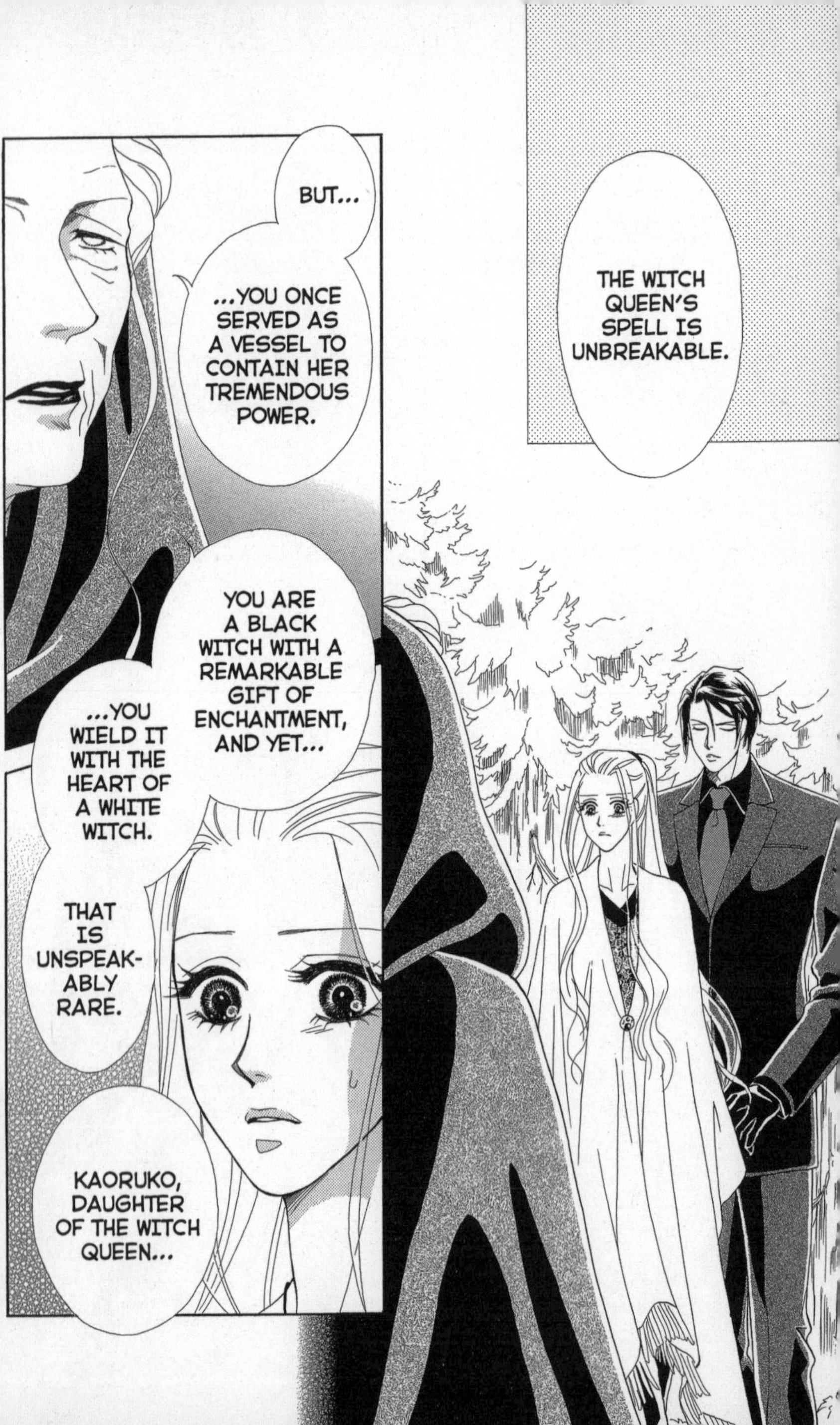
THE WITCH QUEEN'S SPELL IS UNBREAKABLE.
BUT...
...YOU ONCE SERVED AS A VESSEL TO CONTAIN HER TREMENDOUS POWER.
YOU ARE A BLACK WITCH WITH A REMARKABLE GIFT OF ENCHANTMENT, AND YET...
...YOU WIELD IT WITH THE HEART OF A WHITE WITCH.
THAT IS UNSPEAKABLY RARE.
KAORUKO, DAUGHTER OF THE WITCH QUEEN...

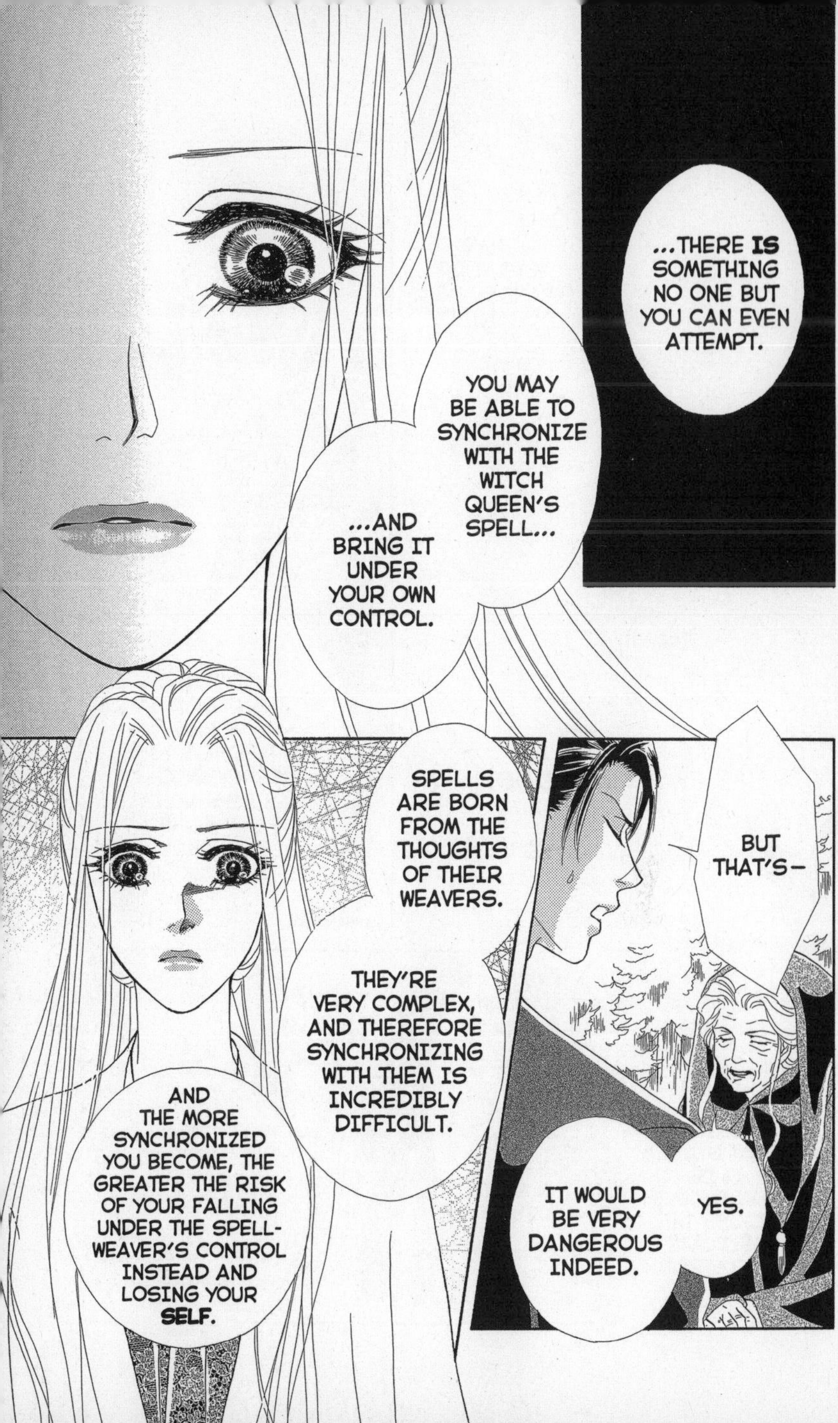
...THERE **IS** SOMETHING NO ONE BUT YOU CAN EVEN ATTEMPT.
YOU MAY BE ABLE TO SYNCHRONIZE WITH THE WITCH QUEEN'S SPELL...
...AND BRING IT UNDER YOUR OWN CONTROL.
BUT THAT'S—
YES.
IT WOULD BE VERY DANGEROUS INDEED.
SPELLS ARE BORN FROM THE THOUGHTS OF THEIR WEAVERS.
THEY'RE VERY COMPLEX, AND THEREFORE SYNCHRONIZING WITH THEM IS INCREDIBLY DIFFICULT.
AND THE MORE SYNCHRONIZED YOU BECOME, THE GREATER THE RISK OF YOUR FALLING UNDER THE SPELL-WEAVER'S CONTROL INSTEAD AND LOSING YOUR **SELF**.

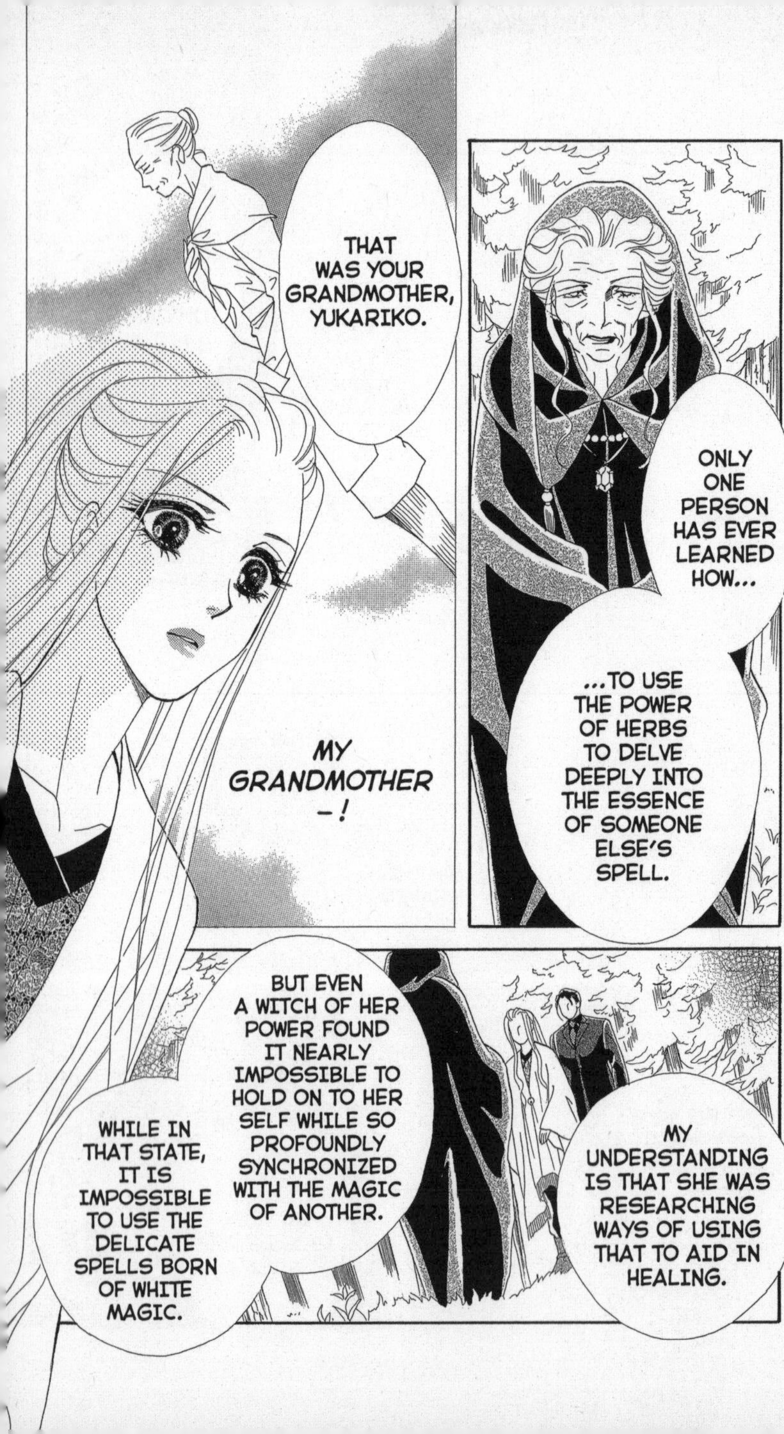
ONLY ONE PERSON HAS EVER LEARNED HOW...
...TO USE THE POWER OF HERBS TO DELVE DEEPLY INTO THE ESSENCE OF SOMEONE ELSE'S SPELL.
THAT WAS YOUR GRANDMOTHER, YUKARIKO.
MY GRANDMOTHER—!
MY UNDERSTANDING IS THAT SHE WAS RESEARCHING WAYS OF USING THAT TO AID IN HEALING.
BUT EVEN A WITCH OF HER POWER FOUND IT NEARLY IMPOSSIBLE TO HOLD ON TO HER SELF WHILE SO PROFOUNDLY SYNCHRONIZED WITH THE MAGIC OF ANOTHER.
WHILE IN THAT STATE, IT IS IMPOSSIBLE TO USE THE DELICATE SPELLS BORN OF WHITE MAGIC.

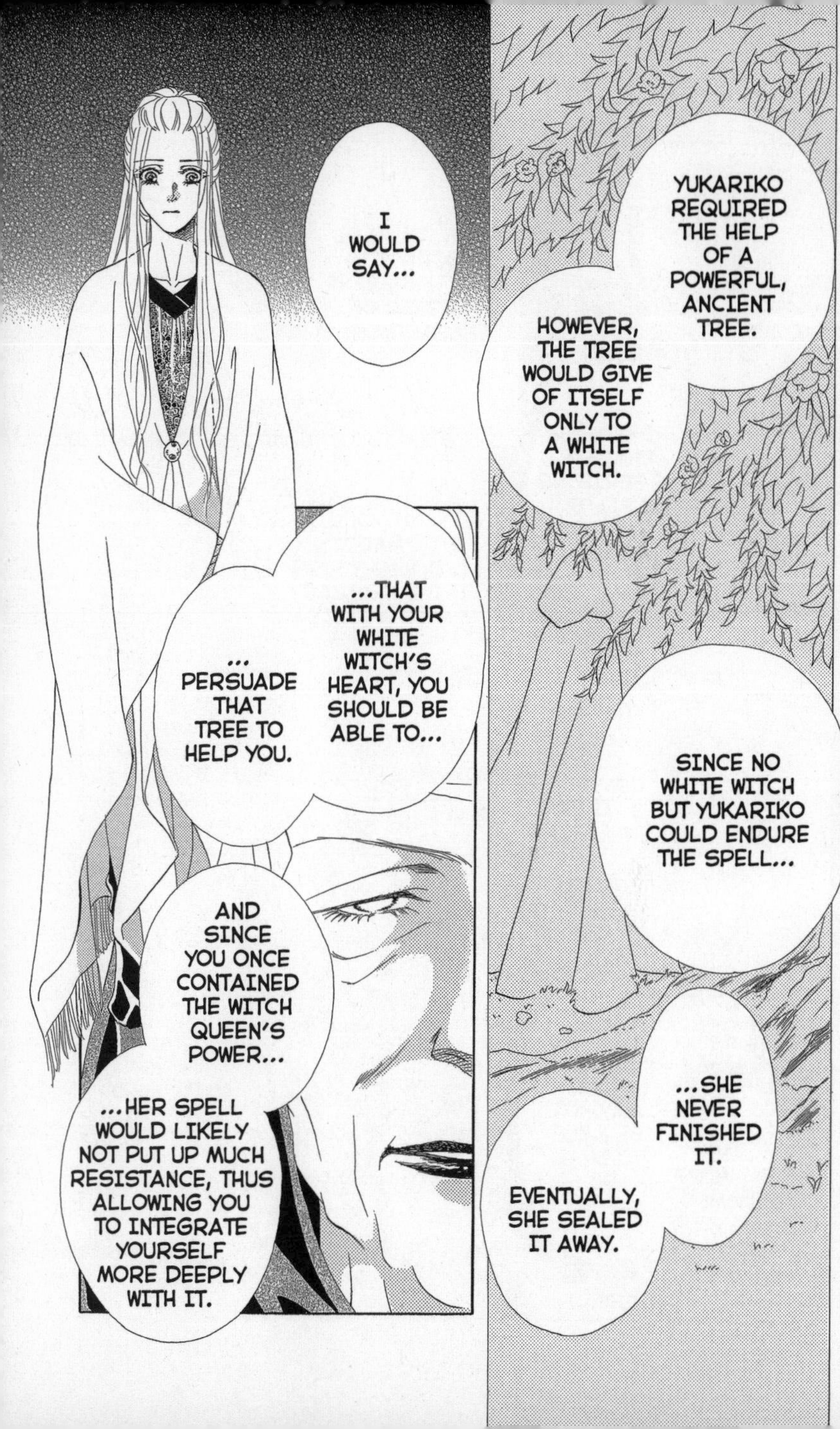
YUKARIKO REQUIRED THE HELP OF A POWERFUL, ANCIENT TREE.
HOWEVER, THE TREE WOULD GIVE OF ITSELF ONLY TO A WHITE WITCH.
SINCE NO WHITE WITCH BUT YUKARIKO COULD ENDURE THE SPELL...
...SHE NEVER FINISHED IT.
EVENTUALLY, SHE SEALED IT AWAY.
I WOULD SAY...
...THAT WITH YOUR WHITE WITCH'S HEART, YOU SHOULD BE ABLE TO...
... PERSUADE THAT TREE TO HELP YOU.
AND SINCE YOU ONCE CONTAINED THE WITCH QUEEN'S POWER...
...HER SPELL WOULD LIKELY NOT PUT UP MUCH RESISTANCE, THUS ALLOWING YOU TO INTEGRATE YOURSELF MORE DEEPLY WITH IT.

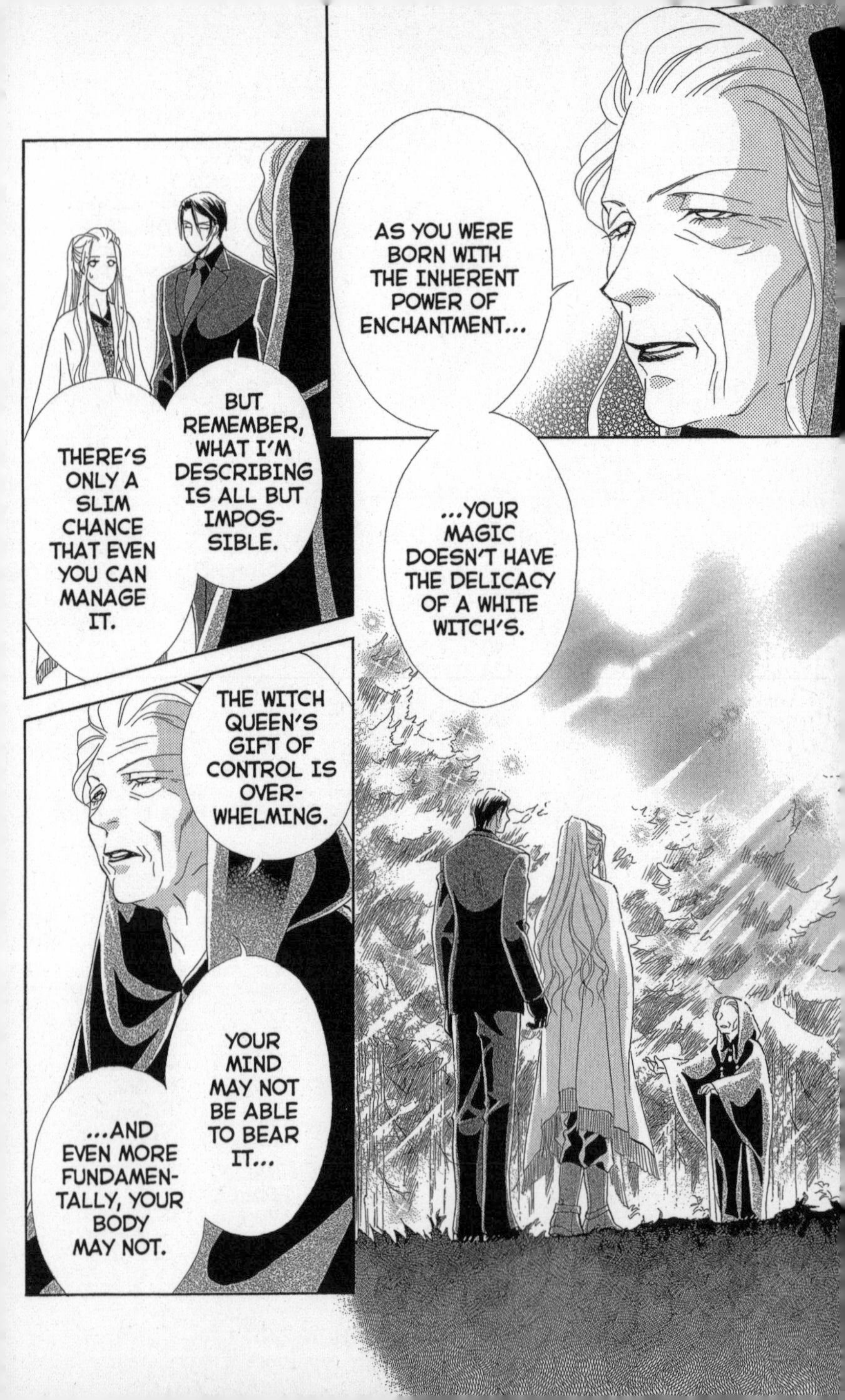
AS YOU WERE BORN WITH THE INHERENT POWER OF ENCHANTMENT...
...YOUR MAGIC DOESN'T HAVE THE DELICACY OF A WHITE WITCH'S.
BUT REMEMBER, WHAT I'M DESCRIBING IS ALL BUT IMPOSSIBLE.
THERE'S ONLY A SLIM CHANCE THAT EVEN YOU CAN MANAGE IT.
THE WITCH QUEEN'S GIFT OF CONTROL IS OVERWHELMING.
YOUR MIND MAY NOT BE ABLE TO BEAR IT...
...AND EVEN MORE FUNDAMENTALLY, YOUR BODY MAY NOT.

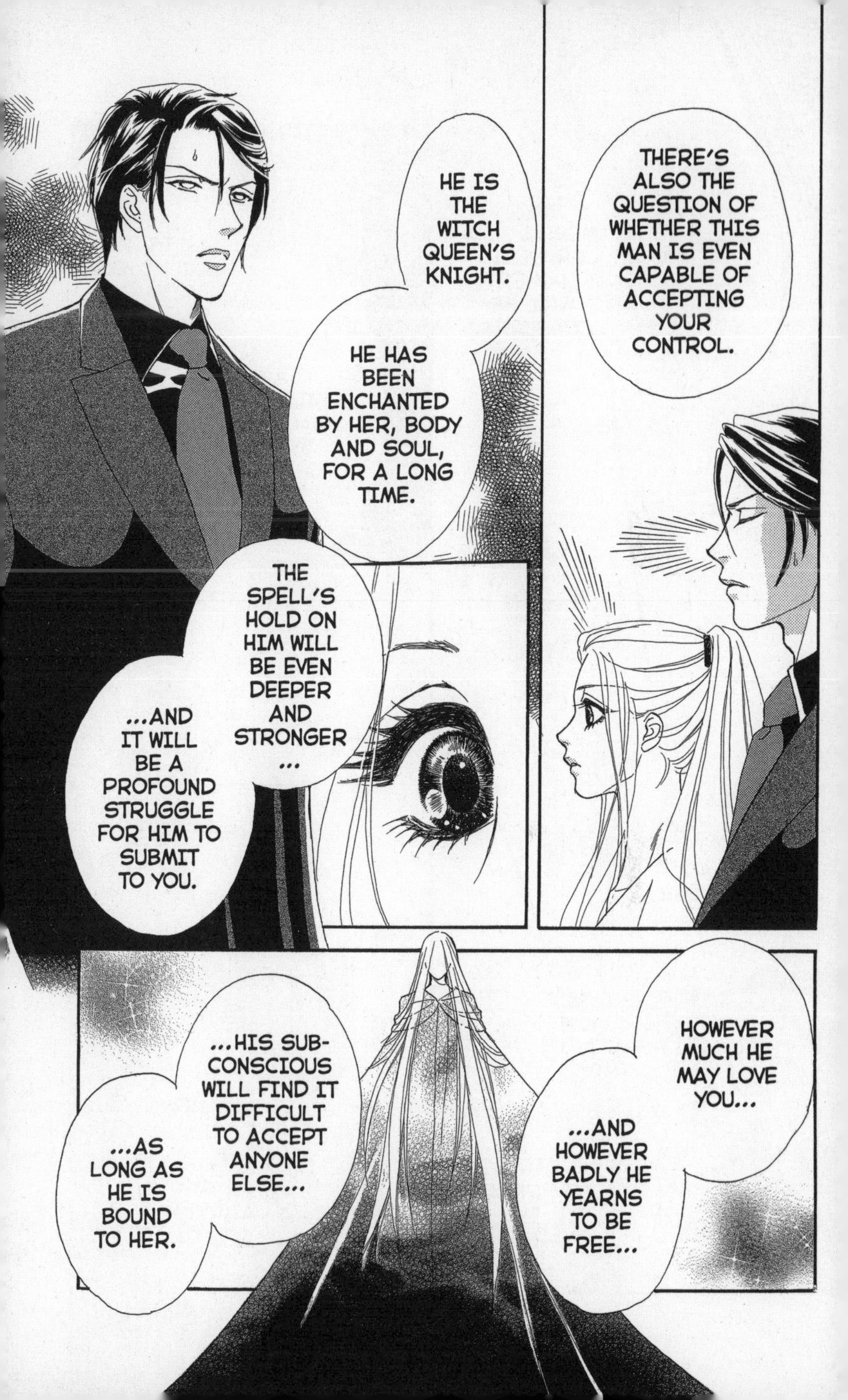
THERE'S ALSO THE QUESTION OF WHETHER THIS MAN IS EVEN CAPABLE OF ACCEPTING YOUR CONTROL.
HE IS THE WITCH QUEEN'S KNIGHT.
HE HAS BEEN ENCHANTED BY HER, BODY AND SOUL, FOR A LONG TIME.
THE SPELL'S HOLD ON HIM WILL BE EVEN DEEPER AND STRONGER...
...AND IT WILL BE A PROFOUND STRUGGLE FOR HIM TO SUBMIT TO YOU.
HOWEVER MUCH HE MAY LOVE YOU...
...AND HOWEVER BADLY HE YEARNS TO BE FREE...
...HIS SUB-CONSCIOUS WILL FIND IT DIFFICULT TO ACCEPT ANYONE ELSE...
...AS LONG AS HE IS BOUND TO HER.

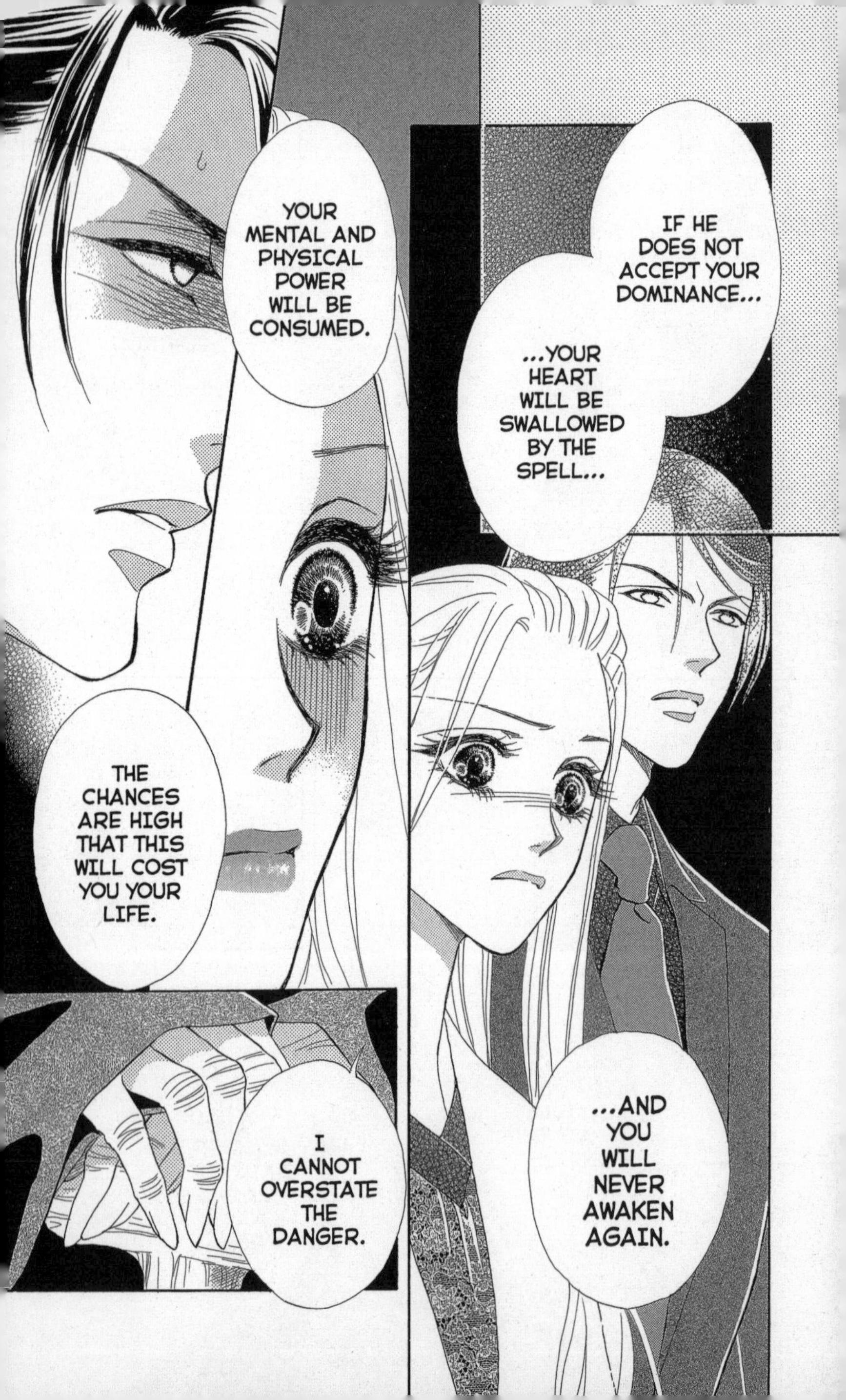
IF HE DOES NOT ACCEPT YOUR DOMINANCE...
...YOUR HEART WILL BE SWALLOWED BY THE SPELL...
...AND YOU WILL NEVER AWAKEN AGAIN.
YOUR MENTAL AND PHYSICAL POWER WILL BE CONSUMED.
THE CHANCES ARE HIGH THAT THIS WILL COST YOU YOUR LIFE.
I CANNOT OVERSTATE THE DANGER.

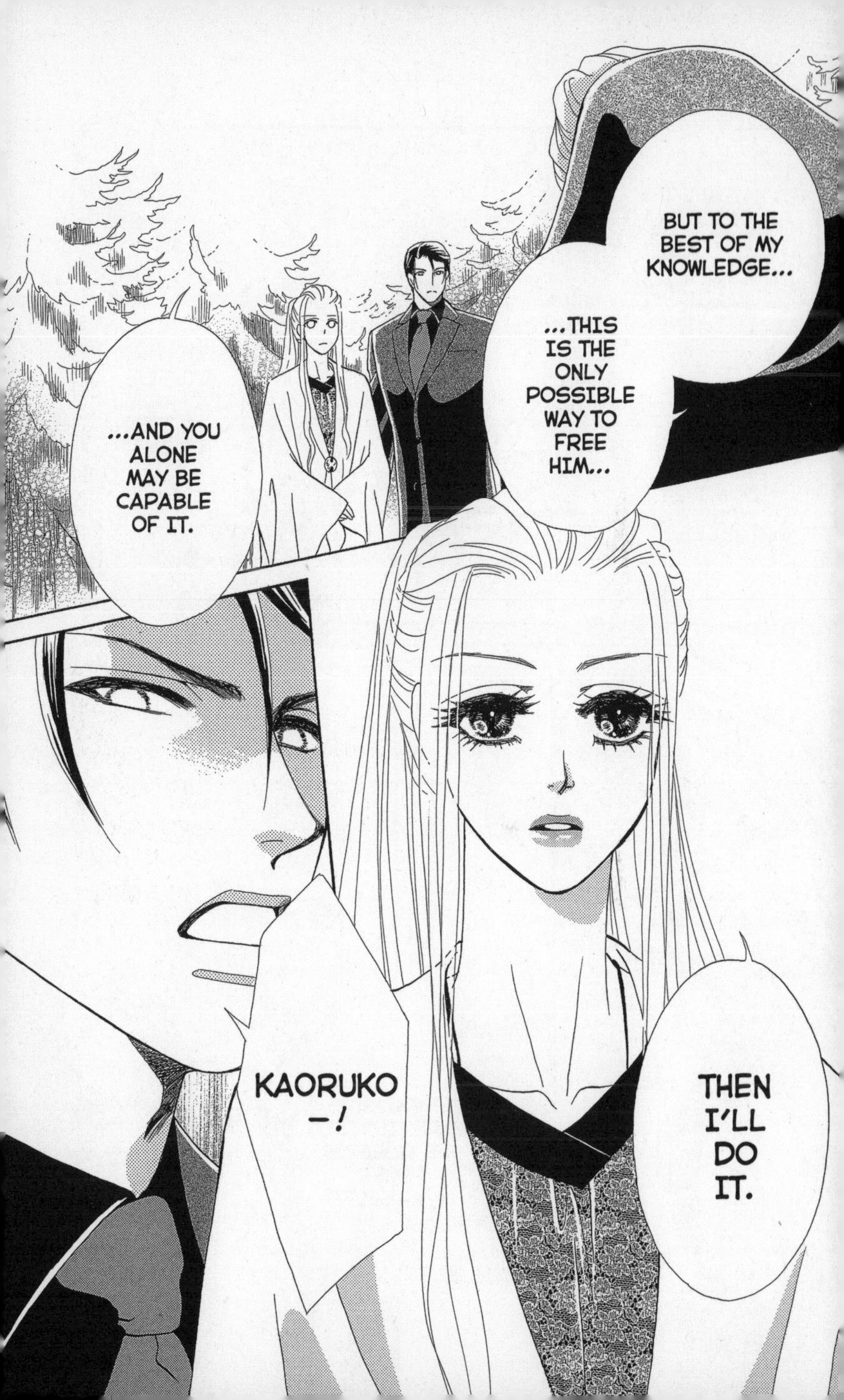
BUT TO THE BEST OF MY KNOWLEDGE...
...THIS IS THE ONLY POSSIBLE WAY TO FREE HIM...
...AND YOU ALONE MAY BE CAPABLE OF IT.
THEN I'LL DO IT.
KAORUKO—!

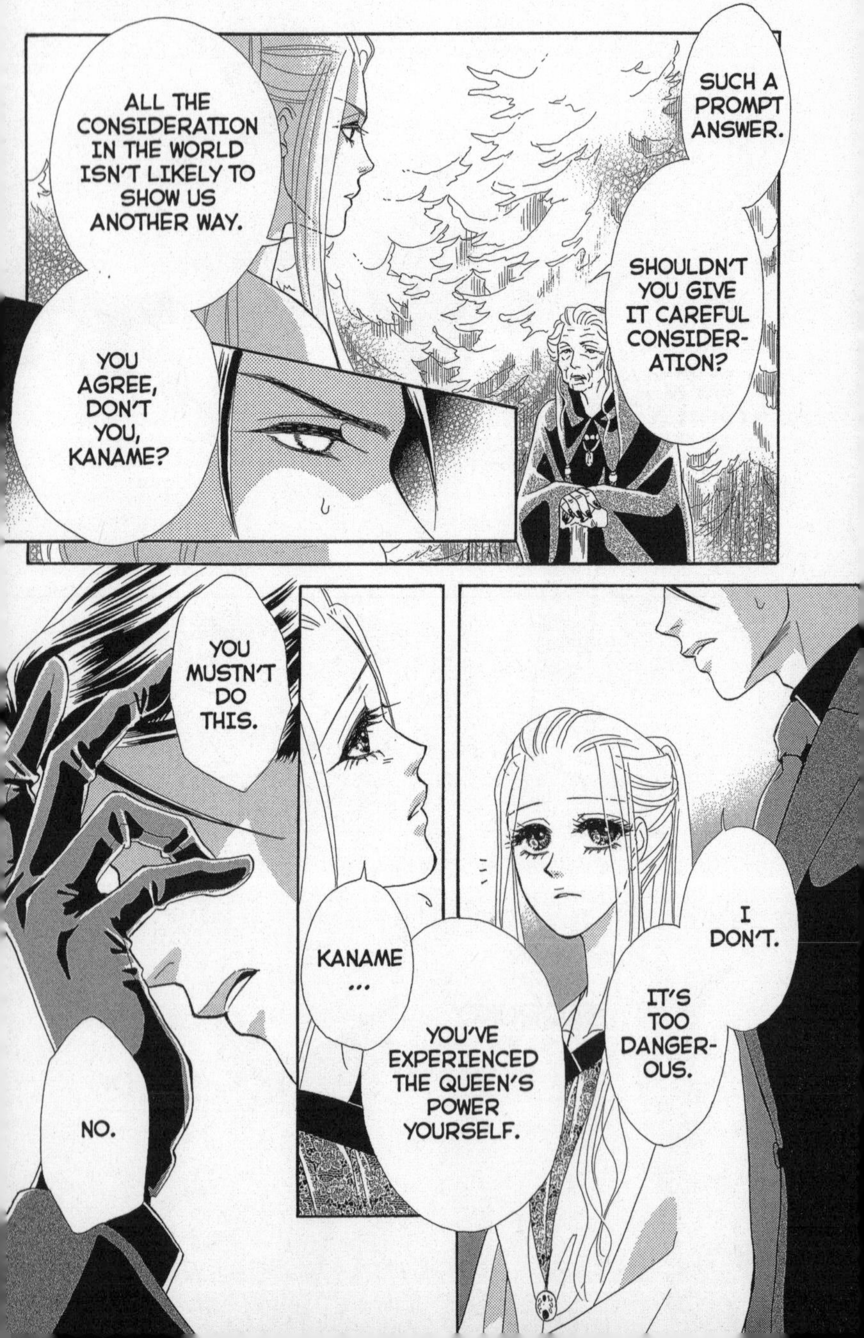
SUCH A PROMPT ANSWER.
SHOULDN'T YOU GIVE IT CAREFUL CONSIDER-ATION?
ALL THE CONSIDERATION IN THE WORLD ISN'T LIKELY TO SHOW US ANOTHER WAY.
YOU AGREE, DON'T YOU, KANAME?
I DON'T.
IT'S TOO DANGER-OUS.
YOU'VE EXPERIENCED THE QUEEN'S POWER YOURSELF.
KANAME ...
YOU MUSTN'T DO THIS.
NO.

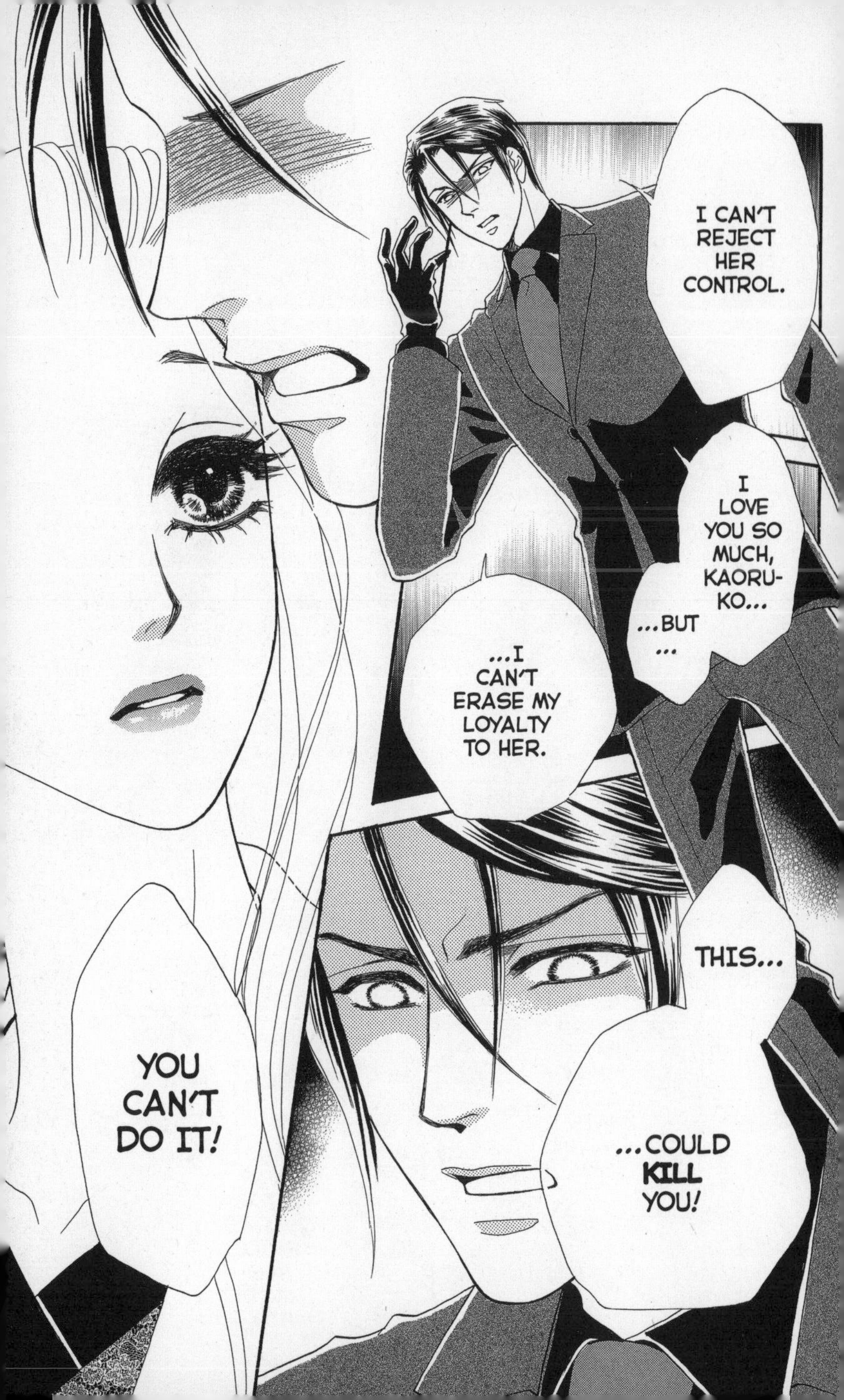
I CAN'T REJECT HER CONTROL.
I LOVE YOU SO MUCH, KAORU-KO...
...BUT ...
...I CAN'T ERASE MY LOYALTY TO HER.
THIS...
...COULD **KILL** YOU!
YOU CAN'T DO IT!

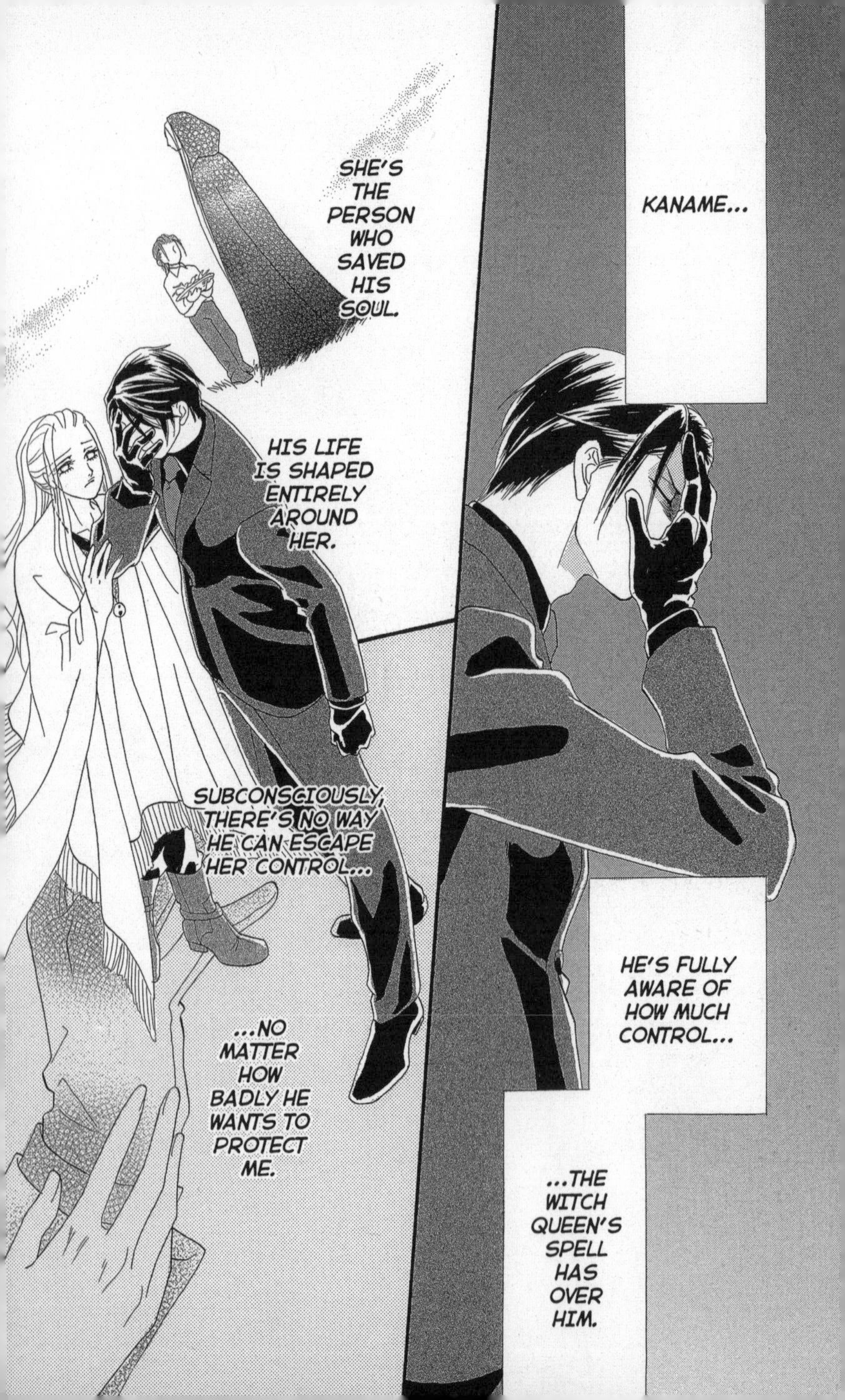
KANAME...
HE'S FULLY AWARE OF HOW MUCH CONTROL...
...THE WITCH QUEEN'S SPELL HAS OVER HIM.
SHE'S THE PERSON WHO SAVED HIS SOUL.
HIS LIFE IS SHAPED ENTIRELY AROUND HER.
SUBCONSCIOUSLY, THERE'S NO WAY HE CAN ESCAPE HER CONTROL...
...NO MATTER HOW BADLY HE WANTS TO PROTECT ME.

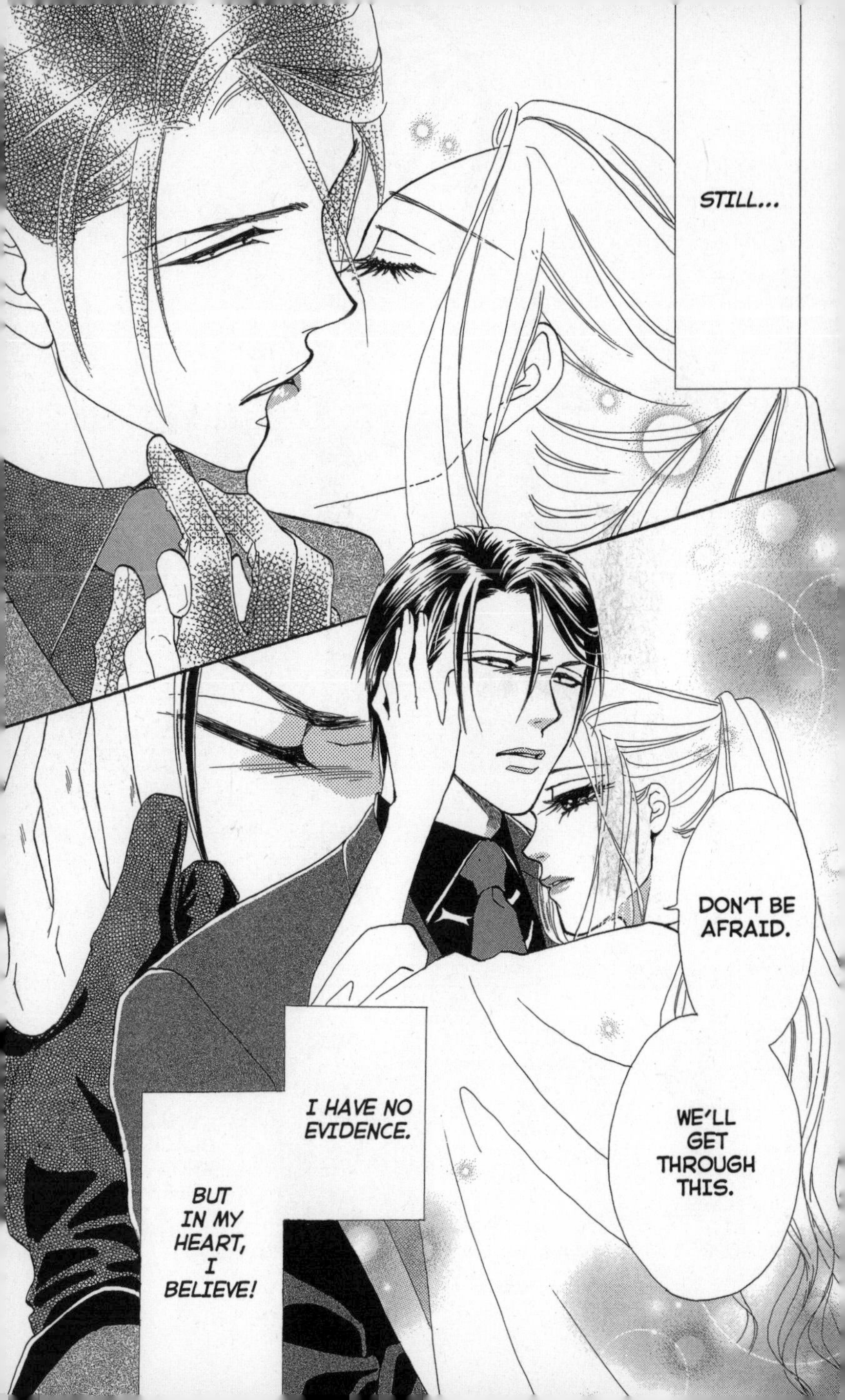
STILL...
DON'T BE AFRAID.
WE'LL GET THROUGH THIS.
I HAVE NO EVIDENCE.
BUT IN MY HEART, I BELIEVE!

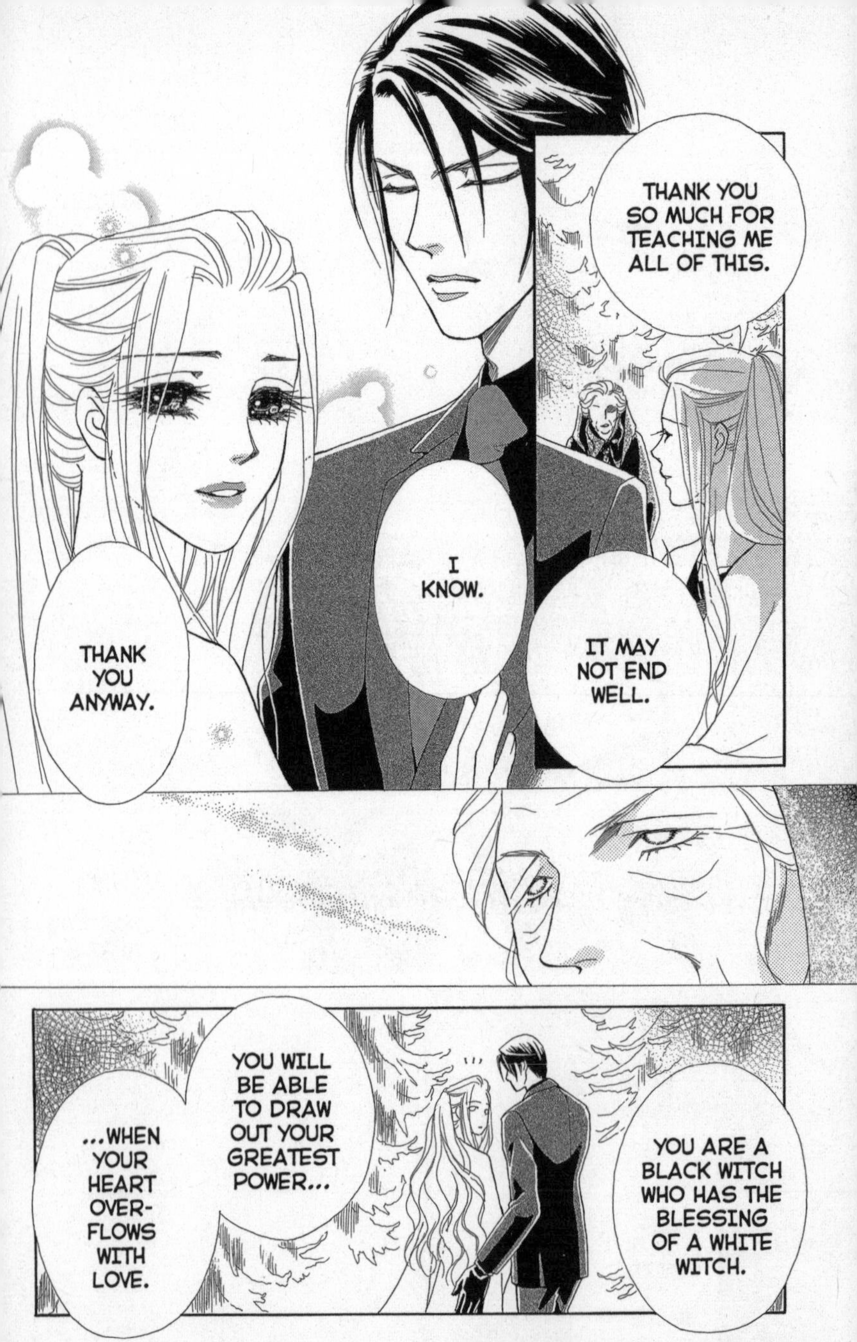
THANK YOU SO MUCH FOR TEACHING ME ALL OF THIS.
IT MAY NOT END WELL.
I KNOW.
THANK YOU ANYWAY.
YOU ARE A BLACK WITCH WHO HAS THE BLESSING OF A WHITE WITCH.
YOU WILL BE ABLE TO DRAW OUT YOUR GREATEST POWER...
...WHEN YOUR HEART OVER-FLOWS WITH LOVE.

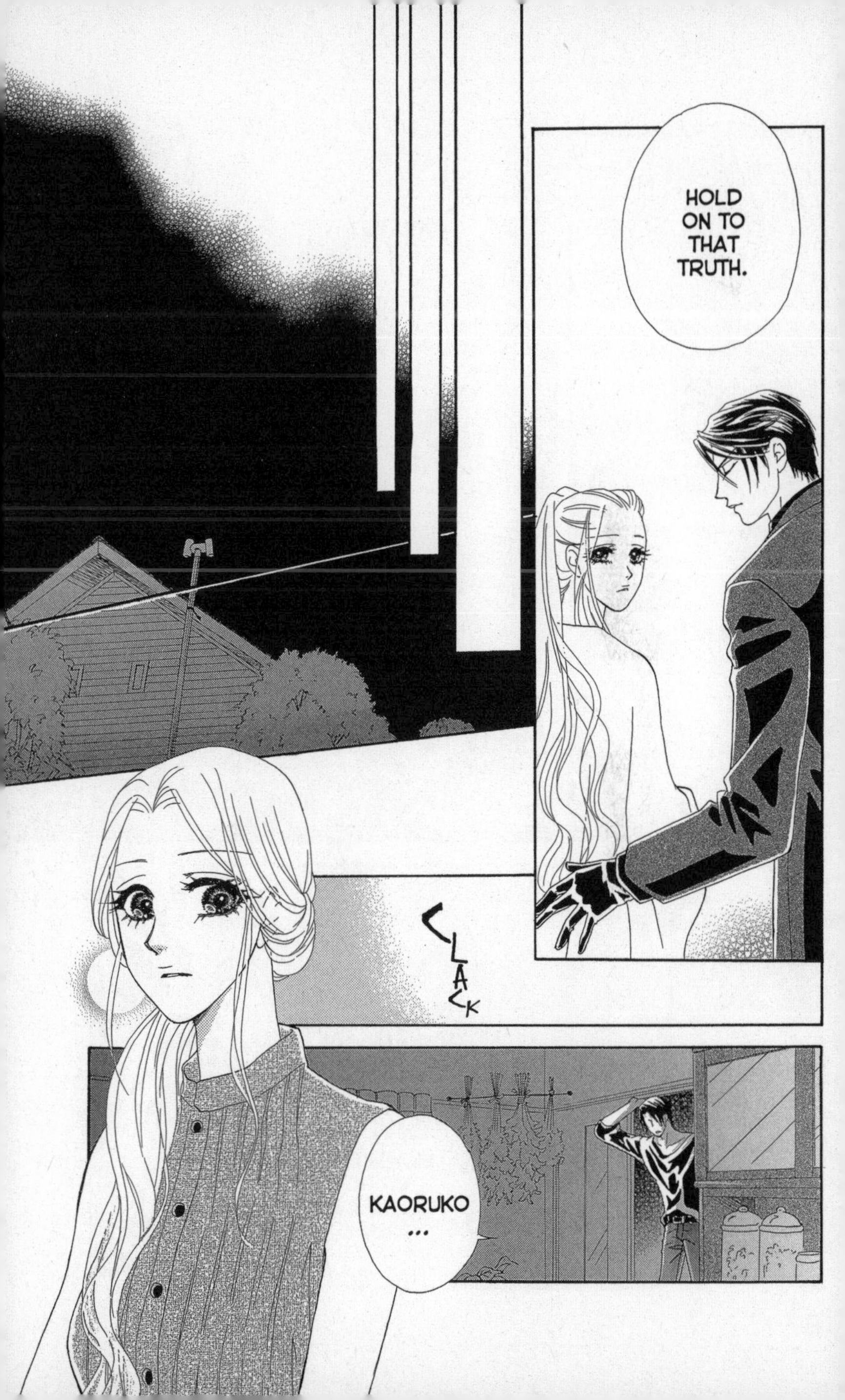
HOLD ON TO THAT TRUTH.
CLACK
KAORUKO ...

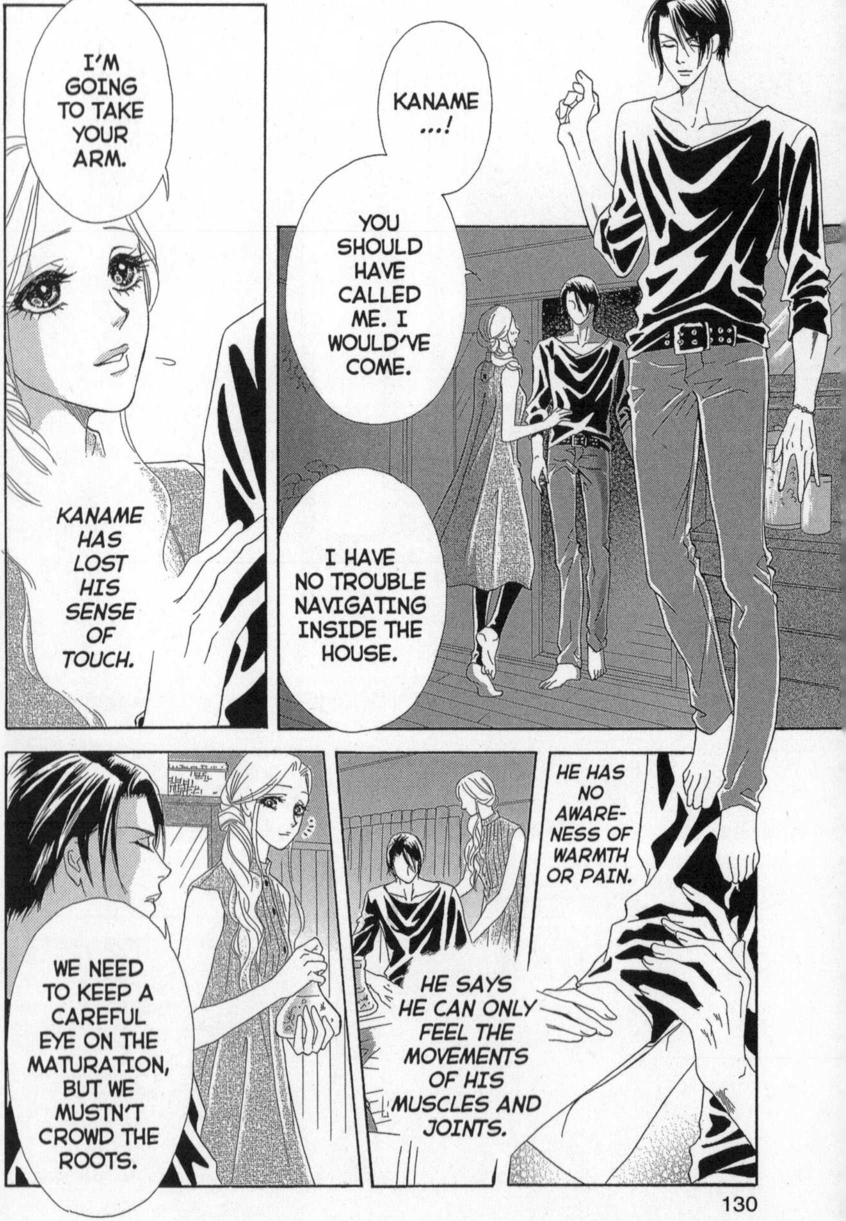
KANAME ...!
YOU SHOULD HAVE CALLED ME. I WOULD'VE COME.
I HAVE NO TROUBLE NAVIGATING INSIDE THE HOUSE.
I'M GOING TO TAKE YOUR ARM.
KANAME HAS LOST HIS SENSE OF TOUCH.
HE HAS NO AWARENESS OF WARMTH OR PAIN.
HE SAYS HE CAN ONLY FEEL THE MOVEMENTS OF HIS MUSCLES AND JOINTS.
WE NEED TO KEEP A CAREFUL EYE ON THE MATURATION, BUT WE MUSTN'T CROWD THE ROOTS.

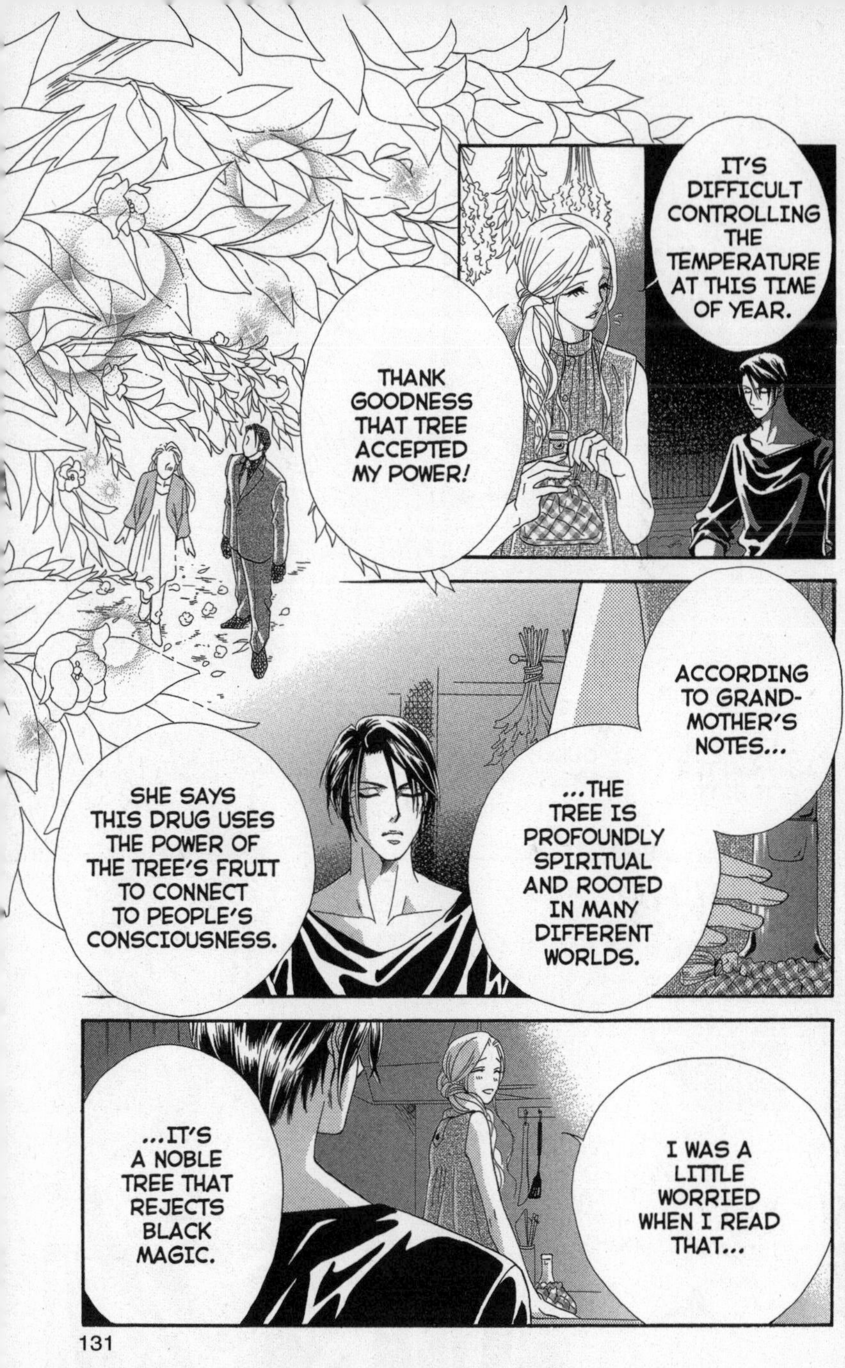
IT'S DIFFICULT CONTROLLING THE TEMPERATURE AT THIS TIME OF YEAR.
THANK GOODNESS THAT TREE ACCEPTED MY POWER!
ACCORDING TO GRAND-MOTHER'S NOTES...
...THE TREE IS PROFOUNDLY SPIRITUAL AND ROOTED IN MANY DIFFERENT WORLDS.
SHE SAYS THIS DRUG USES THE POWER OF THE TREE'S FRUIT TO CONNECT TO PEOPLE'S CONSCIOUSNESS.
I WAS A LITTLE WORRIED WHEN I READ THAT...
...IT'S A NOBLE TREE THAT REJECTS BLACK MAGIC.

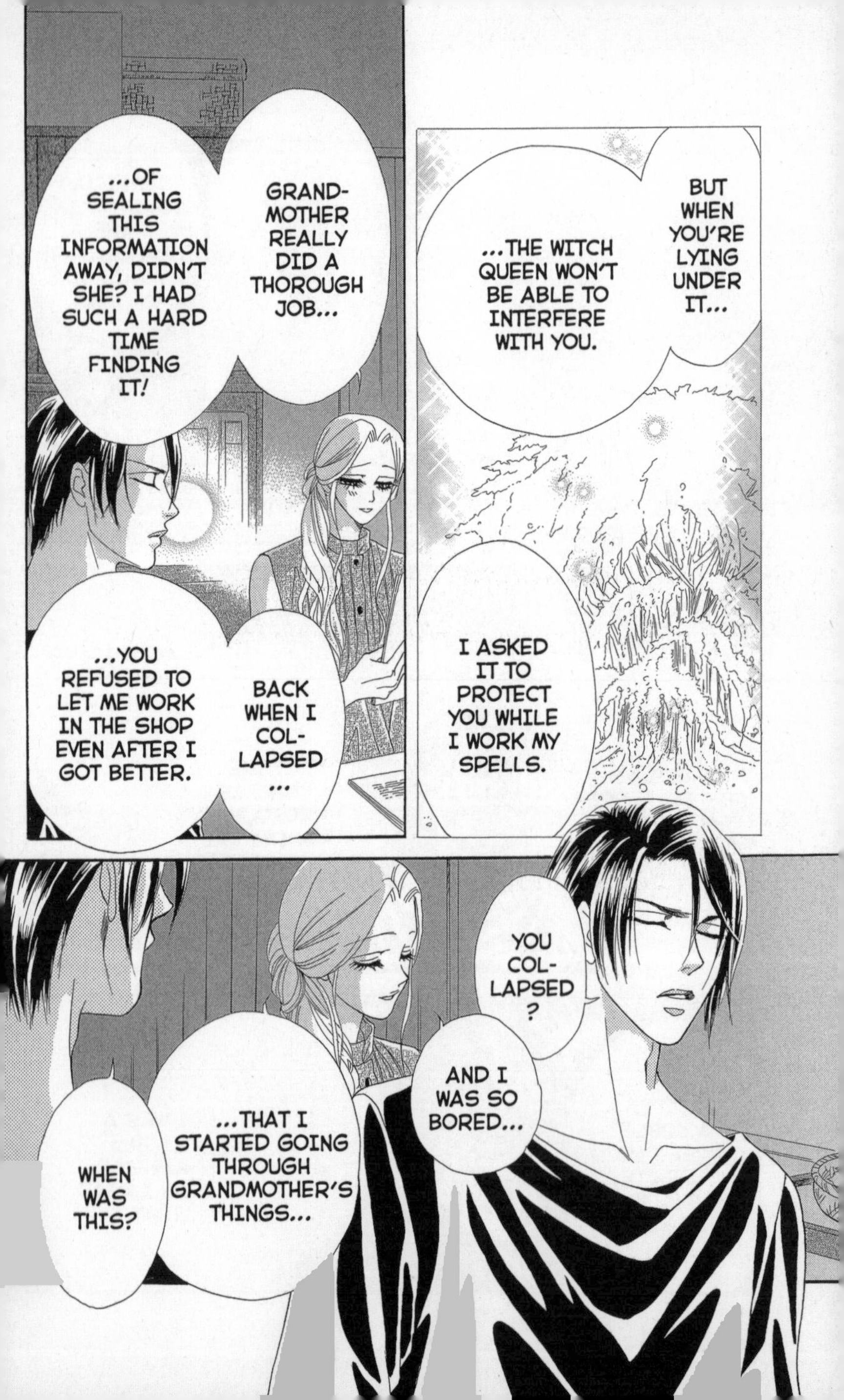
BUT WHEN YOU'RE LYING UNDER IT...
...THE WITCH QUEEN WON'T BE ABLE TO INTERFERE WITH YOU.
I ASKED IT TO PROTECT YOU WHILE I WORK MY SPELLS.
GRANDMOTHER REALLY DID A THOROUGH JOB...
...OF SEALING THIS INFORMATION AWAY, DIDN'T SHE? I HAD SUCH A HARD TIME FINDING IT!
BACK WHEN I COLLAPSED...
...YOU REFUSED TO LET ME WORK IN THE SHOP EVEN AFTER I GOT BETTER.
YOU COLLAPSED?
AND I WAS SO BORED...
...THAT I STARTED GOING THROUGH GRANDMOTHER'S THINGS...
WHEN WAS THIS?

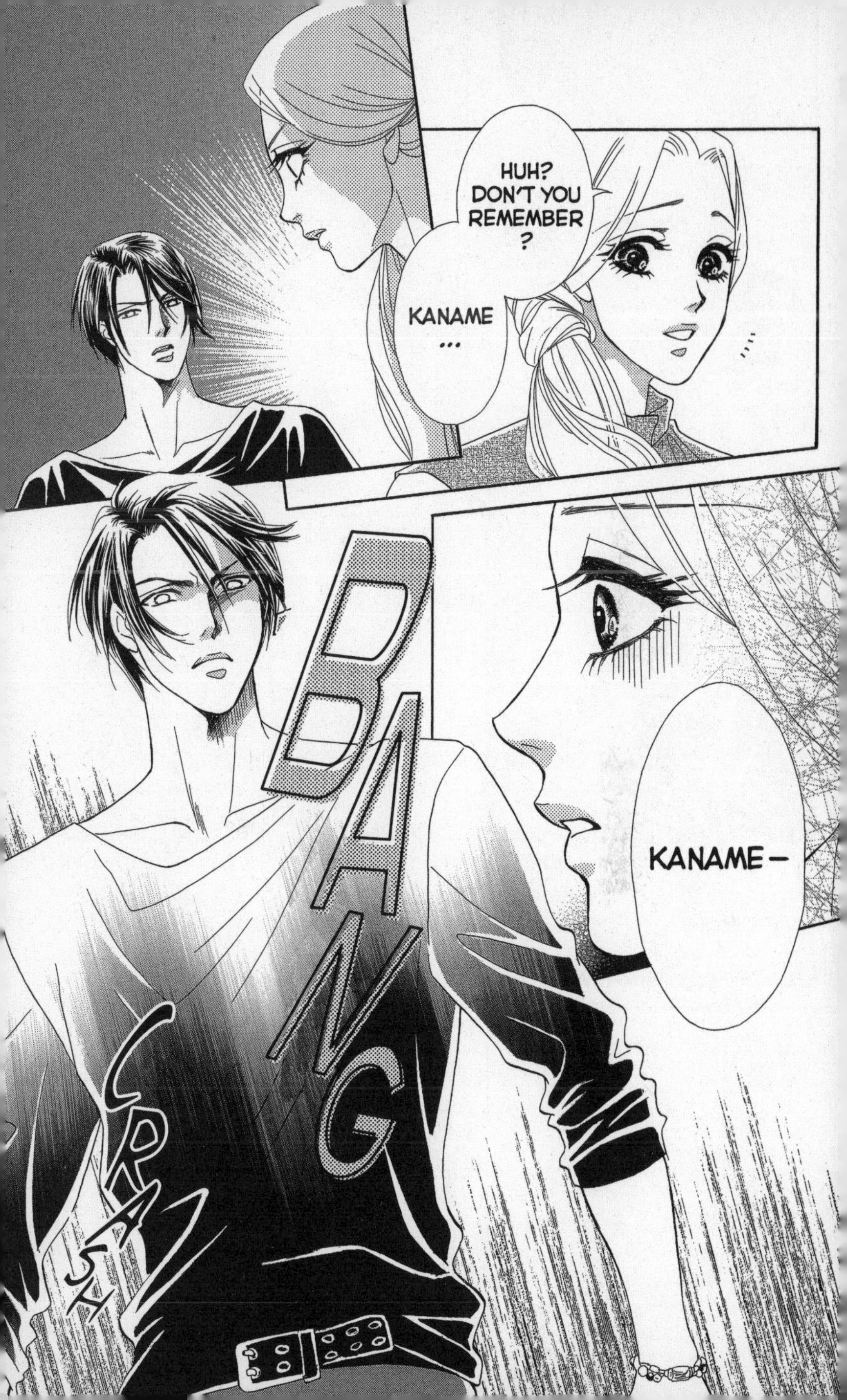
....
HUH? DON'T YOU REMEMBER?
KANAME ...
KANAME–
BANG
CRASH

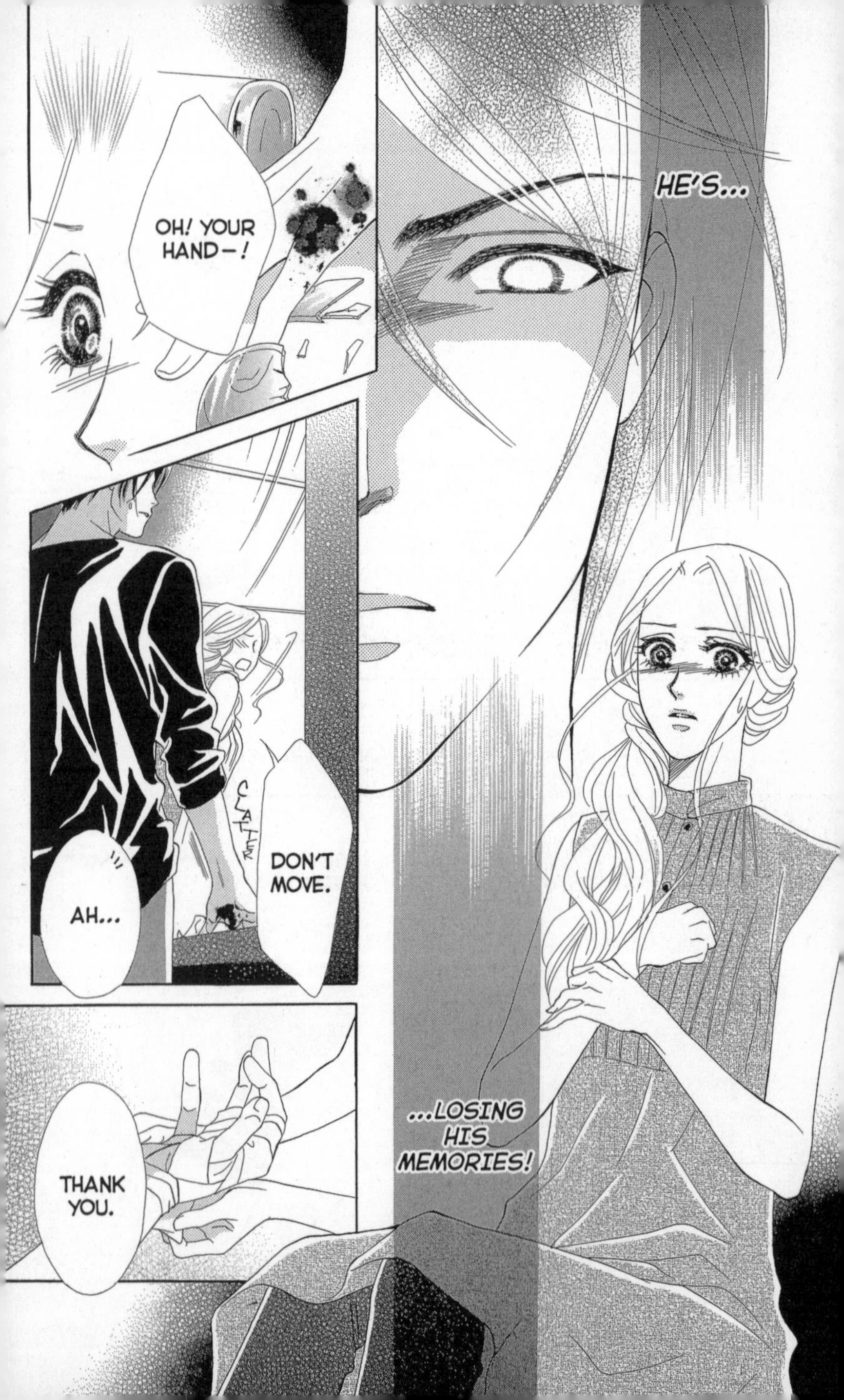
HE'S...
...LOSING HIS MEMORIES!
OH! YOUR HAND—!
DON'T MOVE.
CLATTER
AH...
THANK YOU.

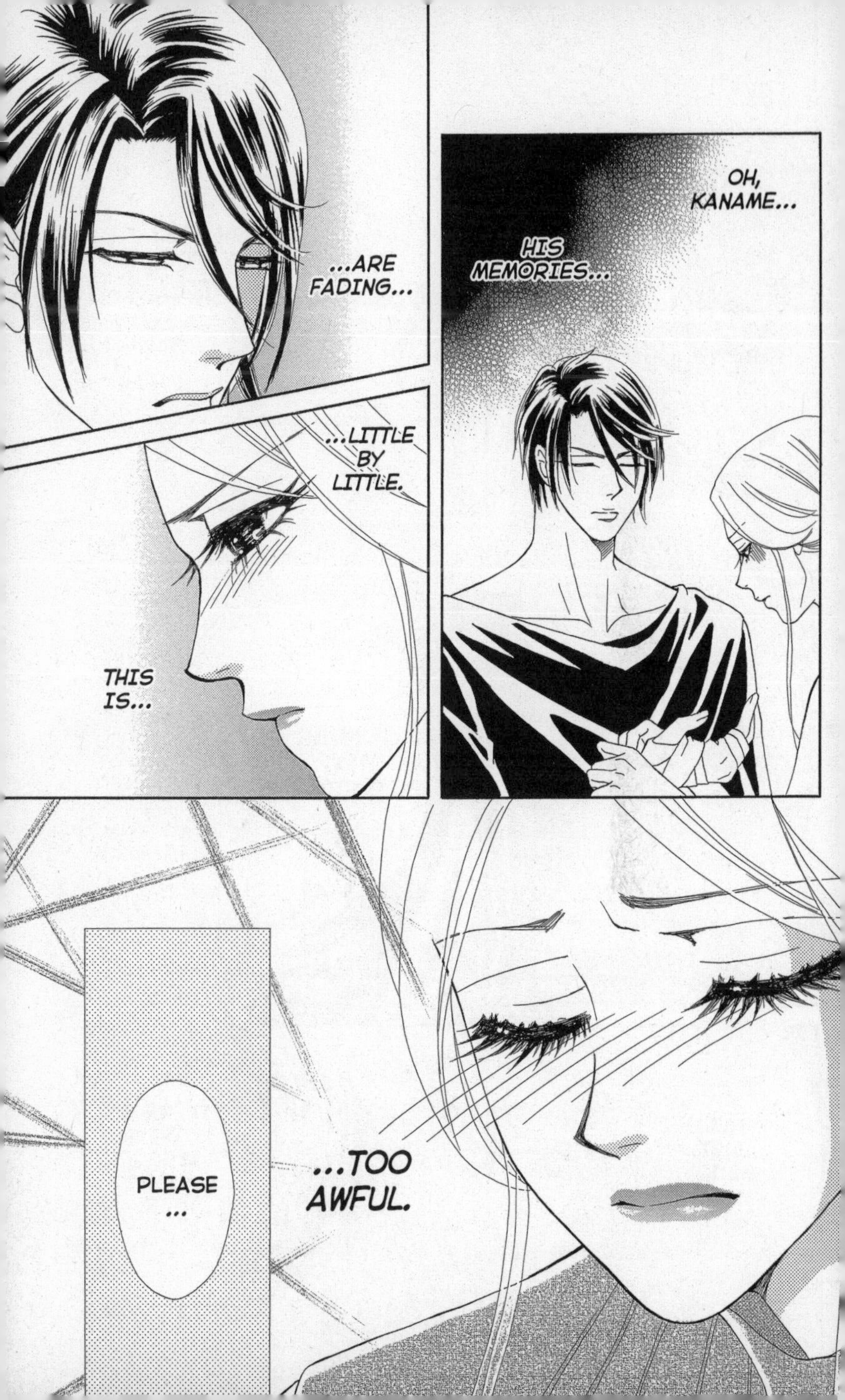
OH, KANAME...
HIS MEMORIES...
...ARE FADING...
...LITTLE BY LITTLE.
THIS IS...
...TOO AWFUL.
PLEASE ...

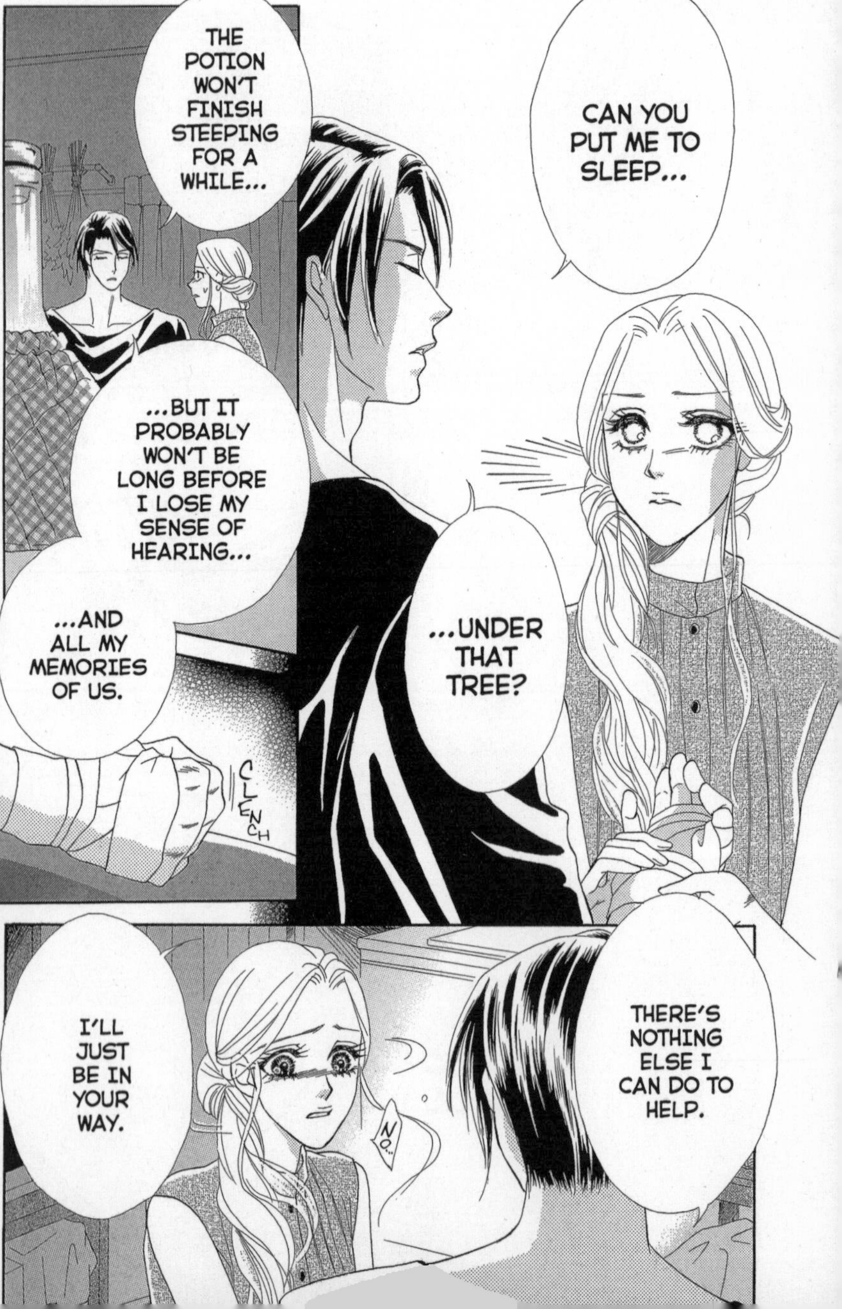
CAN YOU PUT ME TO SLEEP...
...UNDER THAT TREE?
THE POTION WON'T FINISH STEEPING FOR A WHILE...
...BUT IT PROBABLY WON'T BE LONG BEFORE I LOSE MY SENSE OF HEARING...
...AND ALL MY MEMORIES OF US.
CLENCH
THERE'S NOTHING ELSE I CAN DO TO HELP.
NO...
I'LL JUST BE IN YOUR WAY.

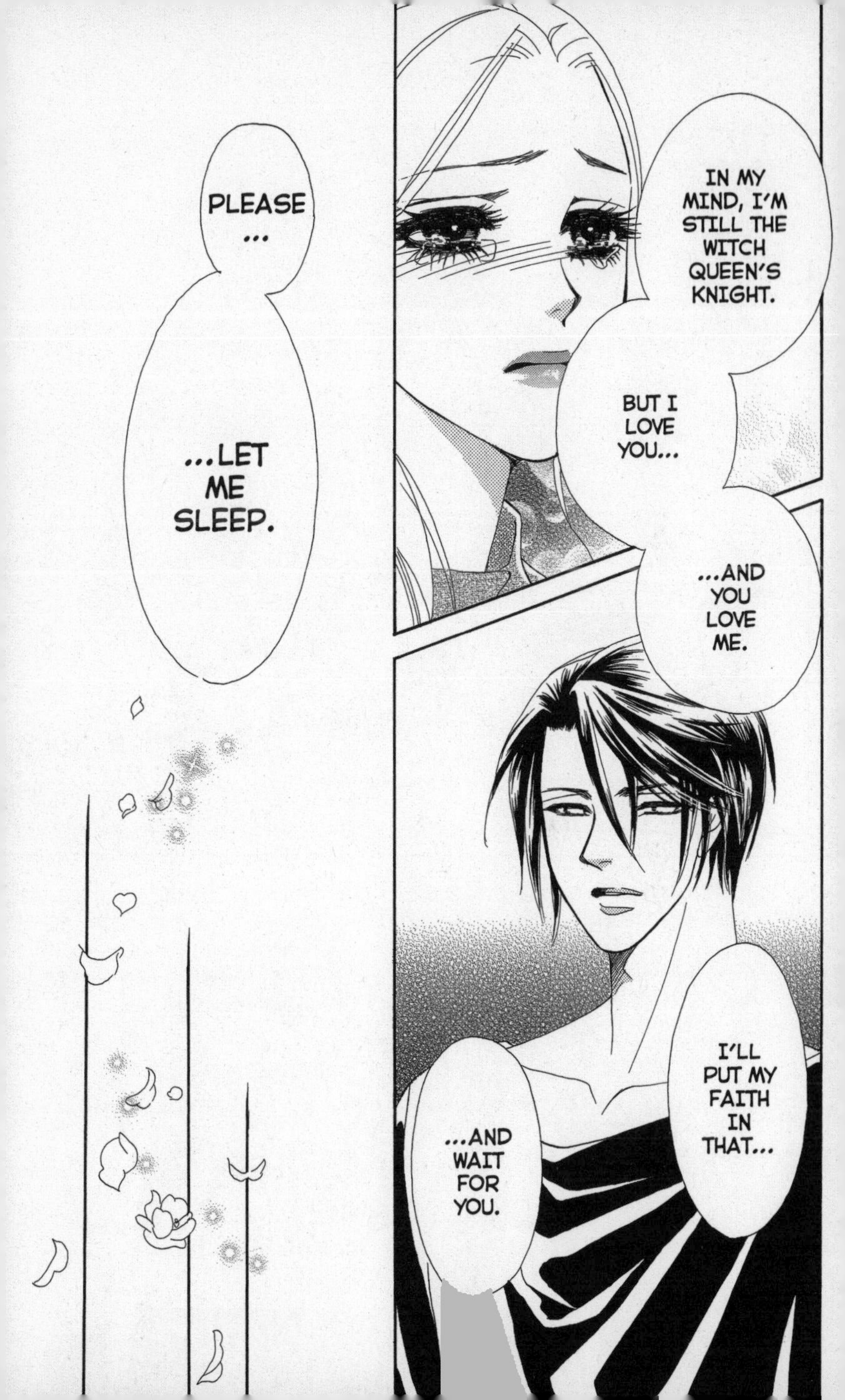
IN MY MIND, I'M STILL THE WITCH QUEEN'S KNIGHT.
BUT I LOVE YOU...
...AND YOU LOVE ME.
I'LL PUT MY FAITH IN THAT...
...AND WAIT FOR YOU.
PLEASE ...
...LET ME SLEEP.

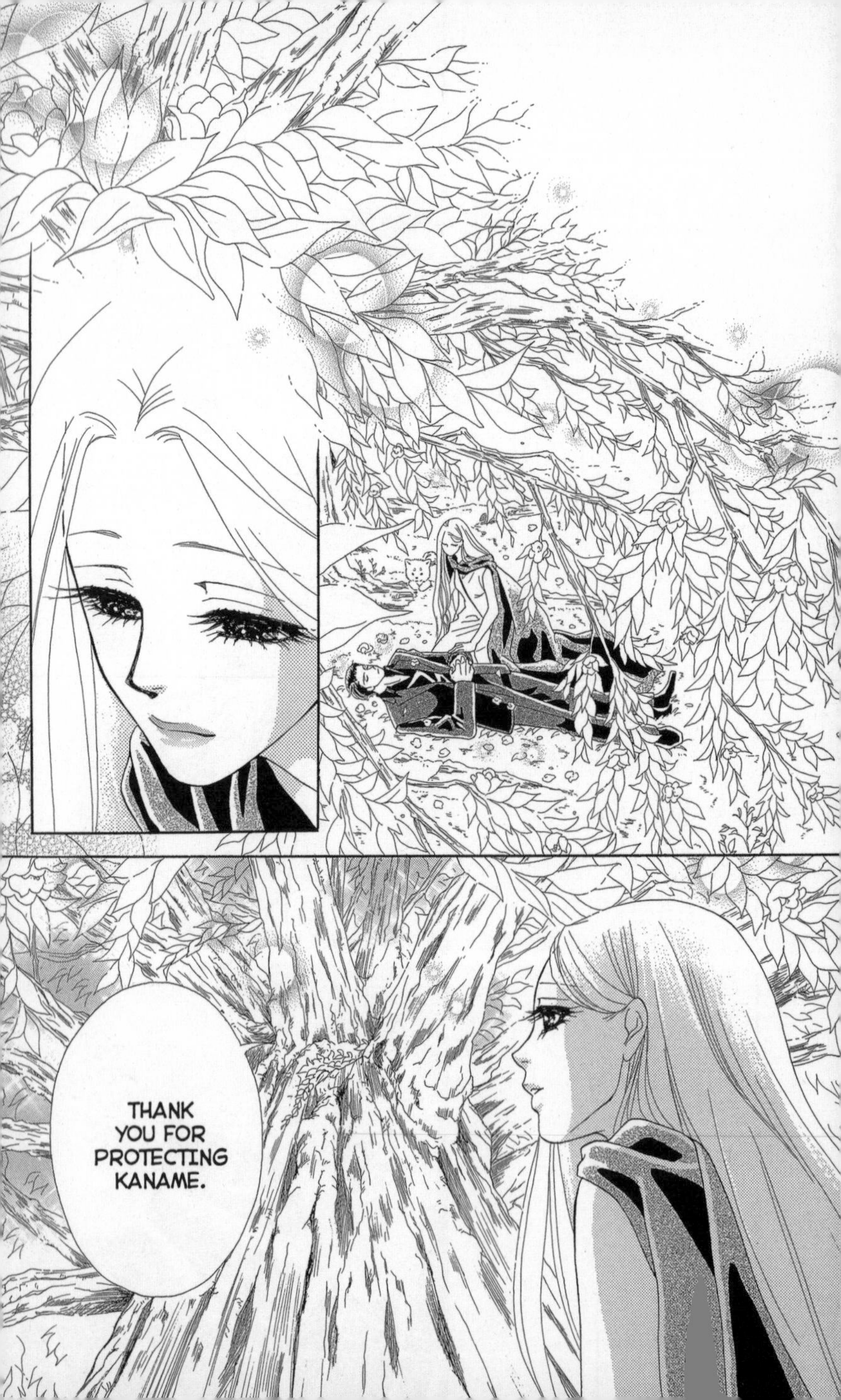
THANK YOU FOR PROTECTING KANAME.

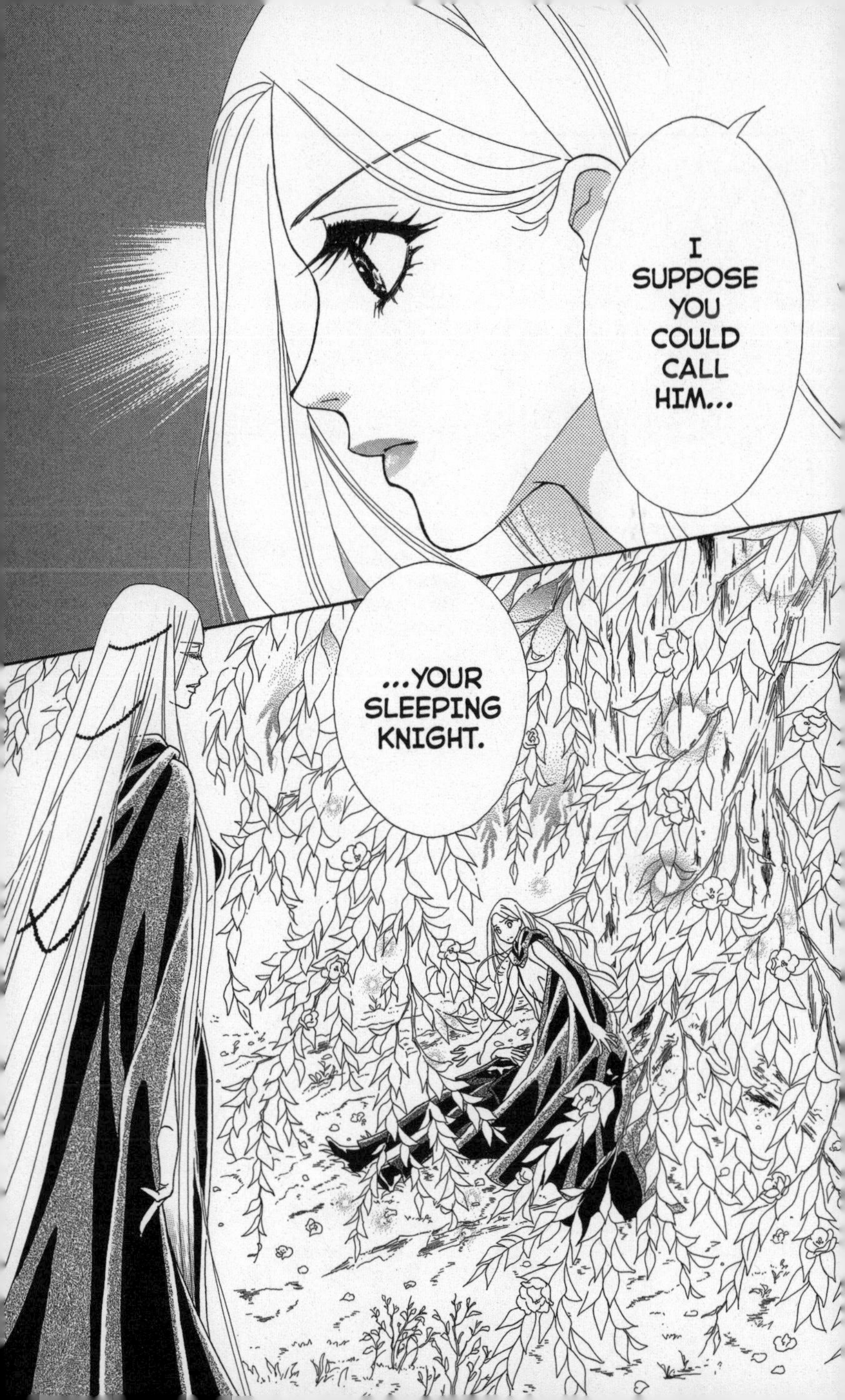
I SUPPOSE YOU COULD CALL HIM...
...YOUR SLEEPING KNIGHT.

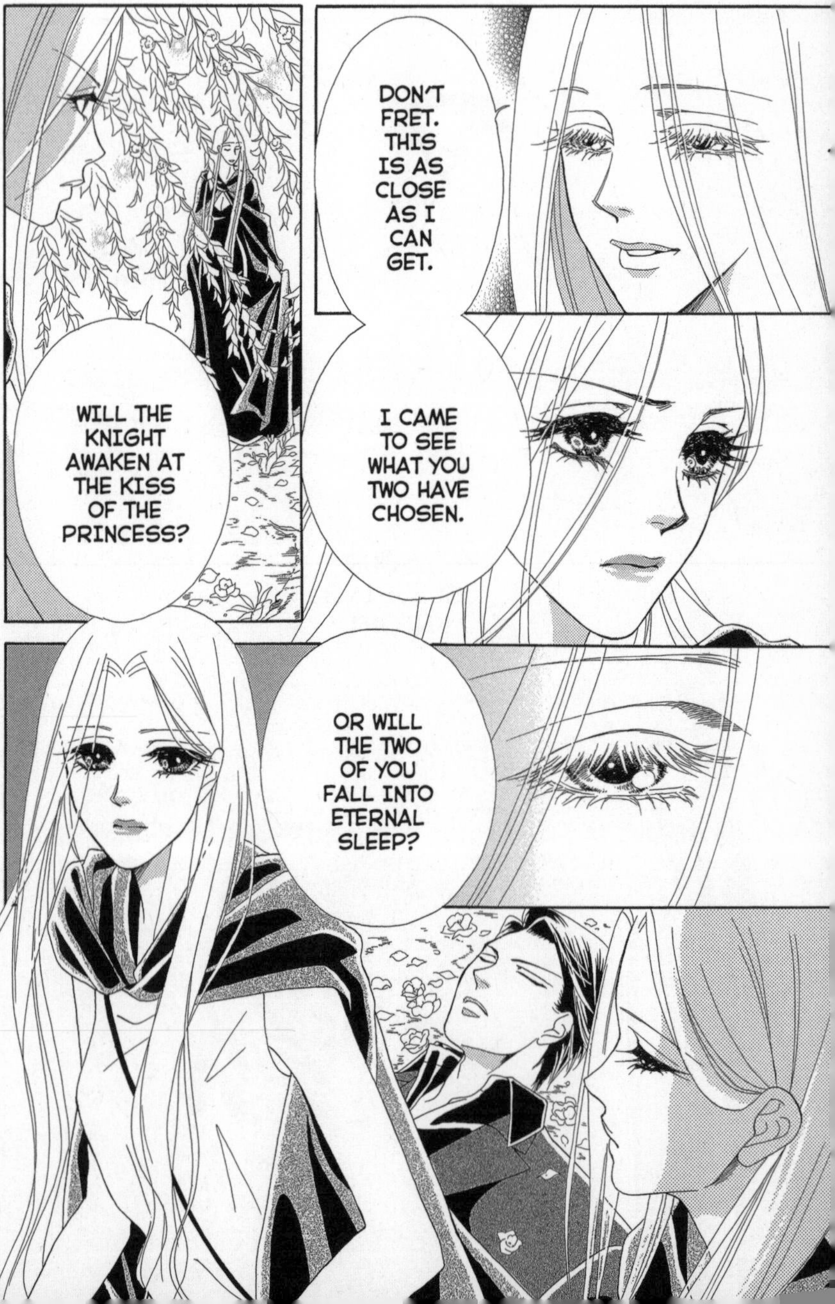
DON'T FRET. THIS IS AS CLOSE AS I CAN GET.
I CAME TO SEE WHAT YOU TWO HAVE CHOSEN.
WILL THE KNIGHT AWAKEN AT THE KISS OF THE PRINCESS?
OR WILL THE TWO OF YOU FALL INTO ETERNAL SLEEP?

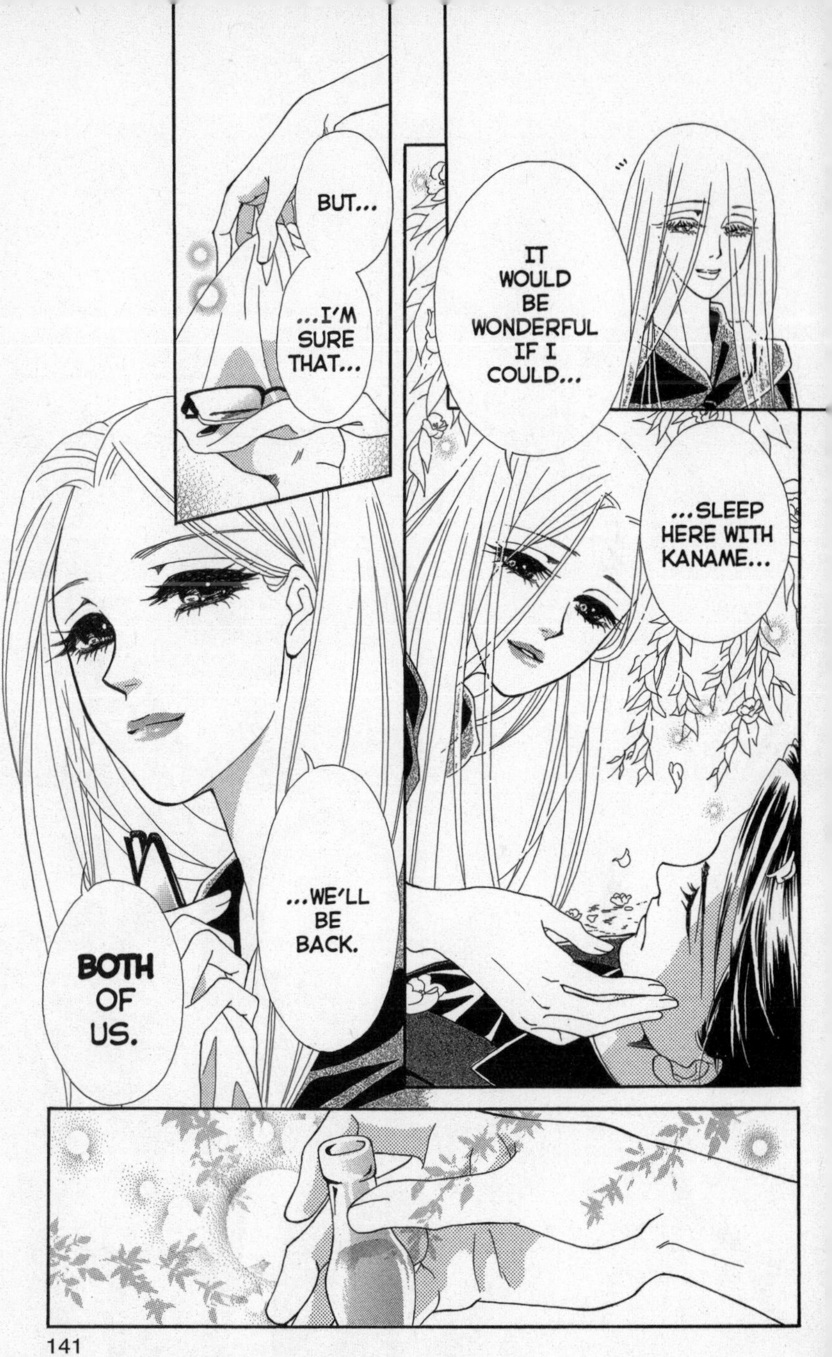
IT WOULD BE WONDERFUL IF I COULD...
...SLEEP HERE WITH KANAME...
BUT...
...I'M SURE THAT...
...WE'LL BE BACK.
BOTH OF US.

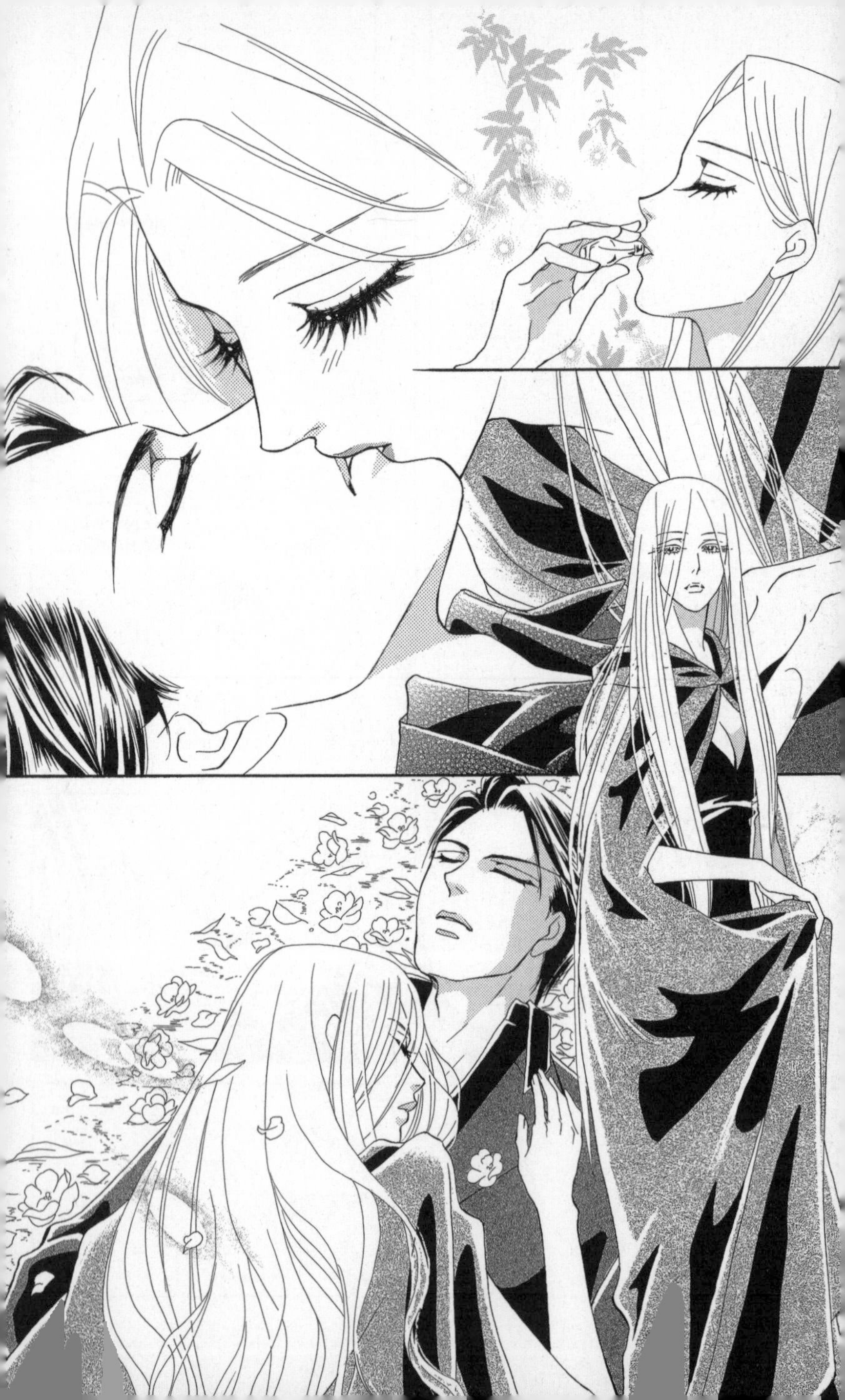

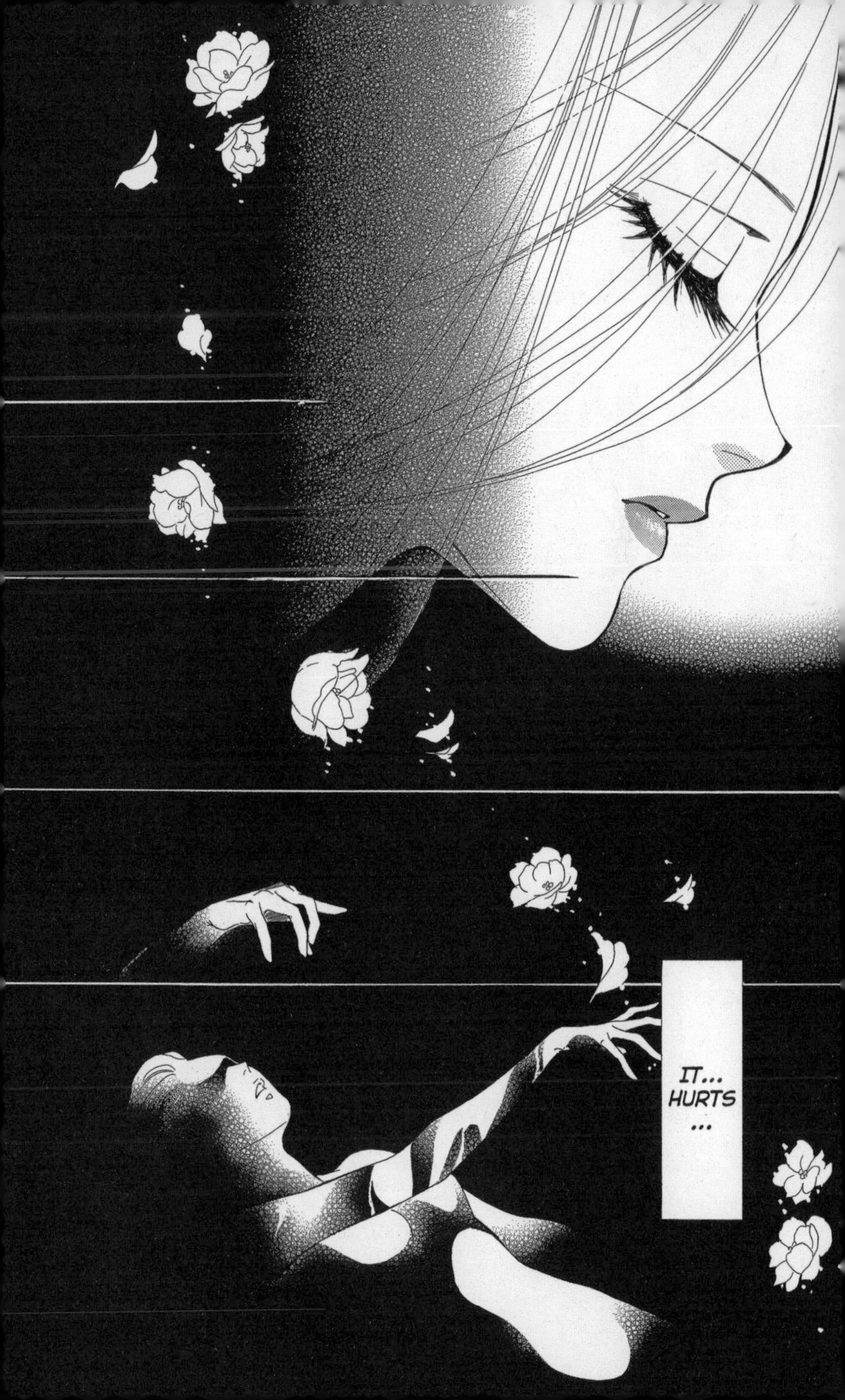
IT... HURTS ...

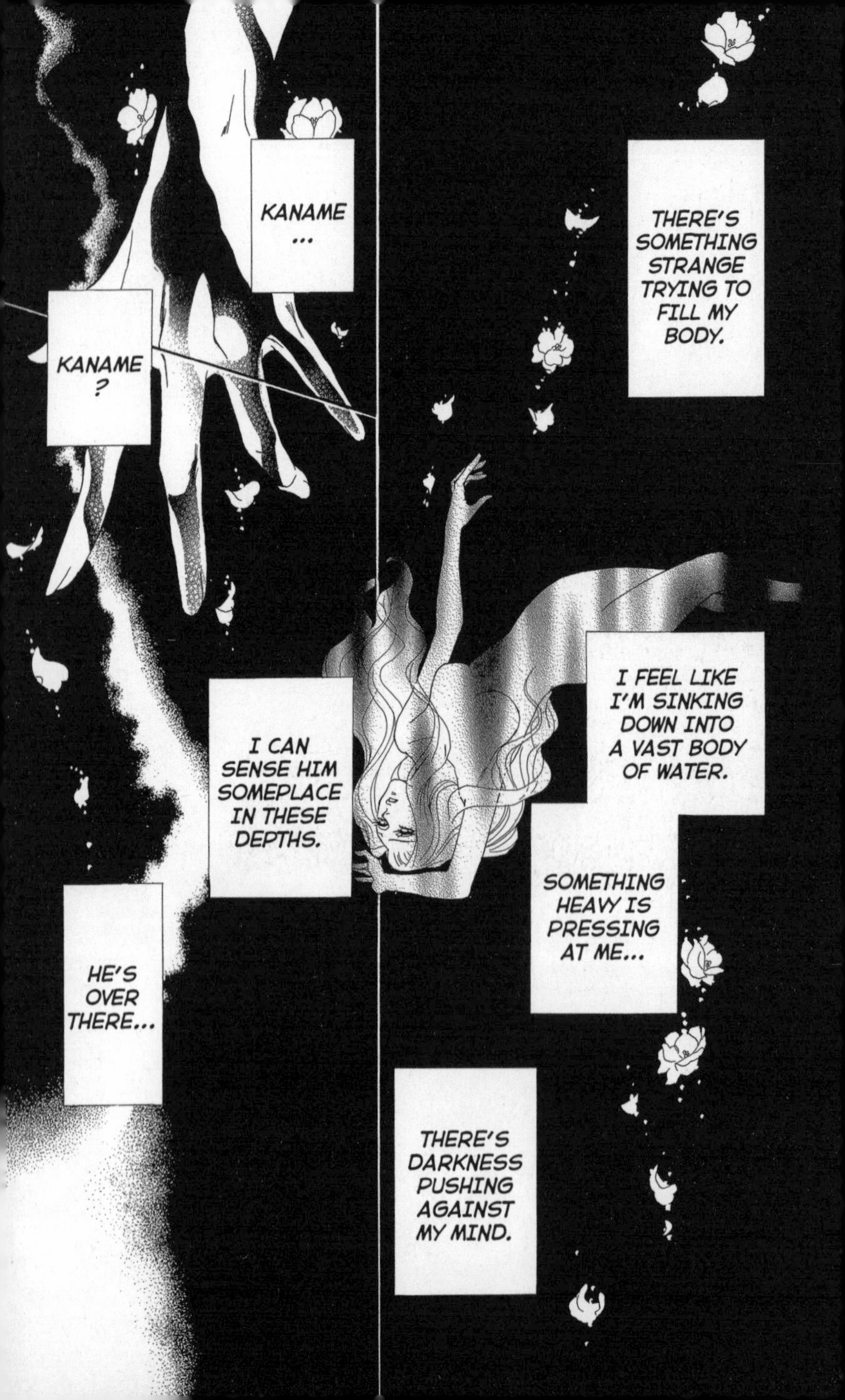
THERE'S SOMETHING STRANGE TRYING TO FILL MY BODY.
KANAME ...
KANAME ?
I FEEL LIKE I'M SINKING DOWN INTO A VAST BODY OF WATER.
I CAN SENSE HIM SOMEPLACE IN THESE DEPTHS.
SOMETHING HEAVY IS PRESSING AT ME...
HE'S OVER THERE...
THERE'S DARKNESS PUSHING AGAINST MY MIND.

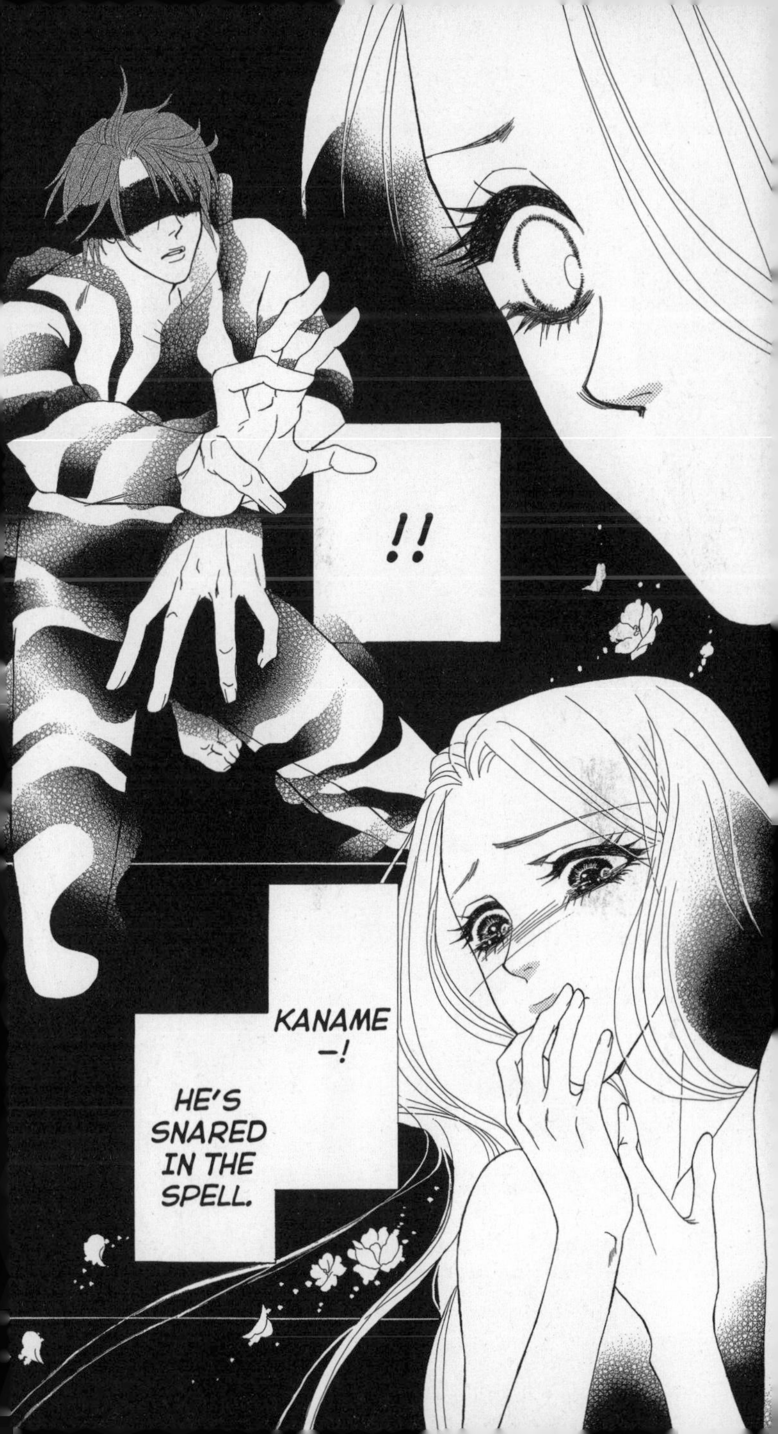
!!
KANAME —!
HE'S SNARED IN THE SPELL.

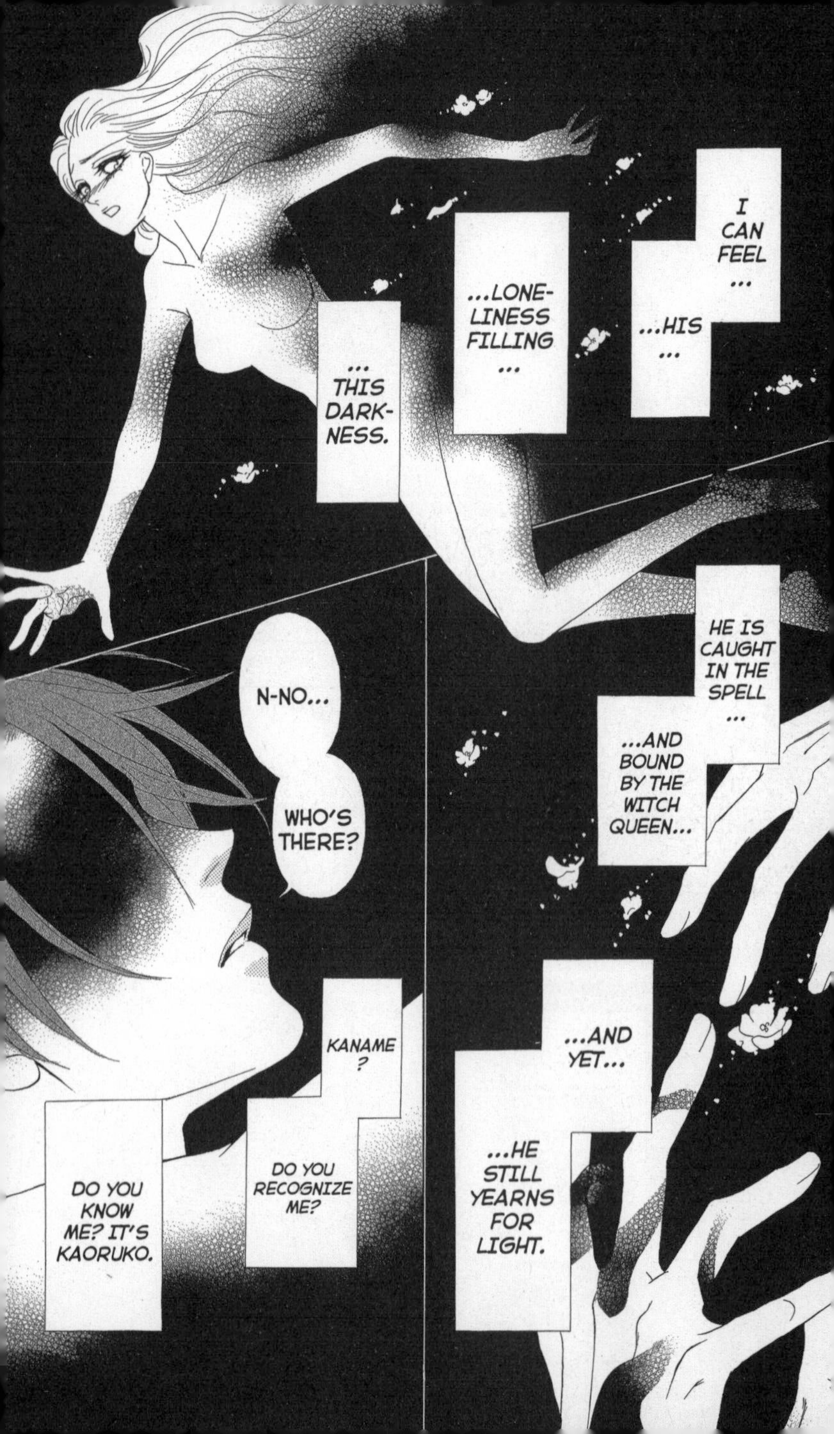
I CAN FEEL...
...HIS...
...LONE-LINESS FILLING...
...THIS DARK-NESS.
HE IS CAUGHT IN THE SPELL...
...AND BOUND BY THE WITCH QUEEN...
...AND YET...
...HE STILL YEARNS FOR LIGHT.
N-NO...
WHO'S THERE?
KANAME?
DO YOU RECOGNIZE ME?
DO YOU KNOW ME? IT'S KAORUKO.

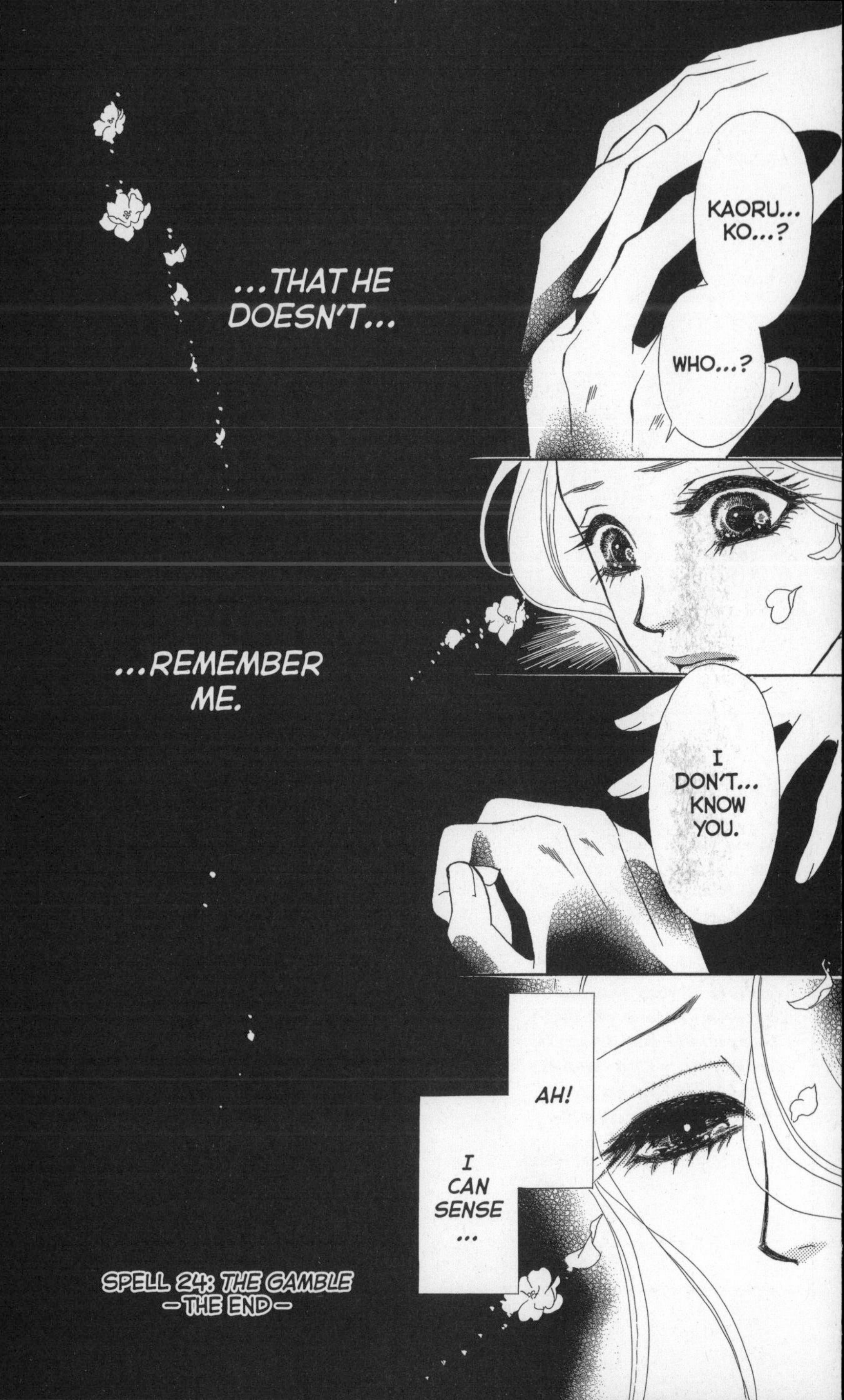
KAORU... KO...?
WHO...?
I DON'T... KNOW YOU.
AH!
I CAN SENSE ...
...THAT HE DOESN'T...
...REMEMBER ME.
SPELL 24: THE GAMBLE
-THE END-

— THE GAMBLE —

This note has nothing to do with the story!

While I was working on this volume, I was also assigned another story to work on: "Pigeon Blood" by Yuki Yoshiwara. It's a story about vampires. She'd done the storyboard, so for the most part, all I had to do was draw it. It was a huge honor, and I had so much fun!

I've mentioned this from time to time, but I'm a big fan of Yoshiwara Sensei. The main reason I originally submitted my work to **Petit Comics** was that they publish her! So it was a very special thing for me to be able to work under her guidance, and she taught me so much.

And then I was even allowed to interview her! Oh, dear... I think I may have used up my lifetime quota of good luck. I'm so grateful to the editors who gave me that job, and to Yoshiwawa Sensei herself.

Whew! It was so exciting that I couldn't help but write a lot about it. (Wry Smile)

— THE APHRODISIAC —

Well, we've reached the last chapter, but this has turned into something of a bonus page... (Ha ha!)

In this final chapter, I feel like I was really able to convey Koko's strength. I especially feel that the scene with all the animals under the ancient tree captured her character as a witch.

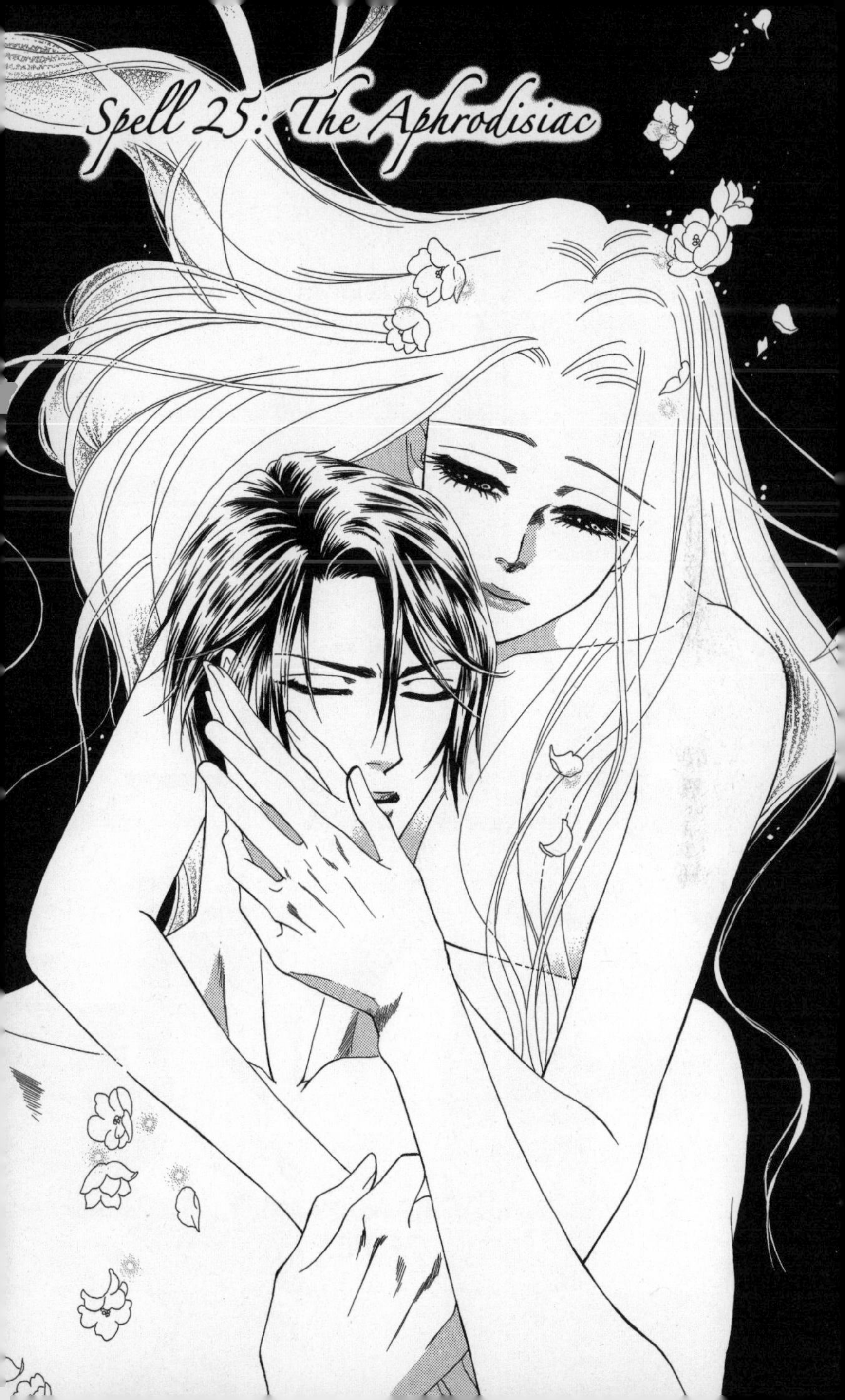
Spell 25: The Aphrodisiac

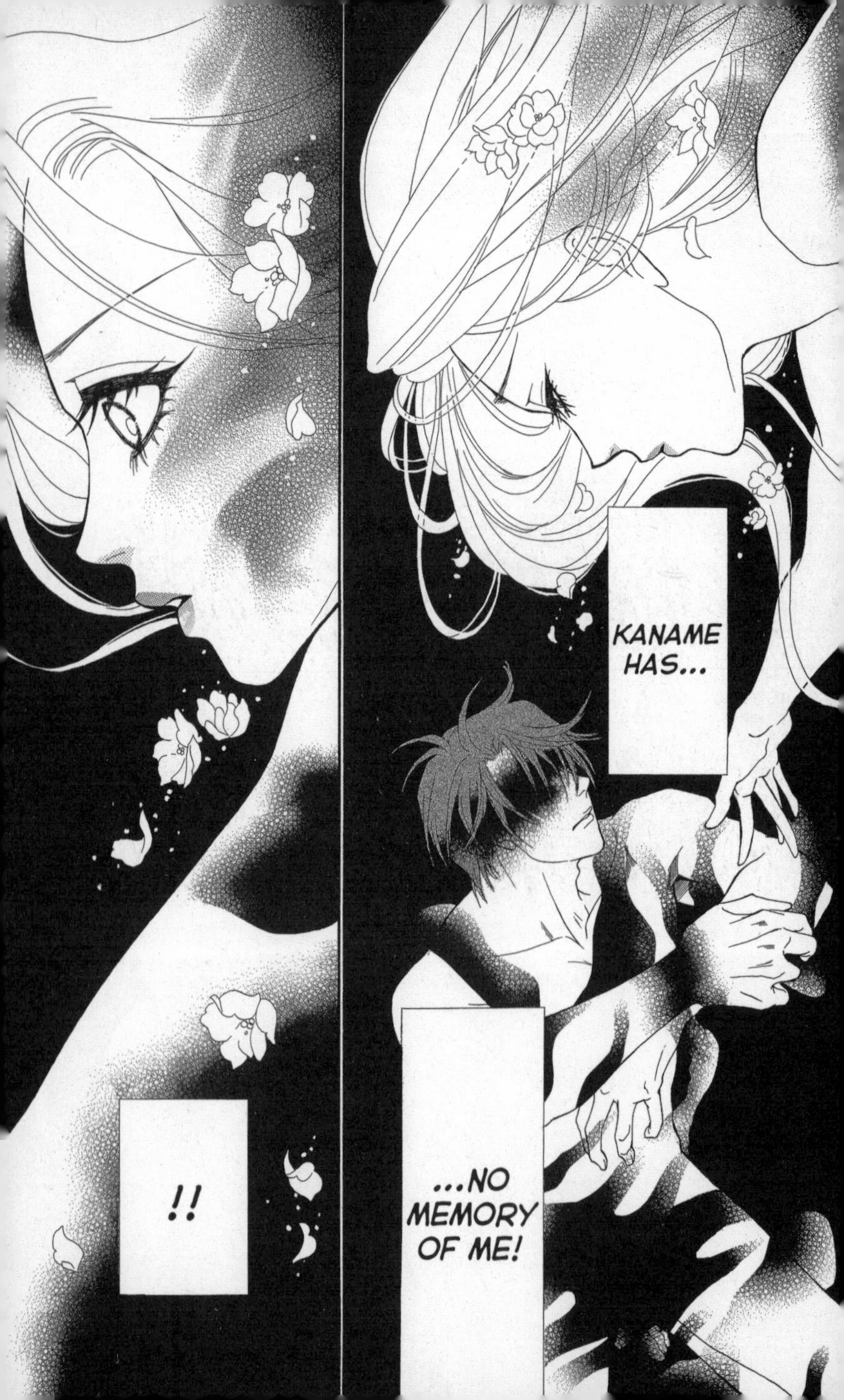
KANAME HAS...
...NO MEMORY OF ME!
!!

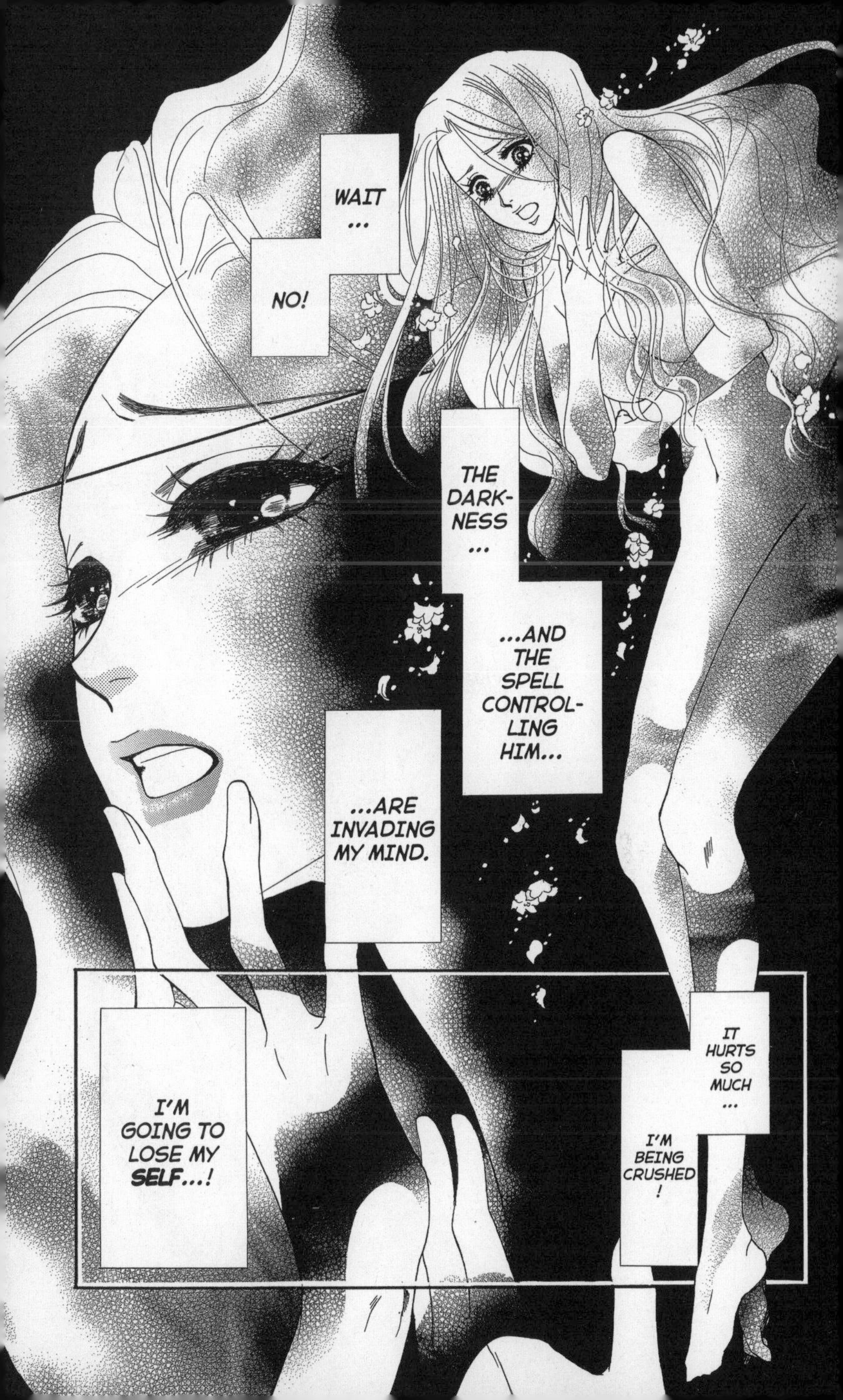
WAIT...
NO!
THE DARKNESS...
...AND THE SPELL CONTROLLING HIM...
...ARE INVADING MY MIND.
IT HURTS SO MUCH...
I'M BEING CRUSHED!
I'M GOING TO LOSE MY **SELF**...!

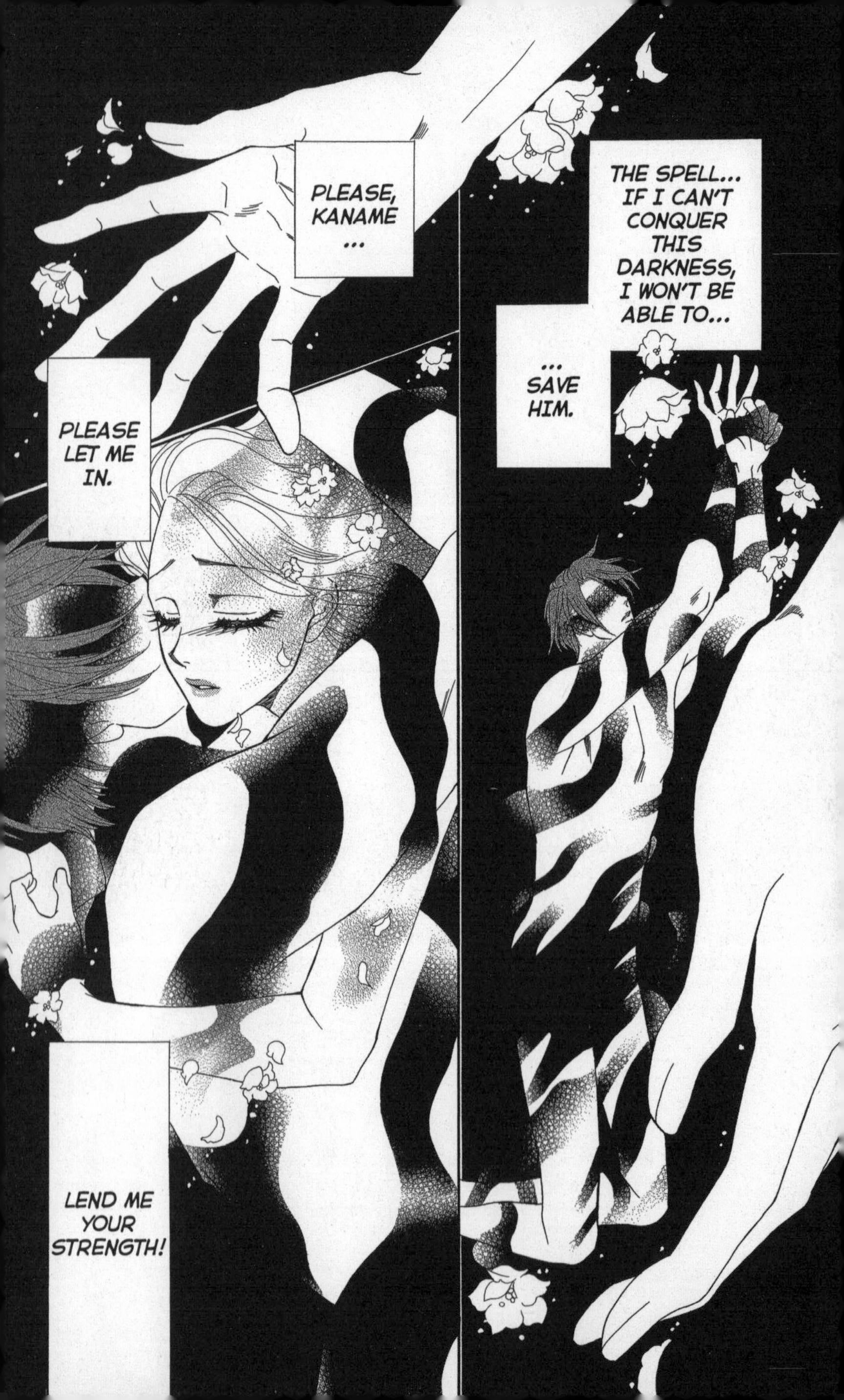
THE SPELL... IF I CAN'T CONQUER THIS DARKNESS, I WON'T BE ABLE TO...
... SAVE HIM.
PLEASE, KANAME ...
PLEASE LET ME IN.
LEND ME YOUR STRENGTH!

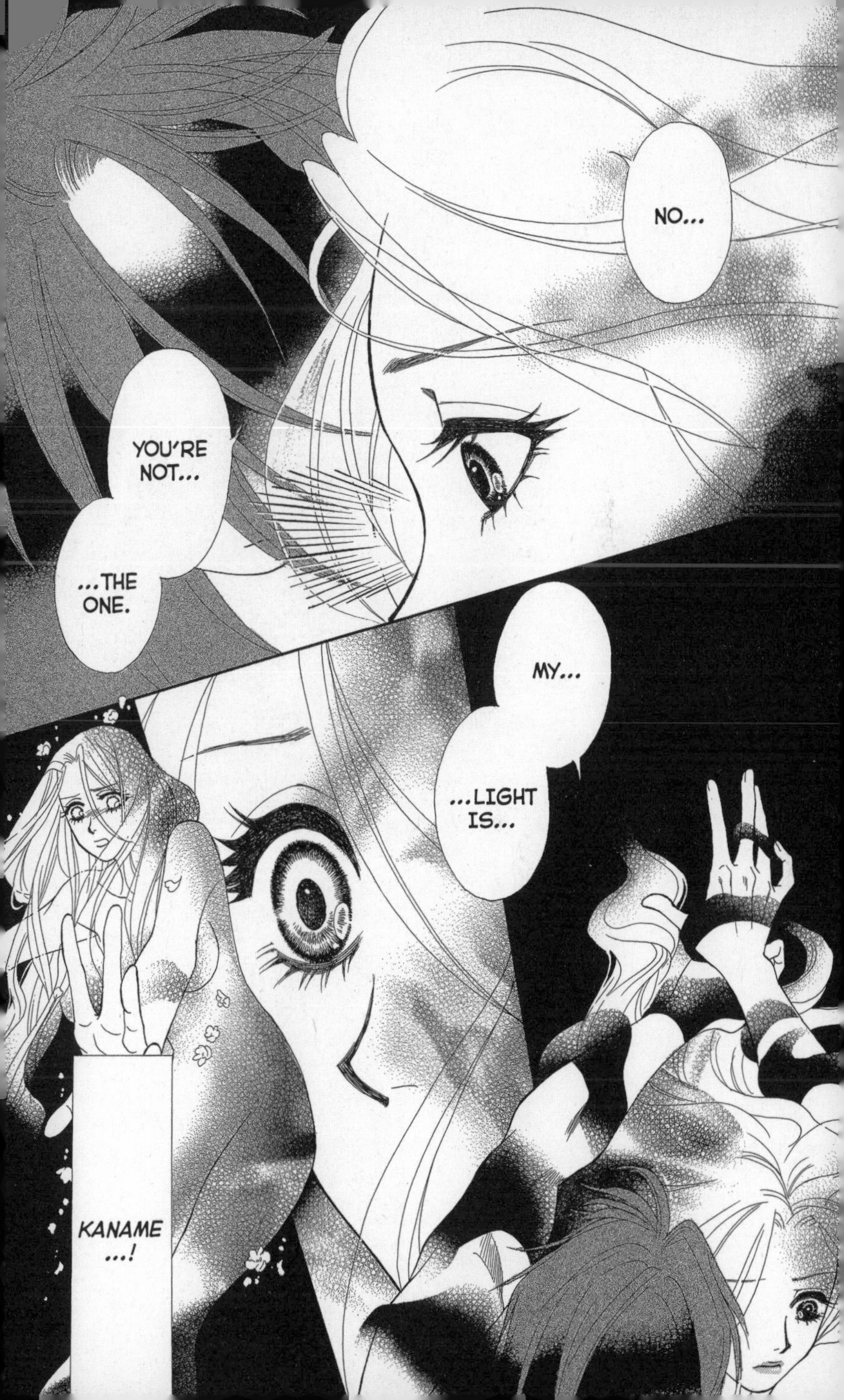
NO...
YOU'RE NOT...
...THE ONE.
MY...
...LIGHT IS...
KANAME ...!

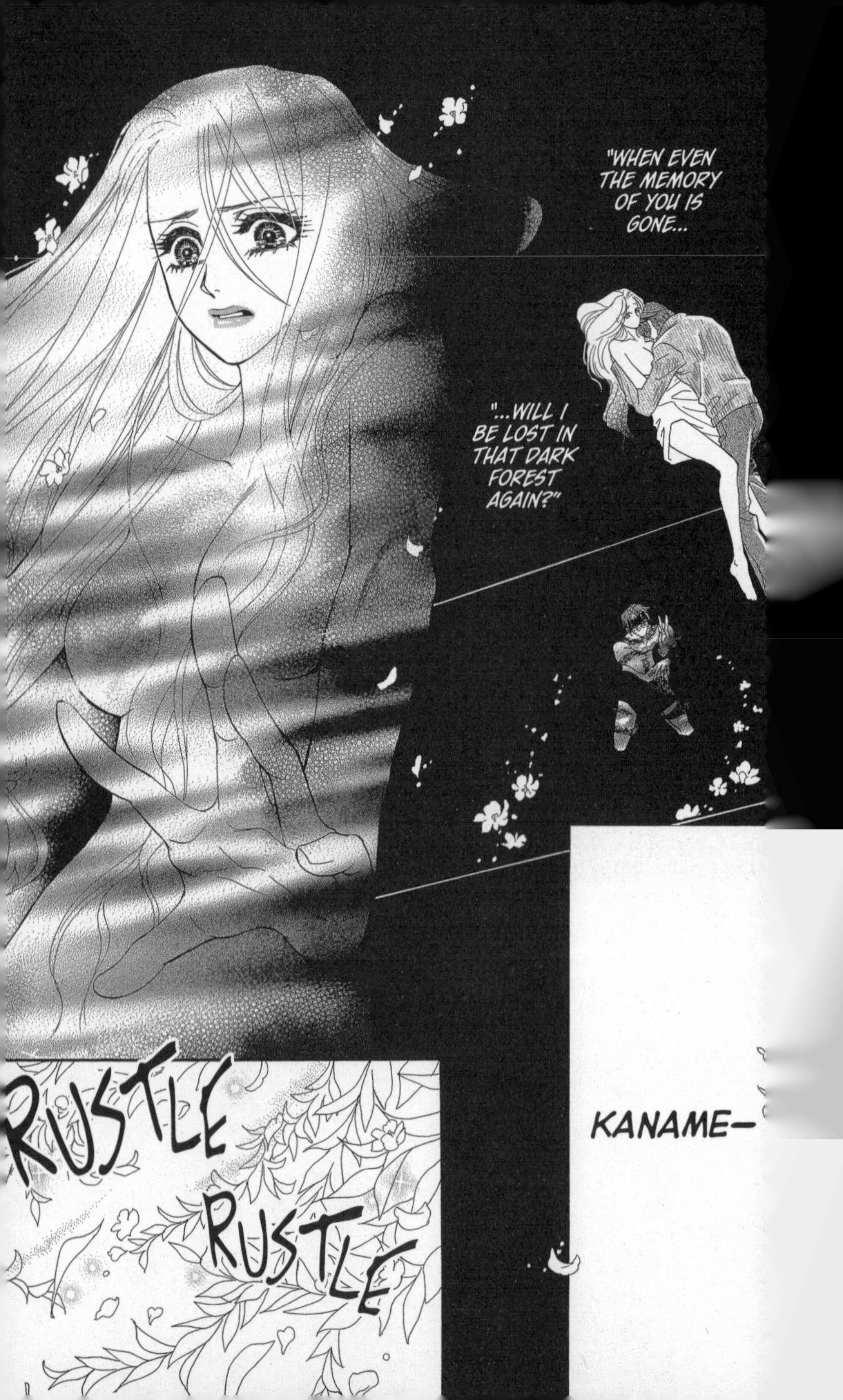
"WHEN EVEN THE MEMORY OF YOU IS GONE...
"...WILL I BE LOST IN THAT DARK FOREST AGAIN?"
KANAME—
RUSTLE
RUSTLE

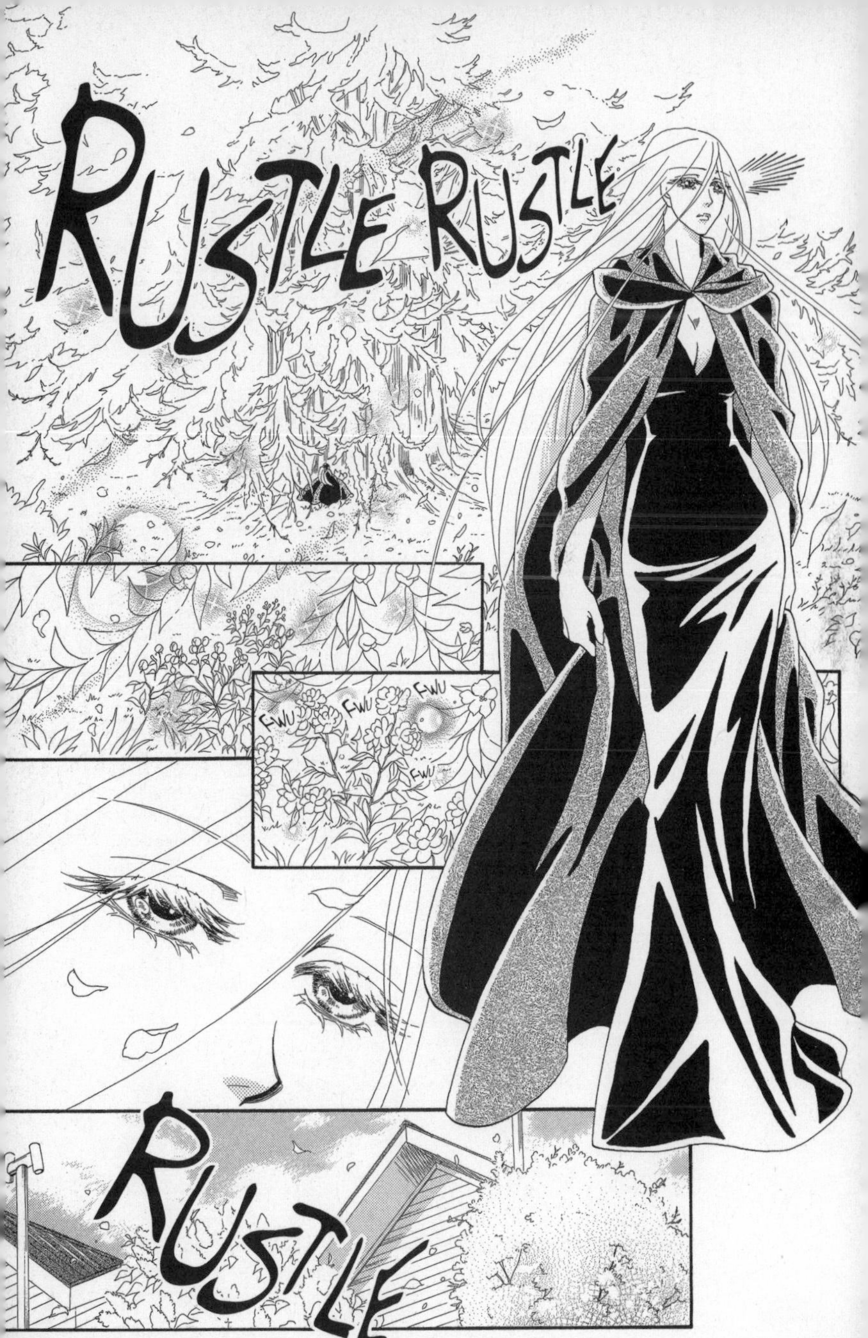
RUSTLE RUSTLE
FWU FWU FWU FWU
RUSTLE

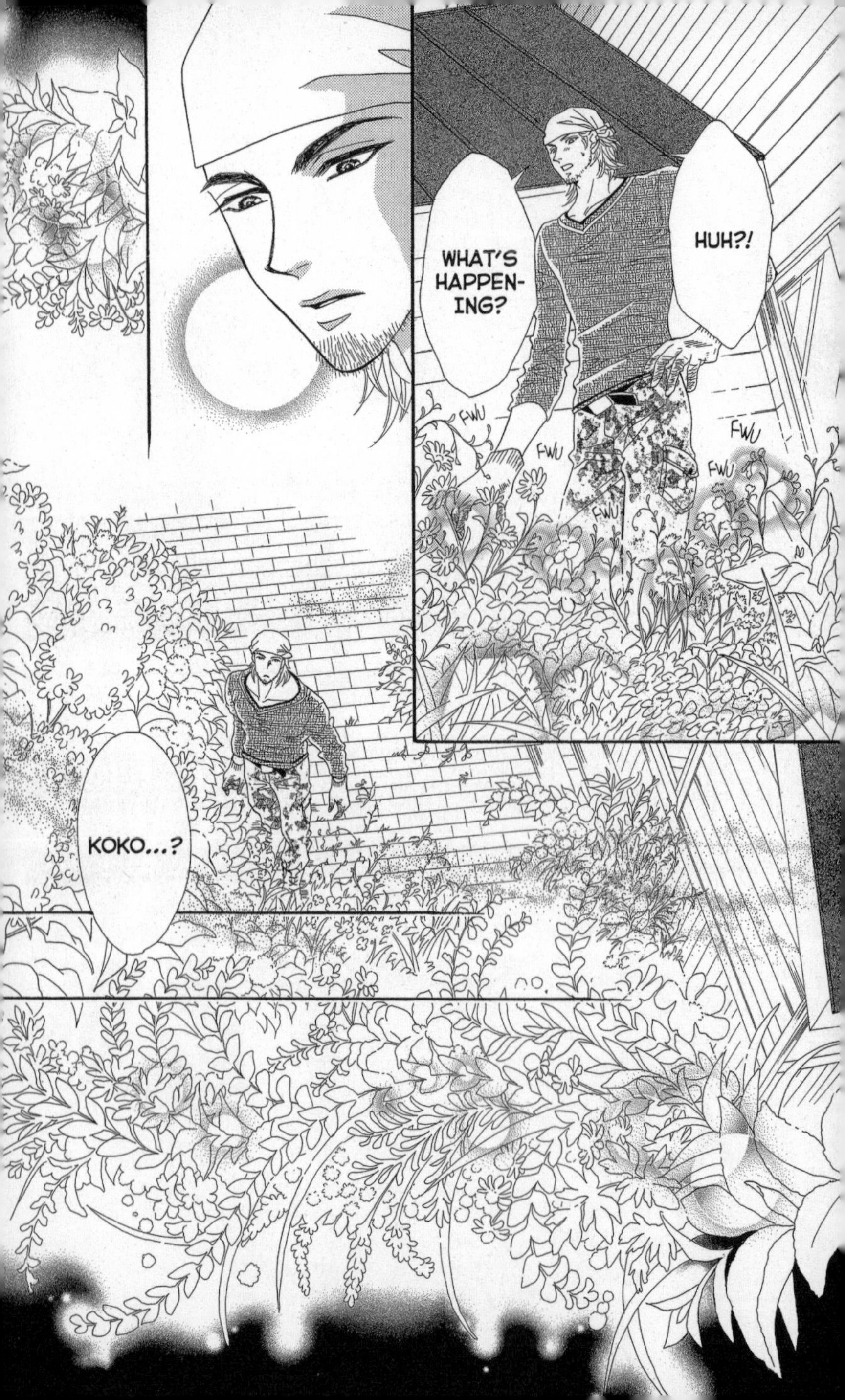
HUH?!
WHAT'S HAPPEN-ING?
FWU
FWU
FWU
FWU
FWU
KOKO...?

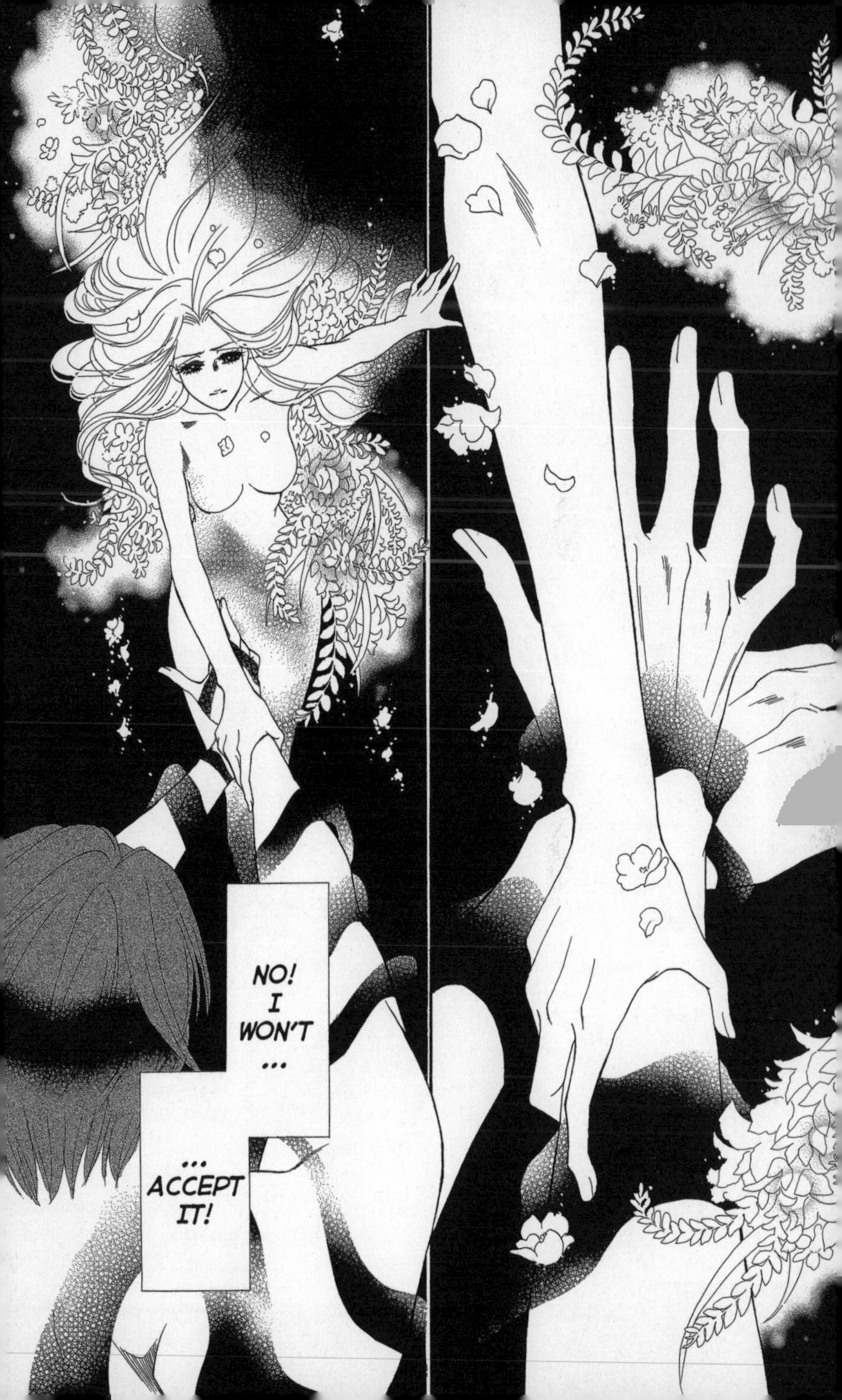
NO! I WON'T ...
... ACCEPT IT!

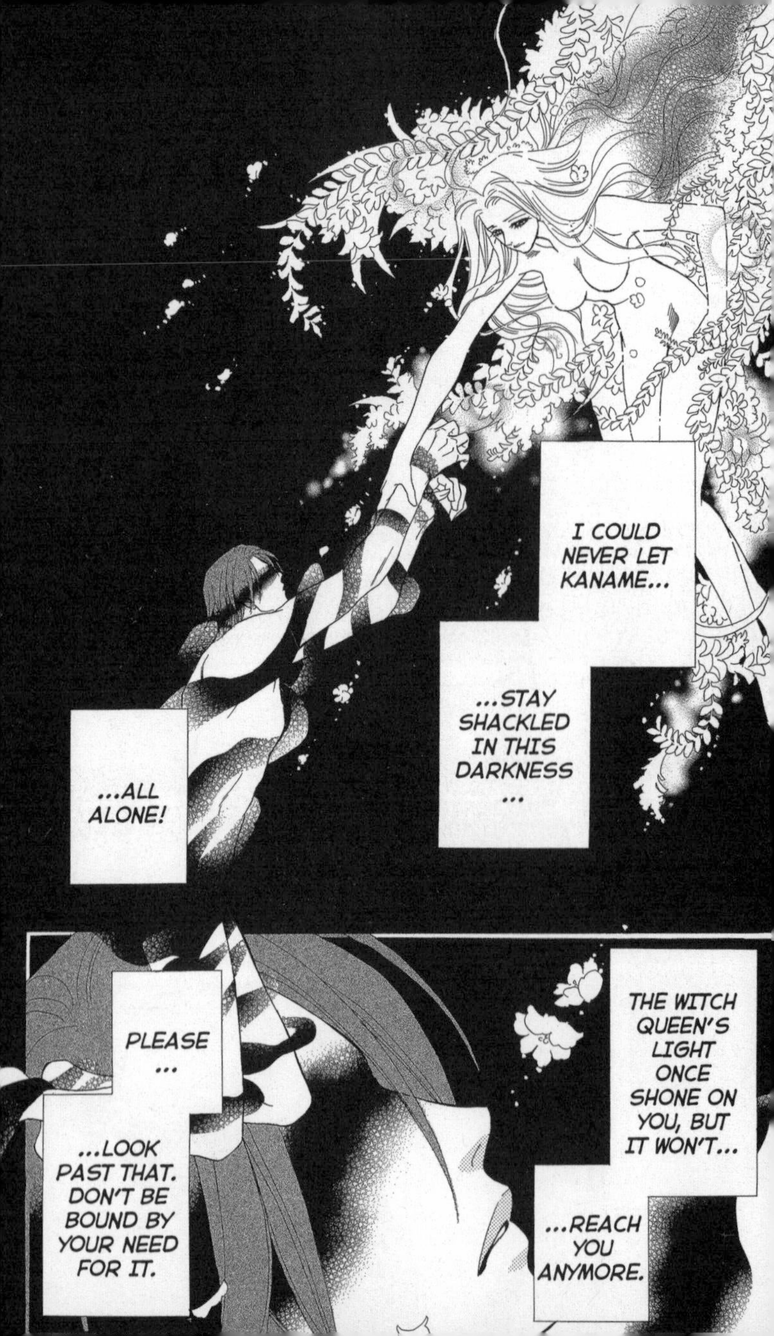
I COULD NEVER LET KANAME...
...STAY SHACKLED IN THIS DARKNESS...
...ALL ALONE!
THE WITCH QUEEN'S LIGHT ONCE SHONE ON YOU, BUT IT WON'T...
...REACH YOU ANYMORE.
PLEASE...
...LOOK PAST THAT. DON'T BE BOUND BY YOUR NEED FOR IT.

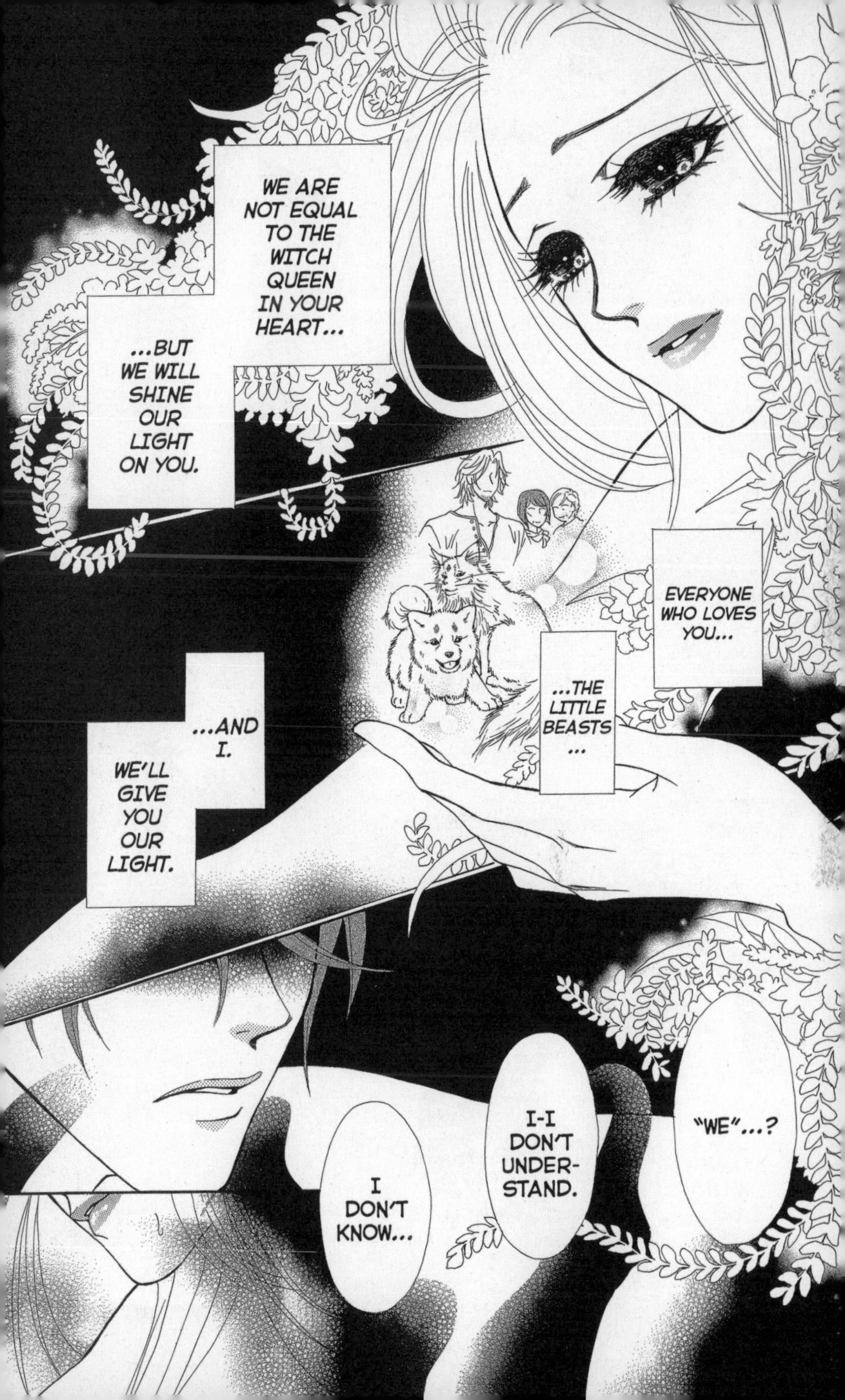
WE ARE NOT EQUAL TO THE WITCH QUEEN IN YOUR HEART...
...BUT WE WILL SHINE OUR LIGHT ON YOU.
EVERYONE WHO LOVES YOU...
...THE LITTLE BEASTS...
...AND I.
WE'LL GIVE YOU OUR LIGHT.
"WE"...?
I-I DON'T UNDER-STAND.
I DON'T KNOW...

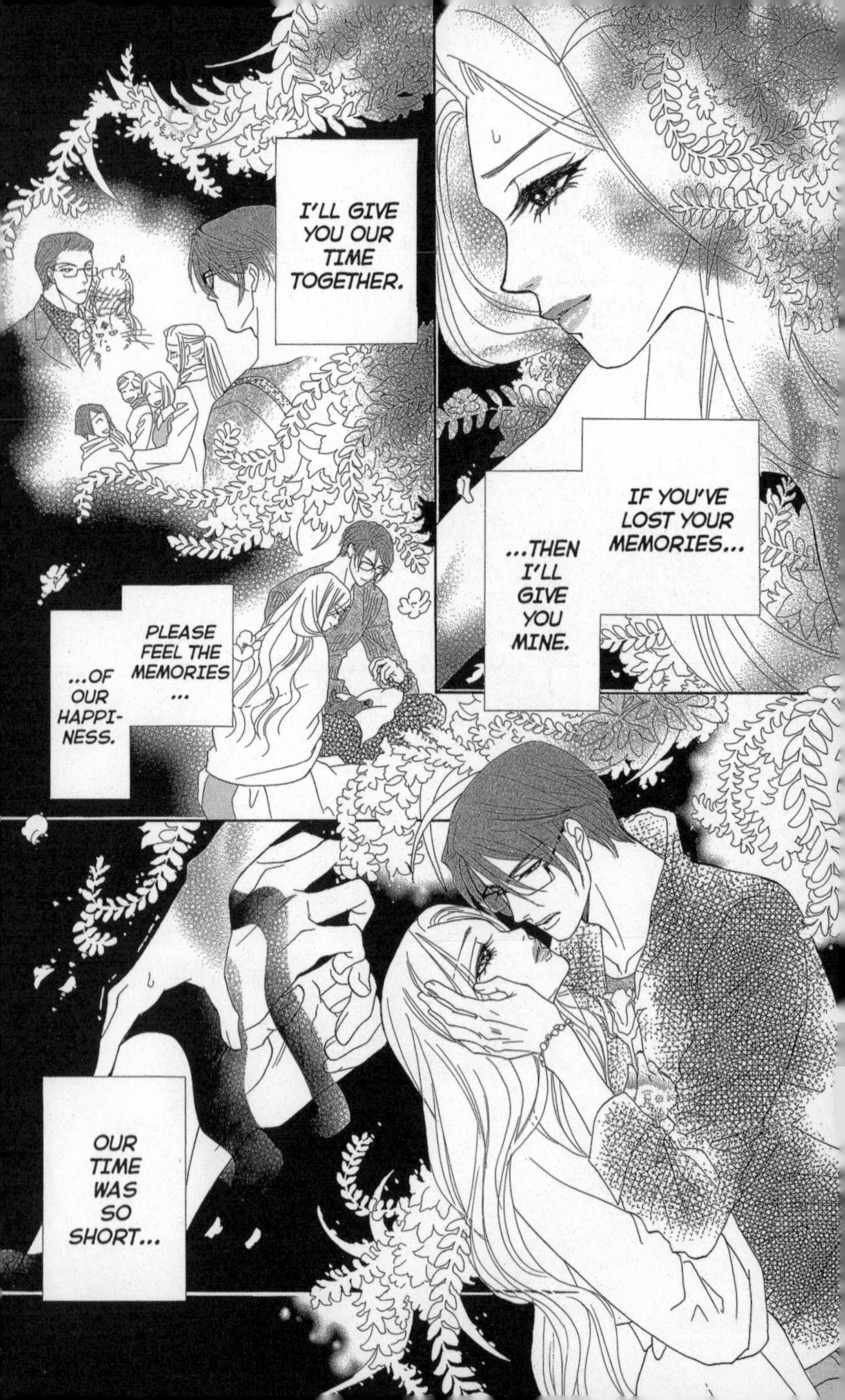
IF YOU'VE LOST YOUR MEMORIES...
...THEN I'LL GIVE YOU MINE.
I'LL GIVE YOU OUR TIME TOGETHER.
PLEASE FEEL THE MEMORIES...
...OF OUR HAPPINESS.
OUR TIME WAS SO SHORT...

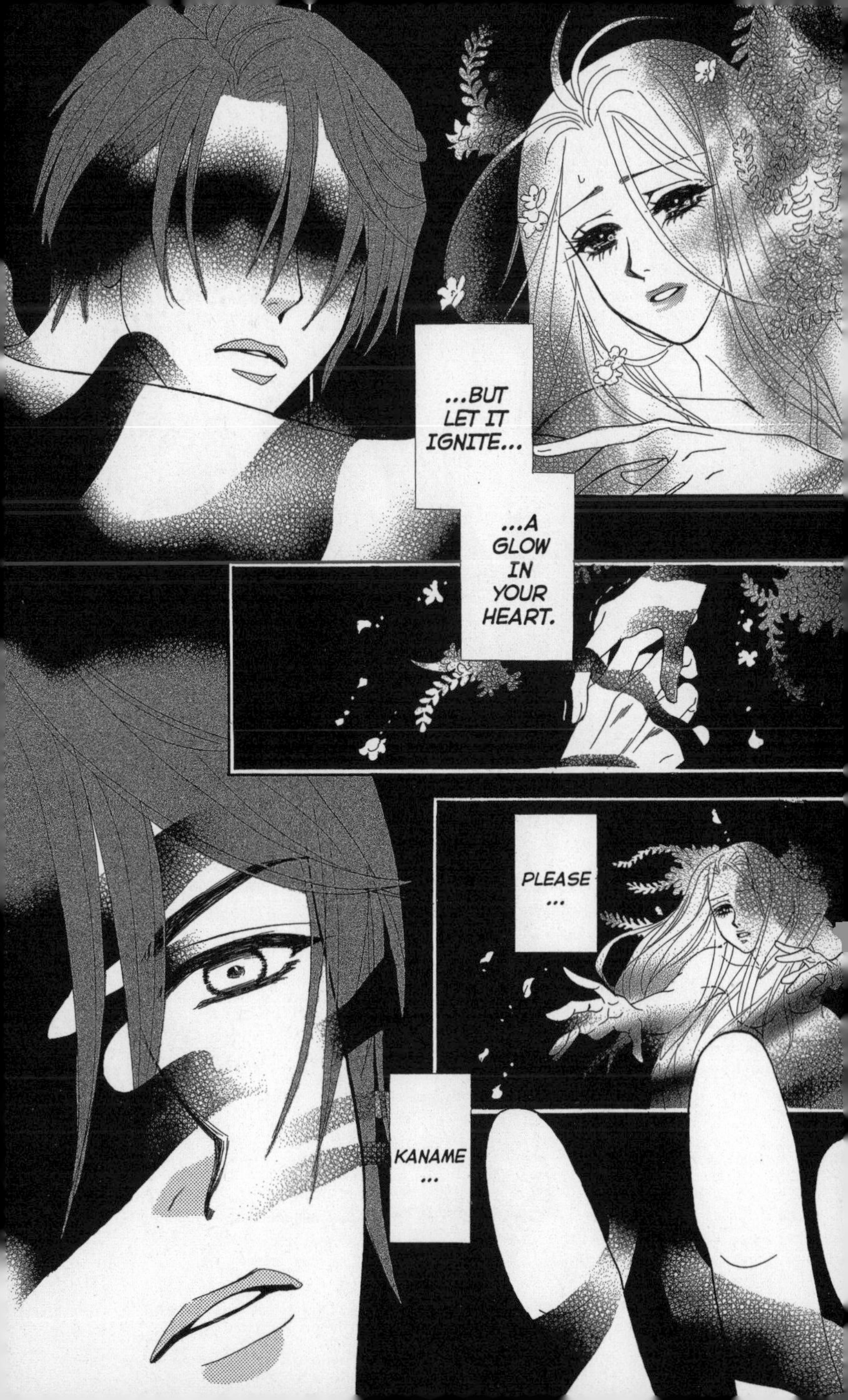
...BUT LET IT IGNITE...
...A GLOW IN YOUR HEART.
PLEASE ...
KANAME ...

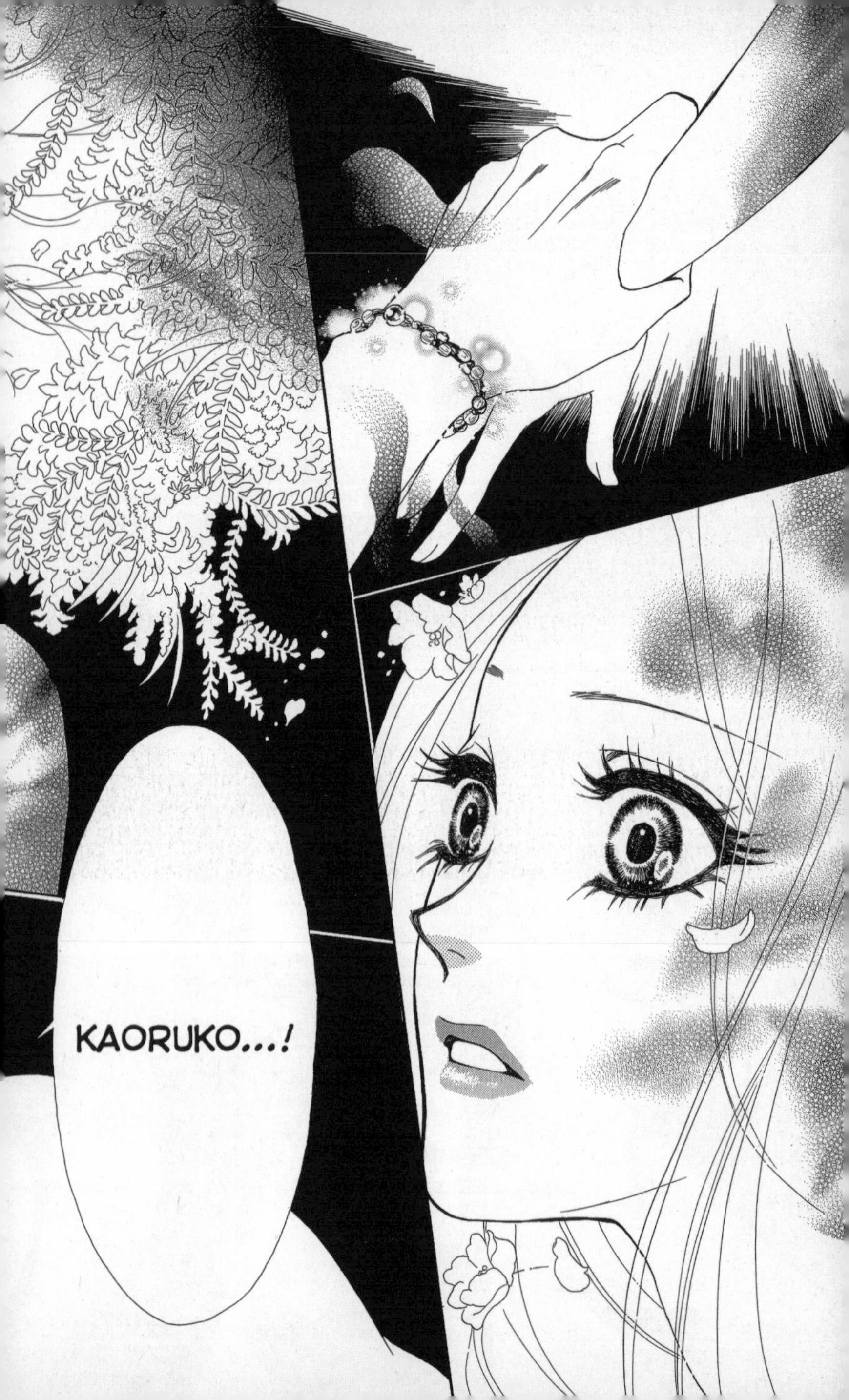
KAORUKO...!

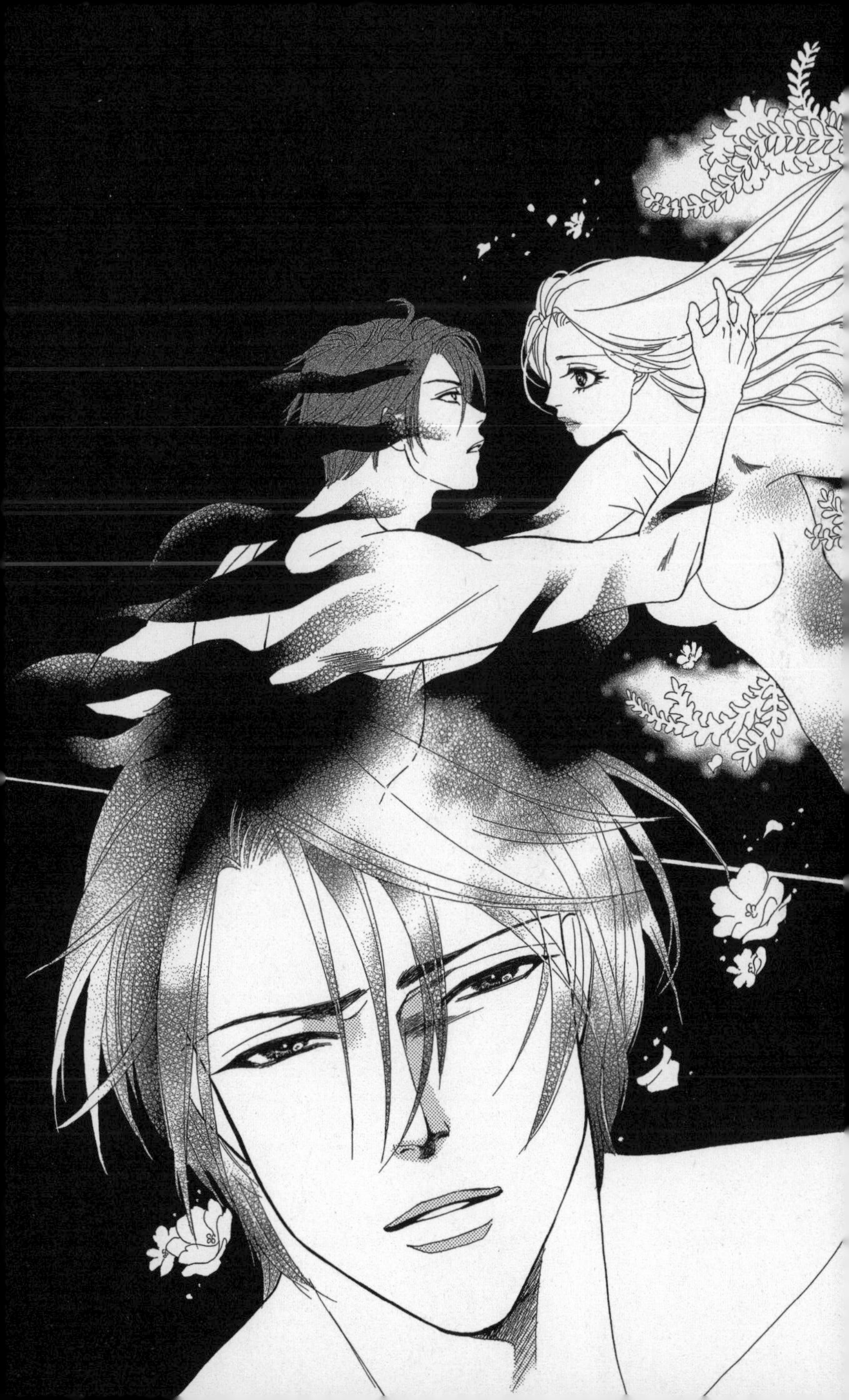

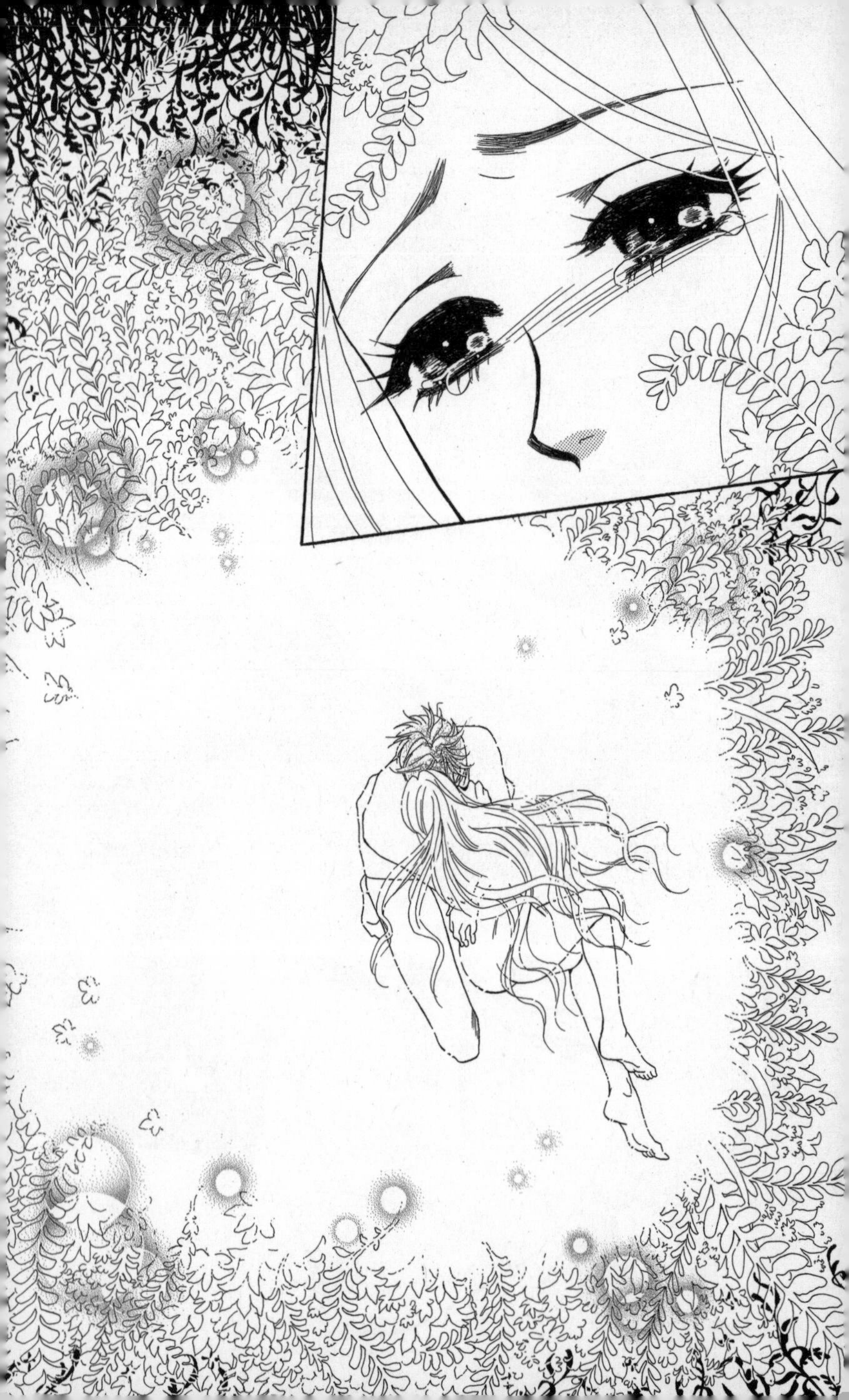

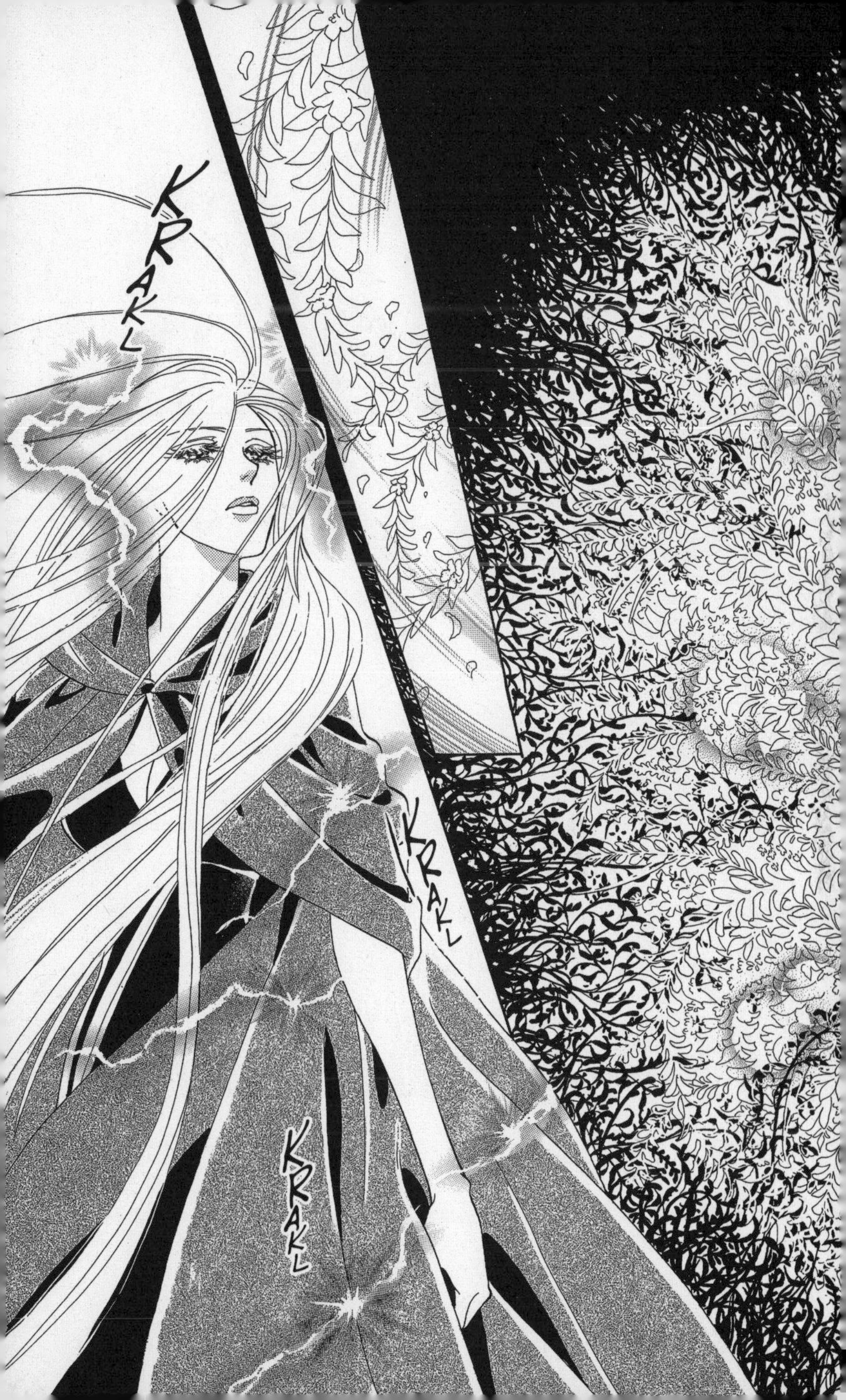
KRAKL
KRAKL
KRAKL

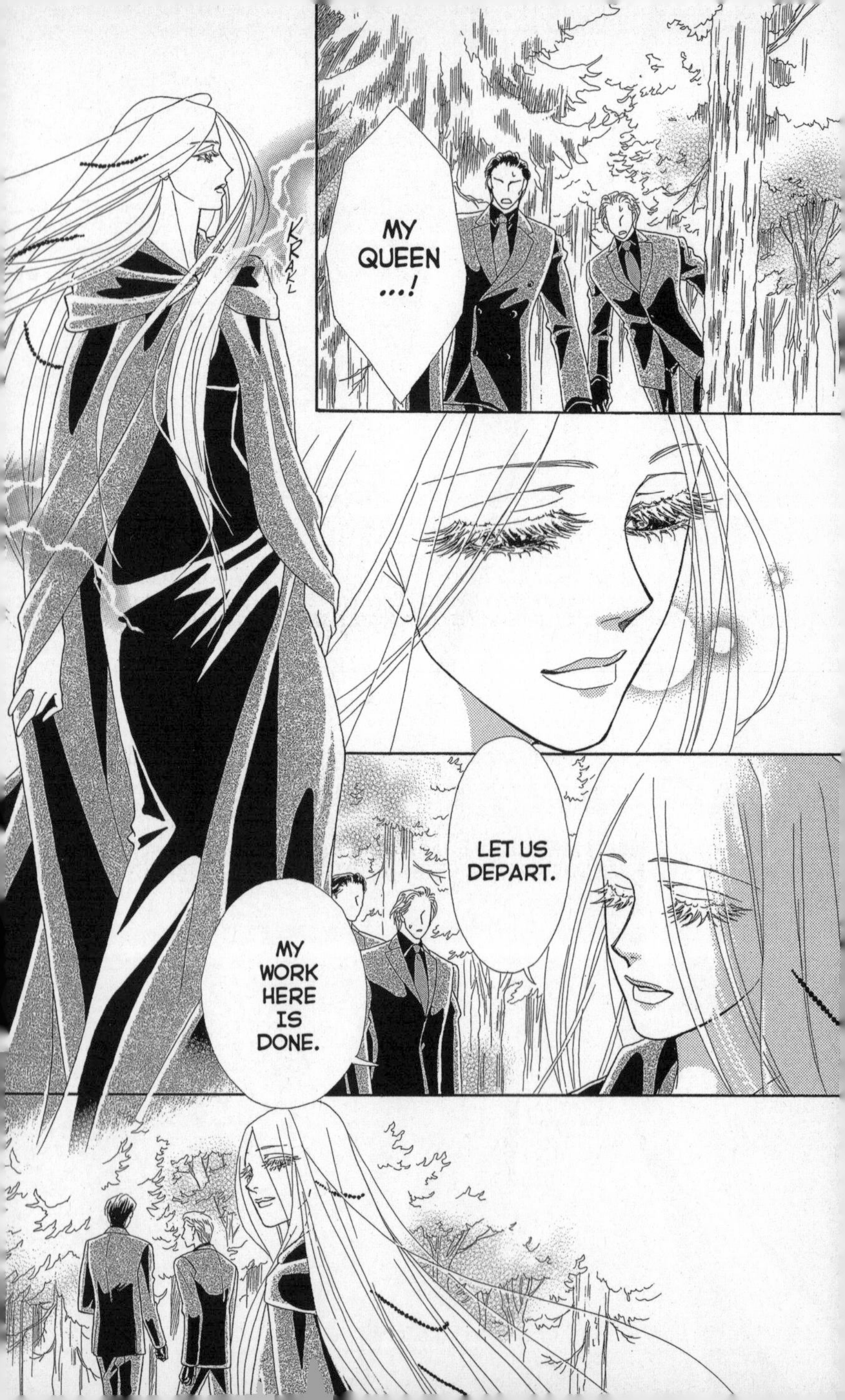
MY QUEEN ...!
LET US DEPART.
MY WORK HERE IS DONE.
KRAKL

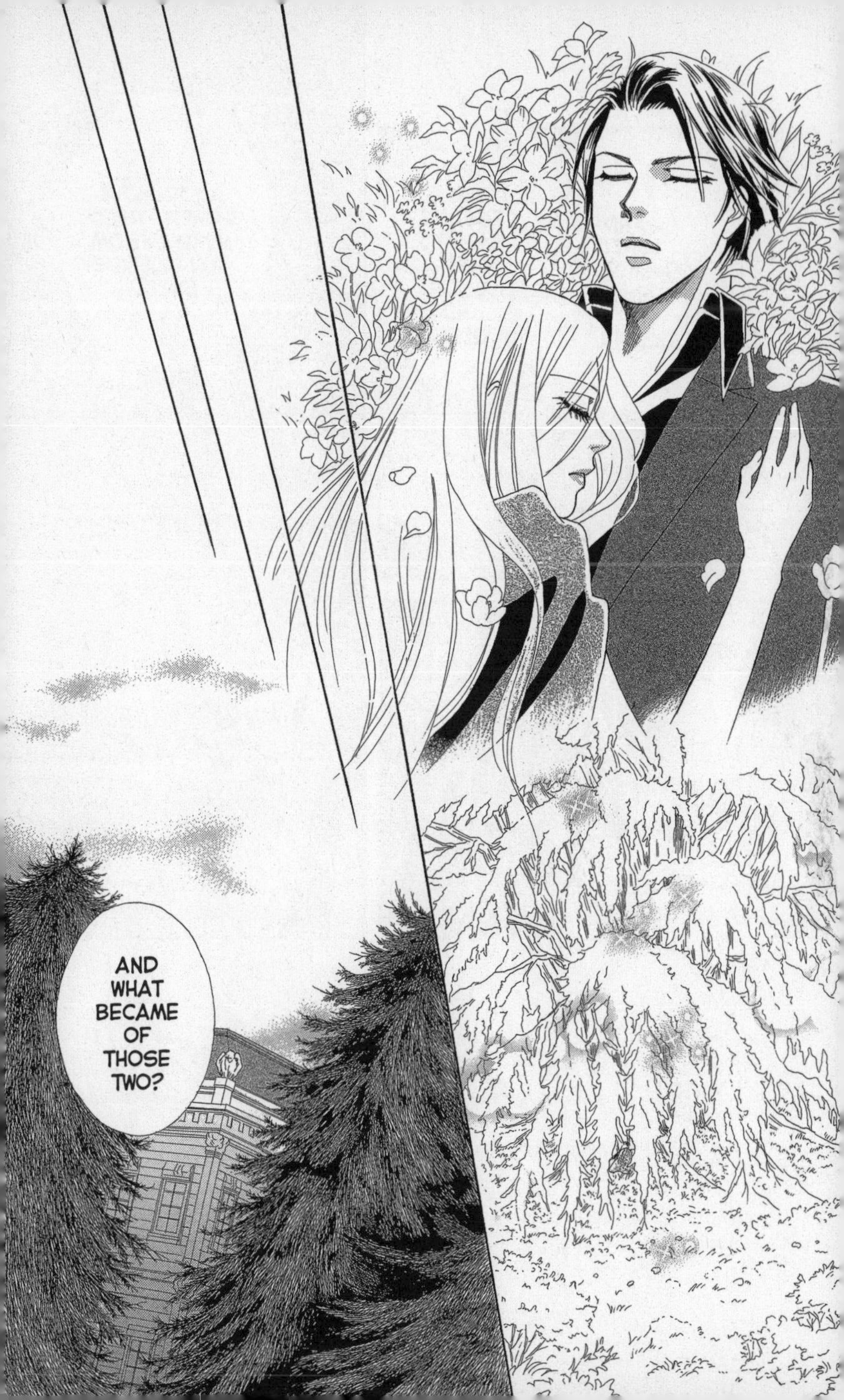
AND WHAT BECAME OF THOSE TWO?

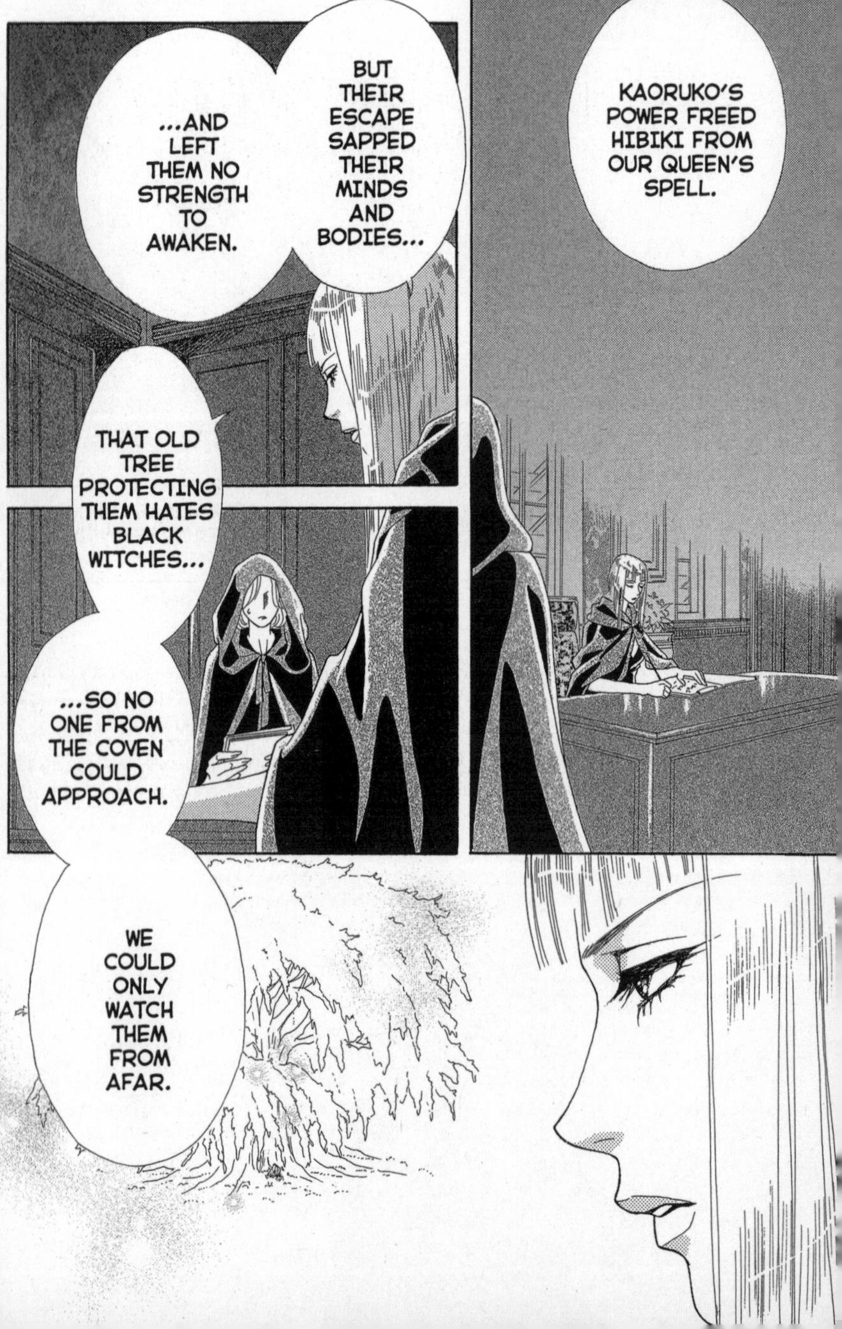
KAORUKO'S POWER FREED HIBIKI FROM OUR QUEEN'S SPELL.
BUT THEIR ESCAPE SAPPED THEIR MINDS AND BODIES...
...AND LEFT THEM NO STRENGTH TO AWAKEN.
THAT OLD TREE PROTECTING THEM HATES BLACK WITCHES...
...SO NO ONE FROM THE COVEN COULD APPROACH.
WE COULD ONLY WATCH THEM FROM AFAR.

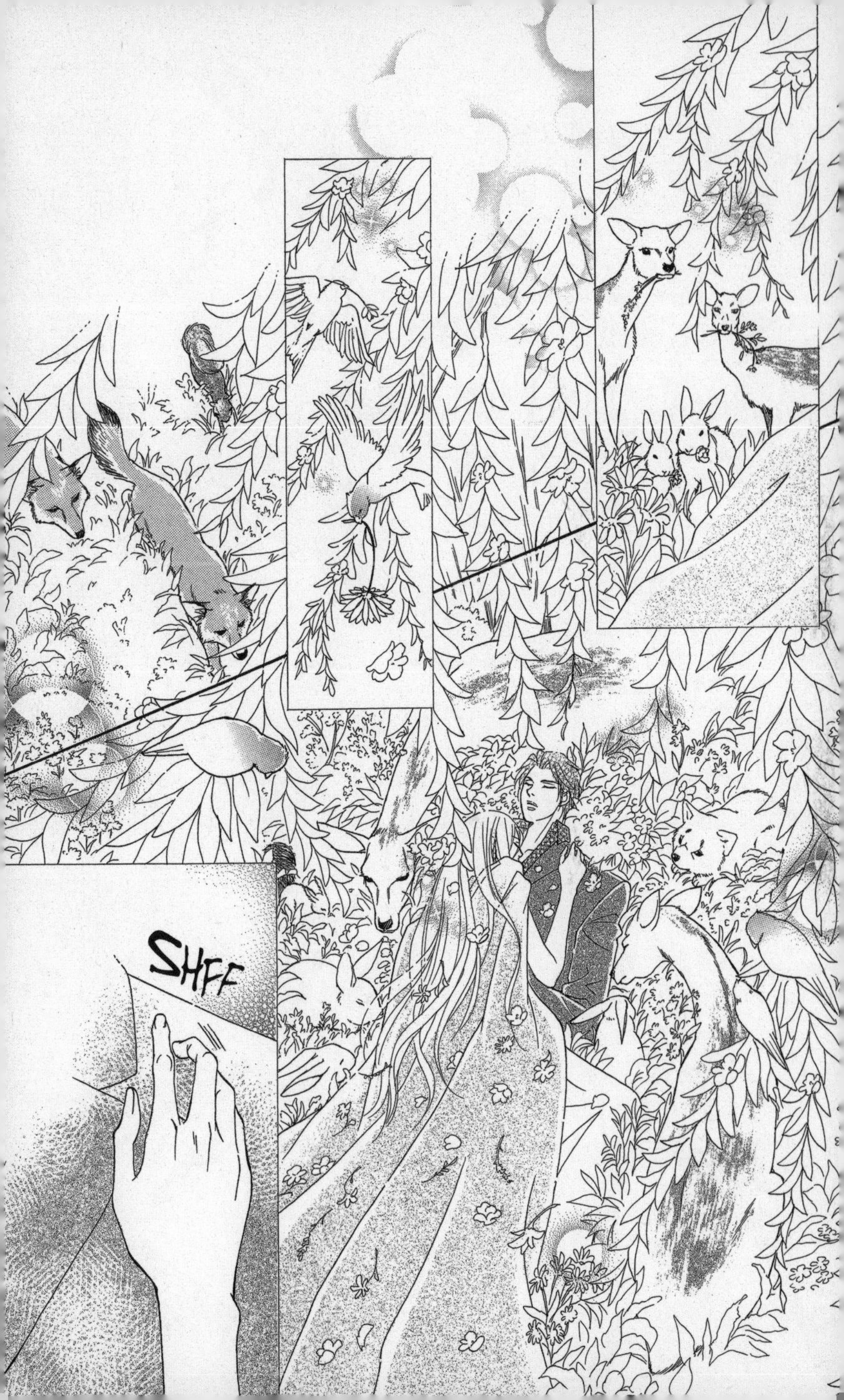
SHFF

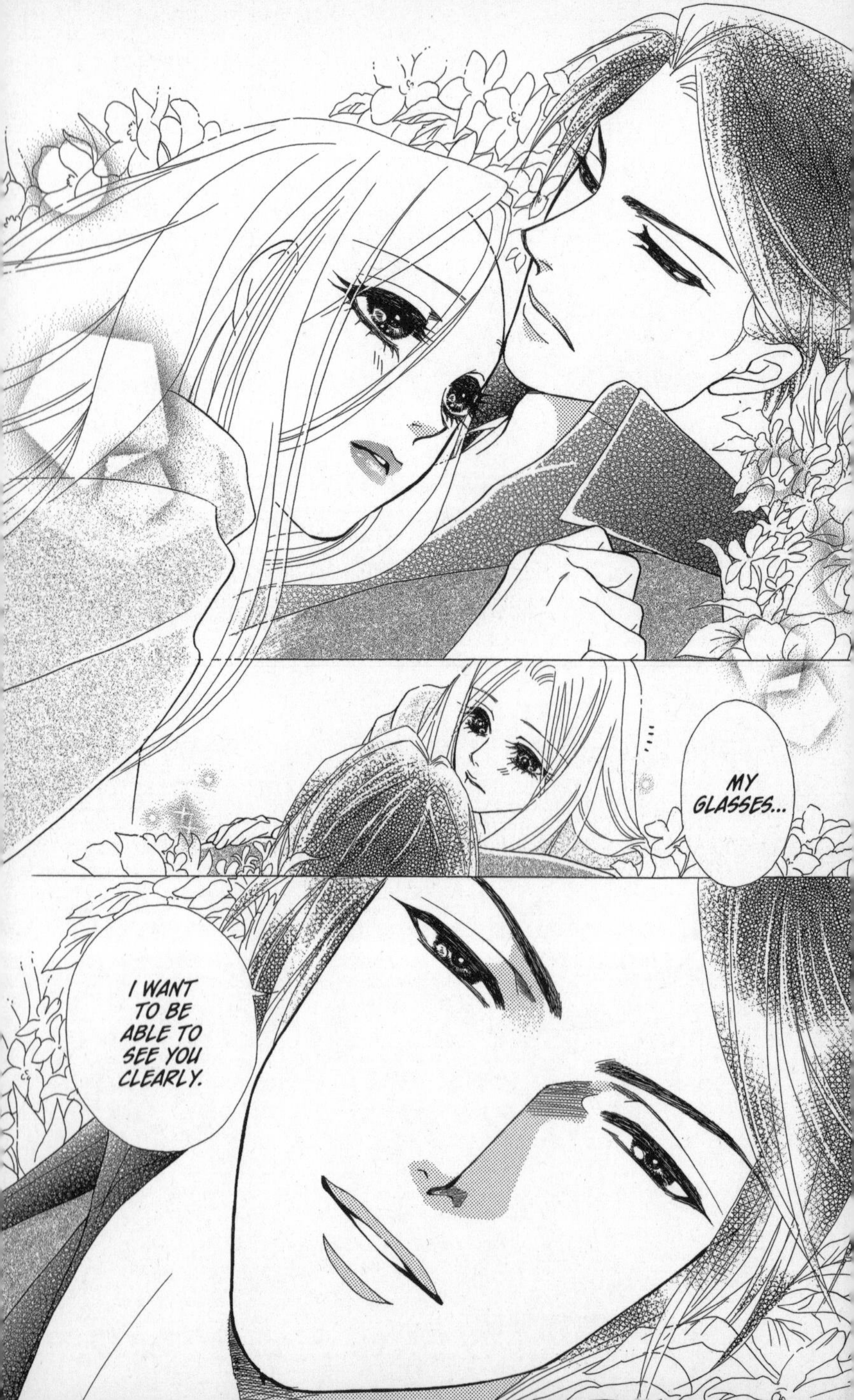
MY GLASSES...
I WANT TO BE ABLE TO SEE YOU CLEARLY.

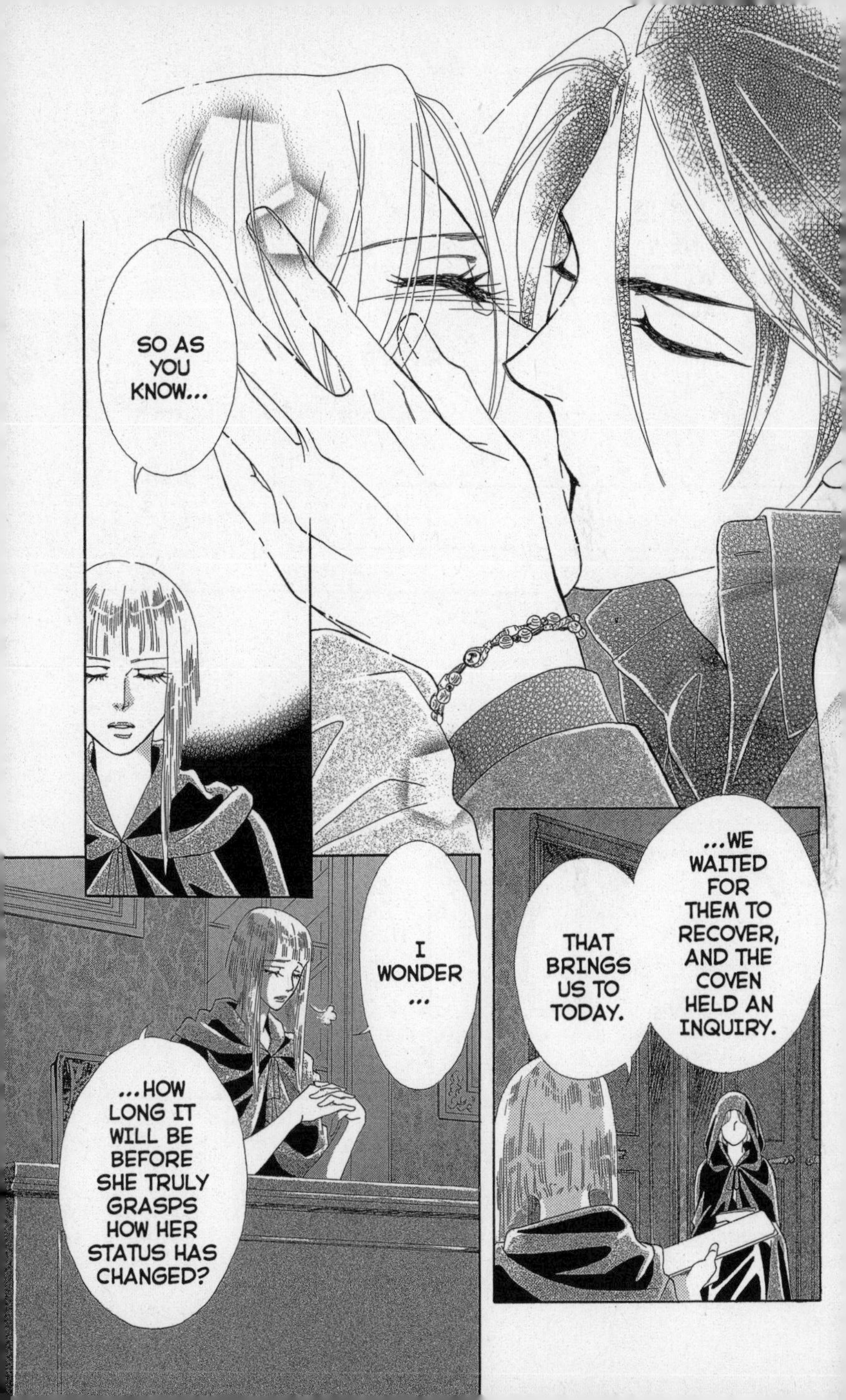
SO AS YOU KNOW...
...WE WAITED FOR THEM TO RECOVER, AND THE COVEN HELD AN INQUIRY.
THAT BRINGS US TO TODAY.
I WONDER...
...HOW LONG IT WILL BE BEFORE SHE TRULY GRASPS HOW HER STATUS HAS CHANGED?

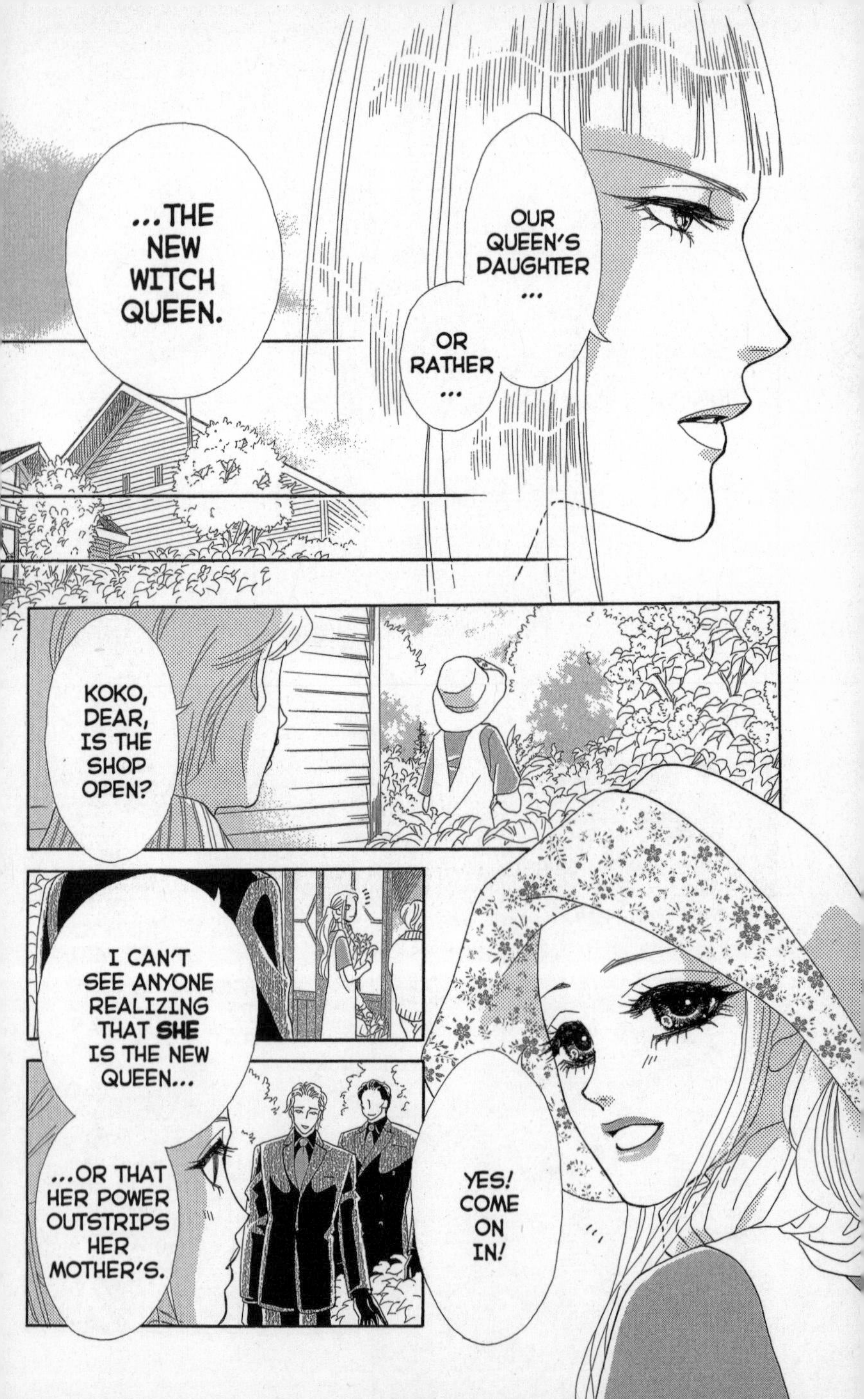
OUR QUEEN'S DAUGHTER ...
OR RATHER ...
...THE NEW WITCH QUEEN.
KOKO, DEAR, IS THE SHOP OPEN?
YES! COME ON IN!
I CAN'T SEE ANYONE REALIZING THAT SHE IS THE NEW QUEEN...
...OR THAT HER POWER OUTSTRIPS HER MOTHER'S.

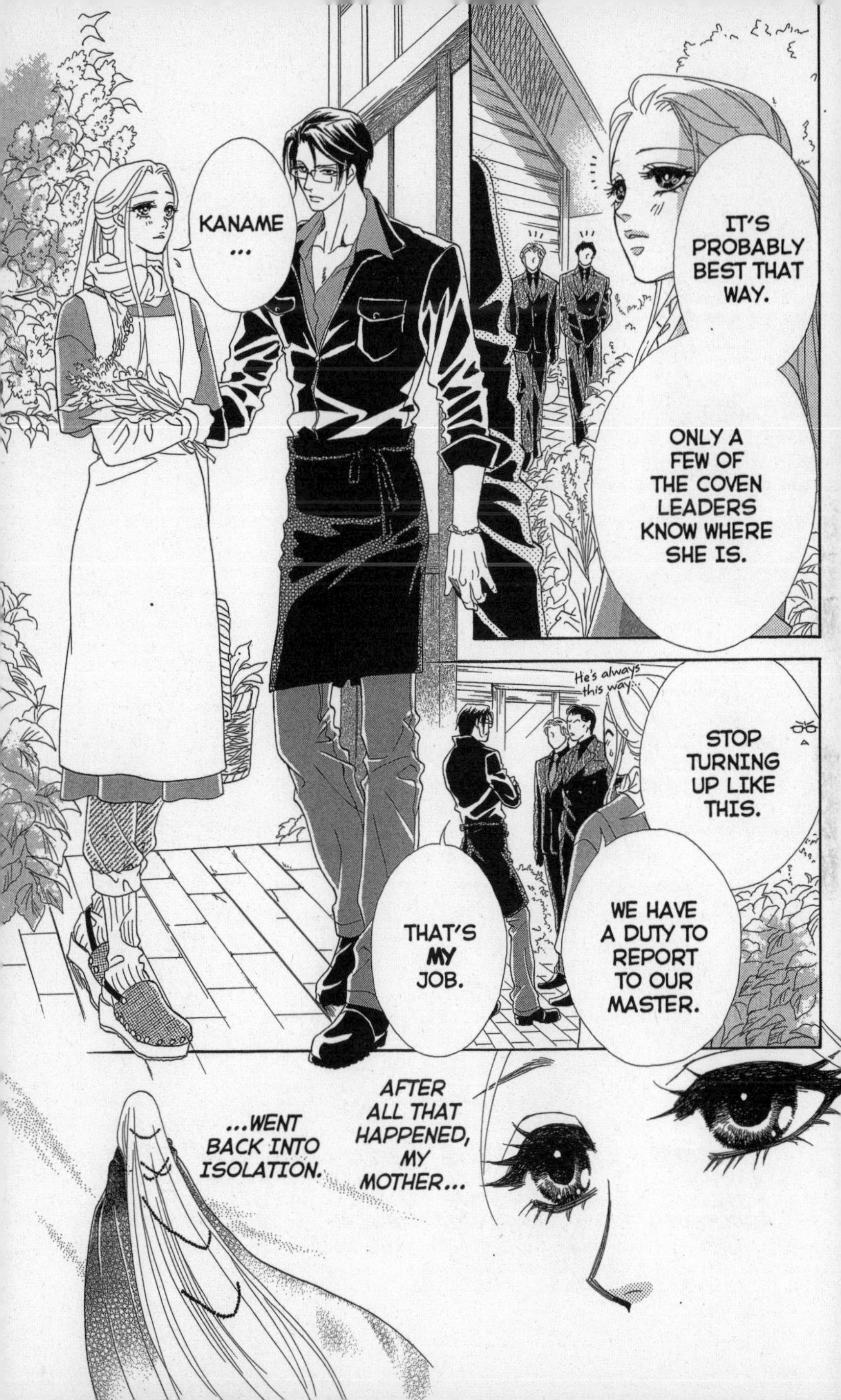
IT'S PROBABLY BEST THAT WAY.
ONLY A FEW OF THE COVEN LEADERS KNOW WHERE SHE IS.
STOP TURNING UP LIKE THIS.
He's always this way...
WE HAVE A DUTY TO REPORT TO OUR MASTER.
THAT'S MY JOB.
KANAME ...
AFTER ALL THAT HAPPENED, MY MOTHER...
...WENT BACK INTO ISOLATION.

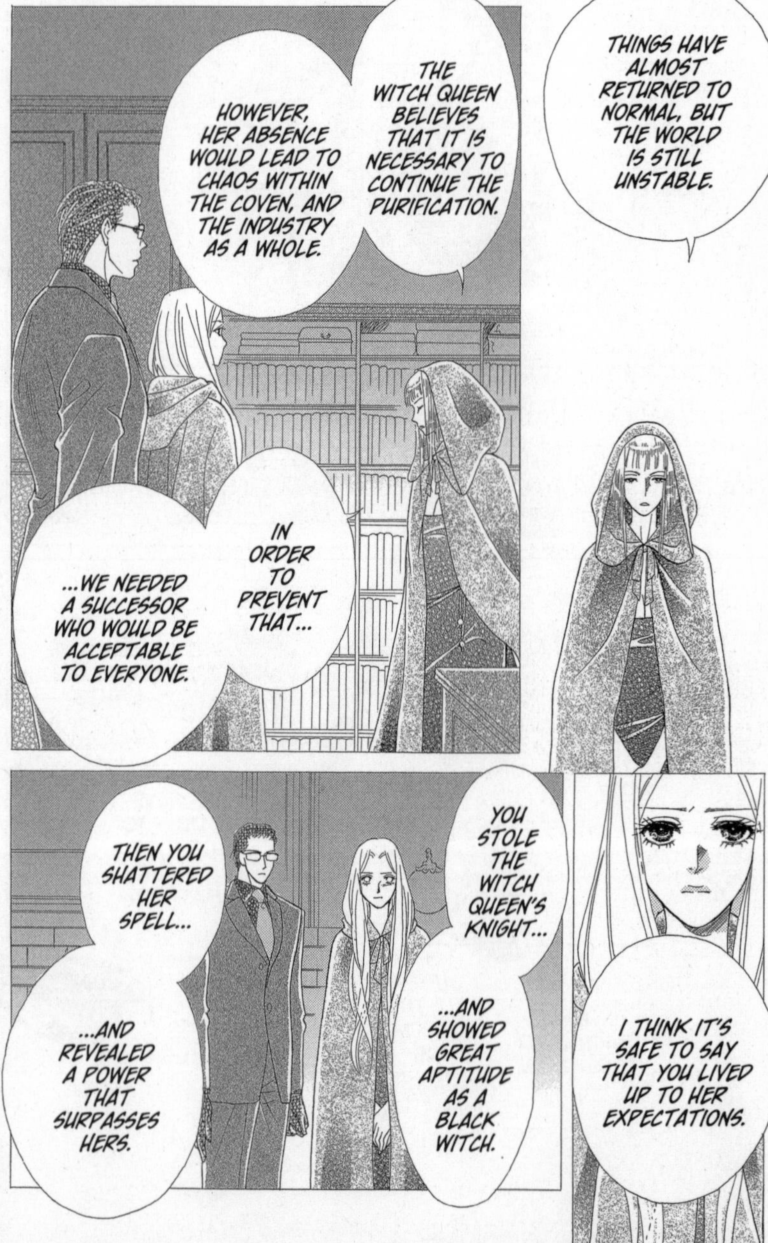
THINGS HAVE ALMOST RETURNED TO NORMAL, BUT THE WORLD IS STILL UNSTABLE.
THE WITCH QUEEN BELIEVES THAT IT IS NECESSARY TO CONTINUE THE PURIFICATION.
HOWEVER, HER ABSENCE WOULD LEAD TO CHAOS WITHIN THE COVEN, AND THE INDUSTRY AS A WHOLE.
IN ORDER TO PREVENT THAT...
...WE NEEDED A SUCCESSOR WHO WOULD BE ACCEPTABLE TO EVERYONE.
I THINK IT'S SAFE TO SAY THAT YOU LIVED UP TO HER EXPECTATIONS.
YOU STOLE THE WITCH QUEEN'S KNIGHT...
...AND SHOWED GREAT APTITUDE AS A BLACK WITCH.
THEN YOU SHATTERED HER SPELL...
...AND REVEALED A POWER THAT SURPASSES HERS.

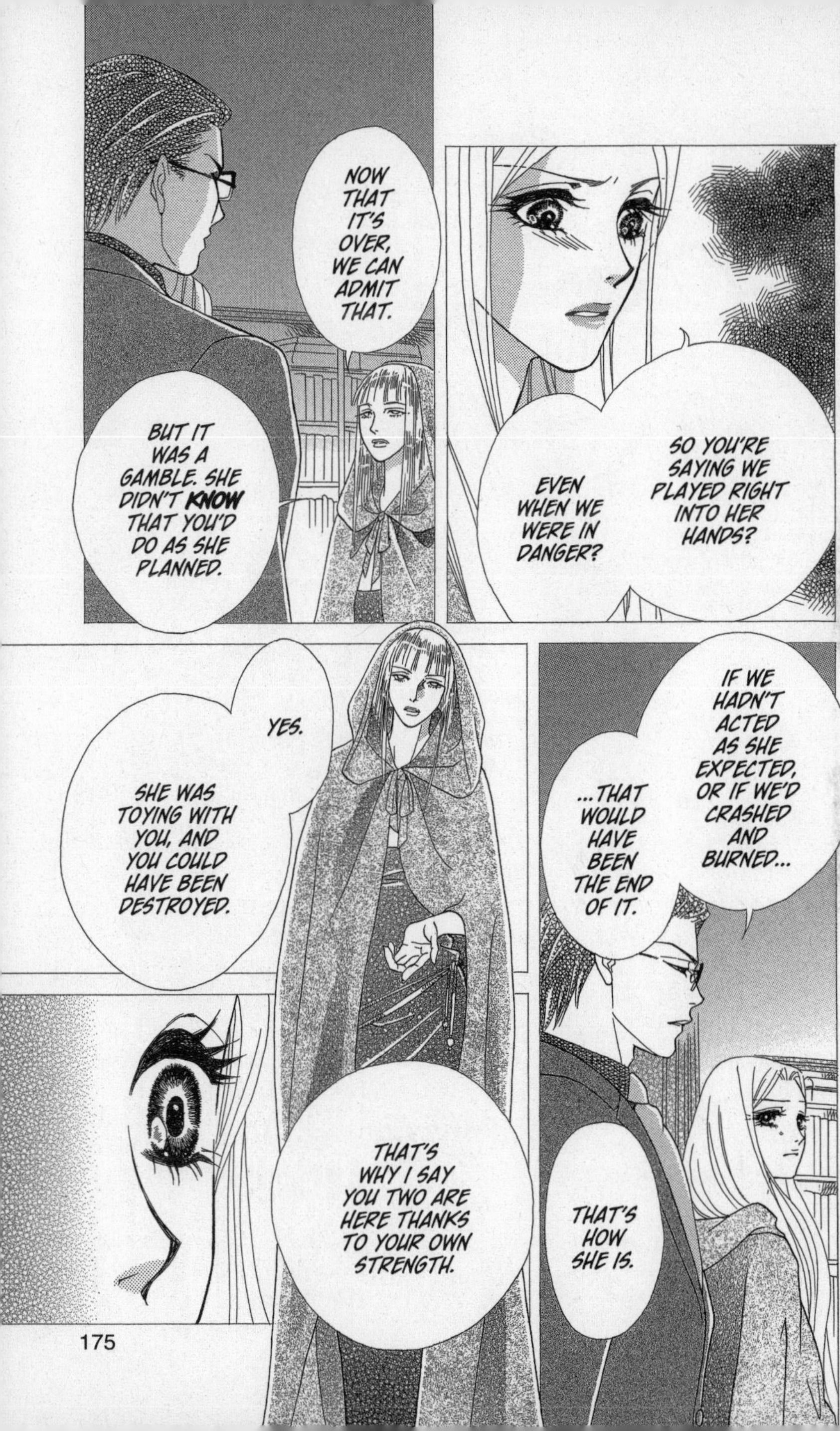
SO YOU'RE SAYING WE PLAYED RIGHT INTO HER HANDS?
EVEN WHEN WE WERE IN DANGER?
NOW THAT IT'S OVER, WE CAN ADMIT THAT.
BUT IT WAS A GAMBLE. SHE DIDN'T **KNOW** THAT YOU'D DO AS SHE PLANNED.
IF WE HADN'T ACTED AS SHE EXPECTED, OR IF WE'D CRASHED AND BURNED...
...THAT WOULD HAVE BEEN THE END OF IT.
YES.
SHE WAS TOYING WITH YOU, AND YOU COULD HAVE BEEN DESTROYED.
THAT'S HOW SHE IS.
THAT'S WHY I SAY YOU TWO ARE HERE THANKS TO YOUR OWN STRENGTH.

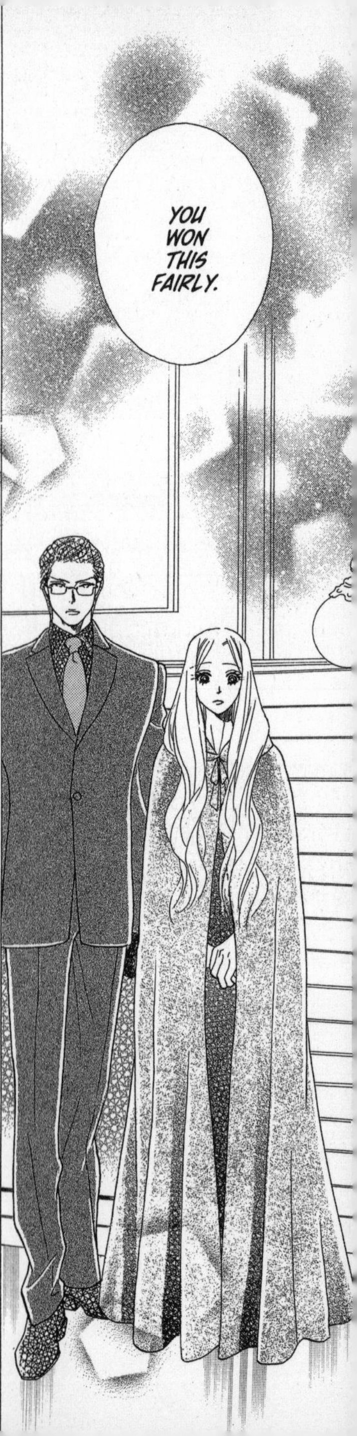
YOU WON THIS FAIRLY.

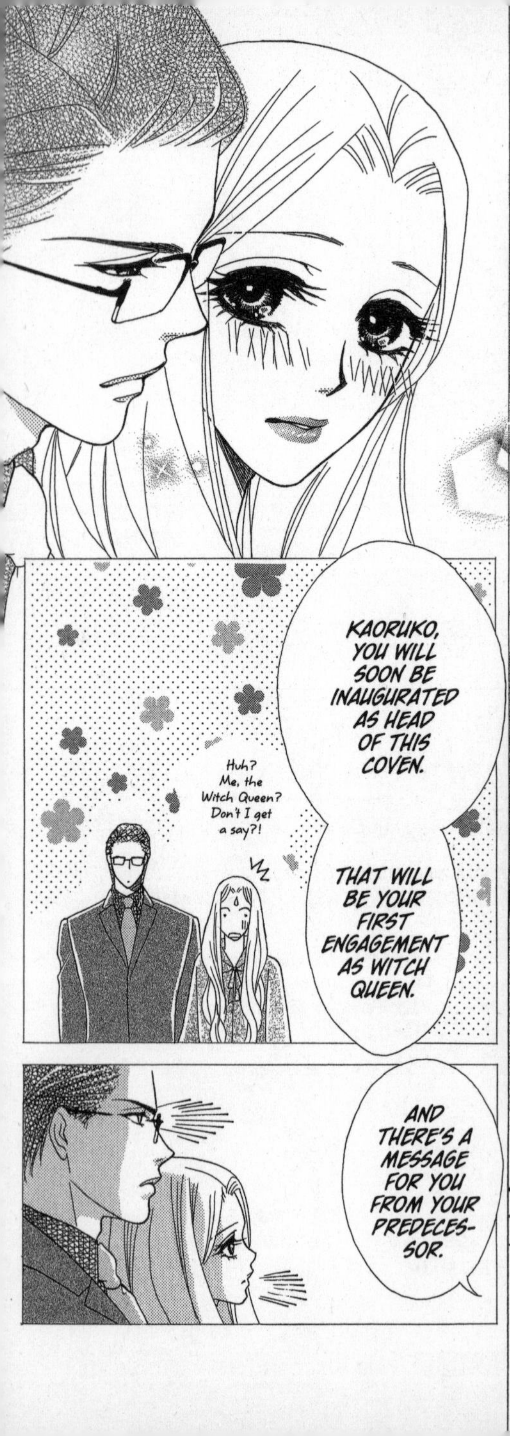
KAORUKO, YOU WILL SOON BE INAUGURATED AS HEAD OF THIS COVEN.
THAT WILL BE YOUR FIRST ENGAGEMENT AS WITCH QUEEN.
Huh? Me, the Witch Queen? Don't I get a say?!
AND THERE'S A MESSAGE FOR YOU FROM YOUR PREDECES-SOR.

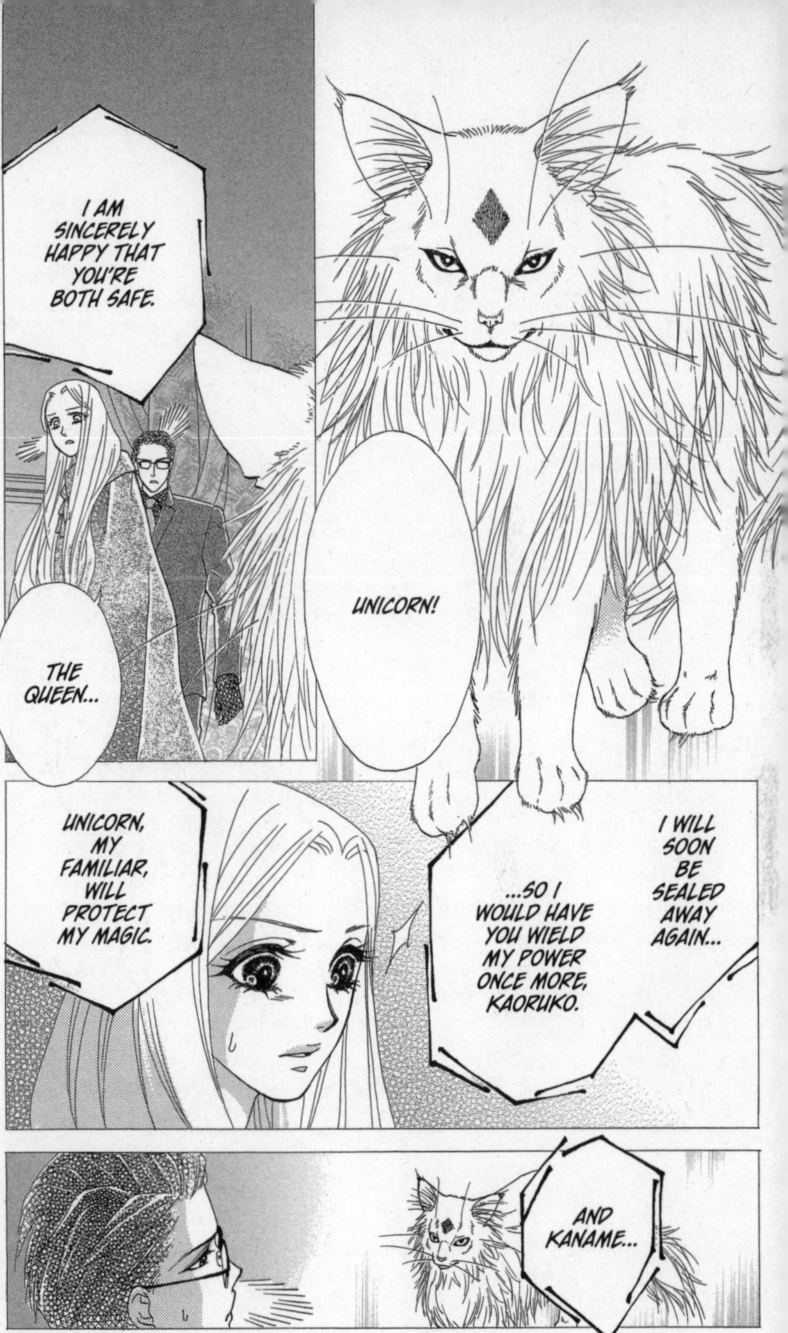
UNICORN!
I AM SINCERELY HAPPY THAT YOU'RE BOTH SAFE.
THE QUEEN...
I WILL SOON BE SEALED AWAY AGAIN...
...SO I WOULD HAVE YOU WIELD MY POWER ONCE MORE, KAORUKO.
UNICORN, MY FAMILIAR, WILL PROTECT MY MAGIC.
AND KANAME...

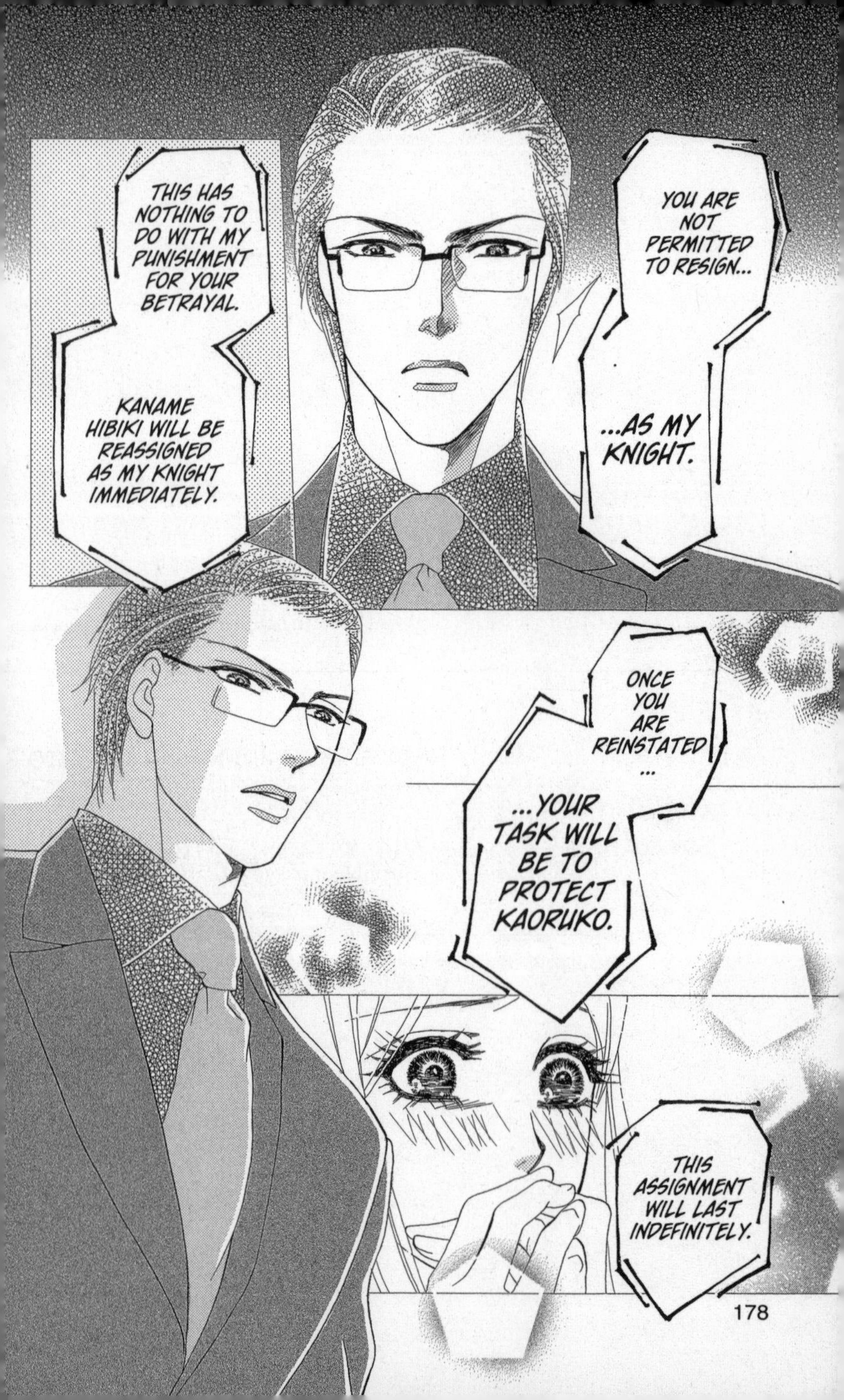
YOU ARE NOT PERMITTED TO RESIGN...
...AS MY KNIGHT.
THIS HAS NOTHING TO DO WITH MY PUNISHMENT FOR YOUR BETRAYAL.
KANAME HIBIKI WILL BE REASSIGNED AS MY KNIGHT IMMEDIATELY.
ONCE YOU ARE REINSTATED...
...YOUR TASK WILL BE TO PROTECT KAORUKO.
THIS ASSIGNMENT WILL LAST INDEFINITELY.

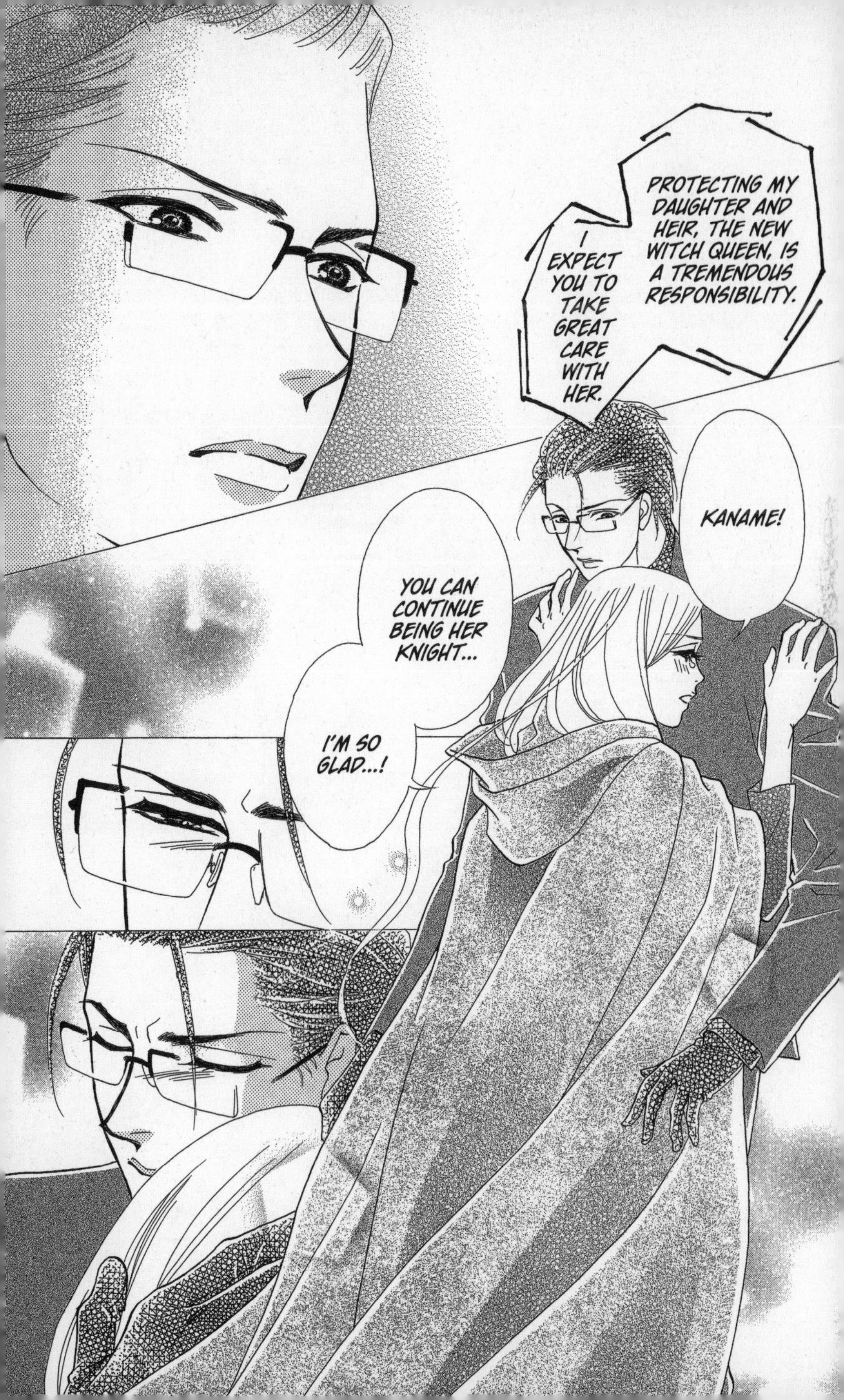
PROTECTING MY DAUGHTER AND HEIR, THE NEW WITCH QUEEN, IS A TREMENDOUS RESPONSIBILITY.
I EXPECT YOU TO TAKE GREAT CARE WITH HER.
KANAME!
YOU CAN CONTINUE BEING HER KNIGHT...
I'M SO GLAD...!

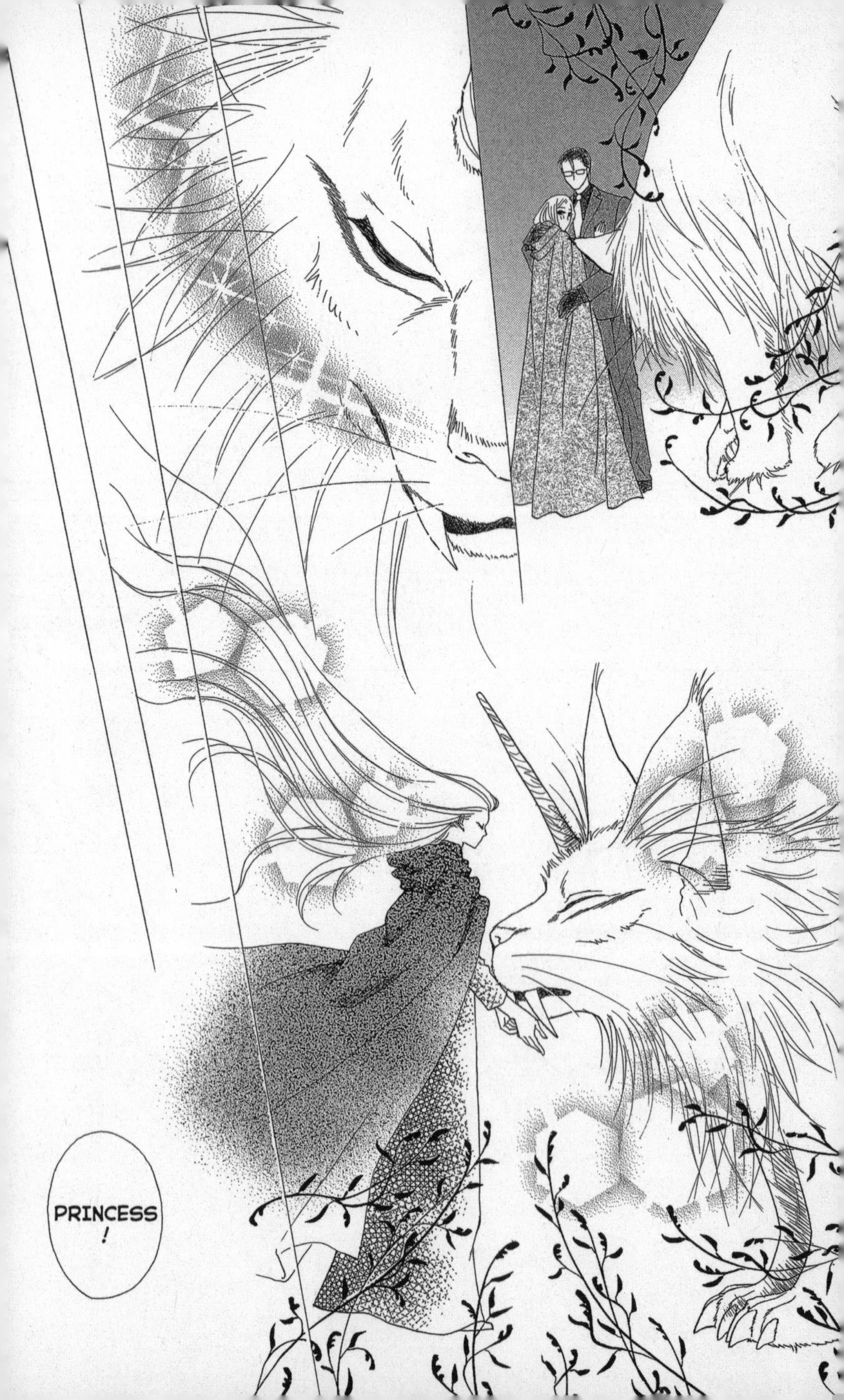
PRINCESS!

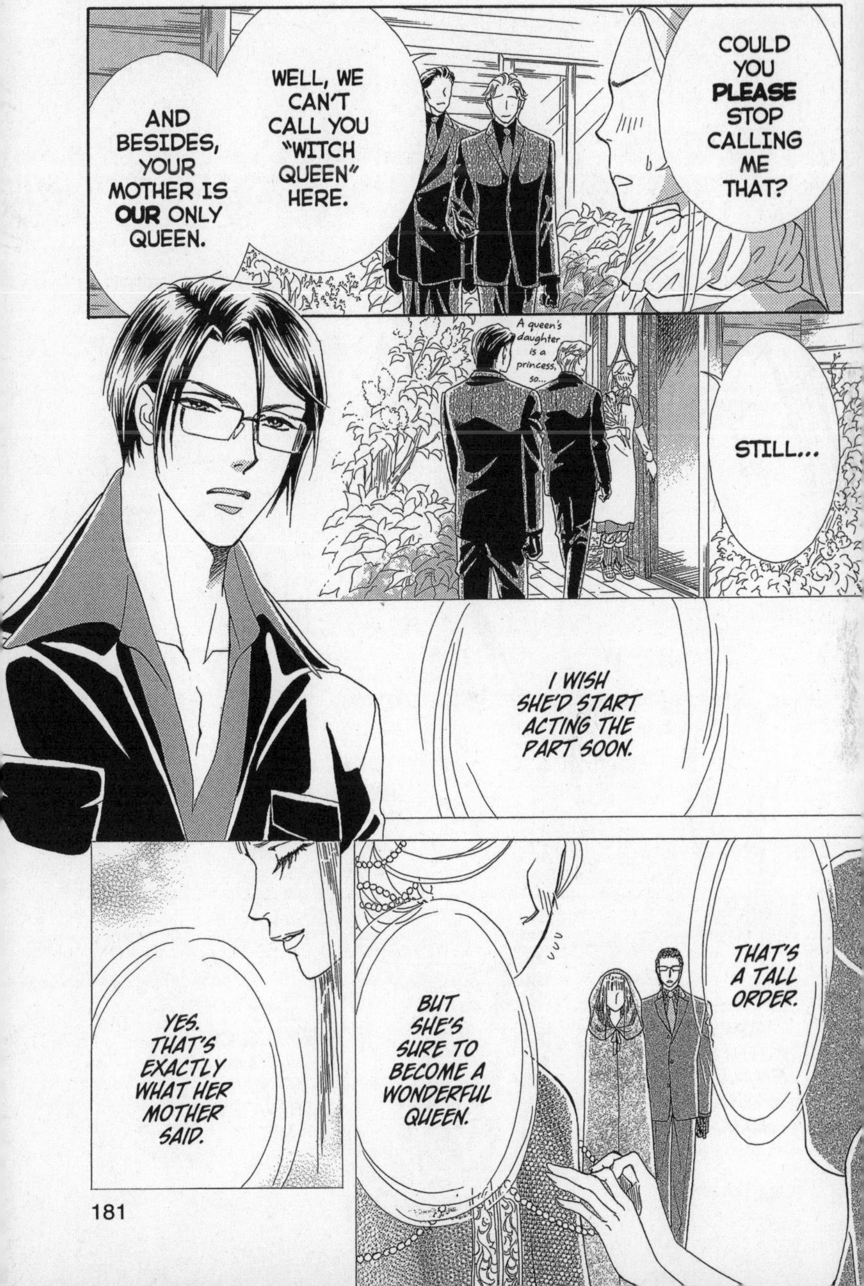
COULD YOU PLEASE STOP CALLING ME THAT?
WELL, WE CAN'T CALL YOU "WITCH QUEEN" HERE.
AND BESIDES, YOUR MOTHER IS OUR ONLY QUEEN.
STILL...
A queen's daughter is a princess, so...
I WISH SHE'D START ACTING THE PART SOON.
THAT'S A TALL ORDER.
BUT SHE'S SURE TO BECOME A WONDERFUL QUEEN.
YES. THAT'S EXACTLY WHAT HER MOTHER SAID.

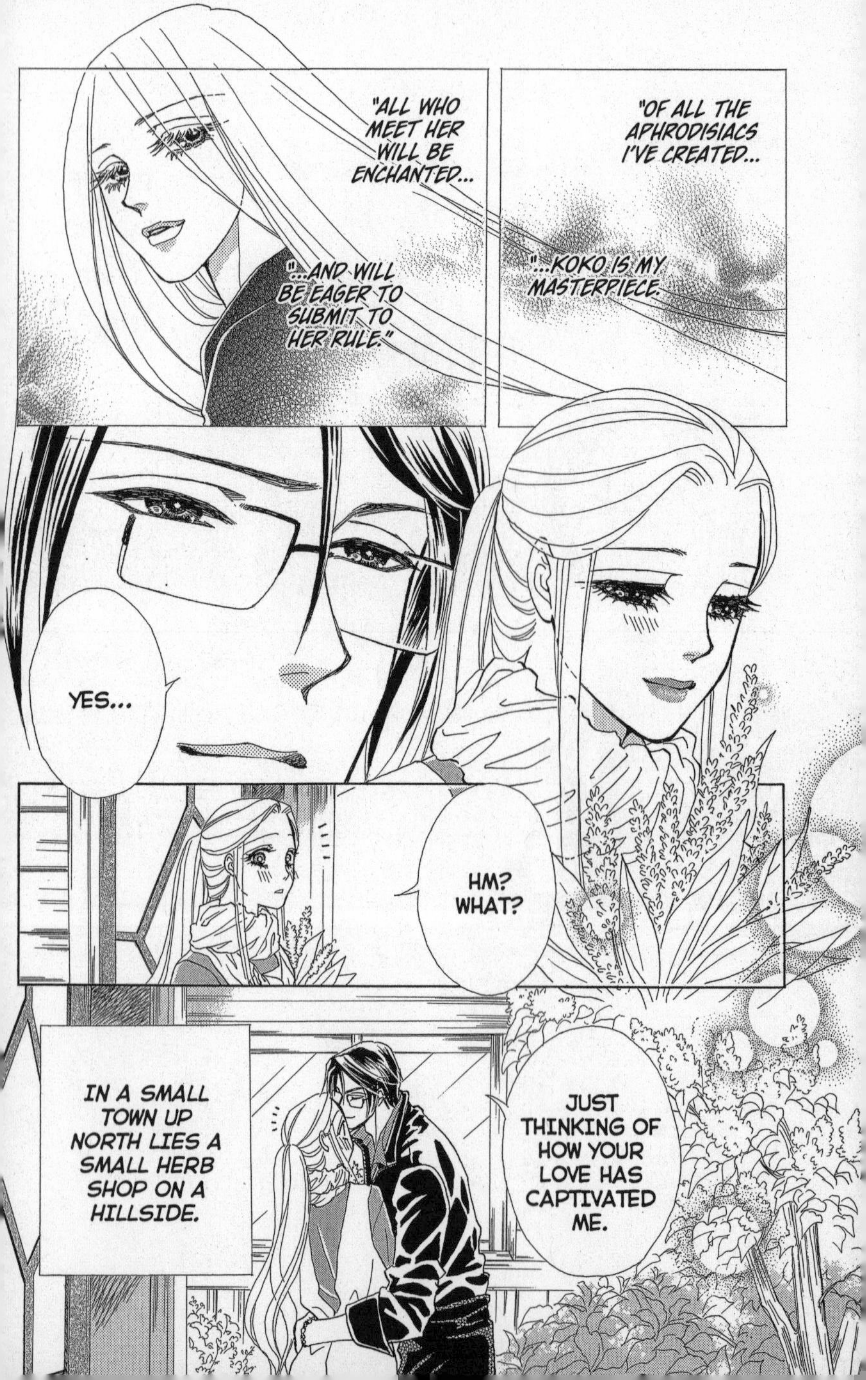
"OF ALL THE APHRODISIACS I'VE CREATED...
"...KOKO IS MY MASTERPIECE.
"ALL WHO MEET HER WILL BE ENCHANTED...
"...AND WILL BE EAGER TO SUBMIT TO HER RULE."
YES...
HM? WHAT?
JUST THINKING OF HOW YOUR LOVE HAS CAPTIVATED ME.
IN A SMALL TOWN UP NORTH LIES A SMALL HERB SHOP ON A HILLSIDE.

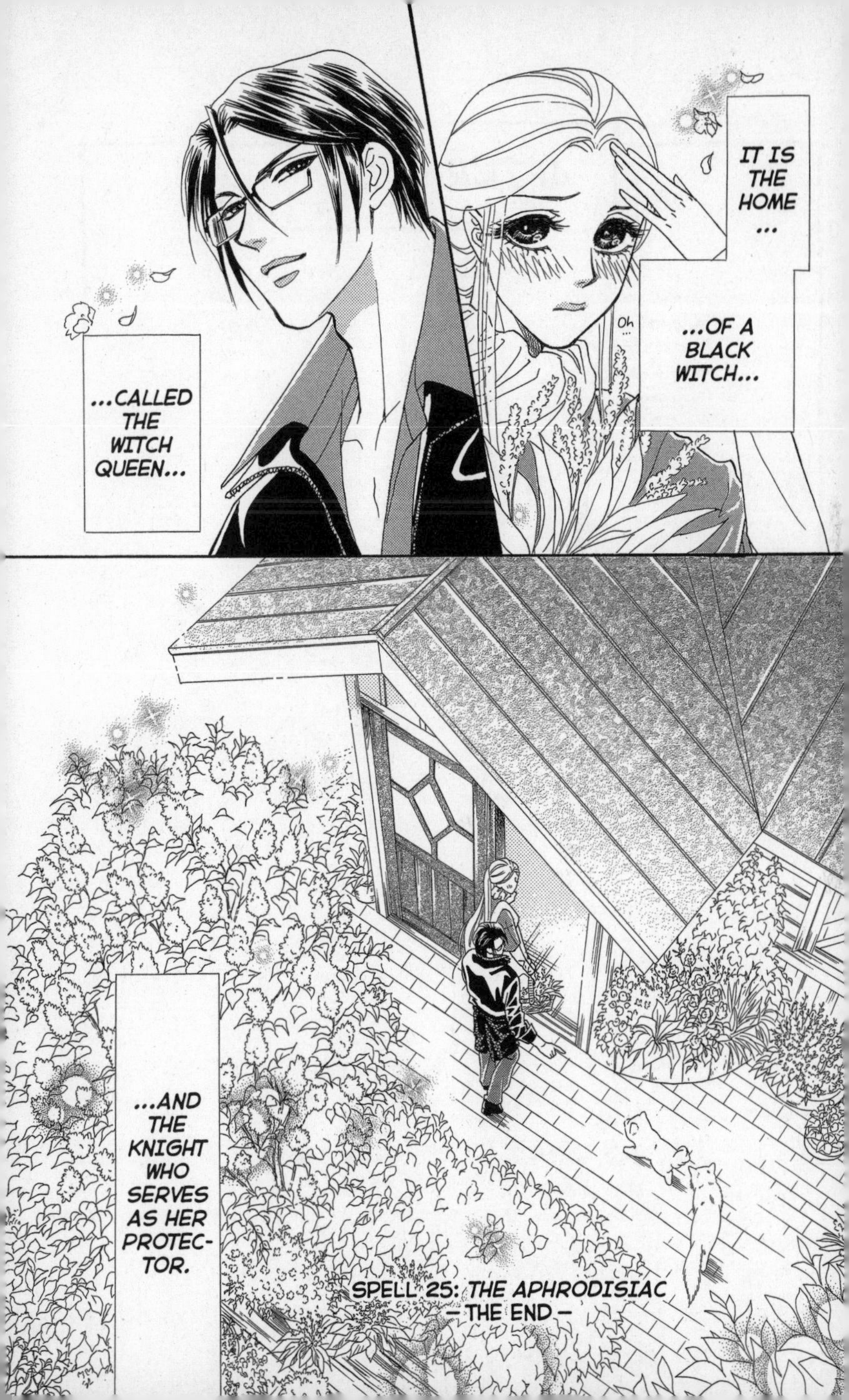
IT IS THE HOME ...
...OF A BLACK WITCH...
Oh...
...CALLED THE WITCH QUEEN...
...AND THE KNIGHT WHO SERVES AS HER PROTEC-TOR.
SPELL 25: THE APHRODISIAC
—THE END—

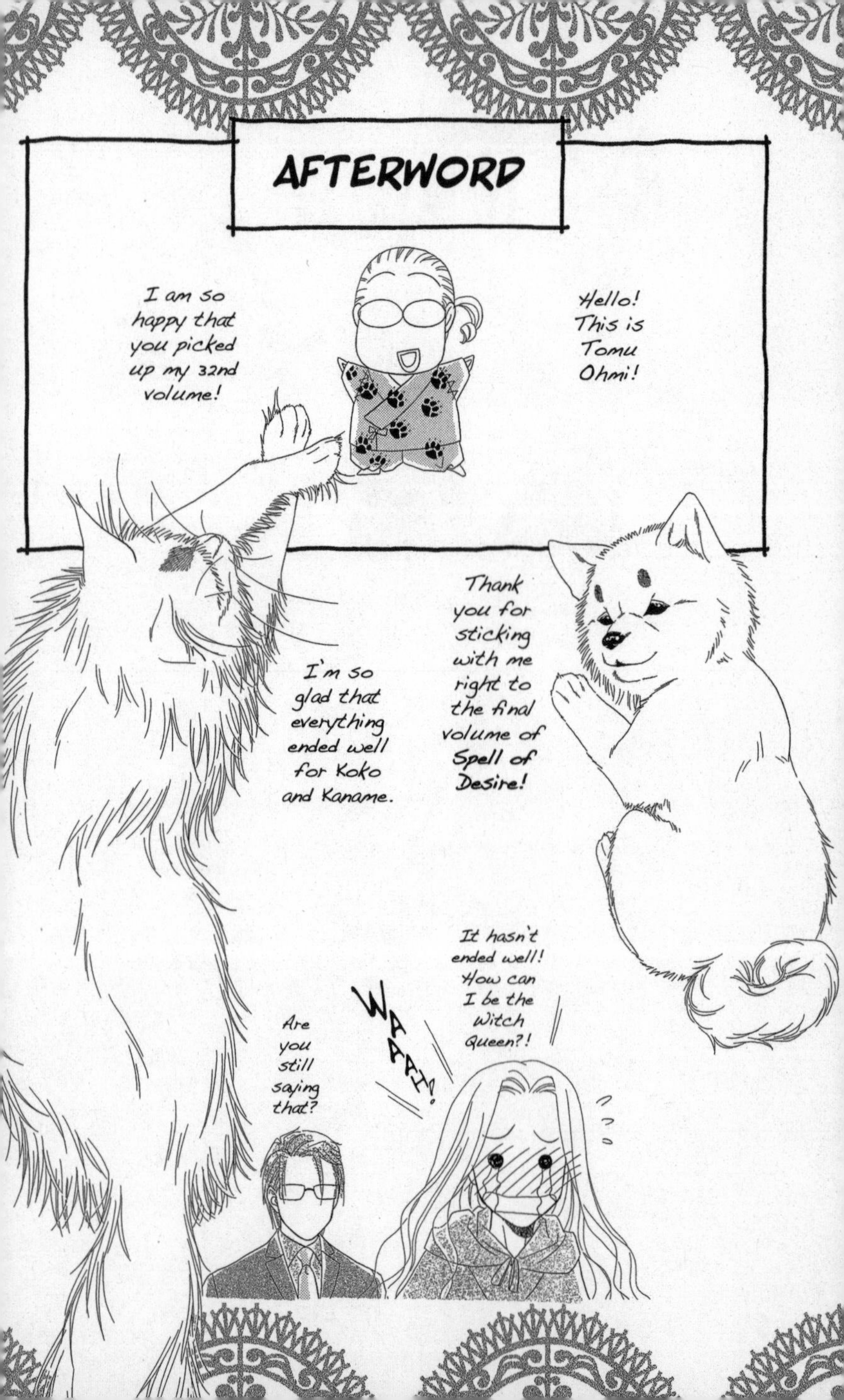
AFTERWORD
Hello! This is Tomu Ohmi!
I am so happy that you picked up my 32nd volume!
Thank you for sticking with me right to the final volume of Spell of Desire!
I'm so glad that everything ended well for Koko and Kaname.
It hasn't ended well! How can I be the Witch Queen?!
WAAAH!
Are you still saying that?

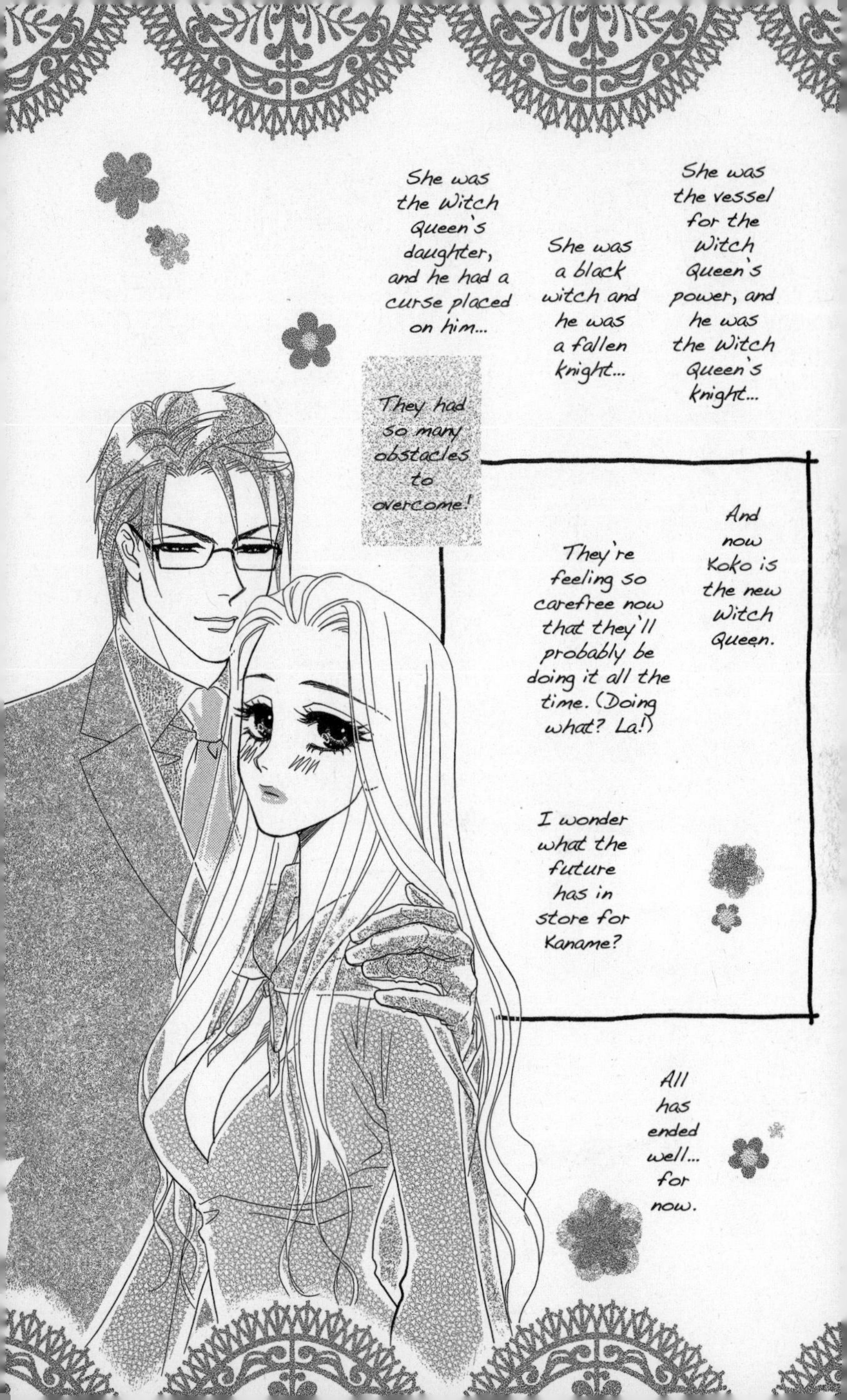
She was the vessel for the Witch Queen's power, and he was the Witch Queen's knight...
She was a black witch and he was a fallen knight...
She was the Witch Queen's daughter, and he had a curse placed on him...
They had so many obstacles to overcome!
And now Koko is the new Witch Queen.
They're feeling so carefree now that they'll probably be doing it all the time. (Doing what? La!)
I wonder what the future has in store for Kaname?
All has ended well... for now.

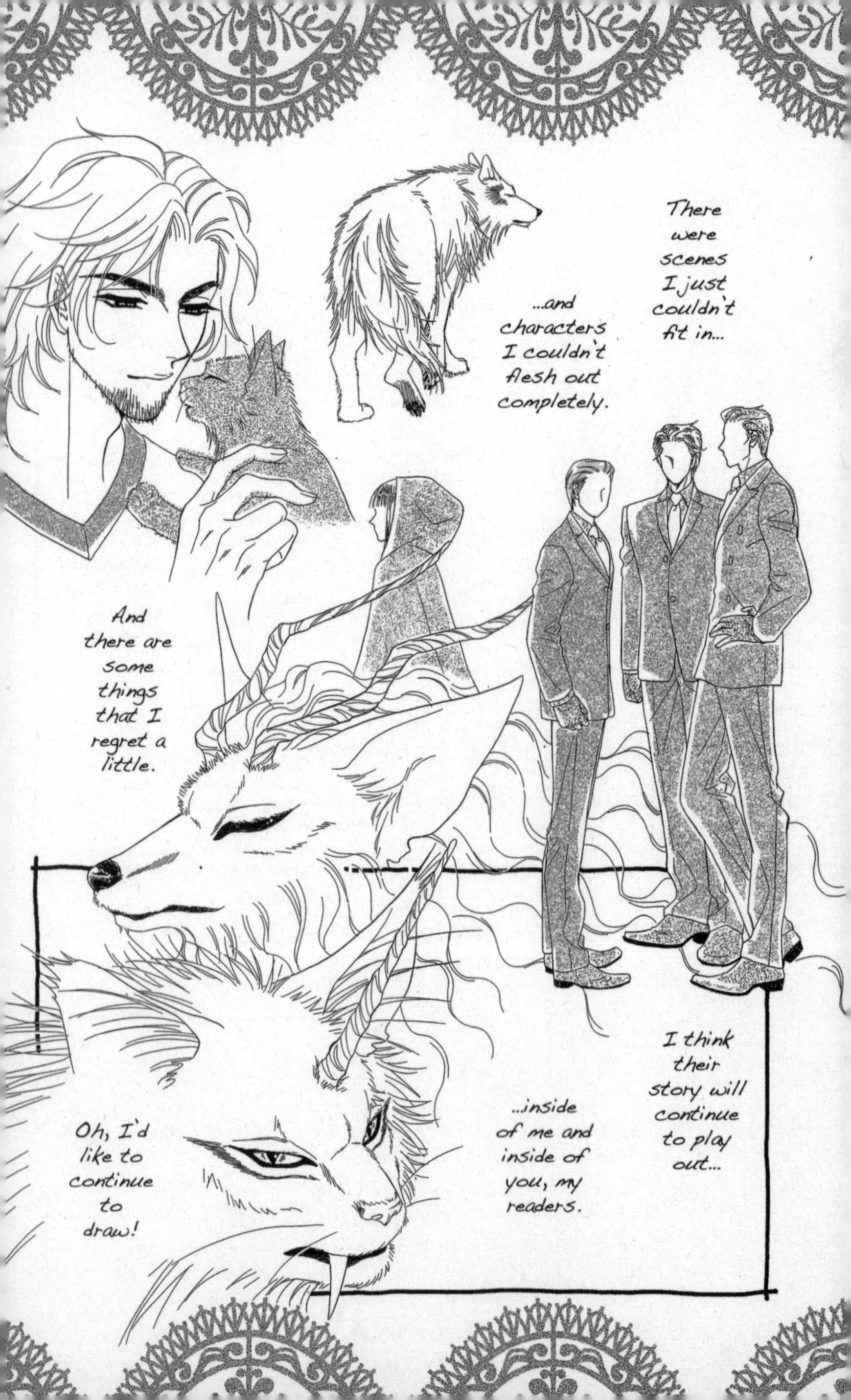
There were scenes I just couldn't fit in...
...and characters I couldn't flesh out completely.
And there are some things that I regret a little.
I think their story will continue to play out...
...inside of me and inside of you, my readers.
Oh, I'd like to continue to draw!

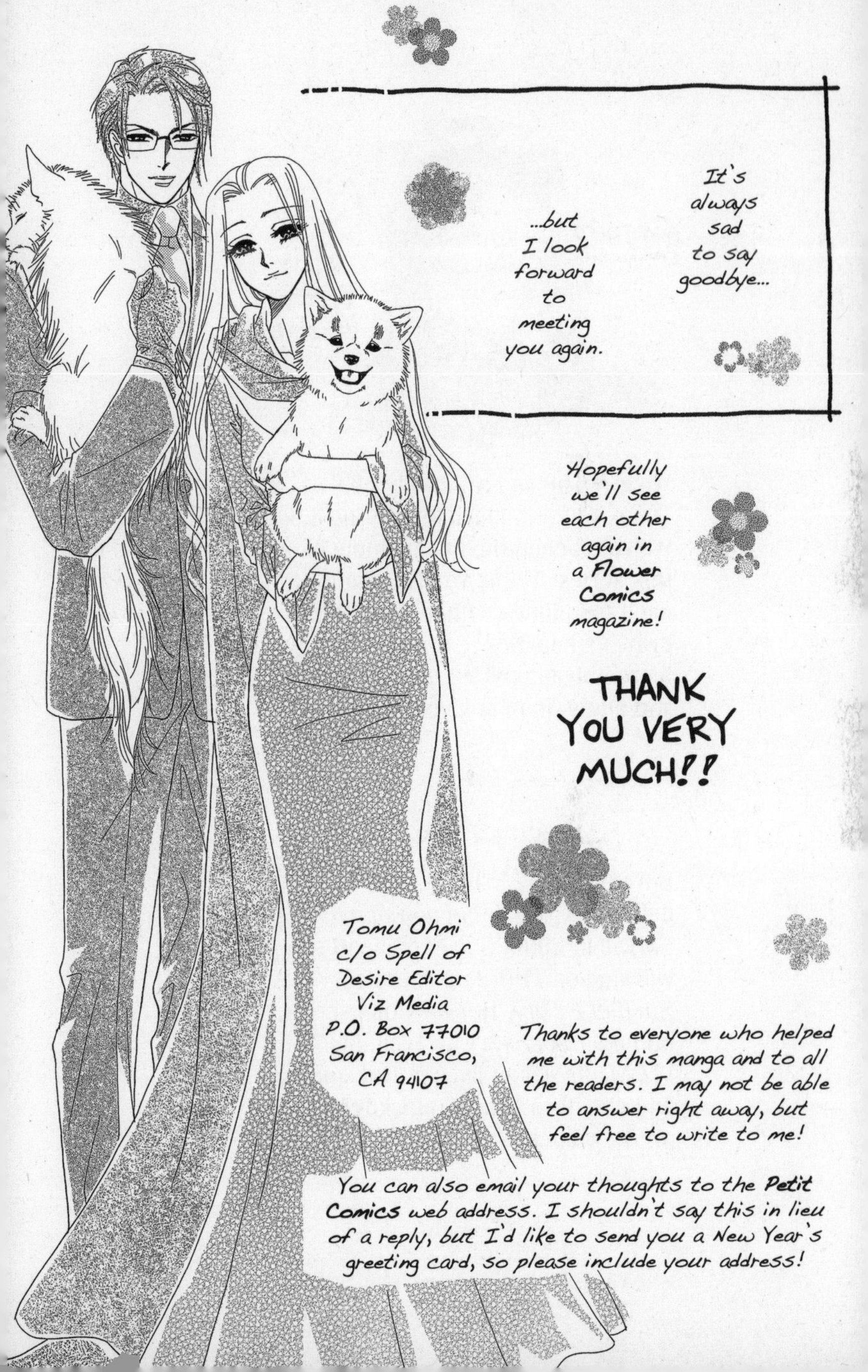
It's always sad to say goodbye...
...but I look forward to meeting you again.
Hopefully we'll see each other again in a Flower Comics magazine!
THANK YOU VERY MUCH!!
Tomu Ohmi
c/o Spell of Desire Editor
Viz Media
P.O. Box 77010
San Francisco, CA 94107
Thanks to everyone who helped me with this manga and to all the readers. I may not be able to answer right away, but feel free to write to me!
You can also email your thoughts to the Petit Comics web address. I shouldn't say this in lieu of a reply, but I'd like to send you a New Year's greeting card, so please include your address!

A WITCH'S FAMILIAR...

...IS A BLACK CAT, OF COURSE!

Wow! ♥ This is my 32nd book!! Thank you very much for picking it up! We've reached the final volume of this series. Thank you for reading each installment. I had a lot of fun drawing beasties in this volume! I'm incredibly happy! ♥ I hope I can see you all again in my next series.

—Tomu Ohmi

Author Bio

Born on May 25, Tomu Ohmi debuted with *Kindan no Koi wo Shiyoh* in 2000. She is presently working on *Petit Comic* projects like *Spell of Desire*. Her previous series, *Midnight Secretary*, is available from VIZ Media. Ohmi lives in Hokkaido, and she likes beasts, black tea and pretty women.

Spell of Desire

VOLUME 5
Shojo Beat Edition

STORY AND ART BY
TOMU OHMI

MAJO NO BIYAKU Vol. 5
by Tomu OHMI

Original Japanese edition published by SHOGAKUKAN.
English translation rights in the United States of America, Canada, the United Kingdom, Ireland, Australia and New Zealand arranged with SHOGAKUKAN.

English Adaptation/Ysabet Reinhardt MacFarlane
Translation/JN Productions
Touch-up Art & Lettering/Monalisa de Asis
Design/Izumi Evers
Editor/Amy Yu

Printed in the U.S.A.

Published by VIZ Media, LLC
P.O. Box 77010
San Francisco, CA 94107

10 9 8 7 6 5 4 3 2 1
First printing, August 2015

www.viz.com

RATED M FOR MATURE

PARENTAL ADVISORY
SPELL OF DESIRE is rated M for Mature and is recommended for ages 18 and up.
ratings.viz.com

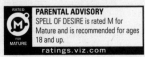

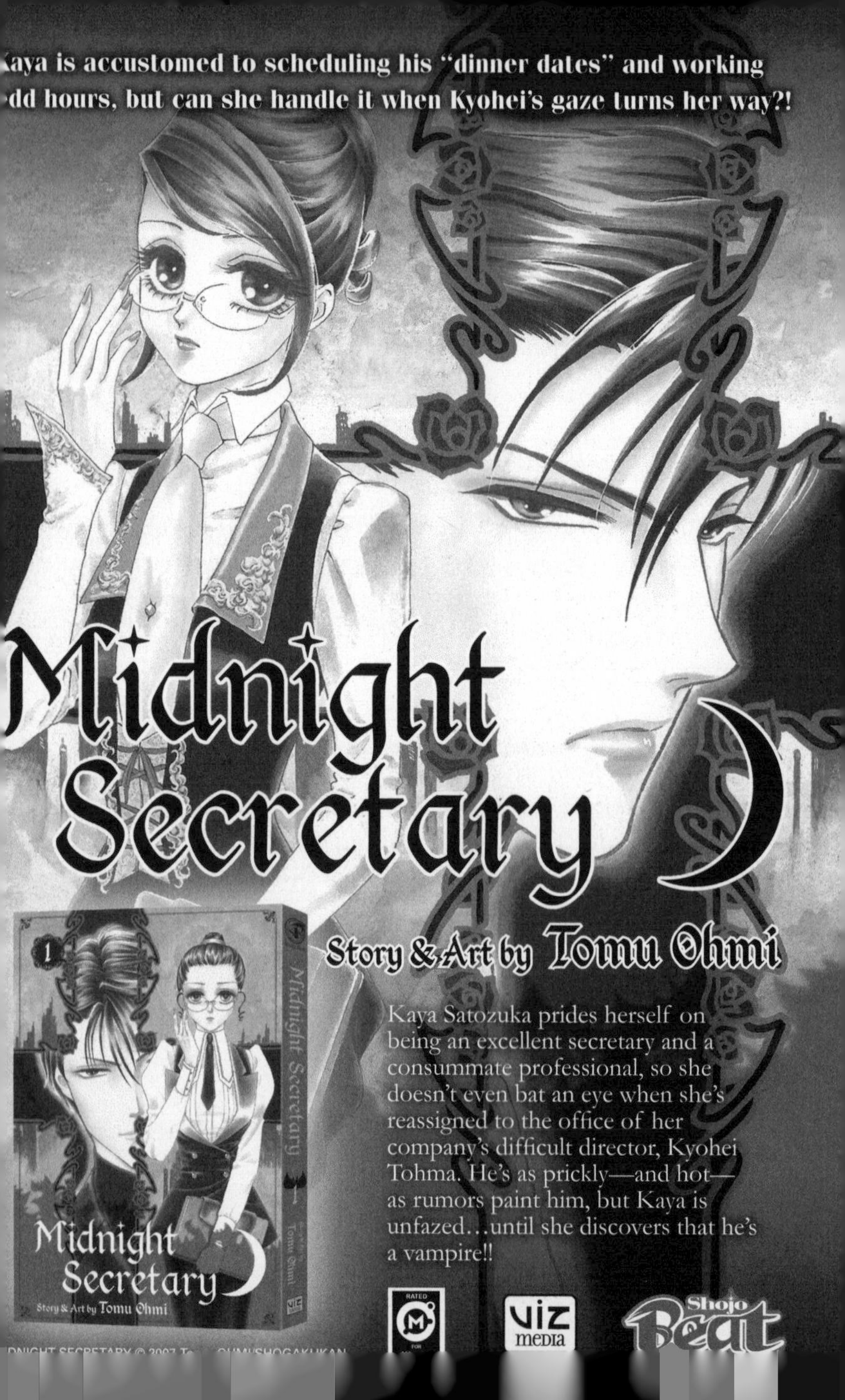
Kaya is accustomed to scheduling his "dinner dates" and working odd hours, but can she handle it when Kyohei's gaze turns her way?!
Midnight Secretary
Story & Art by Tomu Ohmi
Kaya Satozuka prides herself on being an excellent secretary and a consummate professional, so she doesn't even bat an eye when she's reassigned to the office of her company's difficult director, Kyohei Tohma. He's as prickly—and hot—as rumors paint him, but Kaya is unfazed…until she discovers that he's a vampire!!
1
Midnight Secretary
Story & Art by Tomu Ohmi
RATED
M
VIZ media
Shojo Beat

Happy Marriage?!

Story & Art by **Maki Enjoji**

Can two strangers living together find their way to a happy marriage?!

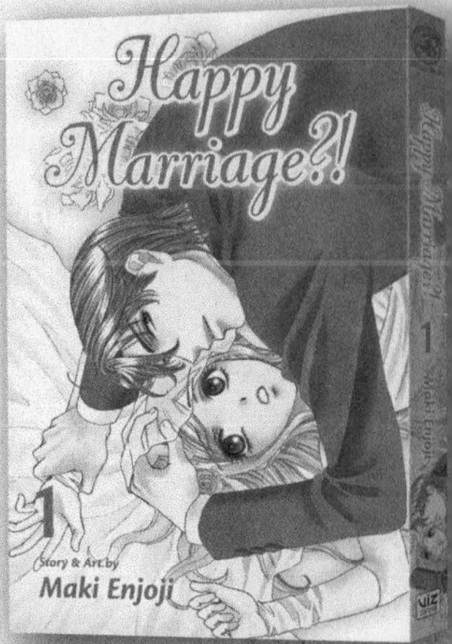

Happy Marriage?!
1
Story & Art by
Maki Enjoji
VIZ

In order to help her father, Chiwa Takanashi agrees to an arranged marriage with the company president, Hokuto Mamiya—a man she doesn't know—at the request of Hokuto's grandfather. Chiwa believes the arrangement isn't binding, but her new partner seems to think otherwise...

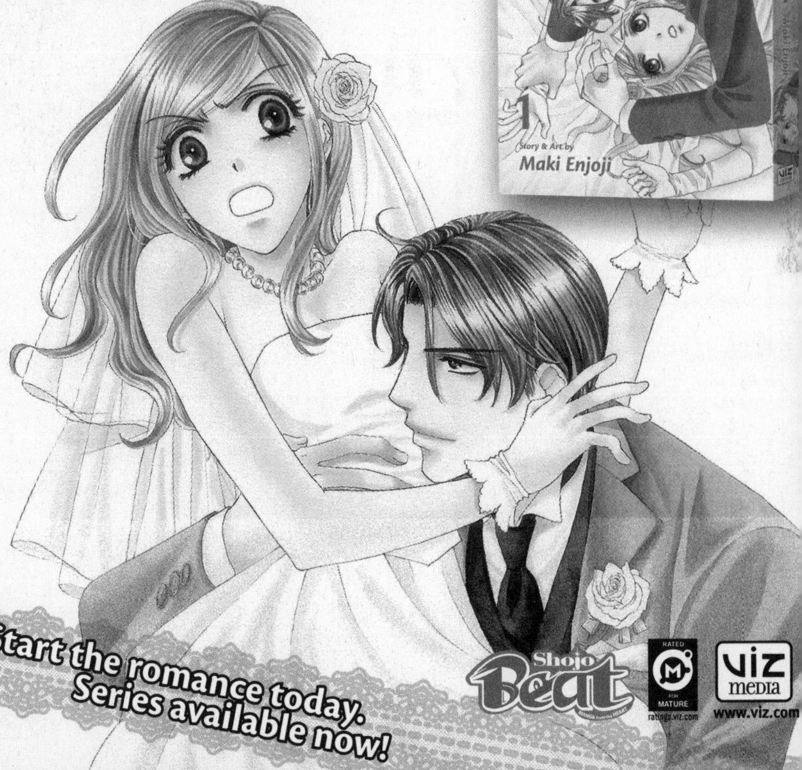

Start the romance today. Series available now!

Shojo Beat

RATED M FOR MATURE ratings.viz.com

VIZ media www.viz.com

This is the last page.

In keeping with the original Japanese comic format, this book reads from right to left—so action, sound effects, and word balloons are completely reversed. This preserves the orientation of the original artwork—plus, it's fun! Check out the diagram shown here to get the hang of things, and then turn to the other side of the book to get started!

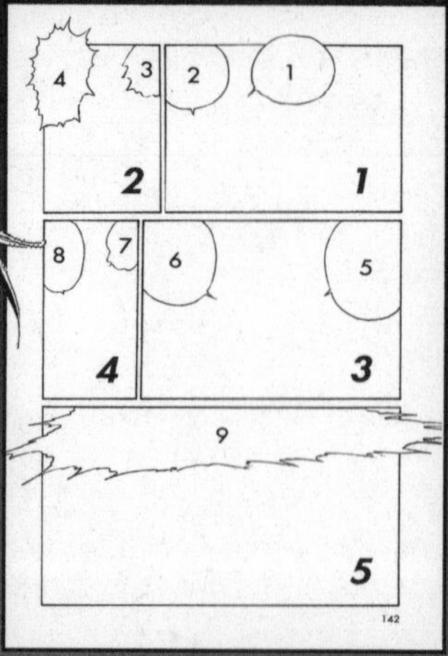
1
2
1
3
4
2
5
6
3
7
8
4
9
5
142

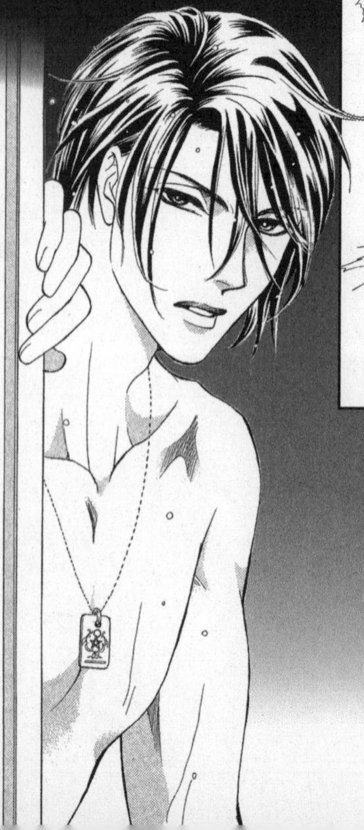

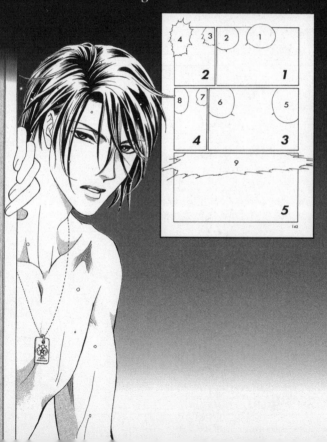